Fourth Edition

Counseling

Theory and Practice

Rickey L. George
University of Missouri-St. Louis

Therese S. Cristiani
University of Missouri-St. Louis

Allyn and Bacon
Boston • London • Toronto • Sydney • Tokyo • Singapore

Series Editor: Raymond Short
Marketing Manager: Ellen Mann
Production Administrator: Marjorie Payne
Editorial Assistant: Christine Shaw
Cover Administrator: Linda Knowles
Composition Prepress Buyer: Linda Cox
Manufacturing Buyer: Louise Richardson
Editorial-Production Service: Chestnut Hill Enterprises, Inc.

This book was previously published under the title *Theory, Methods, and Processes of Counseling and Psychotherapy.*

Library of Congress Cataloging-in-Publication Data

George, Rickey L.
    Counseling : theory and practice / Rickey L. George, Therese S.
Cristiani. – 4th ed.
        p.   cm.
    Includes bibliographical references and indexes.
    ISBN 0-205-15252-X
    1. Counseling.   2. Psychotherapy.   I. Cristiani, Therese Stridde.
II. Title.
BF637.C6G42   1995
158'.3—dc20   94-11091
                                                                      CIP

Printed in the United States of America

10 9 8 7 6 5 4 3 2   99 98 97 96 95

Contents

Preface

This fourth edition of *Counseling: Theory and Practice* is a major revision of the text. In creating this edition we have strived to preserve the strengths of the text that have made it a popular resource for beginning and advanced students for over fourteen years. Thus, its highly readable style and thorough, yet focused, discussion of issues and topics have been maintained. Although all of the text has been updated, most of it has been rewritten or reorganized and two new chapters have been added. Specifically, there is a new chapter, "On Becoming A Counselor," which was added to give students clearer expectations regarding the personal aspects of the counselor education process as well as the personal demands of being a professional counselor. We hope this discussion will assist students in making a good decision with regard to continuing their education in counseling.

Another new chapter co-authored with Brenda-Fay Glik addresses the issues faced by specific client populations. This chapter is a review of the current literature on counseling 1. adult survivors, 2. gay men and lesbians, 3. HIV-infected clients, 4. older adults, and 5. issues related to gender (counseling women and men).

Another significant change has been the addition of a discussion of the various role specializations accredited by the Council for the Accreditation of Counseling and Related Educational Programs (CACREP).

The Ethical Standards of the American Counseling Association are included in the appendices, and the Instructor's Manual has been updated.

The intent of *Counseling: Theory and Practice* on a broader level is to present an overview of the foundations, theories, and practices of counseling without emphasizing a particular theoretical orientation, and thereby to give the reader a well-balanced foundation for further study. It is also our objective to integrate fundamental counseling research in a meaningful and useful way. Therefore, we examine the major findings of those who have studied counseling theory, methods, and processes.

Although the material presented is thorough, we have been selective in what we have chosen to include. It does not include every research finding or every issue in the profession. Rather, it gives broad enough coverage to introduce the reader to the major ideas and to include a comprehensive list of references to provide direction for those students needing more depth.

The response from students over the years has been quite positive. Beginning students appreciate its readability, and more advanced students have found it useful as a study guide for the NBCC test or the state licensure exams. We feel that with the new and updated material the text will continue to be a valuable resource in counselor education.

We acknowledge the contributions of these reviewers, Betty Geis of Southwestern Oklahoma State University and Marty Sapp and Steven W. Ellmann, both of the University of Wisconsin.

We wish to thank our families for their patience and our new editor Ray Short from Allyn and Bacon for his support.

To all of our students who have given personal meaning to this work.

We would like to acknowledge the following individuals whose lives have exemplified all we have tried to teach and who, by being so fully themselves, have expanded the breadth and depth of who we are:

Jim Hurley, Carolyn Pohlmeyer, and Shukry Braik (RLG)

Gina Allen, Brenda-Fay Glik, and Samantha St. Julian (TSC)

P a r t *I*

Introduction to Counseling

C h a p t e r *1*

An Overview to Counseling

Although the profession of counseling is a relatively new field, still in its developing stages, its overall impact on society is growing at a tremendous rate. Increasing numbers of individuals are turning to counselors for help in dealing with the sometimes overwhelming concerns of everyday living, including job-related difficulties or unemployment, marital and family problems, lack of self-confidence, inability to make decisions, educational problems, difficulties in establishing and maintaining relationships, and many others. Thus, the vitality and potential of the counseling profession have never been greater.

At the same time, the relative youth of the profession means that the profession is still changing, redefining its basic goals and purposes as well as its role in our society. Even in defining counseling, one is faced with the fact that various authorities have seen it in different lights. These differences result not only from differences in point of view and in philosophy among the practitioners but also from historical changes and more general perceptions of this process.

Definitions of Counseling

Several elements are common to the many definitions of counseling. One is the notion that counseling is aimed at helping people make choices and act on them. A second is the notion of learning, although there are some sharp differences as to what facilitates learning and how learning occurs. Still another element is that of personality development, with relatively little agreement as to how personality development is best facilitated.

Certainly one of the most novel definitions of counseling is that of Krumboltz (1965), who states that "counseling consists of whatever ethical activities a counselor undertakes in an effort to help the client engage in those types of behavior which will lead to a resolution of the client's problems" (p. 384). This definition clearly emphasizes what the counselor is trying to accomplish—the attainment of client goals—rather than the counseling methods used.

The 1980 American Personnel and Guidance Association (APGA) Licensure Commission's licensing bill, developed to persuade state legislators to license counselors for private practice, defined counseling as "the application of counseling procedures and other related areas of the behavioral sciences to help in learning how to solve problems or make decisions related to careers, personal growth, marriage, family, or other interpersonal concerns" (p. 23).

A final definition is that of Burks and Stefflre, one that seems most appropriate to us. This definition is the following:

> *Counseling denotes a professional relationship between a trained counselor and a client. This relationship is usually person-to-person, although it may sometimes involve more than two people. It is designed to help clients to understand and clarify their views of their lifespace, and to learn to reach their self-determined goals through meaningful, well-informed choices and through resolution of problems of an emotional or interpersonal nature (1979, p. 14).*

This definition, although similar to many previously quoted, indicates that counseling is a relationship, is a process, and is designed to help people make choices and solve problems.

Distinctions Between Counseling and Psychotherapy

One problem facing the counseling practitioner is that of distinguishing between counseling and psychotherapy. Indeed, efforts to distinguish between the two have not met with universal approval. Some practitioners think that such a distinction need not be made and use the two terms synonymously. Others, however, feel that such a distinction must be made. This is particularly true of those who train school counselors, since few would hold that school counselors are ordinarily trained psychotherapists.

However, once the decision to make a distinction between counseling and psychotherapy has been made, the problems begin; the edges of the distinction may blur and agreement on all the particulars is unlikely. Cottone (1992) has pointed out that although distinctions between counseling and psychotherapy may be made according to such factors as the history of each, the type of client and the setting in which the activity takes place, differences in goals, and the seriousness of the client's concern, these distinctions have faded as hospital-based programs now provide "counseling" as well as "therapy" and as individuals trained as counselors are being employed in settings that traditionally have employed psychologists and psychiatrists. In other words, counselors are now providing services that have traditionally been thought of as psychotherapy, and psychotherapists are providing services that have been thought of as counseling. Yet, in spite of this merging of practice, counseling and psychotherapy are different.

As the concepts of these field have changed, so have the definitions. Zeig (1987) described psychotherapy as "being that situation where the therapist helps the patient to empower himself to do something possible which he had been promising himself but had not had the wherewithal to do because he did not really believe it was possible (p. xix)." Although this definition sounds on the surface more like motivation, he later clarifies it by saying that psychotherapy is "about helping people to empower themselves (p. xxvi)." Thus, the emphasis in psychotherapy has become much more of an emphasis on developmental issues, long the domain of counseling, and less on an emphasis of "curing" the mentally ill.

To complicate matters further, the traditional school counseling term "guidance," still used on a limited basis, has a focus very similar to counseling. Based on the concept of using various activities to "guide" students and others into appropriate educational and career decisions, guidance activities have gradually expanded over the years to the point where guidance personnel now include a wide variety of "counseling" activities in their responsibilities, such as personal counseling, group counseling, consulting with teachers and administrators, and family counseling.

Although Blocher (1987) distinguished between counseling and psychotherapy by pointing out that the goals of counseling are ordinarily developmental-educative-preventive, and the goals of psychotherapy are generally remediative-adjustive-therapeutic, the gradual movement of each area of activity toward the other has resulted in guidance being at one end of a continuum and psychotherapy being at the other, with counseling in between. Thus, the distinctions between the three might best be viewed as points on that continuum with regard to various elements: goals, clients, settings, practitioners, and methods. In viewing the three activities in this way, it is important to point out that although the activities of the three may overlap, guidance is more likely to emphasize activities that provide information and direction in terms of career and educational choices; counseling is more likely to emphasize activities that involve supportive, situational, problem-solving, conscious awareness, present-time and short-time concerns; and psychotherapy is more likely to emphasize activities that are reconstructive, depth emphasis, analytical, past-focused, and long-term. Of course, psychotherapy is far more likely to engage in working with individuals with severe psychological problems. However, counselors today are dealing with more severe problems than ever before, including victims of incest, AIDS, and other traumatic illnesses and experiences.

Differences in Goals

In comparing the goals of counseling to the goals of psychotherapy, it seems apparent that a frequent goal of counseling is to help individuals deal with the developmental tasks appropriate to their age. The adolescent who is being helped with problems of sexual definitition, emotional independence from parents, career decision making and preparation, and the other tasks typical of that age in our culture would be receiving counseling. A middle-aged person grappling with these same problems might appropriately be the concern of a psychotherapist.

Within the context of the continuum, the goals of psychotherapy are more likely to involve a quite complete change of basic character structure; the goals of counseling are apt to be more limited, more directed toward aiding growth, more concerned with the immediate situation, and more aimed at helping the individual function adequately in appropriate roles.

Differences in Clients and Settings

When attempts have been made to distinguish counseling from psychotherapy on the basis of the clients each serves, the traditional view has been that the counselor deals with normal persons and the psychotherapist deals with neurotic or psychotic persons. Such a distinction, of course, has many of the same built-in problems in the definition of "normal" as are involved in the distinction between counseling and psychotherapy.

Perhaps part of the difficulty in distinguishing on the basis of the clients served occurs because of the differences in settings. Psychotherapists are more apt to work in hospital settings or in private practice; counselors are more apt to work

FIGURE 1-1   **Counselors must be aware that children at different ages have different social and physical skills to learn**
(Photo by James T. Hurley)

in educational settings. However, as counselors become employed in a wider range of settings and more psychotherapists are employed in school systems and colleges, such a distinction becomes less meaningful. Thus, although counseling may occur more often in educational institutions and psychotherapy more often in medical settings, we cannot always determine which activity is going on by knowing where it is happening.

We take the view that both counseling and psychotherapy utilize a common base of knowledge and a common set of techniques. Both involve a therapeutic process but they differ in terms of the severity of the client's situation, in terms of the client's level of problem and/or functioning. Since the process does not change—only the situation or the client's concern may—we use the terms interchangeably, although we generally use the term *counseling* in this book.

Goals of Counseling

What is the expected result from counseling? Certainly individuals have different perceptions of what can be expected. Individuals preparing to become counselors, those who seek counseling, parents, teachers, school administrators, and governmental agencies all differ in what they hope will result from the counseling experience. Such expectations are, of course, germane to the counseling process. However, the ultimate decision about what the goals of counseling shall be must rest with the counselor and the client as a team.

Five Major Goals

As you will discover in the chapters on the various counseling theories, counseling theorists have not always agreed on appropriate counseling goals. Statements of counseling goals are often general, vague, and saturated with implications. However, the following five major goals are often stated: (1) facilitating behavior change, (2) improving the client's ability to establish and maintain relationships, (3) enhancing the client's effectiveness and ability to cope, (4) promoting the decision-making process, and (5) facilitating client potential and development. These goals are not mutually exclusive, and some are emphasized more often by some theorists than by others.

Facilitating Behavior Change
Almost all theorists indicate that the goal of counseling is to bring about a change in behavior which will enable the client to live a more productive, satisfying life as the client defines it within society's limitations. The way theorists talk about behavior change varies greatly, however. Rogers (1961) sees behavior change as a necessary result of the counseling process, although specific behaviors receive little or no emphasis during the counseling experience.

Dustin and George (1977), on the other hand, suggest that the counselor must establish specific counseling goals. They believe that a shift from general goals to specific goals enables both the client and the counselor to understand precisely the specific change that is desired. They point out that specific behavioral goals have an additional value: The client is better able to see any change that occurs.

Krumboltz (1966) suggests three criteria for judging counseling goals. They are the following: (1) The goals of counseling should be capable of being stated differently for each individual client. (2) The goals of counseling for each client should be compatible with, though not necessarily identical to, the values of his counselor. (3) The degree to which the goals of counseling are attained by each client should be observable.

FIGURE 1-2   **A mother and her daughters discuss their problems with a family counselor**
(Photo by James T. Hurley)

Enhancing Coping Skills

Almost all individuals run into difficulties in the process of growing up. Few of us completely achieve all of our developmental tasks, and the various unique expectations and requirements imposed on us by significant others often lead to problems. Certainly, inconsistency on the part of significant others can result in children's learning behavior patterns that are inefficient, ineffective, or both. These learned coping patterns may serve the individual well in most situations, but in time, new interpersonal or occupational role demands may create an overload and produce excessive anxiety and difficulty for the individual. Helping individuals learn to cope with new situations and new demands is an important goal of counseling.

Promoting Decision Making

To some, the goal of counseling is to enable the individual to make critical decisions. It is not the counselor's job, they say, to decide which decisions the client should make or to choose alternate courses of action. The decisions are the client's, and the client must know why and how the decision was made. The client learns to estimate the probable consequences in personal sacrifice, time, energy, money, risk, and the like. The client also learns to explore the range of values that are related to the situation and to bring these values into full consciousness in the decision-making process.

Counseling helps individuals obtain information and clarify and sort out personal characteristics and emotional concerns that may interfere with or be related to the decisions involved. It helps these individuals acquire an understanding not only of their abilities, interests, and opportunities but also of the emotions and attitudes that can influence their choices and decisions.

Improving Relationships

Much of one's life is spent in social interaction with other individuals, yet many clients have a major problem relating to other people. This problem may be conceptualized as the result of the client's poor self-image, which causes him or her to act defensively in relationships, or it may be seen as the result of inadequate social skills. Whatever the theoretical approach, counselors work with clients to help them improve the quality of their relationships with others. Difficulties with relationships can range from the family and marital problems of adults to the peer group interaction difficulties of the elementary school child. In every case the counselor is striving to help the clients improve the quality of their lives by becoming more effective in their interpersonal relationships.

Facilitating the Client's Potential

Developing the client's potential is a frequently emphasized, although ambiguous, counseling goal. Certainly few theorists would disagree with the idea that counseling seeks to promote the growth and development of clients by giving them the opportunity to learn ways to use their abilities and interests to the maximum. This goal can be viewed as one of improving personal effectiveness. Blocher (1987) suggests that first, counseling seeks to maximize an individual's possible freedom within the limitations supplied by himself and his environment, and second, counseling seeks to maximize the individual's effectiveness by giving him control over his environment and the responses within him that are evoked by the environment.

Such an emphasis means that counselors work to help people learn how to overcome excessive smoking or drinking, to take better care of their bodies, and to overcome shyness, stress, and depression. They help people to learn how to overcome sexual dysfunctions, drug addiction, compulsive gambling, overweight, and fears and anxieties. At the same time, counselors can help people with their interpersonal problems, with emotional problems, and with the development of learning and decision-making skills (Krumboltz and Thoresen, 1976). All of this is part of promoting the *whole* wellness of the individual, including the physical, social, mental, emotional, and spiritual aspects of that person.

Commonality of Goals

The previous description of the kinds of goals that various counselors emphasize fails to recognize certain points about counseling goals. First, as Shertzer and Stone (1974) point out, the goals expressed by differing counseling theorists may reflect their own needs rather than those of the clients. Blackham (1977), however, suggests that while the counselor does provide some direction for the counseling process, both counselor and client decide which goals are to be pursued and how.

Second, perhaps there are more likenesses than differences among the statements of counseling goals. Certainly all of the theorists seem to recognize the broader goal of helping the client to feel better, to function at a higher level, to achieve more, and to live up to his or her potential.

Third, the focus of all counseling goals is the achievement of personal effectiveness that is both satisfactory to the individual and within society's limitations. Thus many of the presumed differences in counseling goals shrink in importance and become simply differences in terms of the criteria used to judge the counselor's effectiveness. In addition, the differences in the way counseling goals are formulated may result from the differences in the way counselors attempt to help clients.

Client Expectations

Before leaving the subject of counseling goals, it is important to note that whether or not a particular counseling experience will be worthwhile to the client will depend on the client's expectations. The client's lack of clearcut understanding of the nature of counseling is a widespread source of inadequate readiness to attack problems. Along with knowing such practical information as length of interviews, probable length of the process, or how to make appointments, the client should understand the limitations and possibilities of counseling. Moreover, the counselor must be aware of his or her own expectations and should encourage clients to talk about their expectations for the counseling experience.

The majority of clients expect counseling to produce personal solutions for them. Those in stressful situations expect that counseling will bring relief. Those who are having difficulty making a particular decision expect counseling to result in a choice. Those who are lonely expect solace and expect to discover ways of improving their interactions with others. Those who want to go to college may view counseling as guaranteeing them admission or even financial aid. Those who are about to fail, either in school or in other ventures, expect failure to turn into success as the result of counseling. Those who seek employment counseling expect quick placement, job satisfaction, and easy promotion (Shertzer and Stone, 1974).

Many clients expect to have something done *to* or *for* them as part of the counseling process. Counselors must communicate to clients that ultimately it is the client who acts, decides, changes, becomes. In addition clients often seek counseling in crisis situations, hoping to find remediation, whereas counselors operate with goals that imply that counseling should be preventive or growth inducing. In these situations counselors must learn to respond to the immediate needs of the client while working toward some intermediate or ultimate goals through the counseling process.

Historical Development of the Counseling Profession

Counseling has emerged and developed as an American product of the twentieth century. Its acceptance and widespread use in the United States far exceed that of other countries, partially because of the American emphasis on the importance of the individual and partially because of American affluence, which allows our society to afford it.

Vocational Guidance Movement

Although no single date can mark the beginning of the counseling movement, counseling may well have begun in 1898 when Jesse B. Davis worked as a counselor with high school students in Detroit. His work with these students' educational and vocational problems is a clear illustration of the early ties of counseling to vocational guidance. Another early pioneer of the movement was Frank Parsons, who founded a vocation bureau in 1908 in Boston, which eventually led to the National Vocational Guidance Association in 1913. One year after Parsons's vocation bureau opened its doors, it established a direct connection with the Boston schools, allying counseling with education as the schools used the services of the new bureau (Rossberg and Band, 1978). During this same period dozens of other schools were experimenting with counseling concepts.

Mental Health Movement

During the same period, other professional developments evolved independently and merged to help form the modern approach to counseling. In particular, the development of the mental health movement became an important part of the whole emphasis on counseling. A book by Clifford Beers, *A Mind That Found Itself*, was published in 1908 and made a profound impression on an awakening society and on the counseling movement. The book sparked concern for the individual; school children came to be viewed as growing, developing organisms and as pliable receptacles for rote memory tasks. In 1909 Beers also supplied the leadership for the formation of the National Committee for Mental Hygiene, which was responsible for or contributed to significant innovations in legislative reform, aftercare, and free clinics for the mentally ill.

During the 1920s and 1930s scientific journals and organizations and child study centers designed to promote the well-being of children came into existence, primarily as the result of the work of G. Stanley Hall of Clark University. Hall, who was a leader in collecting data related to different phases of the mental life of all ages, was also credited with introducing Freudian concepts of child development into American education and psychology. This child-study movement was fourfold: (1) it emphasized the individual as the focal point of study; (2) it stressed the importance of the formative years as the foundation for mature personality development; (3) it pointed out the need for reliable, factual knowledge about children;

and (4) it led to better controlled, more analytical and accurate methods of child study (Shertzer and Stone, 1974).

Standardized Testing

In many ways, developments in mental measurements and other types of human assessment formed the basis for the early technology of counseling practice. Prior to World War I technical efforts in human assessment were basically restricted to the work of individual researchers attempting to measure individual differences in performance on a variety of tasks. The Binet Scales and the American revisions, the appearance of group intelligence tests, and the administration of the first standardized achievement tests are examples of the kind of work that was done to predict success in areas such as academic performance. Interest inventories such as the Strong Vocational Interest Blank emerged. Testing of special aptitudes in music, mechanics, and art was initiated and refined.

Following World War II test "batteries" and large-scale testing programs emerged. But by 1960 many had become highly critical of the practice of using such tests for educational and job selection, believing that current tests penalized members of minority groups who had not had equal educational opportunities.

The testing movement has had a profound influence on counseling: It led to the objective study of individual differences; it enabled scientific investigations to be made into the problems of intelligence; and it facilitated prediction, classification, and placement of individuals. Standardized testing gave the new profession tools that were practical and usable at a time when the tools were needed.

Federal Legislation

Legislation affecting the profession began with the 1917 Smith-Hughes Act and the 1918 Vocational Rehabilitation Act. Both contained provisions either explicitly or implicitly providing for the vocational preparation, education, and guidance of young men and women and veterans. A number of acts passed in the late 1920s and 1930s dealt with vocational education and paved the way for establishing guidance divisions within state departments of education. In 1938 the U.S. Office of Education created the Occupational Information and Guidance Services Bureau. Its publications and research efforts consistently stressed the need for school counselors and the services they provide. Other federal acts gave support to counseling in settings ranging from rehabilitation centers to community agencies.

Two significant pieces of legislation at about midcentury gave still stronger impetus to counseling. The first was the extension of the Vocation Rehabilitation Legislation in 1954, which itself was an extensive revision of the earlier vocational rehabilitation acts. Among other things, it provided enabling legislation and financial support for an extensive program to educate rehabilitation counselors. It provided a legislative mandate for the development of counselors who specialized in assisting the disabled and created a federal source of support that since its inception has provided direct assistance for the education of several thousand counselors and has indirectly affected an equal number in the field.

The second piece of legislation, the National Defense Education Act (NDEA) of 1958, provided funds to strengthen school guidance programs and train school counselors. In 1964 Congress amended Title V of the NDEA to include the preparation of elementary school counselors in institute programs, and financial support was given to elementary school guidance programs at the local level. This amendment also provided funds for the preparation of counselors for higher education settings. Other notable pieces of legislation include the Vocational Education Act of 1963, the 1968 amendments, and subsequent amendments.

Professional Organizations

A major force in the development of counseling as a profession has been the American Counseling Association. In many ways, the growth of the field in numbers and in its acceptance as a helping profession has paralleled the changes in the name of its major professional organization. Originally called the American Personnel and Guidance Association, it was formed in 1951 by merging the National Vocational Guidance Association, the American College Personnel Association, and the National Association of Guidance Supervisors and Counselor Trainers. This merger resulted from a recognition that the activities of the three groups had gradually become very similar in nature and that an integration of the groups would strengthen each of them.

With the change of name to the American Association for Counseling and Development in 1983, the organization recognized the increasing emphasis on individual development and the counselor's role in facilitating that development in a healthy, positive direction. Its change to its present name in 1991 was an indication that the members recognized that counseling as a profession was now fully accepted in American society. By 1993, the American Counseling Association had a membership of over 60,000 and was composed of the following divisions and organizational affiliates:

American College Personnel Association
American Mental Health Counselors Association
American Rehabilitation Counseling Association
American School Counselor Association
Association for Adult Development and Aging
Association for Counselor Education and Supervision
Association for Humanistic Education and Development
Association for Measurement and Evaluation in Counseling and Development
Association for Multicultural Counseling and Development
Association for Religious and Value Issues in Counseling
Association for Specialists in Group Work
Military Educators and Counselors Association
National Career Development Association
National Employment Counselors Association
Public Offender Counselor Association

Many counselors also belong to Division 17 (Counseling Psychology) of the American Psychological Association.

Counselor Credentialing

Problems in Credentialing Counselors

To a large extent, the issue of counselor licensure was forced on counselors by the aggressive action of state psychology licensure boards when they moved to restrict the practice of qualified counseling psychologists and other counselors. The dominant forces among psychologists called for a restriction on which professionals would be allowed to provide nonmedical mental health services, a restriction that would eliminate all but doctoral-trained psychologists. Since such restrictions often limited counseling to those who had been trained in a department of psychology, individuals trained as counselors or counseling psychologists in departments within colleges of education were ineligible for licensure, regardless of the educational level attained or the content of the educational experience.

Running parallel to this problem of a legal prohibition of providing counseling services unless one were a licensed psychologist was a growing concern about providing some quality assurances to the public about anyone who used the title of "counselor." As a result, credentialing concerns by the end of the 1970s had become of primary importance to the profession, and steps were taken to deal with the problems.

Accreditation of Counselor Training Programs

The major problem in the licensure issue, however, was that the counseling profession lacked an effective credentialing process, and as a result, its practitioners were restricted in their opportunities for practicing their profession. In the past, some attention had been given to the preparation standards and certification of counselors, but the emphasis has been on a recommended preparation program. The APGA Professional Preparation and Standards Committee was active in 1960, and standards for the preparation of secondary school counselors were developed in 1964. Yet, no procedure was developed for accrediting preparation programs.

The National Council for Accreditation of Teacher Education, which has been the official accrediting body for teacher preparation programs, has served as the primary structure for accreditation, although its practices have had little impact on the quality of programs. In 1973 the Association for Counselor Education and Supervision (ACES) approved a revised, expanded set of preparation standards that had been carefully formulated. In 1979 the Association for Counselor Education and Supervision began the implementation of a set of guidelines for the accreditation of counselor education programs, and the American Counseling Association is now administering an accreditation program, the Council for the

Accreditation of Counseling and Related Educational Programs (CACREP). This direction has been questioned and evaluated by Wittmer (1988).

CACREP tied together the need to "legitimize" the profession as well as to be a responsible partner to higher education accrediting bodies in verifying that specific counselor training programs met stringent standards in the education of counselors. Focusing on a set of standards designed to verify that a particular counselor training program meets and maintains those standards, CACREP accreditation has become an increasingly important issue for counselor education departments (Vacc, 1992).

The standards used by CACREP for evaluation of counselor preparation programs are organized around eight content areas, clinical experiences, and faculty characteristics. The eight content areas include:

1. *Human Growth and Development*—focusing on an understanding of the nature and needs of individuals at all development levels; normal and abnormal human behavior; personality theory; and learning theory (all) within cultural contexts.

2. *Social and Cultural Foundations*—focusing on an understanding of societal changes and trends, human roles, societal subgroups, social mores and interaction patterns, and differing lifestyles.

3. *Helping Relationships*—focusing on an understanding of the philosophic bases of helping processes, counseling theories and their applications, helping skills, consultation theories and applications, helper self-understanding and self-development, and facilitation of client or consultee change.

4. *Group Dynamics, Processing, and Counseling*—focusing on theory and types of groups, as well as descriptions of group practices, methods, dynamics, and facilitative skills, and including supervised practice.

5. *Lifestyle and Career Development*—focusing on such areas as vocational choice theory, relationship between career choice and lifestyle, sources of occupational and educational information, approaches to career decision-making processes, and career development exploration techniques.

6. *Appraisal of Individuals*—focusing on the development of a framework for understanding the individual, including methods of data gathering and interpretation, individual and group testing, case-study approaches, and the study of individual differences, including ethnic, cultural, and sex factors.

7. *Research and Evaluation*—focusing on such areas as statistics, research design, and development of research and demonstration proposals.

8. *Professional Orientation*—focusing on goals and objectives of professional organizations, codes of ethics, legal considerations, standards of preparation, certification, licensing, and role identity of counselors and other personnel services specialists.

In addition, CACREP requires a practicum with 100 hours of supervised experience and an internship that includes 600 hours of supervised experience.

This emphasis on accreditation of approved counselor training programs is of major importance in the credentialing process of counselors; still, such a procedure fails to provide the legal credentialing for the individual that licensure does. Therefore, the development of licensure standards and approved legislation for those licensure standards in each of the states is a major thrust of the counseling profession today.

Standards for Licensure

Forester (1977) has defined some of the common methods used to credential practitioners of the profession. *Certification* is seen "as a process of recognizing the competence of practitioners of a profession by officially authorizing them to use the title adopted by the profession." Ordinarily such certification is granted by an agency or governmental body after checking the individual's transcripts for evidence that the applicant has completed the specific, required courses in acceptable preparation programs. *Licensure* is "a process authorized by state legislation that regulates the practice and the title of the profession." Because licensure is a legal process, it subjects violators to greater legal sanctions than does certification. The regulations governing licensure are generally far more specific and comprehensive, demanding greater training and preparation, than are the regulations regarding certification. *Accreditation* is "a process whereby an association or agency grants public recognition to a school, institute, college, university, or specialized program of study that has met certain established qualifications of standards as determined through initial and periodic evaluations" (p. 573). Often called "program approval," accreditation often acts to credential graduates of approved programs.

There is no reason to believe that the licensure issue will go away. Rather, recent events suggest that licensure will be required in more and more states, and increasingly higher levels of training will be required for applicants. The most important aspect, however, is the recognition that counselors need an effective credentialing process that will legitimize their professional standing.

The impetus for counselor licensure came from the Association for Counselor Education and Supervision, but by 1975 the American Personnel and Guidance Association had appointed a licensure commission and had begun work on developing resources for groups working toward licensure. In 1976 Virginia became the first state to pass a licensure law; by the spring of 1994, groups in forty states had been successful in getting counselor licensure, registration, or certification legislation passed.

Pros and Cons of Licensure

Certainly the issue of whether counselor licensure is desirable or not generates a great deal of disagreement. Those who support licensing of counselors frequently give the following reasons for doing so: (1) One characteristic of a profession is that it monitors its own members and sets standards for its practice, which licensing would permit counselors to do; (2) licensure would grant increased dignity and prestige to counselors in diverse settings, including education, even though most states are expected to allow school counselors the option of choosing whether or not to become licensed; and (3) licensure would help protect the public's right to be served by a competent, qualified professional whenever counseling is desired.

Opponents of counselor licensure tend to focus on two issues: (1) the potential harm to the profession if licensing becomes more political than professional, with politicians deciding licensing standards; and (2) the potential effect of having licensure standards that reflect what "used to be" rather than what "needs to be"; such standards would serve to stultify rather than encourage growth and development in the training of counselors. Davis (1981), for one, argues that national certification provides greater freedom for counselors and greater protection for the public.

National Board of Certified Counselors

Since 1982, the American Counseling Association (formerly the American Association for Counseling and Development) has been developing a national registry of certified counselors. This system provides for professional recognition of competence by certifying an individual as a "national, certified counselor" when the individual successfully meets the professional standards established. These criteria include the following:

1. Master's or doctorate degree in counseling or a closely related field from a regionally accredited university.
2. At least two years professional counseling experience with a documented supervised counseling experience, and
3. Successful completion of a counselor certification examination.

In addition, certified counselors must show evidence of continuing professional growth and development as counselors in order to be recertified. A 1988 study by Jaeger and Frye showed a positive relationship between the test content and the counselor's job responsibilities.

Similar certification procedures exist in order to be certified as a Certified Clinical Mental Health Counselor by the American Mental Health Counselors Association, as a Certified Career Counselor by the National Vocational Guidance Association, and as a Certified Rehabilitation Counselor by the Commission on Rehabilitation Counselor Certification.

Selected Specialty Areas

An analysis of the various role specialties accredited by CACREP provides an overview of the major areas in which counselors now provide services. These settings have expanded over the years as the needs of clients and society have changed and the field of counseling has expanded.

Peterson and Nisenholz (1991) have pointed out that most master's level counselor training programs are designed to train counseling generalists. However, the CACREP areas of accreditation have recognized and encouraged the need for counselors to pursue a specialty within the generalized training program. This means focusing on a specific specialty area while learning about other aspects of the entire counseling field.

School Counseling

Just a few years ago, the vast majority of individuals studying the field of counseling were planning to be school counselors. Today, a minority are doing so, as the opportunities for counselors to work in other settings have greatly expanded. Yet the first counselor, and often the only counselor, with whom most individuals have contact is the school counselor. Secondary school counselors have provided services for high school students for several decades. Often working with a student load of over four hundred students, secondary school counselors provide help in the areas of career counseling, college planing and college choice, testing, course selection and registration, consultation with teachers, and personal/family problems of the student. Although the use of computers and other comprehensive information systems has provided some relief for secondary school counselors, the student load continues to be very heavy, and combined with the wide range of responsibilities counselors have, their role is very challenging.

A more recent trend has been the recognition of the need for counselors at the elementary school level. A major factor in this trend has been the need for counselors to work with special education teachers in identifying children who need special services and in developing educational plans that are individualized for those children. Of equal importance, however, is the recognition of the need for elementary school counselors to provide support for problem prevention and the development of human potential, including self-esteem. This aspect of the counseling role involves remediation at an early age in order to prevent major problems occurring later. Even elementary school counselors today are dealing with drug use, suicide possibilities, the effects of incest and child abuse, and crucial family problems. Thus these counselors provide in-service training to assist teachers in utilizing guidance interventions and in identifying children who need counseling services. Counselors also consult with teachers and parents in understanding normal child growth and development, as well as in providing alternatives for helping children develop and learn with a minimum of behavioral/emotional difficulties.

Student Personnel Services in Higher Education

Almost all postsecondary institutions of higher learning provide a variety of counseling-related services within such areas as admissions; financial aid; student affairs; special programs for minorities; veterans, women, and individuals with disabilities; academic remedial programs; career planning and placement; academic advising; and counseling centers. Such services are ordinarily limited to the students, faculty, and staff of the institution. Many of these programs have responded to the preventive, as well as the growth, needs of students, offering such programs as assertiveness training, self-esteem development, career planning, and personal growth group experiences. On many campuses, professional counselors live and work in college residence halls and provide some of those services directly to the residents.

Substance Abuse Counseling

The increased use of various mood-altering drugs over the past two decades has resulted in an increasing need for counselors who are trained to provide substance abuse counseling. Due to the extent of the drug problem, a number of new programs and approaches have been established, including drop-in centers, hot lines, peer-counseling programs, crisis intervention programs, rap sessions, and the development of new curricular and visual materials for comprehensive drug education programs. Counselors may be involved in any or all of these approaches from either a remedial or a preventive perspective.

Substance abuse counselors must develop a clear understanding of the dynamics of drug use and abuse, as well as a knowledge of the major approaches to prevention and remediation of substance abuse. Drug use is the consumption of any drug, whether legal (alcohol if over a minimum age), prescribed (especially tranquilizers), over-the-counter (such as diet pills and stay-awake pills), or street-corner and illegal. Abuse, which can occur with any of these drugs, happens when a drug is used improperly to enhance the effects of that drug, such as getting drunk, taking a prescribed drug in excess of physician's directions, or other ways that interfere with the individual's functioning. Dependency occurs when an individual "continues to use mood-altering chemicals, despite the problems their usage causes" (George, 1990, p. 4).

Counseling individuals who abuse various drugs is particularly difficult because the drug use is almost always associated with a variety of other problems in the individual's life. Some individuals abuse drugs in an attempt to "self-medicate," attempting to use drugs to help them deal with, or forget, their problems. Others develop major problems in their lives as the result of their drug abuse. For most, major problems existed in their lives before they began to abuse drugs, and the problems worsened as a result of the drug use. In addition, the individual's denial that he or she has a "problem" is characteristic and is very difficult to break.

Traditionally, individuals who have been able to recover from their substance disorder and stay off alcohol and other drugs for at least a year have been the primary choices for counseling jobs in drug treatment centers. However, as a greater understanding of the relationship between other emotional/psychological problems and drug abuse has developed, a corresponding recognition of the need for professionally trained counselors has emerged.

A specialized area within the field of substance abuse counseling has developed in the past decade, focusing on working with the adult children of alcoholics.

Clear patterns of behavioral and emotional problems have been identified in individuals who grew up in a family environment characterized by the insecurity, uncertainty, and unpredictable behavior of an alcoholic parent. Individuals growing up in this environment have frequently developed problems in coping with stress and in developing and maintaining close relationships. These coping and relationship difficulties require the counselor to help the individuals work through grief, shame, and anger, while learning to accept themselves and express their needs.

Rehabilitation Counseling

Rehabilitation counselors are specialists who work with individuals with disabilities in overcoming their limitations and fulfilling their potentials. These counselors work with individuals with physical handicaps such as vision or hearing impairments, loss of an arm or a leg, and joint problems, as well as individuals suffering from mental and psychological impairments. Individuals recently released from prison and individuals who have completed treatment for substance abuse or psychiatric problems are also frequently in need of rehabilitative counseling.

Rehabilitation counselors must possess a great deal of knowledge and skill in helping individuals with disabilities learn to cope and to function in society. Counselors must understand the nature of the disability, the limitations that result, and the various emotional states that are likely to accompany the disability if they are to establish a therapeutic relationship with the individual and work to provide the kind of assistance needed. Of particular importance is the ability to help the individuals and their family deal with the grief process that typically results from the disability. An understanding of career development as it occurs with an individual with a disability, as well as a knowledge of jobs that can be done with various limitations, is particularly important in helping the person remain, or become, a productive member of society.

Mental Health Counseling

A growing field of counseling is mental health counseling. Working within the context of the mental and human services systems, mental health counselors have become key members of a variety of mental health treatment teams in hospitals and mental health agencies.

Mental health counselors work in the diagnosis, treatment, and prevention of mental and emotional disorders and dysfunctional behavior. They must have a knowledge of various psychopathological disorders, as well as an understanding of the primary approaches for treatment. Frequently working with a psychiatrist, who makes decisions about the use of psychotropic medication, the mental health counselor in hospital settings generally acts as a case manager for the patient during the treatment process. In doing so, the counselor may recommend, for instance, the need for psychological testing, schedule the testing, and utilize the testing results in establishing treatment goals. The counselor becomes the primary provider of individual and group intervention and is often responsible for some type of aftercare following discharge.

Counselors in mental health agencies often provide the same services but with limited contact with the clients. Counselors in these settings are often the key professionals in determining whether or not an individual needs to be hospitalized for treatment. In this setting, counselors are also likely to be involved with community groups and agencies in developing prevention strategies and in promoting community mental health.

Health and Wellness Counseling

In addition to a trend for all counselors to be concerned with the total well-being of clients, including their physical health, an increasing number of counselors are employed in settings where their primary focus is on physical health. Wellness programs, emphasizing nutrition, exercise, or stress management, are important in helping individuals deal with a specific area of their lives in terms of an ongoing prevention of disease and the maintenance of wellness.

Business and Industry

For many years, graduates of counseling programs have found business and industry a possibility for employment, working primarily in personnel departments, and dealing with employment and labor dispute problems. In recent years, however, *personnel* is more likely to be called *human services*, and the scope of the responsibilities for such departments has expanded. Employee assistance programs, career development programs, job placement programs for individuals whose employment has been terminated, and team-building workshops are now routinely provided. Professionally trained counselors are finding their roles in business and industry to be expanding and increasing in value to management.

Employee assistance programs have had a major growth over the past decade. Counselors in this area work with supervisors in training them to identify workers whose performance is suffering and to refer those workers to the EAP office. Counselors then are responsible for diagnosing the problem, determining its severity, and either providing short-term treatment or referring the worker for treatment from a contracted agency. Such a program recognizes the importance of offering help to troubled employees rather than dismissing them and shows far more concern for the individuals.

Private Practice

A large number of people who enter counseling training programs, as well as many who are already employed as counselors, identify a strong desire to enter private practice as a professional counselor. Many counselors in schools and agencies develop a part-time private practice as a step toward a full-time practice.

However, the process of developing and maintaining a private practice requires a great deal of creativity, persistence, and hard work. Counselors in private practice need excellent counseling skills, but they also need marketing ability and managerial skills. Frequently, such counselors must spend as much time making contacts for referrals and handling the administrative details of the practice as they spend providing counseling services. As a result, many counselors who enter private practice return to a school or an agency in order to be able to have more time for counseling itself.

The Role of the Counselor

The role of the counselor has changed in many ways over the past few years. The major settings in which counselors practice have shifted from almost exclusively school and career counseling settings to such areas as private practice, counseling centers, community mental health centers, and hospital/medical settings. The increased number of counselors working in hospitals and clinics has been largely a result of a recognition that counselors have the training desired to work with individuals with substance abuse problems, eating disorders, stress management concerns, and various emotional/psychological difficulties. Working with a team of mental health professionals that often includes psychiatrists, psychologists, and psychiatric nurses, counselors are typically the primary care giver and case manager for patients.

With this development has come an increased emphasis on a holistic model for wellness and prevention that covers the entire life span. This approach, in which counselors are concerned about the "whole person," broadens the focus of counseling to the physical, social, mental, emotional, and, often, spiritual needs of the individual. Counselors are now involved in helping individuals with physical fitness and health habits, at times in specific areas such as weight control clinics or physical exercise programs. Counselors often deal with emotional/psychological issues that may have interfered with positive health habits or with providing the kind of motivation needed to encourage an individual to develop a healthy life style. Related to these functions has been the emphasis on helping clients to learn to facilitate relaxation and positive emotional states as ways of influencing internal bodily functions (Wittmer and Sweeney, 1992).

The social needs of the individual include family relationships, the work environment, friendships, and other activities/relationships that connect each person with the human community. These relationships provide a means by which the individual engages in activities that provide the emotional support of others and that help prevent the sense of loneliness that may lead to depression, low self-esteem, substance abuse, and increased physical problems.

In many ways, counselors probably emphasize the mental development of clients less than the other areas. Yet, by recognizing the relationship between cognition, affect, and behavior, counselors may encourage clients to engage in activities such as reading self-help books or working toward cognitive restructuring of one's belief system about certain events in that person's life. More importantly, however, counselors are beginning to recognize how essential it is to work with clients to stimulate their thinking processes and increase their problem-solving abilities as well as their creativity. Such mental and creative activity is a major part of quality of life.

In many ways, the focus on each of the other four aspects of the whole person relates to the goal of improving the emotional well-being of the individual. This traditional area of concern for the counselor continues to be a primary focus, since individuals generally seek counseling because of the way they "feel" about their lives and/or some event within their lives. The importance of the individual's physical, social, mental, and spiritual needs becomes clear as clients talk about their feelings and the relationship of those feelings to other people and situations in their lives.

The spiritual needs of the person, long considered too value-laden and personal to be part of the counseling process unless the client specifically sought help in this area, is gaining increasing attention as counselors begin to recognize how one's behavior, thoughts, and feelings are connected to one's spiritual beliefs. These spiritual beliefs "represent values that reflect what is considered sacred and essential for the sustenance of life" (Wittmer and Sweeney, 1992, p. 141). For many individuals, religious beliefs are the central core of their spirituality; for others, the set of values that they have developed are central. Spirituality is now seen in counseling as the rules individuals live their lives by, comprised of their beliefs about character, life-style, and reverence for life.

Thus, counselors are engaging in a wider variety of activities designed to facilitate the total growth and development of the individual. Such an approach recognizes that a "band-aid" method of helping with one problem of a client may have only temporary relief for that person if contributing functions in the individual's life continue to create problems. By showing concern with the overall functioning of the individual, the counselor is attempting to help the client become self-sustaining and on the way to become an individual who is able to live and enjoy life to its fullest.

Myers (1992) has pointed out that the strong link that has been established between physical and mental health strongly suggests that preventive mental health interventions can have an impact on both emotional wellness and physical wellness. She supports the idea of counselors providing developmental, preventive, wellness interventions across the life span in order to facilitate mental and physical well-being. This approach, which she calls the "cornerstone of the profession," provides a new paradigm for the role of the counselor today and in the future.

In many ways, this emphasis on the total well-being of the client is what makes the role of the counselor unique. Social workers focus on the social aspects of an individual's life, and clinical psychologists focus on the diagnosis and treatment of individuals with severe emotional/psychological problems. Counselors are more likely to deal with the total life of the person—family, work, leisure, intellectual development, spirituality, and emotional well-being.

Differences in Counseling and Clinical Psychology

The distinction between counseling and psychotherapy parallels the distinction between counseling psychology and clinical psychology. The difference historically has been one of focus, with counseling psychology concerning itself with normalcy and clinical psychology concerning itself with diagnosing the nature and extent of psychopathology, with "uncovering adjustment difficulties and maladaptive tendencies" (Super, 1955, p. 5). However, this distinction has become less clear as counseling psychologists have increased their involvement with chronically emotionally disturbed populations and clinical psychologists have become more involved with the educative and skill-building emphases related to development issues (Herr and Cramer, 1987).

Thus, as Herr and Cramer (1987) point out, there is a blurring of techniques and processes between clinical psychology and counseling psychology with both studying and practicing psychotherapy. They go on to point out that both groups tend to use the same kinds of psychotherapeutic interventions and to overlap in terms of settings and functions. As a result, serious consideration needs to be given to Levy's (1984) proposal for a merger of clinical, counseling, and school psychology into a broader field, which he called *human services psychology*.

Summary

Counseling is viewed as a relationship, as well as a process, and is designed to help people make choices and resolve problems.

Although the distinction between counseling and psychotherapy is difficult to state clearly, differences between the two exist and may best be analyzed by viewing the activities of the two as taking place along a continuum. Counseling is most characterized by terms such as *educational, preventive, short-term,* and *problem-solving;* psychotherapy is more often characterized by terms such as *reconstructive, emphasis on severe emotional problems, remediation,* and *long-term.*

Five general goals of counseling are (1) facilitating behavior change, (2) improving the client's ability to establish and maintain relationships, (3) enhancing the client's ability to cope, (4) promoting the decision-making process, and (5) facilitating client potential and development.

Counseling as a professional activity can be traced back to 1898, when it began as a vocational guidance movement. Other mental health movements contributed to the growth of counseling, as did the development of testing programs. Legislation in the 1950s was particularly important in giving stronger impetus to counseling.

Counseling services are provided by individuals involved in a number of different professions, including social work, psychiatry, clinical psychology, and clergy.

Counselors must work toward giving the institutions in which they work and the clients they serve a better understanding of their role. This role must be personally defined within the institutional guidelines and clearly communicated both to the institution and to the clients.

References

American Personnel and Guidance Association. (1980). *Licensure committee action packet.* Washington, D.C.

Blackham, G. J. (1977). *Counseling: Theory, process and practice.* Belmont, CA: Wadsworth.

Blocher, D. H. (1987). *The Professional Counselor.* New York: Macmillan.

Burks, H. M., & Stefflre, B. (1979). *Theories of counseling* (3rd ed.). New York: McGraw-Hill.

Cottone, R. R. (1992). *Therories and paradigms of counseling and psychotherapy.* Boston: Allyn and Bacon.

Dustin, R., & George, R. (1977). *Action counseling for behavior change* (2nd ed.). Cranston, RI: Carroll Press.

Forester, J. R. (1977). What shall we do about credentialing? *Personnel and Guidance Journal, 55,* 573–576.

George, R. L. (1990). *Counseling the chemically dependent.* Englewood Cliffs, NJ: Prentice Hall.

Herr, E. L., & Cramer, S. H. (1987). *Controversies in the mental health professions.* Muncie, IN: Accelerated Development.

Krumboltz, J. D. (1965). Behavioral counseling: rationale and research. *Personnel and Guidance Journal, 44,* 383–387.

Krumboltz, J. D. (1966). Behavioral goals of counseling. *Journal of counseling psychology, 13,* 153–159.

Krumboltz, J. D., & Thoresen, C. E. (Eds.). (1976). *Counseling methods.* New York: Holt, Rinehart & Winston.

Jaeger, R. M. , & Frye, A. W. (1988). An assessment of the job relevance of the National Board for Certified Counselors examination. *Journal of Counseling and Development, 67,* 22–26

Levy, L. H. (1984). The metamorphosis of clinical psychology: Toward a new charter as human services psychology. *American psychologist, 39,* 486–494.

Myers, J. E. (1992). Wellness, prevention, development: The cornerstone of the profession. *Journal of counseling and develoment, 71,* 136–139.

Patterson, C. H. (1980). *Theories of counseling and psychotherapy* (3rd ed.). New York: Harper & Row.

Peterson, J. V. & Nisenholz, B. (1991) *Orientation to counseling* (2nd ed.) Boston: Allyn and Bacon.

Rogers, C. (1961) *On becoming a person.* Boston: Houghton Mifflin.

Rossberg, R. H., & Band, L. (1978). *Historical antecedents of counseling: A revisionist point of view.* In J. C. Hansen (Ed.), *Counseling process and procedures.* New York: Macmillan.

Shertzer, B., & Stone, S. C. (1974) *Fundamentals of counseling* (2nd ed.). Boston: Houghton Mifflin.

Vacc, N. A. (1992). An assessment of the perceived relevance of the CACREP standards. *Journal of counseling and development, 70,* 685–687.

Wittmer, J. (1988). CACREP or APA: A counselor educator's personal view. *Counselor education and supervision, 27,* 291–294.

Wittmer, J. M., & Sweeney, T. J. (1992). A holistic model for wellness and prevention over the life span. *Journal of counseling and development, 71,* 140–148.

Zeig, J. K. (1987). Introduction: The evolution of psychotherapy. In J. K. Zeig. (Ed.), *The evolution of psychotherapy.* New York: Brunner/Mazel.

Chapter 2

On Becoming a Counselor

A career in counseling differs significantly from a career in most other professions. Unlike law, medicine, engineering, political science, or accounting, counselors use themselves as instruments of therapeutic change. Although counseling obviously requires mastery of skills and knowledge of theory, the counseling process is more dependent on who the counselor is than on what the counselor knows or can do.

What makes an effective counselor, and what is the training process to become one? Is it possible to develop the qualities or characteristics associated with effective counseling, or are these qualities inherent? Most beginning counselors in training wonder whether they have chosen a profession in which they can be successful.

The journey to effective counseling is not as clearly defined as the accumulation of courses toward an advanced degree in some other areas. Although there is a prescribed course of study, it has been said that effective counselors are not trained to counsel. Rather, they become effective through a process that may include many components: formal courses, self-growth, personal therapy, supervision, and actual practice. Due to the complexity of this learning process and the fact that each student brings to the process a unique life experience, there are differences in how long it takes to become effective, and the journey, for many, is a complex transformative process.

Personal Characteristics of Effective Counselors

This chapter discusses the desired qualities of effective counselors and explores the process of counselor education, values in counseling, and other issues related to choosing a profession in counseling.

What are the qualities associated with effective counseling? Counseling theorists and researchers have given these questions as much attention as any in the field of counseling. Carkhuff and his associates (Carkhuff, 1969a, 1969b; Truax and Carkhuff, 1967; Carkhuff and Berenson, 1977) isolated through extensive research investigations the "core conditions" of effective counseling. To summarize, this research found that fully functioning counselors demonstrated high levels of these qualities regardless of their theoretical orientation. The core conditions include empathy, genuineness, positive regard, and concreteness. These core conditions will be discussed in detail in Chapter 7.

In addition to the core conditions, other personal traits of the counselor have been found to be very important. The Association of Counselor Education and Supervision (1964) indicated that the counselor should have six basic qualities: belief in each individual, commitment to individual human values, alertness to the world, open mindedness, understanding of self, and professional commitment.

Combs and his coworkers (1969) concluded from a series of studies that the major differences between effective and ineffective counselors were their personal beliefs and traits. These findings led Combs to conclude that the major "technique" of counseling was the *self-as-instrument*; the counselor's self or person became the major facilitator of positive growth for clients. In addition, Combs studied some basic beliefs that counselors held concerning people and their ability to help themselves. He found that effective counselors perceived other people as *able* rather than unable to solve their own problems and manage their own lives. Effective counselors also perceived people as *dependable, friendly,* and *worthy.* They were also more likely to identify with *people* rather than things, to see people as having an adequate *capacity to cope* with problems, and to be more *self-revealing* than self-concealing.

Combs and Soper (1963) found that effective counselors perceived their clients as capable, dependable, friendly, and worthy, and perceived themselves as altruistic and nondominating. Rogers (1961) concluded from his experiences and his reviews of research that the counselor's theory and methods were far less important than the client's perception of the counselor's attitudes. Rogers was pointing out that the effective counselor must be an attractive, friendly person, someone who inspires confidence and trust.

The research suggests that one approach to determining counselor effectiveness is to look for characteristics of personal effectiveness. Allen found that "the effective counselor is a person who is on relatively good terms with his own emotional experience and that the ineffective counselor is one who is relatively uneasy in regard to the character of his inner life" (1967, p. 39).

Following is a composite list of qualities that are present in highly effective counselors. This discussion must begin with an analysis of effective individuals. Over the years, a number of models of human effectiveness have been presented from which a composite model can be drawn. It must be reiterated that these are characteristics generally found in effective counselors. The list is incomplete and still evolving. The model is presented as a stimulus for present and prospective counselors as a goal toward which they should strive. These same qualities may also be seen as goals for clients to attain a result of the counseling process.

Effective counselors are open to and accepting of their own feelings and experiences. Such individuals do not try to control their emotional reactions but are able to accept their feelings as they are. Openness, as used in this context, means being open to oneself, not necessarily revealing oneself to everyone with whom one comes in contact. Much of our experience teaches us to deny our feelings. Small boys are told "big boys don't cry." Even adults are discouraged from expressing their feelings openly. Pressures are applied not to feel depressed or not to be angry. Effective counselors can accept within themselves feelings of sadness, anger, resentment, and other feelings that are ordinarily considered negative. By accepting these feelings as they are without denying or distorting them, effective counselors have greater control over their behavior. Because they are aware of their emotional reactions, they can choose how they wish to act, rather than permitting their feelings to affect their behavior without their conscious awareness.

Persons learn to be accepting of their experiences (1) if the significant individuals in their lives model such acceptance and (2) if they are not punished for their feelings. Counselors have a positive effect on clients when the client's undesired emotional reactions—boredom, anger, anxiety, depression—are accepted.

Allowing clients to have negative feelings is far more effective in promoting positive growth than telling clients that they are foolish to feel the way they do, logical though such arguments may be.

Effective counselors must be self-aware. In addition to being open to and accepting of their feelings, effective counselors are introspective and in touch with their own issues and actively work to resolve them. They must know their strengths and weaknesses and accept themselves. Counselors who are not aware of their own issues can be very harmful to clients by using their clients to meet their own personal needs. For example, a counselor who seeks personal power may encourage clients to become dependent in the relationship. Counselors who do not establish healthy, satisfying friendships may not create appropriate boundaries with clients and may, therefore, encourage clients to see them socially.

Effective counselors are aware of their own values and beliefs. They know what is important to them and have determined the standards by which they wish to live. Thus, they can make decisions and choose alternatives that are consistent with their value systems. More important, a clear value system allows individuals to find a meaningful role for their lives and gives them guidelines for relating to the people and things around them. They can avoid ineffective and inconsistent patterns of behavior and instead engage in more positive, purposeful, and rewarding behavior.

Effective counselors are open-minded. They are aware of their own personal values and at the same time must be able to resist forcing their values on clients. This means that counselors are deeply appreciative of and accepting of human differences and do not need to impose their values on others. This nonjudgmental attitude must be communicated verbally and nonverbally, and it must be genuine.

Effective counselors are risk-takers. These individuals are willing to be vulnerable and take interpersonal risks. They do not hide behind a professional facade. They are willing to be honest and direct with others and are free to challenge clients when appropriate. These individuals are self-disclosing and transparent. They are congruent verbally and non-verbally. They are free to express caring, warmth, and support.

Effective counselors are able to develop warm and deep relationships with others. They can prize other individuals—their feelings, their opinions, their persons. This feeling is caring, but a nonpossessive caring with little evaluation or judgment. The other person is accepted with few conditions. Most of us experience a certain amount of fear toward feeling warmth toward another person. We fear that if we let ourselves freely experience such positive feelings toward another, we will become trapped and therefore vulnerable. Other persons may take advantage of us; they may make demands that we are unable to reject; they may reject our feelings by failing to reciprocate. So we keep our distance, rarely permitting ourselves to get deeply connected to another person. Effective counselors are less vulnerable to such fears because they recognize that the risk involved is worth the value to be gained. They therefore respond to other people more freely, developing close relationships with those who share their interests and values. They have wide freedom of choice in developing such relationships because of their ability to care and their relative lack of fear of intimacy.

Effective counselors allow themselves to be seen as they actually are. This characteristic results in an attitude of realness or genuineness. When individuals gain awareness of and accept the feelings they are experiencing, they need not impose feelings on others nor put up a facade to make people think they are something they are not. Authentic people are willing to be themselves and to express, in their words and in their behavior, the various feelings and attitudes they hold. They do not need to present an outward facade of one attitude while holding another attitude at a deeper level. They do not pretend to know the answers when they do not. They do not act like loving persons at moments when they feel hostile. They do not act as though they are confident and full of assurance when they are actually frightened and unsure. On a simpler level, they do not act well when they feel ill.

Part of the difficulty for most individuals is that, the energy spent on playing a role or presenting a facade prevents them from using that energy for accomplishing tasks and solving problems. In addition, effective persons, by presenting their authentic selves to others, are more able to develop cooperative relationships with others, thus gaining support for problem-solving tasks. They have less need to puff up their own importance, to blow their own horn. They can share the limelight; therefore, they are able to secure the help of others.

Effective counselors accept personal responsibility for their own behaviors. Rather than denying the way they are and blaming others, effective counselors can handle their failures and weaknesses. They recognize that, although many situations are largely caused by factors beyond their control, they are responsible for their actions in these situations. Recognizing that they can determine, in large part, their own behavior gives them the freedom to consciously choose either to conform to external group control or to ignore those controls, with that choice based on well-considered reasons.

This acceptance of personal responsibility also means that these individuals are able to accept criticism in a much more constructive way. Instead of constantly defending themselves, effective counselors view criticism as a desirable feedback mechanism permitting them to lead more effective, constructive lives. They stand by their behaviors rather than "passing the buck" or blaming others.

Effective counselors have developed realistic levels of aspiration. Ordinarily, persons raise their goals slightly as a result of success and lower their goals after failure. In this way they protect themselves from both too easy achievement and continued failure. Sometimes this self-protective mechanism is thrown out of balance, and individuals either set their goals too high, which results in inevitable failure, or too low, which robs them of a sense of achievement, no matter what they do.

Effective counselors, on the other hand, are able to set obtainable goals and take failure in stride. Because they are aware of their own skills and abilities, they can accurately estimate what to expect from themselves. Their acceptance of their experiences—both positive and negative—enables them to evaluate previous goals realistically and to use this evaluation to establish future goals.

Effective counselors are curious about personality and human behavior. Counselors are aware of the complexity of personality. They have knowledge of theories of personality, and their theoretical framework guides their practice. They can conceptualize a model of human behavior.

Effective counselors have a sense of humor. Because of the serious and intense nature of the counseling process, counselors must be able to maintain a perspective and be able to share with clients the humor of the human condition.

Effective counselors are intuitive. Counselors who trust themselves and are free to make deep contact with others can respond spontaneously to clients based on their intuition. They take in many nonverbal cues and often respond to a client without a conscious awareness of where the response comes from. They simply "know" at an intuitive level what might be going on with a client and trust these intuitions enough to share them.

Personal characteristics of effective counselors:

1. Are open to and accepting of their own feelings and experiences.
2. Are self-aware.
3. Are aware of their own values and beliefs.
4. Are open-minded.
5. Are risk-takers.
6. Are able to develop warm and deep relationships with others.
7 Are able to allow themselves to be seen by others as they really are.
8. Accept personal responsibility for their own behaviors.
9. Develop realistic levels of aspiration.
10. Are curious about personality and human behavior.
11. Have a sense of humor.
12. Are intuitive.

The Process of Counselor Education

From the discussion of the characteristics of effective counselors, it is clear that becoming an effective therapist is a process combining personal exploration and growth with mastery of knowledge and skills training. Because of the demands on the personhood of the counselor, not everyone who enters a counselor education program is well suited for a career in the counseling profession. How do beginning students know if there is a match between their own personalities and the requirements of the field of counseling? This is a complex issue because of the wide range of needs/interests that motivate individuals to pursue a career in counseling.

Many students enroll in a graduate program in counseling because they have had a career in another helping profession such as teaching or nursing and have enjoyed the one-to-one contact with individuals. They have typically found themselves functioning in a "helping" capacity and have received feedback that others can trust them. They are sensitive and caring individuals who genuinely care about others. Other students are searching for a career change and decide to try out counseling because others have usually sought their advice or counsel.

Another growing group of entering students have been clients themselves and are interested in "paying back" the help they have received. These students bring into the program a high level of self-awareness and some experience of the counseling process itself. Although previous experience as a client may, indeed, be a real strength, it is also important for these students to be sure that they have grown enough to be able to be therapeutic to others. Counseling is a serious profession. There is great potential for helping others, but the potential for harm is even greater. It is imperative that "wounded healers" have worked through their own issues and are able to set themselves aside so they can accurately perceive the client's world. Although most counselors are continuously striving to grow and become more effective through their own self-development, it is critical that counselors in training are far enough along in their growth process that they can focus their energy on others.

Many students enter their first counseling classes expecting what they have previously encountered in their educational experiences. They are prepared to read, master material, listen to lectures, and regurgitate facts on examinations. They expect to be challenged academically and may be concerned about their cognitive ability. It is, therefore, often surprising and disconcerting when they encounter the process-oriented experience of counselor education. Having previously focused on academic performance, they may experience confusion and disorientation when they enter classes that focus on their personal growth and development. It can be quite threatening to learn that not only will they be expected to master material and acquire skills, but most importantly they will be expected to embark on an intense personal journey of self-exploration. This journey, which may begin in their first counseling class, will possibly lead to accelerated personal change.

This personal change process that often accompanies a graduate program in counseling can be exciting and exhilarating as well as frightening and confusing. Counseling programs trigger the intense exploration of self and an examination of one's personal relationships. Such exploration requires a delicate balance between support and challenge. Most students and their families are not prepared for the pervasive impact of entering a graduate program that demands personal introspection and growth. The entire family actually enrolls in a change process, which may be quite unpredictable and even dangerous. So, one wonders what to expect when the door to personal change is opened so wide that it may cause a total restructuring of one's life (Seashore, 1975).

The basis for such dramatic change typically stems from a shift in personal values as well as from the development of interpersonal skills that changes one's expectations for the quality and depth of personal relationships. As students begin exploring themselves and developing new relationships with other students in training, they typically begin re-examining their marriage and personal friendships and may try to re-negotiate or even withdraw from their primary support system. This can be perceived as a paradox of the training process. At a time when students are under enormous pressure to be highly successful and competent, they are required to open up and expose the most vulnerable aspects of themselves. And, they must do this when they have abandoned their life-long support systems and have not had time to build new relationships that are grounded in more current values and styles of communication. Thus, students find themselves in an emotional dilemma: They must try to grow and change when they are letting go of the relationships that have given them their stability and security. Even if students are able to salvage their closest relationships, there is fertile ground for conflict due to the lack of understanding, and perhaps the sense of threat or envy that their significant others experience. Due to these challenges to one's most intimate relationships, students may experience anger, depression, resentment, and even loss of relationships (Seashore, 1975).

Most students do not anticipate such dramatic ramifications from their enrollment in a graduate program in counseling. However, once the student's previously held values are challenged, a change process is put in place, and there is no turning back. Students may experience a growing sense of isolation or even desperation as they confront aspects of their marriage and significant relationships that cannot go unexplored. In sum, because the program requires enormous personal energy and also provides the opportunity for the exploration of deep personal concerns and for intense personal encounters, it can be treacherous territory.

The impact of the program on returning students may be even more dramatic. Many of these students may have functioned competently in the field as professionals and may find themselves feeling threatened, incompetent, confused, frightened, and generally overwhelmed. The high levels of stress and anxiety combined with severe blows to their ego may reach levels that actually block learning. Additionally. they may experience being used and/or abused by faculty due to their professional skills and competence. In other words, returning students suffer the additional stress of starting over, of comparing themselves to those who are brighter or have more credentials, and of questioning their previously recognized competence. In essence, they are beginning again.

From a more positive perspective, a counselor education program offers students the opportunity to engage in a transformative process that may be terrifying in its initial phases but that has the potential for restructuring one's life and increasing the potential for depth and meaning. The rewards of change at this intense personal level match the pain and struggle. Students who are aware of some of the possible adjustments and emotional hurdles may be able to navigate their course with fewer negative effects.

Personal Values in Counseling

The issue of what role the counselor's values should play in the helping relationship has been widely debated in the professional literature. Counselors certainly need to be in touch with their own personal values and, as stated earlier, their behavior should be guided by their belief system. Should counselors expose their values to clients? What are the risks involved? Can a counselor's values be exposed without being imposed on the client? Corey and Corey (1989) assert that the counselor's values will be communicated in the relationship at some level (either verbally or non-verbally), and that it is preferable for the counselor to expose them directly. Corey and Corey (1989) make it clear that exposing values is different from imposing one's value system. Others assert that the counselor's values should be a part of the therapeutic relationship. There are numerous concerns in this regard. The therapeutic process is grounded in the therapist's ability to deeply accept the client regardless of the client's and counselor's personal differences. Many clients' concerns boil down to their personal struggle with their values and their inability to know and act on what they honestly believe. The therapist is in an extremely influential position, and the slightest judgment or criticism can powerfully impact clients' feelings about themselves and their decisions. It has been suggested by Belkin (1984) that the primary value to which counselors must commit themselves is personal freedom. Freedom is an ideal that propels the individual to certain types of actions. Freedom allows the individual to determine what direction in which to move. It allows the individual to be creative, to make choices and be responsible for them. Freedom also commits clients to assuming responsibility for their actions and the consequences. Blocher (1987) states that one of the primary goals of counseling is to help the client maximize this freedom so that clients can choose directions, settings, and situations that will best facilitate their growth.

Perhaps the debate over the role of the counselor's values in the therapeutic relationship is really one of semantics. Most practitioners would probably agree that some values are communicated by the counselor in the therapeutic relationship whether or not the counselor wishes to do so. There are probably different categories of values, some of which should be communicated and others which should not. The type of values that are potentially helpful in the therapeutic relationship are what Egan (1977) has called "interpersonal values". Most therapists communicate that they value introspection, self-awareness, personal freedom, and as Corey and Corey (1989) have said, the importance of painful experiences in self-understanding and healing. These interpersonal values teach clients how to grow and change and how to develop more effective interpersonal relationships. These values seem inherent in the therapeutic process and are significant in terms of client growth.

The interpersonal values seem significantly different from another category or level of values that is more specific to each individual's life choices. The values might include those around sexual preference, abortion, hard work, monogamy, etc. Although the therapist will probably have personal preferences in these areas as well, it seems critical that their views are not exposed or imposed on the client. If one of the primary goals of counseling is to promote client self-discovery and an internal locus of control, it seems fundamental that therapists strive to help clients' determine their own values and beliefs without needing clients to think and act like them. Counselors must be extremely careful to remain neutral so that clients can come to know who they are without being influenced. Therapists who expose or impose these values on clients are violating their human freedom and run the risk of being responsible for life choices that may be harmful to clients. The greatest potential damage in the area of counselors' exposing/imposing their values is that clients may feel judged or criticized in the relationship. Criticism at such a core level by a person as significant as a therapist can thwart any attempt at self-actualization on the client's part.

On Becoming a Counselor

As implied in this chapter, self-exploration, introspection, and self-understanding are a fundamental part of the process of becoming a counselor. This self-knowledge can be developed through a variety of ways: academic courses, self-growth groups, workshops, and personal counseling. It is important, if not critical, that all counselors in training experience being a client. This affords them the opportunity to understand what it is like to be a client; to know what a client needs from a counselor; to feel the anxiety and vulnerability of disclosing oneself to a stranger; and to explore their own issues and themes in a therapeutic context.

Self-exploration and introspection do not end with graduate training. They are an essential part of the lifestyle of a counselor. Counselors must continue to stay in touch with themselves as long as they continue to see clients.

Another important aspect of becoming a counselor involves learning to value "process." Rather than focusing one's time and energy on the outcomes or products of learning, counselors must learn to appreciate the learning process itself. As counselors learn, grow, explore, and gain insight into themselves, they need to observe how they get through the experience. This level of reflection will assist them with clients who are struggling to gain similar levels of self-understanding. Processing interactions, experiences, and feelings, and learning to draw connections and identify themes, are essential to becoming a counselor. If we have not done this in our own lives, we cannot facilitate the process for others.

At yet another level, becoming a counselor involves a commitment to others. This genuine concern for another's well-being is not a role one plays when at the office. It is a lifestyle that permeates the counselor's interactions regardless of context. Although counselors are obviously compensated for their concern, they do not switch that concern on and off depending on a time schedule. For a counselor to be effective, they must give deeply and compassionately to others. This level of commitment of one's personal resources can be both an incredible gift as well as a serious and potentially dangerous drain of one's self. This is, perhaps, the most difficult course to navigate as a professional in this field. How can I give so deeply of myself and not lose me in the process? It is essential that counselors struggle with this question. They will not be effective if they withhold themselves in the therapeutic context, and they will not be effective if they give of themselves so deeply that there is nothing left. None of us have endless supplies of emotional and psychological energy. It is essential that we nurture ourselves and find ways to restore all that we give. Obviously, we do not all take care of ourselves in the same way. Some of us need to spend time alone. Others are nourished through deep and intimate friendships; others might need to get away to the woods or ocean. As counselors, we all need to know what fills us, what nourishes us, so that we can continue giving. Ideally, in addition to finding and using our personal resources, counselors will maintain a supervisory relationship in which they can discuss their clients and any personal issues that might be triggered by the counseling relationship. If supervision is not available, counselors could establish a professional network or organize group case consultations. Many counselors continue their own therapy so they have a place to go to be listened to and to process the issues clients trigger in their own lives. All these activities help prevent counselor burnout and help ensure that counselors are receiving as they give. It seems important that agencies or counseling practices look for ways to offer support for their staff. These could include balancing client contact hours with other activities: supervision, in-service training, or perhaps offering body massage. As counselors, we must constantly monitor ourselves and our needs, if we hope to be effective. If we don't, we not only risk burnout or in the most serious instances, suicide; we also cannot give to clients at therapeutic levels. Unfortunately, too many private practitioners get caught in the financial aspects of running a business and begin seeing far more clients than they can be effective with. Counselors have a responsibility to themselves and to their clients to manage a client load that does not overextend them.

In summary, becoming a counselor is an incredible journey that involves a lifelong commitment to others. Students considering this profession must assess whether their interpersonal values and personal resources are adequate to meet the intense emotional and psychological demands of professional counseling. Although the personal demands are high, the rewards are incredible. Professional counselors have the unique life experience of being able to touch others deeply and participate in a transformational process. Changing others' lives at this level and connecting with others this intimately is extremely challenging and richly satisfying.

Summary

In this chapter we have explored the qualities of effective counselors; the process of counselor education; the role of the counselor's values in the counseling relationship as well as what it means to become a professional counselor. Students considering a career as a professional counselor are encouraged to engage in a deep process of self-exploration so as to better facilitate this process for clients.

References

Allen, T. (1967). Effectiveness of counselor trainees as a function of psychological openness. *Journal of Counseling Psychology, 14,* 35–40.

Association for Counselor Education and Supervision, (1964). The counselor: Professional preparation and role. *Personnel and Guidance Journal, 42,* 536–541.

Belkin, G. (1984). *Introduction to counseling* (2nd ed.) Dubuque, Iowa: Wm. C. Brown.

Blocher, D. H. (1987). *The professional counselor.* New York: Macmillan.

Carkhuff, R. R. (1969a). *Helping and human relations: A primer for lay and professional helpers. Vol. 1: Selection and training.* New York: Holt, Rinehart and Winston.

Carkhuff, R. R. (1969b). *Helping and human relations: A primer for lay and professional helpers. Vol. 2: Practice and research.* New York: Holt, Rinehart and Winston.

Carkhuff, R. R. & Berenson, B. G. (1977). *Beyond counseling and therapy* (2nd ed.). New York: Holt, Rinehart and Winston.

Combs, A., & Soper, D. (1963). The perceptual organization of effective counselors. *Journal of Counseling Psychology, 13,* 77–81.

Combs, A., Soper, D., Gooding, C., Benton, J. Dickman, J., & Usher, S. (1969). *Florida studies in the helping professions.* Gainesville: University of Florida Press.

Corey, G. & Corey, M. S. (1989). *Becoming a helper.* Monterey, CA: Brooks Cole.

Egan, G. (1977). *You and me: The skills of communicating and relating to others.* Belmont, CA: Wadsworth.

Rogers, C. (1961). *On becoming a person.* Boston: Houghton Mifflin.

Seashore, C. (1975). In grave danger of growing: Observations on the process of professional development. Paper presented to candidates and faculty of Washington School of Psychiatry Group Psychotherapy Training Program.

Truax, C. B. & Carkhuff, R. R. (1967). *Toward effective counseling and psychotherapy.* Chicago: Aldine.

Part *II*

Theoretical Approaches to Counseling

Chapter *3*

Psychoanalytic Foundations

Chapters 3, 4, and 5 give a brief overview of the theoretical foundations of some of the counseling approaches in use today. The approaches summarized in these chapters have been chosen because they have attained significant support in the field.

The impact of psychoanalytic thought on the field of counseling and psychotherapy is summarized to provide insight into the way the study of human behavior has developed over the years. Chapters 4 and 5 are divided according to the emphasis of the theories—feelings or thoughts and behaviors. Each approach recognizes and deals with both aspects, but places a primary emphasis on one of the two.

Only an introduction to these approaches is given in these chapters; prospective counselors are urged to study each approach in much greater depth and to explore other approaches that seem relevant.

Chapter 6 discusses theory in greater detail—its nature, function, and purpose—and will provide some comparisons of these theories as a beginning point for the counselor in developing a personal theoretical model.

Sigmund Freud

While Freudian theory is not considered to be entirely relevant to present counseling practice, it is essential to understand the influential role it has played in current theoretical conceptualizations. A close examination of the theories presented here will reveal that many are extensions or modifications of Freudian thought. Here we will explore the basic constructs of Freud, and we will summarize the significant contributions of his followers Adler, Horney, and Sullivan, and the ego analysts. Due to the limitations of space in this text, interested readers are encouraged to read the original works of each of these important theorists.

Sigmund Freud, in an effort that spanned more than forty years, developed what is thought to be the first comprehensive theory of personality. This theory was revised over the years as a result of Freud's experience in his clinical practice. Psychoanalysis, then, is not only a theory, but also a method of therapy.

Freud's views of the importance of the unconscious were at odds with previously held views of behavior. These views, which emphasized conscious processes, were thought to be totally inadequate by Freud, who viewed the unconscious as a huge region of feelings, urges, and passions which exerted control over conscious behavior. Thus he developed techniques, such as free association and dream interpretation, to enable the therapist to tap these unconscious but powerful determinants of behavior.

The works of Freud are far too numerous to list. Important introductions to Freudian thought would include Brenner's (1974) *An Elementary Textbook of Psychoanalysis*, and Hall's (1954) *A Primer of Freudian Psychology*.

Structure of Personality

Personality, according to Freud, is composed of three systems: the id, ego, and superego. These systems are interrelated, and behavior is a function of the interaction among them.

The Id

Freud regards the id as the original system of personality, consisting of all that is inherited at birth, including the instincts. Within the id lies the reservoir of psychic energy which fuels the other two systems, the ego and the superego. The id is in direct contact with bodily processes, represents the inner world of subjective experience, and operates to reduce tension. Because the id cannot tolerate tension, it discharges it immediately and returns the organism to a homeostatic state. This principle of tension reduction is called the *pleasure principle*. Thus, the id functions to satisfy the needs of the organism by decreasing pain and increasing pleasure, with no concern for external realities or morality.

The Ego

Because the id is the driving force of the personality and functions at an unconscious level with no concern for external reality, the ego exists to make transactions with the objective world of reality. That is, it is the responsibility of the ego to make decisions about which instincts to satisfy and to somehow mediate between the conflicting demands of the id, the superego, and the real world. The ego is thus in control of the actions of the organism, and it employs intellect and reason to satisfy the organism's needs. The ego is said to operate by the *reality principle*.

The Superego

The superego represents the moral and traditional values of society which are communicated to the child by the parents. As children, we are rewarded by our parents for good behavior and punished by them for wrongdoing. Thus the behavior for which we are punished becomes part of our "conscience," and positive behavior becomes part of our ego-ideal. The superego, then, is comprised of these two subsystems: the "conscience," which punishes us with guilt, and the "ego-ideal," which rewards us with pride. The functions of the superego include restraining the impulses of the id, convincing the ego to substitute moralistic goals for realistic ones, and striving for perfection.

In summary, personality, according to Freud, is a complex energy system consisting of the interaction between the driving forces of the id and the restraining forces of the ego and superego. The id, which houses the reservoir of psychic energy, strives to satisfy its needs according to the pleasure principle, while the ego seeks to mediate the impulses of the id with the superego and the external world.

View of Human Nature

Freud viewed the human organism as a complex energy system with psychic energy distributed among the three systems and behavior being a function of these unconscious forces. His view of human nature, then, is highly deterministic, since individuals are controlled by their biological drives and instincts; man is biological and, therefore, unsocialized and irrational.

The instincts consist of psychic energy, the reservoir of which is originally housed in the id. Freud classified the instincts into two broad categories, the life instincts and the death instincts. The *life instincts* include those which are necessary

for the organism to survive, such as hunger, thirst, and sex. These instincts operate using a form of energy called *libido;* the term originally referred primarily to
sexual energy but later was used more broadly to refer to all of the life instincts.
The *death instincts* are related to aggression and destruction. While Freud knew
less about the death instincts, he believed that they were motivating forces in
behavior.

Layers of Personality

One of Freud's most significant contributions was his emphasis on the unconscious. Freud likened the mind to an iceberg, with consciousness being represented by the small part above the water and the unconscious region being the
large area beneath the surface. Thus the unconscious houses all memories, experiences reactions, feelings, and needs that are not in our awareness. Freud thus believed that most of our psychological functioning is not in our awareness; hence
the need for a therapeutic model that could gain access to these important influences on behavior (Corey, 1991). The unconscious is a critical construct in psychoanalytic thought; it is essential to therapeutic growth that motivations and other
repressed material be brought to a conscious level of awareness, so that the person
can understand the roots of the symptoms and decide whether or not to change. In
other words, to understand human behavior the therapist must be able to reveal
the unconscious (Nye, 1981).

Thus the layers of personality in Freud's "topography of the mind" are the unconscious, the preconscious, and the conscious. The preconscious includes material that is just beneath the surface and is reasonably accessible if we give it some
thought. The conscious includes material that is at an immediate level of awareness, and the unconscious houses the basic determinants of personality (Nye,
1981).

Ego-Defense Mechanisms

One of Freud's most important contributions to psychology was his conceptualization of the ego-defense mechanisms. As previously discussed, Freud viewed
personality as an energy system with psychic energy being distributed among the
id, ego, and superego. The id originally had all of the psychic energy. Because the
ego needs psychic energy to function, a state of conflict exists between the driving
forces of the id and the restraining forces of the ego and superego. Most of the time
the outer world functions to satisfy the wishes of the ego. Sometimes, however, the
outer world threatens the ego, and when the ego receives this excessive stimula-
tion, it is flooded with anxiety.

Anxiety may exist in three forms: reality anxiety, neurotic anxiety, and moral
anxiety. *Reality* anxiety is caused by real dangers in the external world. *Neurotic*
anxiety results from fear that the instincts will get out of control and cause the individual to do something for which he will be punished. *Moral* anxiety is a fear of
the conscience. In other words, people with strong superegos feel guilty when they
do something that violates the moral code (Hall and Lindzey, 1978).

Anxiety serves an important function. It warns the individual of impending danger by signaling the ego that unless appropriate measures are taken, the ego may be overthrown (Hall and Lindzey, 1978). Anxiety, therefore, is a state of tension that can motivate the individual to action. When the ego cannot deal with anxiety through appropriate and rational methods, it resorts to unrealistic measures—the ego-defense mechanisms.

We employ defense mechanisms when we are in situations in which the ego is threatened. These mechanisms are, therefore, essential for helping us to cope with failure and to maintain a positive self-image. In fact, in a traumatic situation in which the experience is repressed, the repression serves to protect the ego from severe damage. In this situation the defense mechanisms are fundamental to the individual's psychological survival. In other instances, however, such as a succession of job-related failures, the ability to rationalize these failures may actually prevent the individual from taking appropriate measures to improve his behavior and enhance his success. Thus, the ego-defense mechanisms can operate to protect the individual, or they can serve as blocks to the self-growth that occurs when one faces problems or mistakes and learns to adequately cope with them.

While there are many ego-defense mechanisms, Anna Freud (1946) states that there are four principle defense mechanisms: repression, projection, reaction formation, and fixation and regression. Here we will define these four and seven others.

1. *Repression* Repression is one of the earliest Freudian concepts. It involves the removal of painful or dangerous thoughts and experiences from consciousness. Thus a highly traumatic event, such as witnessing one's mother's murder, is not forgotten but is removed from one's awareness, producing amnesia. Often the repression of an event or experience is not complete, and such repressed desires may be revealed through dreams or slips of the tongue. In certain instances, such as the traumatic incident cited above, repression may be temporary and may protect the individual until other resources or methods of coping are available. Unfortunately, repression can also be used to enable the individual to deceive himself and evade learning more effective methods of dealing with the problem. Thus energy that could be used to enable the individual to cope effectively on a daily basis is tied up in maintaining the defensive posture.

2. *Projection* Projection involves transferring blame for our own short-comings onto others as well as attributing to others our unacceptable desires or impulses. A student who fails an exam attributes the failure to the poor quality of the test. Or the sibling who pushes and shoves her brother exclaims that the brother actually started the fight.

3. *Reaction Formation* This is a defensive reaction in which a dangerous impulse is replaced by a feeling or behavior pattern that is just the opposite. Thus a mother who hates her child might "smother" the child with love and affection. Another example might be someone who crusades against various vices or exhibits other forms of extreme intolerance. A reaction formation is characterized by compulsiveness and extravagant showiness (Hall and Lindzey, 1978).

4. *Fixation and Recession* Personality development involves passage through a series of well-defined stages. At each stage there is a certain amount of frustration

and anxiety. If the anxiety of the next stage is too great, the individual's development may be halted (Hall and Lindzey, 1978). A related mechanism of defense is that of regression. Regression is a reaction to stress that involves reverting back to a less mature level of adjustment in order to feel safe and secure and to get one's needs met. For example, an older child at the birth of a sibling will sometimes revert to bed wetting or request a bottle in order to acquire attention. In severe forms of regression, the individual retreats from reality to a developmental stage that is less demanding or stressful. An illustration might involve a woman in her early twenties who, unable to meet the demands of her marriage and family, regresses to infantile levels of behavior and assumes a fetal position.

5. *Denial* Denial involves the refusal to acknowledge unpleasant realities by ignoring their existence. Many of us refuse to acknowledge the reality of death; some deny criticism; others ignore a physician's diagnosis or prognosis. Denial is used to protect ourselves from the stress, but it also prevents us from facing the very real conflicts and problems of our daily existence.

6. *Rationalization* Rationalization involves coming up with logical, ethical, or socially approved reasons for our behavior; this enables us to do things that are sources of conflict for us. For example, after we've had a stressful experience, we might spend money on a glamorous trip rather than spending the savings on home repairs. When turned down for a position, we convince ourselves that the job really was not what we wanted. In this sense, rationalization softens the blow of disappointments and enables one to deal with experiences without serious damage to one's ego.

7. *Sublimation* Channeling aggressive or sexual impulses into socially acceptable activity is the basic principle of sublimation. Thus someone who has a lot of aggressive feelings might choose to play football. Some cultural achievements are attributed to sublimation of sexual urges.

8. *Identification* While identification as a defense occurs as part of the individual's normal development, it is used to enhance self-worth. Individuals who have poor self-concepts or who feel basically inadequate might associate with successful organizations or causes in order to improve their sense of acceptability; for example, one might identify with athletic teams or with social clubs that impart status.

9. *Compensation* Compensatory behavior can have either a positive or negative influence on one's adjustment. It involves masking weaknesses or feelings of inferiority by developing other aspects of one's physique or personality. A student who is slow academically might develop a pleasing personality, while someone who has suffered a physical disability might excel in another area of physical fitness. In other words, positive traits are exaggerated in order to make up for those that negatively influence the individual's self-concept.

10. *Displacement* In this defensive reaction, there is a shift of emotion from the original target to a safer one. Work-related stresses may be taken out at home. Children experiencing excessive family problems might act out their frustrations by abusing other children in the classroom. A father whose marriage is empty of emotional closeness and whose needs are not met in other ways might beat his child because the child is unable to satisfy him in an emotional sense.

11. *Introjection* This reaction involves taking on the attitudes and values of others in an attempt to control one's own behavior and to act in an acceptable manner so as to protect oneself. In the German concentration camps, prisoners' previous values and identifications were broken down and new "Nazi" norms were adopted for survival's sake.

Stages of Development

Freud considered the first five years of life to be quite important in the development of the child's personality. These first five years are followed by a latency period during which the dynamics are somewhat stabilized. At the onset of adolescence, the dynamics become active again (Hall and Lindzey, 1978).

Each developmental stage is dominated by a specific zone of the body. The first three stages, the oral, anal, and phallic, are referred to as the pregenital stage. The final stage of maturity, which occurs during adolescence, is the genital stage.

Oral Stage

The first year of life is called the oral stage. During this stage the primary source of gratification for the infant is through eating, which stimulates the lips and oral cavity, sensitive erogenous zones. Adult character traits are sometimes related to the two basic oral activities, incorporation of food and biting. That is, pleasure from oral incorporation may be displaced to the pleasure gained from acquiring possessions (Hall and Lindzey, 1978). Biting is sometimes displaced as sarcasm. Through the defenses of displacement and sublimation, modes of oral functioning provide the basis for the development of many attitudes and character traits (Hall and Lindzey, 1978). Additionally, the infant's relationship to the mother will influence the development of dependence/independence in adulthood.

Anal Stage

The anal region exerts considerable influence over personality development during the ages of one to three. With the onset of toilet training, typically during the second year of life, the infant experiences the external regulation of an impulse for the first time. That is, the child must learn to delay the gratification that comes from defecation. Parental attitudes toward toilet training are important and very influential in the development of future personality traits. Children learn to use their bodily functions to control their parents. Strict attitudes toward toilet training are said to produce retentive personalities—personalities, in other words, that are cruel or obstinate. If, on the other hand, the parents praise the child's bowel movements, the child may become creative and productive.

Phallic Stage

The focus of personality development from the age of three to the age of five or six is the genital area. During this time the child receives pleasure through masturbation, and there are several possible psychological developments, including castration anxiety, penis envy, and the Oedipus complex, which Freud considered to be one of his greatest discoveries.

As the boy experiences increased tension and excitation in his genitals, masturbation increases. If his parents attempt to stop the masturbation, he may fear loss of his penis as a punishment. This is particularly possible if he observes a female, who does not have a penis. Castration anxiety is also related to the unconscious incestuous desires that children develop for parents of the opposite sex. As the male child experiences these desires for his mother, he fears that his father will punish him by cutting off his penis. This is the now-famous Oedipus complex, which, if properly resolved, results in more acceptable forms of affection, as well as a strong identification with father (Corey, 1991).

The female counterpart to the Oedipus complex is called the Electra complex. Girls begin to transfer their feelings of love from mother to father during this stage. The absence of a penis in mother causes negative feelings or penis envy. The girl begins to compete with mother for father's attention and affection. Once she realizes she cannot compete, she begins to identify with her mother, taking on some of her behavioral characteristics (Corey, 1991).

Parental attitudes are, once again, most important during this psychosexual stage of development. Acceptance of the child's natural sexual curiosity lays the foundation for the development of adult attitudes toward sexuality, intimacy, and sex role identification.

Latency Stage

The latency period occurs between the ages of six to twelve and is basically a period of rest. The child moves from a narcissistic orientation to more socialized interaction. The focus during this period is on outside interests and relationships.

Genital Stage

During adolescence, children move into the genital stage, provided they are not fixated at an earlier stage of development. At this time the child begins moving into adulthood, replacing self-love with love of others. Heterosexual relationships become increasingly more important, as does the ability to form intimate relationships with members of the same sex. The adolescent begins to develop a sense of responsibility and moves gradually out of the realm of parental influence.

The Therapeutic Process

Role of Therapist

The role of the therapist is to assume a neutral position with the patient so that the patient will develop a *transference relationship*. Thus, patients project onto the analyst feelings they have had toward significant others in their lives. It is felt that the transference relationship will provide more material for therapy as unresolved conflicts, feelings, and experiences are relived. Analysts, therefore, share very little about themselves with the patient. The session is characterized by the patient's deeply reflecting on past experiences while lying on a couch, with the therapist primarily remaining silent, except when making appropriate interpretations. The major therapeutic goal is to enable clients to gain insight into their problems through the uncovering of unconscious material.

Therapeutic Techniques

Several techniques—including interpretation, dream analysis, transference, and free association—are employed by psychoanalysts to uncover unconscious material.

Interpretation, which is used in the other techniques, has to do with the analyst's explaining to the patient the meanings associated with the uncovered unconscious material. These interpretations have a significant role in the patient's development of insight into problems and experiences.

Dreams are used by psychoanalytic therapists to gain access to the unconscious. The patient describes dreams to the analyst, and these dreams are then interpreted through the symbols that appear in them.

As has been described, the analyst strives to remain neutral in the relationship so that the patient will project onto the analyst unresolved feelings and experiences with others. The *transference relationship* allows patients to work out conflicts that are retarding their emotional and psychological growth.

Because it is necessary to tap the unconscious, analysts often use *free association* as a technique. Patients, while lying on a couch, are asked to spontaneously share whatever thoughts, words, expressions, or feelings come to mind, without censorship. These associations are interpreted by the analyst, who notes sequencing, blocking, and disruptions.

Contributions

While Freudian theory has been the object of much attack, and while the application of Freudian thought to counseling per se is limited, the importance of Freud's contributions to both psychology and counseling must not be under-estimated. Among the significant contributions are the following:

1. The identification of the defense mechanisms has significantly influenced our understanding of abnormal behavior and the role of anxiety; this will be discussed in more detail at the conclusion of this chapter.
2. The elaboration of both the developmental stages and the influence of early childhood experience has impacted contemporary views of development and child rearing.
3. Freud's creativity, originality, and observations of human behavior gave us our first theory of personality.
4. Psychoanalysis as an approach to therapy is the foundation from which many contemporary theoreticians have generated their approaches.
5. Assessment instruments and techniques have been influenced by Freudian thought.

Criticisms

The attacks against Freud and his theory have been numerous. Among the most common criticisms are the following:

1. Freud's view of human nature was very negative and far too deterministic and mechanistic.
2. The strong emphasis on early childhood experiences makes it possible for patients to deny responsibility for their problems.
3. The role of interpersonal experiences and relationships was virtually ignored.
4. Women have strongly rejected the concept of penis envy.
5. Much criticism has been levied against the empirical procedures used by Freud, including the facts that he carried out no scientifically controlled studies and that his method of record keeping was incomplete.
6. Freud's emphasis on instinctual drives, particularly sex, was too strong.

Both the contributions and criticisms of Freudian thought are extensive. Here we have outlined a few of the most common of each. At the end of the chapter, we will explore in more depth the relationship between Freudian theory and other contemporary counseling approaches.

Neo-Freudian Theorists

Freud was surrounded by a group of followers, including Alfred Adler and Carl Jung, who eventually left the close circle and developed opposing views. Adler is said to have been the first analyst to reject Freud's view of sexuality in favor of an emphasis on the social nature of humans. Karen Horney, Eric Fromm, and Harry Stack Sullivan are the other psychoanalysts who developed a social-psychological view, which helped bridge the gap between Freud and contemporary psychoanalysts. While each of these theorists adapted and extended Freudian theory, they have made their own distinct contributions. Due to the limitations of space, we will discuss the theory of Alfred Adler, and review the significant contributions of Horney and Sullivan.

Alfred Adler

Alfred Adler, a charter member of Freud's Vienna Psychoanalytic Society, split with Freud in 1911 because his views were at variance with Freud's. When he left the small group of followers who made up the Vienna Psychoanalytic Society, he formed his own group, known as Individual Psychology. The basic contention between Freud and Adler centered around Adler's disagreement with a sexual etiology of neuroses and belief that individuals were motivated by social responsibility and need achievement, not driven by the inborn instincts. Adler's views were well received initially, but later his popularity decreased. In the past twenty years, however, there has been a renewed interest in his views, and many counselors, particularly those working with children, have become ardent followers. Rudolf Dreikurs (1897–1972) contributed much to Adler's work, especially through the development of specific counseling techniques. Important sources of information about Adler's work are *The Practice of Individual Psychology* by Adler, and *The Individual Psychology of Alfred Adler* by Ansbacher and Ansbacher. Another excellent resource on Adlerian counseling is *Adlerian Counseling and Psychotherapy* by Dinkmeyer, Pew, and Dinkmeyer.

View of Human Nature

Adler's view of human nature was much more positive than Freud's. Rather than viewing humans as being motivated by instinctual drives, Adler felt that humans were motivated by social, interpersonal factors. Adler saw people as having control over their lives, with each individual developing a unique life style. Adler believed that behavior is goal directed and purposive and that life goals motivate human behavior. The most important life goals involve overcoming feelings of inferiority and striving for security. The attempt to master feelings of inferiority provides the motivation for striving for perfection and creativity. From these basic concepts, it follows that Adler's emphasis is on conscious, rather than unconscious, process, with individuals assuming responsibility for their life decisions (Corey, 1991).

Striving for Superiority

Adler believed that all human beings have "striving for superiority" as their life goal. The drive toward superiority is similar to the concept of self-actualization. It has nothing to do with achieving a position of status in society; rather it is, according to Adler, "the great upward drive." This upward drive pulls the individual through the developmental stages. It is important to note that individuals develop their own forms of achieving perfection which are related to the concept of feelings of inferiority (Hall and Lindzey, 1978).

Feelings of Inferiority and Compensation

All individuals suffer from feelings of inferiority; these feelings, whether they stem from psychological or social problems or actual physical disability, motivate individuals to strive for perfection. Humans, then, are pushed by feelings of inferiority and pulled by feelings of superiority, and we tend to compensate for the areas of weakness or disability by developing a lifestyle that allows us to be successful.

Lifestyle

No two individuals develop the same style of life. As stated above, the lifestyle is based on the individual's feelings of inferiority and the particular way it which the individual strives to overcome a weakness. The lifestyle is a result of judgments the individual makes about the status of the self. The judgments of self in relation to one's perception of status in the world begin to form patterns of behavior that become one's lifestyle (Hansen, Stevic, and Warner, 1982). By the age of four or five, the style of life has been formed, and future experiences are merely integrated into it. Examples of lifestyle development would be a physical weakling becoming an athlete, or a withdrawn child developing his or her intellect.

Family Constellation

One of Adler's most popular and useful contributions was his observation of family constellation and birth order. Adler placed a great deal of emphasis on early childhood experiences and, in line with his views on social determinants of personality, observed very carefully the influence of position in birth order on personality and lifestyle. In fact, he felt that birth order was an important determinant of the child's perceptions of the world outside the family.

Basically the concept of family constellation has to do with the child's interactions with and perceptions of the family group. Children are affected by others, just as they affect or influence them. The relationship is dynamic and interactive, and children's perceptions of the family environment greatly influence how they come to view themselves.

Alder sought to associate characteristics with position in birth order. For example, many only children are pampered and are accustomed to having things their way. First children have to be first in order to maintain superiority over other children and may feel "dethroned" at the birth of the second child. Second children never have their parents' undivided attention and constantly have to look at the child ahead, who is more advanced. The second child is trying to catch up and, if the first child is very successful, may become discouraged. The youngest child resembles an only child and is usually spoiled.

Early Memories

Adler used the adult's earliest recollections to help him understand style of life. He made interpretations of style of life based on these early memories. He felt that memory is biased and that only significant events are remembered; these recollections, then, are good indicators of present attitudes.

The Counseling Process

The relationship between the counselor and the client received recognition by Adler. He believed that the counselor should feel warm and accepting toward the client; empathy was considered to be an important factor in the establishment of the therapeutic climate. The relationship was viewed as a collaborative one in which equal partners work out and agree upon specific goals.

The next stage of the counseling process is the assessment phase. During this stage, the counselor works to assess the client's style of life through an understanding of the client's beliefs, feelings, goals, and motives. Empathy enables the counselor not only to develop the relationship but also to understand the beliefs underlying the feelings. The counselor probes the client's early childhood to assess sibling relationships and the child's perception of his place in the family. Early recollections are used to further the life-style investigation. The assessment procedure enables the counselor to identify the client's "basic mistakes" and interpret how they are presently influencing the client.

In the third stage the counselor emphasizes the development of insight into problems through an awareness of mistaken goals and self-defeating behaviors. The counselor is confrontive in pointing out hidden purposes and using interpretation to facilitate insight. While insight is viewed as important, the emphasis is on changes in behavior. As the counselor interprets the clients' lifestyle, it is hoped that they will come to understand their role in creating their problems, so that they can see how to improve their present situation.

During the final stage of counseling, the counselor orients the client toward action. Clients are encouraged to take risks and try out new behaviors, to take responsibility for their lives, and to make new decisions that will enable them to reach their goals.

The above discussion is a summary of the phases of the counseling process as presented by Dinkmeyer, Pew, and Dinkmeyer (1979). For a more thorough description, counselors are encouraged to consult this important resource.

Contributions

1. The Adlerian view of human nature is essentially positive.
2. The relationship between the counselor and the client is valued.
3. The concept of family constellation has been useful and has yielded important research investigations.
4. Adlerian theory is used by parent-education groups.
5. The concept of natural consequences has influenced child-rearing practices.

Criticisms

1. Adlerian counseling is dependent on insight to influence change. That is, clients' experiences and life-styles are interpreted to them, and this intellectual understanding is supposed to result in behavior change.
2. The counseling process is basically educative rather than therapeutic. Clients' feelings, as related to insight, are not considered to be important.
3. Although it is done in the context of a supportive environment, Adlerian confrontation can be perceived as highly judgmental.
4. Counselors at the elementary level who use an Adlerian approach tend to limit their counseling to dealing with discipline problems, because Adlerian methods provide an efficient method for handling the misdirected goals of children, which result in behavior problems.

Karen Horney

Horney parted with Freud over his deterministic, mechanistic approach and his emphasis on instinctual drives. She emphasized, instead, the concept of anxiety, which she felt grew out of the child's feelings of isolation and helplessness. The real root of anxiety lies in the parent-child relationship, with anxiety being produced by anything that disturbs the child's fundamental security (Hall and Lindzey, 1978).

According to Horney, the insecure children handle their feelings by developing irrational (neurotic) solutions to the problem. These solutions compensate in some way for the emotional and psychological losses they've experienced, and may become permanent personality characteristics. The ten neurotic needs are listed; readers are encouraged to consult Horney's original writings listed in the reference section.

Ten Neurotic Needs

1. The neurotic need for affection and approval.
2. The neurotic need for a partner who will take over one's life.
3. The neurotic need to restrict one's life within narrow borders.
4. The neurotic need for power.
5. The neurotic need to exploit others.
6. The neurotic need for prestige.
7. The neurotic need for personal admiration.
8. The neurotic need for personal achievement.
9. The neurotic need for self-sufficiency and independence.
10. The neurotic need for protection and unassailability.

It is important to understand that, for the neurotic, these needs are not easily met. In most cases, the need simply cannot be satisfied because of the deep inner conflict that lies at its source.

After defining the ten neurotic needs, Horney classified them into three basic orientations: moving toward people (need for love), moving away from people (need for independence), and moving against people (need for power). She distinguishes between normal individuals and neurotics by stating that normal individuals resolve their conflicts by integrating the three orientations, while neurotics rely exclusively on one of the orientations. Horney feels that all conflicts are avoidable if the child is reared in a loving, accepting home in which warmth, trust, and affection characterize the parent-child relationship (Hall and Lindzey, 1978).

Horney parted significantly from Freud in her view that conflict is environmental and arises out of the individual's social surroundings. Possibly her greatest contributions were this awareness of the impact of environment in the role of psychological dysfunction, and her identification of neurotic needs and the psychological dynamics involved in neuroses.

Harry Stack Sullivan

Harry Stack Sullivan differs greatly from Adler and Horney both in his background and training and in his theoretical views. Sullivan was born and trained in America and never had direct contact with Freud. His unique approach to psychiatry was the first to emphasize the role of interpersonal relationships. He describes his approach and theory in *The Interpersonal Theory of Psychiatry* (Sullivan, 1953). His views of the importance both of interpersonal relationships and of the role of the therapist as an involved participant in the interview have significantly influenced present counseling theory and practice.

Personality, according to Sullivan, actually exists only through the individual's interactions with others. Processes such as thinking, perceiving, and even dreaming are considered to be interpersonal.

The self-system develops out of the anxiety experienced in interpersonal relationships, which originally stems from the mother-infant relationship. Individuals learn that if they please their parents, they will be praised (the good-me self), and that if they misbehave, they will be punished (the bad-me self). The self protects from anxiety and guards security. The self-system will avoid information that is not consistent with its organization, and thus it is protected from criticism. The self-system may lose its ability to be objective and may prevent the individual from accurately assessing his behavior. If the individual experiences much anxiety, the self-system will become inflated and will prevent the individual from growing and interacting with others in healthy relationships (Hall and Lindzey, 1978). Here we see some possible antecedents of Rogers' self theory and note the link between Freud's view that while anxiety stems from different sources, the ego (self) deals with it by distorting reality through use of the defense mechanisms.

Some believe that Sullivan's most unique contributions were in the area of cognitive processes. He delineated the following three modes of experiencing: *prototaxic, parataxic,* and *syntaxic.*

Prototaxic—involves experiences that have no connection or meaning for the experiencing individual. Infants undergo this kind of experiencing.

Parataxic—involves seeing a relationship between events that occur simultaneously, but that have no actual relationship. Superstitions are examples of parataxic thought processes.

Syntaxic—involves the use of language in which commonly agreed-upon verbal symbols enable communication.

Sullivan's theory of personality emphasized stages of development but differed from Freudian thinking with regard to the role of sexuality. His view of development emphasized social factors and consisted of the following six stages: infancy, childhood, juvenile era, preadolescence, early adolescence, and late adolescence.

One of Sullivan's major contributions was his view of the therapeutic interview. He made a significant departure from Freud and the so-called neoanalysts in viewing the interview as a highly personal and interpersonal experience in which the therapist functions as a "participant observer." The role of the therapist as conceptualized by Sullivan emphasizes the therapist as a person, with a focus on the communication between the therapist and patient. In other words, Sullivan acknowledged that the therapist's attitudes, feelings, doubts, or personal difficulties influence the interaction in the interview. Obviously, then, the therapist cannot assume a strictly observational stance.

The psychiatric interview consists of four stages—the formal inception, reconnaissance, detailed inquiry, and the termination. These stages are briefly summarized as follows:

1. *The Formal Inception* The therapist is viewed as an interpersonal relations expert. In the initial phase of therapy, the primary task is to determine the nature of the patient's problem and to begin a communication process in which the therapist is sensitive to nonverbal behavior, including voice tone, speech rate, and changes in volume. Sullivan emphasized that the patient has a right to expect to benefit from the experience, even from the initial session. Emphasis is placed on relationship building.

2. *Reconnaissance* During this phase the therapist structures sessions to gather factual information about the past, present, and future of the patient. The goal is to develop some hypotheses regarding the patient's problems.

3. *The Detailed Inquiry* Both questioning and listening are techniques that assist the therapist in sorting through tentative hypotheses and selecting the one that is most accurate. Information regarding the patient's functioning in all areas is collected.

4. *The Termination* A summary of the therapist's learnings about and observations of the patient characterizes this last stage. The therapist may also prescribe some guidelines for the patient following termination.

As previously stated, Sullivan's influence on contemporary counseling theory and practice is most obvious in his humanistic view of the psychiatric interview. He was a very creative thinker and was among the first to change the role of the therapist from a removed observer and interpreter of the patient's experience, to an active, involved participant in an interpersonal relationship. His emphasis on the therapist, as a person and on the power of the relationship in facilitating client change was probably an antecedent of humanistic thinking, which resulted in the development of client-centered therapy.

New Directions

The Ego Analysts

The ego analysts, while greatly influenced by Freud, have departed from Freudian theory in several significant ways. First, the ego analysts give consideration to the role of social and cultural influences on behavior. Second, they view the ego as functioning autonomously from the id. According to Heinz Hartmann (1958, 1964), a leader in ego psychology, the ego analysts believe that the ego develops separately from the id and is not dependent on the id for energy. Once developed, the ego resists reattachment to the id. Third, the ego analysts are concerned with normal functioning and believe that behavior is environmentally influenced and is relatively independent of instinctual impulses. And finally, the ego has at its disposal the cognitive processes of thinking, perceiving, and remembering, which help it adapt to the real world.

The stages of development from this view are best exemplified by Erik Erikson's (1963) psychosocial stages. The process, according to Erikson, goes through eight stages, the first four of which resemble Freud's, and the last four of which recognize the development of cognitive processes and the expanding role of the ego. Basically, Erikson states that each of the developmental stages consists of a crisis which must be successfully passed through. Success or failure at these critical points influences personality development.

According to Hall and Lindzey (1978), one of Erikson's greatest contributions is the psychosocial theory of development, which states that the life stages are formed by the interaction of social influences with the physically and psychologically maturing organism.

Summary

It has been the purpose of this chapter to explore Freudian theory, to summarize the contributions of Adler, Horney, and Sullivan, who are important links to present counseling practice, and to briefly explore the ego analysts as a contemporary extension of Freudian thinking.

In the section on Freud, we discussed his view that personality is a complex energy system consisting of the driving forces of the id and the restraining forces of the ego and superego. The reservoir of psychic energy is housed in the id, which functions by the pleasure principle. The instinctual impulses of the id are mediated by the ego and the superego, as well as by the external world. Personality, then, is a highly mechanistic and deterministic system, and behavior is largely a result of instinctual drives and unconscious processes. When the ego can no longer satisfy the demands of the ego and is flooded with anxiety, it employs defense mechanisms to enable it to cope. Repression, projection, reaction formation, fixation, and regression were discussed, along with several other commonly used defense mechanisms. Freud believed that personality developed in five psychosexual stages: oral, anal, phallic, latency, and genital. He utilized techniques such as interpretation, dream analysis, transference, and free association.

Each of the other theorists included in this chapter departed in some important way from Freudian thinking. Alfred Adler, Karen Horney, and Harry Stack Sullivan developed social-psychological views which rejected Freud's view of sexuality, placed greater emphasis on environmental and interpersonal factors, and bridged the gap with the ego-analytic view which is receiving attention today.

While Freudian theory differs in many ways from the contemporary affective approaches to counseling presented in the following chapters, there are some interesting linkages between Freud and Rogers, the counseling theorist who most significantly departed from Freudian thought.

The importance placed on feelings is the most obvious similarity between Freud and Rogers. Freud used techniques with both cognitive components (recall of early memories, interpretation, and making the unconscious conscious) and affective ones (transference and the corrective emotional experience) to facilitate client insight. It is important to note, however, that insight involved more than cognitive understanding. It also involved the client's emotional reexperiencing of the event. Freud emphasized the emotional working through of feelings associated with past traumatic events. Blocked feelings had to be discharged through catharsis. Rogers also strongly emphasizes feelings and encourages clients to experience in the interview the very real feelings associated with their experiences. Thus, a goal of counseling, according to Rogers, is for clients to move from reporting feelings to actually feeling them with the therapist; Rogers uses empathy to accomplish this. It is interesting to note that empathy at its highest levels has both an affective and a cognitive component. That is, empathy involves the identification of feelings and a stimulus for the feelings. Empathy not only brings feelings to awareness but, when most effective, also greatly facilitates clients' insight into their experiences. Here we see that change in the client, from both a Freudian and a Rogerian perspective, is most influenced not by cognitive or intellectual processes, but through feelings. This is an important similarity between the approaches.

Another interesting point of convergence between Freudian and Rogerian theory has to do with the importance of anxiety as it influences the self (ego). Freud believed that the ego coped with a flood of anxiety through use of the defense mechanisms. Rogers, without using the term anxiety, states that experiences that the self cannot integrate into the self-concept become denied or distorted. The denials and distortions of experience, according to self theory, result in defensive behavior. The self is coping through the use of defense mechanisms, but not in ways that are healthy and growth producing. Acceptance allows the self to be freed from anxiety and judgment, and the self-concept can change to integrate these previously threatening feelings and experiences. Thus, the goal of client-(person-) centered therapy is to relax the self-structure through empathy and unconditional positive regard in order to allow for the total integration of experience and the reduction of defensive behavior. The goal of psychoanalysis, according to Freud, is to reduce anxiety so that the ego can function without defenses.

While a comparison between Freud and Rogers can be drawn, the two were quite different in a number of important ways. Freud emphasized psychological dysfunction and held very deterministic and mechanistic views of personality and change processes; Rogers, on the other hand, emphasized psychological growth and healthy functioning with very positive views of the change process. While their therapeutic goals and their emphasis on the importance of feelings in the change process may be similar, their therapeutic approaches and techniques are quite different. That is, both seek to help individuals achieve a new level of integration; both encourage clients, through the therapist-patient relationship, to re-live their experiences with an emphasis on feelings; and both enable clients to gain insight into themselves and their problems. Rogers accomplished this through accepting, understanding, listening, and empathizing; Freud used the techniques of transference, interpretation, early memory recall, and dream analysis.

Freud's influence on contemporary counseling theory and practice is apparent. One must appreciate the creativity and originality of his thinking. Indeed, he laid the foundation for all of the theories that will be discussed in the following chapters.

References

Adler, A. (1925). *The theory and practice of individual psychology* (Paul Radin, Trans.). London: Routledge and Kegan Paul Ltd.

Ansbacher, H., & Ansbacher, R. (1956). *The individual psychology of Alfred Adler.* New York: Basic Books.

Brenner, C. (1974). *An elementary textbook of psychoanalysis.* Garden City, NY: Anchor Press.

Corey, G. (1991). *Theory and practice of counseling and psychotherapy* (4th ed.). Monterey, CA: Brooks/Cole.

Dinkmeyer, D., Pew, W., & Dinkmeyer, D., Jr. (1979). *Adlerian counseling and psychotherapy.* Monterey, CA.: Brooks/Cole.

Erikson, E. (1963). *Childhood and society* (2nd ed.). New York: Norton.

Freud, A. (1946). *The ego and the mechanisms of defense.* New York: International Universities Press.

Hall, C. (1954). *A primer of Freudian psychology.* New York: NAL (Mentor).

Hall, C. & Lindzey, G. (1978). *Theories of personality.* New York: John Wiley.

Hansen, J., Stevic, R. & Warner, R. (1982). *Counseling: Theory and process* (3rd ed.). Boston: Allyn and Bacon.

Hartmann, H. (1958). *Ego psychology and the problem of adaptation.* New York: International Universities Press.

Hartmann, H. (1964). *Essays on ego psychology: Selected problems in psychoanalytic theory.* New York: International Universities Press.

Nye, R. (1981). *Three psychologies* (2nd ed.). Monterey, CA: Brooks/Cole.

Sullivan, H.S. (1953). *The interpersonal theory of psychiatry.* New York: W. W. Norton.

Chapter 4

Affective Approaches to Counseling

FIGURE 4-1   Carl Rogers
(The Bettmann Archive, Inc.)

This chapter will focus on affective approaches to counseling, in which the counselor focuses on the client's feelings and gives secondary consideration to thoughts and behaviors. Person-centered therapy and Gestalt therapy will be discussed, along with a brief analysis of existential therapy and holistic counseling.

Person-Centered Therapy

Background

Person-centered therapy was developed by Carl Rogers in reaction to the traditional, highly diagnostic, probing, and interpretive methods of psychoanalysis. *Counseling and Psychotherapy* (Rogers, 1942) was the first attempt to present his new approach, one which emphasized the importance of the quality of the relationship between the client and the therapist. Rogers saw the therapist as the creator of a facilitative environment that would allow the client to move toward self-growth. Of his many books, *Client-Centered Therapy* (1951) and *On Becoming a Person* (1961) are considered classics.

The person-centered approach evolved from client-centered therapy, which was originally called *nondirective therapy*. Cottone (1992) reports that Rogers used the term *person-centered* as a result of his faith in the individual and the need to see others from a positive, nonclinical standpoint. The person-centered term also allowed a wider range of applications—teaching, administration, organizational behavior, marriage and parenting, and interpersonal relations in general.

View of Human Nature

When Rogers began developing his therapy, the basic belief among therapists was that individuals were basically irrational, unsocialized, and self-destructive, and had little control over themselves. Rogers rejected this view and emphasized that the individual can "guide, regulate, and control himself" (1959, p. 221). He pointed out that these views had been formed as a result of his experiences in psychotherapy; they did not precede his therapeutic experiences. Rogers's views can be organized into four basic areas: (1) a belief in the dignity and worth of each individual, (2) a perceptual view of behavior, (3) a tendency toward self-actualization, and (4) a belief that people are good and trustworthy.

Belief in the Dignity and Worth of Each Individual

Rogers is strongly committed to the belief that all persons should have the right to their own opinions and thoughts and should be in control of their own destiny, free to pursue their own interests in their own way as long as they do not trample on the rights of others. Rogers sees this democratic ideal, which underlies all his ideas about humanity, as having both practical utility and moral value. He also believes that a democratic society's needs are best served by social processes and social institutions that encourage the individual to be an independent, self-directing person.

Perceptual View of Behavior

Rogers clearly emphasizes that the ways in which individuals behave and adapt to situations are always consistent with their perceptions of themselves and their situations. He even states that "man lives essentially in his own personal and subjective world, and even his most objective functioning, in science, mathematics, and the like, is the result of subjective purpose and subjective choice" (1959, p. 191). As a result, the self-concept becomes an important aspect of one's perception. Since the self is the center of one's experiences with the environment, one's perceptions of, and interactions with, the environment change as the sense of self changes. Rogers feels that, in general, one's experiences are either (1) organized into the self-structure, (2) ignored because they are inconsistent with the sense of self, or (3) perceived distortedly because they are not harmonious with self-perceptions.

Thus those who are developing their full potential are able to accept the subjective aspects of self and to live subjectively, relying on their own subjective sense of evaluation rather than depending on external sources of evaluation.

Tendency Toward Self-Actualization

Rogers has gradually increased his emphasis on the inherent tendency of people to move in directions that can be described roughly as growth, health, adjustment, socialization, self-realization, and autonomy. He calls this directional tendency the *actualizing tendency*, and he defines it as "the inherent tendency of the organism to develop all its capacities in ways which serve to maintain or enhance the organism" (1959, p. 196).

This conception, while relatively simple, is all-encompassing. In fact, Rogers sees this actualizing tendency as applying to all life—animals and plants as well as people. Thus the essential nature of life is that it is an active process in which the organism interacts with its environment in ways designed to maintain, to enhance, and to reproduce itself.

Rogers emphasizes several ideas by his stress upon this actualizing tendency. First, the actualizing tendency is the primary motivating force of the human organism. Second, the actualizing tendency is a function of the total organism rather than of one or more parts of that organism. People do have specific needs and motives, but Rogers points out that the ways in which a person seeks to meet these needs enhances rather than diminishes self-esteem and other strivings of the total organism. In this sense Rogers's conception is similar though not identical to Maslow's hierarchy of needs.

Third, this stress on the actualizing tendency suggests a broad conception of motivation, including the usual needs and motives but emphasizing the individual's tendency to physical growth and maturation, the need for close interpersonal relationships, and the tendency of the individual to impose herself on her environment—that is, to move in directions of autonomy and away from external control.

Finally, individuals have both the capacity to actualize themselves and the tendency to do so. These capacities are released under the proper conditions. Hence, the counseling process is not aimed at doing something *to* or *for* the individual; rather it is aimed at freeing the individual's capacities for normal growth and development. The counseling theory developed by Rogers simply attempts to specify the conditions that allow this freeing process to occur.

Belief That People Are Basically Good and Trustworthy

Throughout his writings Rogers uses such words as *trustworthy, reliable, constructive,* or *good* to describe the inherent characteristics of people. Rogers knows that people sometimes behave in untrustworthy ways, that they are capable of deceit, hate, and cruelty. But he believes that these unfavorable characteristics arise out of a defensiveness that has alienated individuals from their inherent nature. This defensiveness is the result of a widening incongruence between the individuals' ideal selves—the way they believe they ought to be, and their real selves—the way they think they are. As this incongruence becomes greater, individuals are less open to their own experiences, tending to distrust them, and they attempt to hide both from others and from themselves. However, Rogers points out that as defensiveness diminishes and individuals become more open to all of their experiences, they tend to behave in ways that are seen as being socialized and trustworthy, striving for meaningful and constructive relationships with others.

Key Concepts

Rogers believes that person-centered therapy is on stronger theoretical ground than other kinds of therapy because of its close relationship to a well-developed theory of personality. In his writings Rogers has presented a series of nine formal propositions which clearly outline the underlying personality theory for a person-centered approach.

All individuals exist in a continually changing world of experience of which they are the center (Rogers, 1951). This description of the private world of each individual's experience is sometimes called the *phenomenal field.* It includes all that the individual experiences, although these experiences are only occasionally conscious. The important aspect of this proposition is that only the individual can completely and genuinely perceive this world of experience. No one else can fully understand the experience of another who is rejected by a friend or unable to find a job. We can observe other individuals, even measuring their reactions to various stimuli, but we can never know in full and vivid detail how they are experiencing and perceiving any given situation.

Individuals react to their phenomenal field as they experience and perceive it. This perceptual field is, for the individual, "reality" (Rogers, 1951). What this means, of course, is that individuals do not react to reality as it may be perceived by most people around them, but rather they react to reality as they perceive it. Such a proposition clearly supports the person-centered idea of understanding the individual's phenomenal field from his perception as a major part of the therapeutic process.

Behavior is basically the goal-directed attempt of individuals to satisfy their needs as experienced, in their phenomenal field as perceived. This proposition, then, ties in with the second proposition by emphasizing that individuals do not react to some absolute reality; they react to their perceptions of that reality. Rogers observed that a man dying of thirst in a desert, for instance, will struggle as hard to reach a mirage as he will to reach a real body of water. Thus, reality for any individual is that individual's perception of reality, regardless of whether or not it has been tested and confirmed.

The best vantage point for understanding behavior is from the internal frame of reference of the individual. Rogers includes within this internal frame of reference the full range of sensations, perceptions, meanings, and memories available to consciousness. Thus, to understand another individual from this internal frame of reference is to concentrate on a subjective reality that exists within that individual at any given time.

To achieve this understanding requires empathy. On the other hand, simply understanding another individual from an external frame of reference is to view the individual without empathy, as an object, usually with the intent of emphasizing objective reality. Persons become objects in that we make no empathic inferences about their subjective experiences. Even when the counselor's internal frame of reference may more closely approximate objective reality than the client's, it is still only the counselor's perception of objective reality, which tends to ignore the client's subjective experience of reality.

The student who feels that her teacher has treated her unfairly, for example, will act as though the teacher's treatment really was unfair. Whether or not an objective analysis of that treatment will agree with the student's perception is irrelevant, except perhaps for the self-satisfaction of the teacher. As long as the student believes that the teacher treated her unfairly, she will continue to behave as if the treatment really was unfair. To bring about a change in her behavior, Rogers suggests that her perception of that situation must first change, since her behavior is the result of her perception of the situation.

Most ways of behaving adopted by the individual are consistent with the individual's concept of self. The self-concept is basic to the person-centered system. For Rogers the self-concept describes an organized picture consisting of the individual's perception of himself alone and himself in relation to other persons and objects in his environment together with the values attached to those perceptions. Such a picture does not always exist at a level of awareness, but that picture is always available to awareness. Thus, by definition, the self-concept excludes unconscious self-attitudes that are not available to consciousness. In addition, the self-concept is considered to be fluid and changing, a process rather than a fixed entity.

The incongruence that often occurs between an individuals' conscious wishes and his behavior is the result of a split between the individuals' self-concept and his experiences. Rogers emphasizes some specific terms when he talks about this incongruence, particularly in referring to the development of certain needs. Rogers points out that as the individual gains an awareness of self, he also develops a need for positive regard and positive self-regard. Obviously these two needs are closely related. When the individual feels loved or not loved by significant others, he develops positive or negative feelings about himself.

When the incongruence between the individual's self-picture and the individuals' experiences is very wide, a state of anxiety exists. Rogers believes that this state of anxiety can be best understood by seeing it as the result of the incongruence between the individual's ideal self and real self. As these two pictures of self diverge, the individual becomes more and more upset with herself and also fears that others will see her as inadequate and worthless. The anxiety comes from a fear that others will recognize her basic inferiority.

To lower an individual's anxiety, the self-concept must become more congruent with the individual's actual experiences. To state it differently, one's ideal self and real self must become more similar. One can change by creating conditions that are less threatening to one's self and that encourage one to assimilate denied and distorted experiences, and by sharing these with a significant person so that one can receive positive feedback that one is a worthwhile, able individual.

The fully functioning individual is completely open to all experiences, exhibiting no defensiveness. Such an individual experiences unconditional positive self-regard. The self-concept is congruent with the experiences, and the individual is able to assert his basic actualizing tendency.

Process and Goals

Person-centered counseling can be described as an *"if, then"* approach to counseling: *If* certain conditions exist, *then* a definable process is set in motion, leading to certain outcomes or changes in the client's personality and behavior. The basic premise of person-centered counseling, then, is that once the proper conditions for growth are established, the client will be able to gain insight and take positive steps toward solving personal difficulties. In the person-centered view, the following conditions are both necessary and sufficient for counseling.

Conditions for Growth

Psychological Contact.   Rogers suggests that the first essential condition for effective counseling is that two persons be in contact. He defines this contact as a situation in which each person makes a difference in the experiences of the other. From the very beginning, then, Rogers is setting the groundwork for a two-way interaction rather than a process where the counselor does something *to* or *for* the client.

Minimum State of Anxiety.   The second necessary condition is that the client be in a state of incongruence, feeling vulnerable or anxious. As mentioned before, the client's incongruence between his self-concept and his actual experiences causes this anxiety. Rogers believes that the more anxious the individual is about this incongruence, the more likely successful counseling will take place. In effect, this means the individual must be uncomfortable enough to want to change.

Counselor Congruence.   The counselor must be congruent or genuine in the relationship. Rogers talks of the counselor's being authentic—or real—in the sense that what the counselor is experiencing internally must be consistent with the messages the counselor is communicating to the client externally. This allows the counselor to be aware of and honest about the kinds of feelings the client is eliciting.

Unconditional Positive Regard.   The counselor must experience unconditional positive regard for the client. This genuine acceptance of all aspects of the client's self-experiences is central to the client-centered counselor. Such unconditional positive regard for an individual means respecting the person, regardless of the different values the counselor might place on certain behaviors. To maintain such feelings for a person, counselors must be nonevaluative. They do not judge one behavior as being positive and another negative; rather, they accept the client as an individual, regardless of the client's behaviors. Rogers believes that when this condition is provided for the client, the client comes to believe that she is a person of worth, a person capable of growth.

Empathic Understanding.   The counselor must experience empathic understanding of the client's internal frame of reference. Recognizing that no one can ever fully understand what an individual is experiencing internally, Rogers emphasizes that the counselor must develop a highly accurate understanding of the client's internal frame of reference. It is the counselor's attempt to put himself in the place of the client that is important. Although the counselor can never become the client, the counselor must try to understand as if he were the client himself.

Client Perception.   Finally, the client must perceive, at least to a minimal degree, the counselor's unconditional positive regard and empathic understanding. It is not enough that the counselor genuinely accept the client, and understand

and empathize with the client's situation. Acceptance and understanding will have value only if they are communicated so that the client perceives that they are present.

Outcomes

In the person-centered view, the counselor must allow the client to set the goals. The person-centered counselor believes that individuals have an innate motivating force, the need for self-actualization, that will enable them to develop and regulate their own behavior. The counselor who sets goals for the client would be interfering with the basic nature of the individual. In Rogers's view, such a counselor is unable to help the individual learn self-reliance. In essence, the goal of the person-centered counselor is to establish the proper therapeutic conditions to allow the normal developmental pattern of the individual to be brought back into play.

In a more specific sense, the goal of person-centered counseling is to help the clients become more mature and to reinstitute the movement towards self-actualization by removing the obstacles. The objective, then, is to free individuals from anxiety and doubts that prevent them from developing their own resources and potential. Thus, counseling is simply a process of releasing an already existing force in a potentially adequate individual.

Rogers (1951) recognizes that the existence of those necessary and sufficient conditions for effective counseling do result in a process that leads to certain outcomes. As a result of these conditions, the client is less defensive and more congruent and open to his experiences. He is more realistic, objective, and extensional in his perceptions, and consequently, more effective in problem solving. The client's vulnerability to threat is reduced because of the increased congruence of self and experience.

The client's perception of his ideal self is more realistic, more achievable. As a result of the increased congruence of self and experience, his real self becomes more congruent with his ideal self; hence all tension is reduced and the degree of positive self-regard is increased.

The client perceives the locus of evaluation and the locus of choice to be within himself. He feels more confident and more self-directing; his values are determined by his own valuing process.

The client experiences more acceptance of others. He accepts more behaviors as belonging to himself and conversely has fewer behaviors that he denies as part of his own self-experience. Others see his behavior as more socialized and mature.

Implementation: Techniques and Procedures

The development of person-centered therapy shifted the focus from *what* the therapist does, to *who* the therapist is, particularly the philosophy and attitudes. Certainly the primary emphasis is on the counseling relationship itself. In terms of the role that the counselor assumes in this process, Raskin and Rogers (1989) stated that the basic theory was simply that if the counselor successfully communicated genuineness, unconditional positive regard, and empathy, then change would occur. No other techniques were particularly important. Interestingly, Kirschenbaum (1991) reported that up to just before his death, Rogers continued to believe that these same three helping conditions, which he had first insisted were essential over four decades earlier, were still the core of a counseling approach that actually worked in the real world. Thus the person-centered counselor is simply viewed as a facilitator who allows the individual to move toward an inherent tendency of growth and development toward the process of full functioning (Cottone, 1992).

There are, however, certain emphases within this counseling approach. One is the emphasis on the here-and-now of the individual's existence, both inside and outside of the counseling relationship. The counselor does not need a knowledge of the nature and history of the client's difficulties. What has happened in the individual's past to cause the present difficulties is not important to the counselor; how the client is now operating is. As a simple illustration, consider a client who feels hatred for her brother. The person-centered approach takes the position that it makes little difference that this hatred developed because of a particular situation. Rather, how the client now feels toward her brother and how her feelings affect her whole pattern of behavior are important. Thus one emphasis is to help the client focus on her present feelings by expressing them verbally.

This emphasis on the here-and-now replaces diagnosis in counseling. Diagnosis is considered undesirable because it suggests that certain individuals have the power to decide what is right for all individuals. It also violates the belief that all individuals are self-determining beings, responsible for their own actions. Likewise, diagnosis in counseling is inappropriate because only the client can diagnose the difficulty. Only the client can accurately see the internal frame of reference. It is dangerous for counselors to attempt diagnosis, no matter how accurate they feel their perception of the client's internal frame of reference may be. Finally, diagnosis implies a denial of the unique qualities of each person. To diagnose is to place individuals in categories, and the person-centered counselor wants to avoid this trap. Instead, the counselor responds to the individual as a unique person with a potential for self-diagnosis and remediation.

Another major emphasis of the person-centered approach is a concentration on the emotional rather than the intellectual elements in the relationship. Pure knowledge is not seen as helping the client; the impact of knowledge may be blocked from awareness by the emotional satisfactions that the individual achieves through the present behavior. Intellectually, the client may know what the real situation is but, because the client responds emotionally, this knowledge does not help to change behavior. Although clients ordinarily begin talking about particular situations and emphasize the factual content of those situations, person-centered counselors attempt to help clients focus on feelings about themselves, other people, and events that take place in their world. The counselor then feeds back to clients as accurately as possible the feelings they are expressing in the hope that they will be able to view these feelings more objectively.

Since the emphasis of person-centered counseling is not on techniques but on the ability of the counselor to establish a relationship in which the necessary conditions outlined earlier are present, the counselor must be a patient and expert lis-

tener, one who fully accepts each individual by offering an atmosphere of unconditional positive regard and empathic understanding. The counselor attempts to
help the client develop insight by encouraging free expression and then reflecting
these feelings. In this process no specific problem, information, or other intellectual elements are emphasized; the focus is on the current state of the individual.

If the counselor follows this process, then the necessary and sufficient conditions for counseling are established. Clients will be able to go through the process
of articulating their feelings, developing insight and self-understanding, and finally, developing new goals and modes of behavior. Counseling may end at this
stage, but the process continues. The client has simply been returned to a state that
allows the lifelong process towards self-actualization to continue. The individual
is once again in control. The external conditions of worth have disappeared, and
the organismic valuing process has taken its proper place as the evaluator of experiences and the controller of behavior.

Boy and Pine (1982), however, suggest that the person-centered viewpoint has
been expanded and that there are two phases to this effective person-centered relationship. The first phase consists of those dynamics that have been traditionally
identified by Rogers as essential in building a therapeutic, facilitative, and substantive relationship—empathy, acceptance, genuineness, liberality, involvement,
sensitive listening, and equalizing. The second phase, which depends on the effectiveness of the relationship built in the first phase, centers on the needs of the
client. Although they give but little emphasis and clarification to this phase and the
needs of clients, they do point out that clients often need the intervention of counselors to obtain such basic needs as a job, adequate housing, and access to governmental agencies. Such an expansion, which is highly consistent with what person-
centered counselors are doing, enables the counselor to be more flexible and
concrete in meeting client needs once the therapeutic relationship has been fully
established. In addition, the development of the person-centered approach over
the years has included a change to a more active, direct, and confrontational role
for the counselor (Blocher, 1987).

Contributions and Limitations

The person-centered approach makes several unique contributions to counseling
effectiveness. Its emphasis is on providing clients with the kind of facilitative environment in which the focus is fully on their concerns. As a result, they can sense
that they are being listened to as they receive responses from the therapist that involve feedback of what they have communicated. Person-centered counseling emphasizes reflective listening, as the counselor adopts the internal frame of reference of the client. Further, if clients feel they are being heard without being judged
or evaluated, they are likely to express even deeper feelings, thus leading to further self-exploration and self-understanding of attitudes, beliefs, and feelings. In
addition, person-centered counselors consciously avoid taking responsibility for
decision making by clients, leaving that responsibility with clients and thus helping them recognize their own power over themselves. Lastly, the person-centered

concepts are applicable to a wide variety of helping situations, as well as to daily living itself .

Person-centered counseling does have some limitations. Some counselors oversimplify the major concepts of the theory and limit their own repertoire of responses to reflections and empathic listening. As a result, they often fail to distinguish between the use of techniques and the use of their own personality, their self-as-instrument. Another limitation: clients often fail to understand what the counselor is trying to accomplish. Such clients, since they are unaware of any positive effects resulting from their interactions with the counselor, may withdraw from the counseling process. In addition, person-centered therapy appears to be less effective with persons who do not voluntarily seek counseling, who have limited contact with reality, or who have difficulty communicating.

Gestalt Therapy

Gestalt therapy, developed by Frederick Perls, is a therapeutic approach in which the therapist assists the client toward self-integration and toward learning to utilize his energy in appropriate ways to grow, develop, and actualize. Perls's most important books include *Gestalt Therapy Verbatim* (1969a), *In and Out of the Garbage Pail* (1969b), and *Gestalt Therapy: Excitement and Growth in the Human Personality* (Perls, Hefferline, and Goodman, 1951).

View of Human Nature

Like person-centered therapy, Gestalt therapy views people as essentially phenomenological. Passons (1975) lists eight assumptions about the nature of humanity that form the framework for the Gestalt approach.

1. A person is a composite whole made up of interrelated parts. None of these parts—body, emotions, thoughts, sensations, and perceptions—can be understood outside the context of the whole person.
2. A person is also part of his own environment and cannot be understood apart from it.
3. A person chooses how to respond to external and internal stimuli, is an actor on his world, not a reactor.
4. A person has the potential to be fully aware of all sensations, thoughts, emotions, and perceptions.
5. A person is capable of making choices because of this awareness.
6. People have the capacity to govern their own lives effectively.
7. People cannot experience the past and the future; they can only experience themselves in the present.
8. People are neither basically good nor bad.

It is clear from these eight assumptions that Gestalt theorists share with Rogers an optimistic view that people are capable of self-direction. However, Perls also emphasized that individuals must take responsibility for their own lives. He believed that the motivation for this process was the result of an inherent goal of self-actualization. All other needs were viewed as stemming from and grounded in this basic need to actualize oneself (Perls, 1969a). Unlike Rogers, however, this striving for self-actualization is present-centered, rather than future-focused. Gestaltists believe that a healthy personality exists when a person's experiences form a meaningful whole (gestalt), where there is smooth transition between those sets of experiences that are immediately in the focus of awareness and those sets that are in the background. Thus, one has the capacity to know one's own balance and to attend to one's own needs as these needs emerge. Therefore, the purpose of Gestalt therapy is to increase the client's self-awareness, since awareness is, in itself, therapeutic. Perls believed that, with awareness, the most important unfinished business would emerge to be dealt with.

Key Concepts

Probably the most significant concept in Gestalt therapy is the now. For Perls, this is related to awareness in that one becomes aware of what one does by becoming aware of what one is doing now and by remaining in this awareness, letting the experience flow through the total senses. By allowing oneself to fully experience the present moment, the individual is able to allow "organismic self-regulation" to take over and to eliminate self-manipulation, environmental control, and other factors that interfere with this natural self-regulating process. This attainment of awareness as it relates to the present is the basic goal of Gestalt therapy. Perls (1969a) in fact indicates that "awareness per se—by and of itself—can be curative" (p. 16).

This emphasis on experiencing the here-and-now is certainly a major contribution of the Gestalt approach, one which has greatly influenced other theories. Other affective approaches, as well as the major behavioral approaches and the cognitive approaches, have placed increasing focus on the present, either in terms of feelings, behaviors, or thinking. This here-and-now orientation provides the basis for an I-thou relationship, which includes an emphasis on addressing someone directly (even if absent) instead of talking about that person to the counselor (Gladding, 1988).

Anxiety from the Gestalt point of view is the gap between the now and the later. Perls suggests that individuals experience anxiety because they leave the security of the present and become preoccupied with the future, frequently expecting bad things to happen. As a result, living with a focus on the future often results in not seeing what is at hand. Whether this leads to daydreams—fleeing from the present into better times—or catastrophizing—excessive worrying about what might happen—the impact on the present is real and can be dealt with only by "presentizing" these into current awareness (Passons, 1975).

Similar problems occur when individuals focus on the past. In particular, focusing on the past often relates to blaming the past as being responsible for what is happening now. By using past events and experiences as a scapegoat, clients place responsibility for their current behavior onto the past and thus avoid present responsibility. This avoidance of living in the present prevents individuals from having the energy or time for creative adjustments and changes that could make the present more satisfying. In addition, the past is over and cannot be reexperienced other than in fantasy and is usually dealt with in the past tense, leaving the past in the past. Gestalt therapists attempt to presentize the past by using fantasy to bring the past into the present. This is done by asking the clients to relate past events as if they were occurring at the moment. By reexperiencing the past as if it were happening now, clients are frequently able to reexamine those events and gain a new perspective for the meaning of those events for their lives.

This is particularly true in dealing with unfinished business or interrupted experiences of the past. Perls (1969a) emphasizes the need to relive or reexperience situations from the past about which clients have unexpressed feelings such as anger, pain, anxiety, grief, guilt, resentment, alienation, and so on. Even though these feelings are unexpressed, they are associated with distinct memories of specific events in which the client did not attain closure or did not resolve the matter. Perls points out that simply having an intellectual awareness of these events is not enough, but that clients must fully experience these events and work through the feelings involved.

Another key concept for the Gestalt view is that of *growth* or *maturation*, which Perls (1971) defined as ". . . the transcendence from environmental support to self-support" (p. 30). Thus maturity is seen in terms of process rather than in terms of product and involves the individual's taking on the functions necessary for self-support and learning to mobilize her own resources for dealing with the environment effectively. This necessitates learning to make creative adjustments, in which an active, dynamic, and changing self is able to respond both to environmental pressures and to inner emergent needs.

Process and Goals

Gestaltists believe that individuals seek counseling because their psychological needs are not being met. They expect the counselor to provide environmental support and often attempt to manipulate the counselor into doing so. However, Gestalt therapists seek to assist clients in discovering that they need not be dependent upon others, but that they can become independent beings. This involves helping clients to become responsible for themselves and to work toward achieving integration, in which there is a bringing together of all the parts of themselves that they have disowned. This integration enables one to function as a systemic whole comprised of feelings, attitudes, thoughts, and behaviors. Energy previously directed toward the playing of roles is released for the individual's self-regulating capabilities. All of this is a process, on-going and never completed. As Perls (1969a) points out, "Integration is never completed; maturation is never completed. It's an ongoing process forever and ever . . . . There's always something to be integrated; always something to be learned" (p. 64).

Passons (1975) has divided the kinds of problems that individuals experience into six areas: lack of awareness, lack of self-responsibility, a loss of contact with environment, inability to complete Gestalts, disowning of needs, and dichotomizing dimensions of the self.

Lack of awareness is usually a problem for people with rigid personalities. The image they have established to maintain the delicate balance between self and self-image causes them to lose contact with the *what* and *how* of their behavior. They simply exist, moving through life from day to day with an uneasy feeling of non-fulfillment.

Lack of self-responsibility is related to lack of awareness but takes the form of trying to manipulate the environment instead of manipulating the self. Instead of striving for independence or self-sufficiency, characteristics of maturity, the individual strives to remain in a dependency situation.

Loss of contact with the environment is also related to the first problem area, lack of awareness. This problem can take two forms. The first occurs when an individual's behavior has become so rigid that no input from the environment is accepted or incorporated. Such individuals withdraw from contact with the environment, including other people. Such a withdrawal prohibits them from meeting their needs and from moving toward a state of maturity. A second form is manifested by those who need so much approbation that they lose themselves by trying to incorporate everything from the environment, becoming almost totally subsumed by the self-image.

Inability to complete Gestalt or to complete unfinished business is another area that accounts for many problems brought to counseling. Unfinished business causes the individual to continue to strive to complete the business, even in her current activities. However, when these unfinished situations within us become powerful enough, they cause difficulties and prevent us from dealing with current situations. "The individual is beset with preoccupation, compulsive behavior, wariness, oppressive energy, and much self-defeating activity" (Polster and Polster, 1973 p. 36).

Disowning of needs occurs when someone acts to deny a need. Passons (1975) points out that in our society individuals commonly deny their need to be aggressive; since this need is generally socially unacceptable, individuals tend not to express it. Instead of moving energy into constructive behavior, people deny the existence of some need and thereby lose the energy it produces.

Dichotomizing dimensions of the self takes the form of people perceiving themselves at one end of a possible continuum. An example would be the woman who sees herself only as being weak, who never fully realizes that she has both strengths and weaknesses. The best-known split is what Perls called "top dog, underdog." The top dog is that part of the individual characterized as moralistic, perfectionistic, and authoritarian. The top dog strives to get the individual to behave as others expect. The underdog represents the desires of the individual and operates as the defensive and dependent part of the personality. Individuals who listen only to the top dog and fail to recognize and meet their own needs will have an internal conflict.

Each of the six problem areas is related directly to conflicts within the self, conflicts usually resulting from an inability to bring together individual needs and

FIGURE 4-2   Working with resistant clients sometimes results in a need for confrontation
(Photo by James T. Hurley)

environmental demands. Problems arise when individuals fail to utilize their own capacity for self-regulation and expend their energies in attempting to avoid frustration by depending upon others, by acting helpless, and by manipulating the environment in other ways. Thus one step in the process is for the counselor to frustrate the client's demands for support and help so that the client is forced to rely on his own resources. Of course, the client may resist this transition from external to internal support.

At the point at which the client is unable to manipulate the counselor into solving his problems and is unwilling to move toward self-support, an impasse occurs. The client is stuck, unable to experience his feelings because of the threat involved. For example, the client who is confused, frustrated, or blocked is seen by Perls (1969a) as being in an impasse. At this point the counselor identifies the impasse and provides an accepting situation, a "safe emergency," in which the client can feel safer in working toward self-support. Actually, Perls points out that most clients do *not* want to go beyond the impasse, since it is easier to keep things the way they are. Therefore, the counselor must facilitate the process in an active, propulsive manner so that the client is forced to recognize and deal with his impasse in order to get in touch with, and work through, his frustrations.

Gestalt therapy has several important goals. Certainly the most significant goal is helping individuals assume responsibility for themselves, rather than carrying out duties according to another's expectations. The aim is to challenge the client to move from "environmental support" to "self-support."

A second major goal is achieving integration. An integrated person functions as a systematic whole comprising feelings, perceptions, thoughts, and a physical body whose processes cannot be divorced from the more psychological components. When one's inner state (emotions) and behavior match, little energy is wasted, and one is more capable of responding appropriately to meet one's needs.

As was pointed out earlier, the achievement of self-regulation and integration requires awareness. Awareness is seen as both necessary and sufficient for change. Perls (1969a) emphasized that once one is aware, "the organism can work on the healthy Gestalt principle: that the most important unfinished situation will always emerge and can be dealt with" (p. 51). Consequently, awareness is always an underlying aim of the counselor.

Implementation: Techniques and Methods

From the very beginning the Gestalt counselor strives to challenge clients to assume responsibility for their own actions. The counselor quickly attempts to communicate to the client that, although the counselor wants to facilitate the client's growth and self-discovery, the counselor cannot make the changes for the client. In essence, the counselor seeks to force the client into open and honest interaction, refusing to tolerate the games that the client may play with people outside counseling. Such an interaction sets the conditions that will facilitate the client's growth and awareness.

The essential technique at the disposal of the Gestalt counselor is the establishment of what Perls calls a "continuum of awareness." This continuum of awareness is seen as being required for the organism to work on the healthy Gestalt principle that the most important unfinished situation will always emerge and must be dealt with. The counselor does this by integrating the client's attention and awareness, by helping him assimilate into his structure of self the totality of his experiences. A major technique of the Gestalt counselor is deliberately playing provocative games with the client, games intended to force the client to confront and acknowledge feelings that have been so arduously avoided. As Perls (1969b) suggests, individuals who are experiencing difficulty cannot see the obvious. They are full of avoidances and resistances that keep them from full awareness. Perls suggests that clients reach an impasse that they don't want to work through. Such impasses involve unsatisfied needs or unfinished business that clients believe they lack the resources to resolve. The counselor, rather than providing answers to the client's problems, seeks to force the client to work through the impasse—first by structuring the situation so that the impasse comes into the open, then by frustrating the client by refusing to give what is sought. In this situation the counselor's goal is to help the client recognize that the impasse exists in the mind and that the client does have the ability to resolve the impasse. In effect, the counselor is telling the client, "You can and must be responsible for yourself." This will then result in individuals liking themselves more (Dolliver, 1991).

Gestalt counseling, like person-centered counseling, does not attempt to reconstruct the past or uncover the unconscious motivations of the client. Gestalt counselors focus on the present. They believe that people who tend to intellectualize about the past or future are generally having difficulty with the present and are using these discussions to resist the counselor's attempt to deal with current functioning; therefore, counselors can gain their most important information about clients by what they observe during interaction with the client. Gestalt counselors must be able to pick out discrepancies between verbal and nonverbal expressions and feed these expressions back to clients, making clients more aware of their own behavior and emotions. This here-and-now orientation is further encouraged by the counselor who asks such questions as "What is your right hand doing now?" or "How does your voice sound now?" The counselor never asks "why" because why questions encourage intellectualization, whereas "how" and "what" questions focus attention on current functioning. In both cases the counselor is seeking to get the client to become more aware of feelings, behaviors, emotions, and sensations in the moment to moment of *now*. At the same time, the counselor is attempting to discover what the client is trying to avoid and in what areas of functioning the client is suffering from internal conflicts.

In addition to the techniques of frustrating the client and fostering here-and-now orientation, Gestalt counselors also use experiential games that increase individuals' self-awareness and awareness of their impasses, then help them reintegrate themselves. This last step is the most crucial, for if individuals are stripped of all their defenses and given no new ways of behavior, they will be even more vulnerable to outside forces than they were prior to counseling. Following are some of those that appear on both lists and seem appropriate for use by counselors.

Specific Techniques

Use of Personal Pronouns.   Clients are encouraged to use *I* instead of words like *it, you,* or *we* when talking about themselves. This helps clients to own their own behavior. For example, the client might say, "I didn't have many dates this year. Next year it will be different." The counselor might respond with *"It* will be different? Who are you talking about?" The client might then respond "Me. *I'll* be different."

Converting Questions to Statements.   Clients often use questions to keep the focus off themselves or to hide what they are really thinking. The client who asks, "Do you really believe that?" is generally saying, "I don't think you believe that." Forcing clients to make statements makes them declare their own belief systems and forces them to take responsibility.

Assuming Responsibility.   The client is sometimes asked to end all expressions of feelings or beliefs with, "and I take responsibility for it." Sometimes clients are encouraged to assume responsibility by having them change "can't" to "won't," or by changing "but" to "and." For instance, "I want to lose weight, but I just keep eating a lot," sounds different when it is stated, "I want to lose weight, and I just keep eating a lot." By changing the *but* to *and* the client is verbalizing the responsibility. This assumption of responsibility helps clients to see themselves as having internal strength, rather than relying on external controls.

Playing the Projection.   When a client projects something onto another individual, especially the counselor, the counselor asks the client to play the role of the other person. For instance, when a client says to the counselor, perhaps as the result of the counselor structuring a frustration situation, "I have the feeling you don't really like me," the counselor may ask the client to play the role of the counselor and to express what she believes the counselor is feeling. By doing this the client recognizes that her feelings toward the counselor are being projected in a way that affects what she believes the counselor is feeling toward her.

The Empty Chair.   In the empty chair technique, clients are given the opportunity to act out the way they would like to behave toward another person, pictured as sitting in the empty chair. This role playing helps clients get in touch with parts of themselves that they were either unaware of or have denied. In addition, the client may also be rehearsing a new role that will be tried outside of counseling. The rehearsal strengthens the client's belief that the new behavior can be carried out. The empty chair technique can also be used when the client is caught between conflicting parts of her personality (top dog, underdog; passive, aggressive). In this situation, the counselor may instruct the client to play both roles, sitting in one chair for one role and sitting in the second chair for the second role. The client carries on a verbal dialogue between the two parts, switching seats to represent the part of the personality being portrayed. Such a dialogue brings the conflict into the open so that the individual can inspect and resolve it.

A variety of other techniques are used by Gestalt counselors. The ones above are frequently used and are representative of many other techniques.

Contributions and Limitations

Gestalt counseling is particularly effective in avoiding the kind of games clients often play with counselors. Its focus on helping clients to experience all their present feelings more fully avoids allowing clients to use helplessness as an excuse. Gestalt counseling is a confrontive and active approach, stressing the *what* and *how* of behavior and leading to the acceptance of personal responsibility for behavior. Clients are able to work through the barriers that have prevented them from expressing the unfinished business that has interfered with effective contact with themselves and others.

Cottone (1992) suggests that the Gestalt counselor enters into dialogue to take the client and the counselor to full experiencing and awareness in interpersonal interaction. He goes on to say that "where Carl Rogers is loving, Perls is making love. Where Albert Ellis is defining the irrational, Perls is living irrationality with the client. All concerns are 'brought to' and 'lived in' the present" (p. 144).

Limitations of Gestalt counseling include its failure to develop a solid theory and an apparent "coldness" on the part of the counselor toward the client. Perls seemed to discount the value of a systematic discussion of therapy and to discourage research to evaluate the effectiveness of Gestalt counseling, with the danger that Gestalt therapy would become a collection of jargon and techniques that the counselor uses on the client. Polster (1990), in particular, has worked to remedy this criticism. In addition, although Perls was often viewed as inhumane in application of his technique (Cottone, 1992), Polster has incorporated a humanistic interpersonal spirit into Gestalt counseling that allows the counselor to be loving and confrontive at the same time.

Existential Therapy

Unlike most therapeutic approaches, existential therapy is not closely tied to one person. Primarily the product of European existential philosophers, existential counseling consists of numerous approaches that emphasize the philosophical concerns of what it means to become fully human. Major American exponents of this approach include May, Van Kaam, Frankl, and Yalom. Their most important works are *Man's Search for Himself* (May, 1953), *Existential Psychology* (May, 1961), *The Art of Existential Counseling* (Van Kaam, 1966), *Man's Search for Meaning* (Frankl, 1959), and *Existential Psychotherapy* (Yalom, 1980).

Existential theory focuses on the human condition. Rather than a system of techniques used to influence clients, this approach is primarily an attitude that stresses the understanding of persons. Hence, it is not a school of therapy nor is it a unified and systematic theory.

May (1961) has proposed six essential characteristics which constitute the nature of an existing person.

1. Humans are centered in themselves. Neurosis is only one method the individual uses to protect his own center or existence.
2. Humans have the character of self-affirmation, or the need to preserve their centeredness. The preservation of this centeredness takes will.
3. Humans have the possibility of moving from centeredness to participation with other beings. The moving from centeredness to participation involves risk.
4. Awareness lies on the subjective side of centeredness. Humans are able to be subjectively aware of that with which they are in contact.
5. Humans have a unique form of awareness called self-consciousness. Awareness means knowledge of external dangers and threats, and conscious-

ness has to do with one's experience with oneself as the subject who has a world.

6. Humans have the characteristic of anxiety, the feeling of one in a struggle against that which would destroy one's being.

To these six characteristics Frankl (1959) adds a seventh.

7. The primary force in one's life is one's search for meaning. Each person must have a unique and specific meaning, one that can be fulfilled by that person alone. One's striving toward existence takes will.

Existential theory emphasizes concepts that are more philosophical than those in most therapies. Existentialists see human beings as capable of self-awareness, a unique and distinctive capacity that allows them to think and decide. For the existentialist, the more awareness a person has, the greater the person's possibilities for freedom. Thus, the power to choose among alternatives is an essential aspect of being human. This freedom to choose and to act becomes a responsibility. This, of course, implies that one is responsible for one's existence and one's destiny; they are not the result of deterministic forces of conditioning.

The awareness of freedom and responsibility gives rise to existential anxiety, which is a basic human attribute. The knowledge that one *must* choose, despite an uncertain outcome, results in anxiety. Existential anxiety also results from the awareness of being finite and from facing the inevitable prospect of death. Awareness of death gives the present moment significance, because one realizes one has only a limited time to actualize one's human potential. Existential guilt, then, is the result of failing to become what one is fully able to become. Since no one ever fully fulfills his potential, guilt is universal and is therefore a condition of existence. This existential guilt, however, is a positive force, since it leads to humility, sensitivity in personal relationships, and creative utilization of one's potentialities (May, 1953).

Existential therapists recognize that individuals seek counseling for any of several reasons, but they believe a major reason is that clients seek to expand their psychological world in one way or another. The client's world is unique, and the counselor must understand it to assist the client. The counselor encourages the client to unfold his world in the encounter so that both client and counselor can begin to understand it, and the client can act upon the possibilities inherent in it. Thus the counselor's main task is not only to show the client where, when, and to what extent the client has failed to realize his potential, but also to attempt to help the client *experience* this existence as fully as possible. Technique loses importance, as existential therapists utilize whatever procedure seems appropriate based on their understanding of the client's *being* (May, 1961). The existential counselor's role is to be authentic, to expose herself to clients so that the client can become aware of commonalities of qualities between the two of them (Meier and Davis, 1992).

Because honesty is an essential characteristic of an existential encounter, counselors must expose their true selves, and they cannot view the client as an object to be manipulated or exploited. The counselor's ability to be human enables clients to become aware of similar qualities in themselves. Through this process individuals will recognize their potentials and achieve self-growth, because that becomes their responsibility.

In existential counseling knowledge and insight are presumed to follow commitment; this is the direct opposite of most other counseling approaches. Thus, existential therapy does not ask *how to,* but looks for the underlying meaning in the client's statement as well as the myths and symbols in the client's psychology and being (May, 1987). Finally, most existentialist counselors do not believe in viewing individuals as divided into conscious and unconscious parts. They hold that what is often called the unconscious is part of the individual's being and that the unconscious is too often used to rationalize behavior and responsibility and thus to avoid the realities of one's existence. The aim of existential counseling is to enable individuals to accept responsibility for themselves.

Basically, the goal of existential therapy, if there is a single goal, is to help the client find and develop meanings in life as a way of reducing the anxiety associated with the threat of *nonbeing.* This is generally accomplished in two stages. In the first stage, the client must recognize his freedom of choice, being capable of choosing both that which is right for him and that which is not. This freedom must be fully recognized, leaving behind various restricting ideas, such as that of believing that only adhering to parental views is acceptable. Once the client accepts this freedom and the resulting variety of possibilities he can explore, the second stage is entered, in which the client learns to accept responsibility for his decisions by recognizing his need to see how the consequences of his choices make a profound impact on his existence. Thus the emphasis is on the client's realizing the importance of responsibility, awareness, freedom, and potential (Gladding, 1988).

Existential counseling puts little emphasis on techniques. The emphasis is on flexibility and versatility; what the counselor does depends entirely on the nature of the client's difficulty. The existential counselor recognizes that psychological forces take their meaning from the existential situation of the client's immediate life. Each client's behavior is seen and understood in the light of the client's existence as a human being.

Frankl (1959) did include the technique of paradoxical intention, which requires clients to intend that which they anticipate with fear. For example, the individual who has difficulty sleeping may be asked to practice staying awake. This is a reversal of the client's attitude toward the situation, especially if it is carried out in as humorous a setting as possible. Such a reversal brings out a change of attitude toward the symptom, enabling the client to gain some distance from the symptom, to view the troubling situation with detachment. The goal of the existential counselor, then, is to bring clients to the point where they cease to flee from or to fight their symptoms, and instead exaggerate them. As a result, the symptoms diminish and clients are no longer haunted by them.

Summary

Affective approaches to counseling focus primarily on the way clients feel, particularly about themselves. Counselors with an affective approach believe that if the feelings of clients change, their behavior will also change. This chapter presents three theoretical models, as well as brief summaries of two others.

Person-centered therapy stresses the need for self-acceptance by clients. To facilitate this self-acceptance, the counselor must experience empathic understanding of the client's world and then communicate genuine acceptance of the client's feelings about that world. The relationship between the counselor and the client is of major importance.

Gestalt therapy stresses the importance of clients' gaining awareness of their present experiences and of how they prevent themselves from feeling and experiencing the present. With this awareness clients are able to assume greater responsibility for their own behavior and to work through the barriers that have prevented them from expressing the unfinished business which has interfered with effective contact with themselves and others.

Existential therapy stresses the philosophical concerns of what it means to become fully human. Highly philosophical in its concepts, existential counseling aims at having clients experience their existence as authentic by becoming aware of their own existence and potentials and of how they can act on their potentials.

References

Blocher, D. H. (1987). *The professional counselor.* New York: : Macmillan.

Boy, A. V., & Pine, G. J. (1982). *Client-centered counseling: A renewal.* Boston: Allyn and Bacon.

Cottone, R R. (1992). *Theories and paradigms of counseling and psychotherapy.* Boston: Allyn and Bacon.

Dolliver, R. H. (1991). Perls with Gloria re-revisited: Gestalt techniques and Perls's practices. *Journal of Counseling and Development, 69,* 299–304.

Frankl, V. (1959). *Man's search for meaning.* New York: Washington Square Press.

Gladding, S. T. (1988). *Counseling: A comprehensive profession.* Columbus, OH: Merrill.

Kirschenbaum, H. (1991). Denigrating Carl Rogers: William Coulson's last crusade. *Journal of Counseling and Development, 69,* 411–413.

May, R. (I953). *Man's search for himself.* New York: NAL.

May, R. (Ed.). (1961). *Existential psychology.* New York: Random House.

May, R. (1987). Therapy in our day. In J. K. Zeig (Ed.). *The evolution of psychotherapy.* New York: Brunner/Mazel.

Meier, S. T., & Davis, S. R. (1992). *The elements of counseling* (2nd ed.). Pacific Grove, CA: Brooks/Cole.

Passons, W. R. (1975). *Gestalt approaches in counseling.* New York: Holt, Rinehart and Winston.

Perls, F. (1969a). *Gestalt therapy verbatim.* Moab, UT: Real People Press.

Perls, F. (1969b). *In and out of the garbage pail.* Moab, UT: Real People Press.

Perls, F., Hefferline, R., & Goodman, P. (1951). *Gestalt therapy: Excitement and growth in the human personality.* New York: Dell.

Polster, E. (1990). Gestalt therapy: Humanization of technique. Paper presented at the second "Evolution of Psychotherapy" conference in Anaheim, CA, December, 1990.

Polster, E., & Polster, M. (1973). *Gestalt therapy integrated: Contours of theory and practice.* New York: Brunner/Mazel.

Raskin, N. J. & Rogers, C. R. (1989). Person-centered therapy. In R. J. Corsin, & D. Wedding (Eds.). *Current Psychotherapies.* Itasca, IL: F. E. Peacock.

Rogers, C. R. (1942). *Counseling and psychotherapy.* Boston: Houghton Mifflin.

Rogers, C. R. (1951). *Client–centered therapy.* Boston: Houghton Mifflin.

Rogers, C. R. (1959). A theory of therapy, personality, and interpersonal relationships, as developed in the client-centered framework. In S. Koch (Ed.). *Psychology: A study of a science.* New York: McGraw-Hill.

Rogers, C. R. (1961). *On becoming a person.* Boston: Houghton Mifflin.

Van Kaam, A. (1966). *The art of existential counseling.* Wilkes-Barre, PA: Dimension Books.

Yalom, I. D. (1980). *Existential psychotherapy.* New York: Basic Books.

Chapter 5

Cognitive-Behavioral Approaches to Counseling

This chapter will emphasize the client's thinking process as it relates to behavior and to psychological and emotional difficulties. The synthesis of cognitive and behavioral approaches has occurred as theorists and practitioners have recognized that both approaches were dealing with inner cognitive processes such as thoughts, perceptions, and covert speech as a means of guiding actions that would lead to a more satisfying emotional state. Counselors who subscribe to a cognitive-behavioral approach engage in active, directive teaching as a means of reeducating the client to understand the cognitive input of the emotional disturbance; they seek to change clients' thinking so that they abandon irrational thinking or learn to anticipate possible benefits or aversive consequences to a specific behavior. As such, the counselor places far less emphasis on the relationship itself and takes the role of a teacher-persuader.

Rational-Emotive Therapy

Probably the most consistent attempt to introduce logical reasoning and cognitive processes into counseling was that of Albert Ellis, who developed rational emotive therapy (RET). Ellis stresses thinking, judging, deciding, analyzing, and doing; he puts little emphasis on feeling. Ellis himself has written numerous books and articles about RET; the most important are *Reason and Emotion in Psychotherapy* (1962) and *A Guide to Rational Living* with Robert A. Harper (1961).

View of Human Nature

The rational-emotive view of people is dominated by the principle that emotion and reason—thinking and feeling—are intricately entwined in the psyche. RET stresses that all normal humans think, feel, and act, and that they do so simultaneously. Their thoughts affect, and often create, their feelings and behaviors. Their emotions affect their thoughts and actions. Their acts affect their thoughts and feelings. Thus in order to change any one of the three, it is necessary to modify one or both of the other two. Ellis (1974) thus insists that he emphasizes all three: cognitive, emotive, and behavioral. His writings, however, emphasize the thinking process.

However, in 1992, Ellis insisted that his views had often been distorted. He stated that he does not assume that the emotional response to an event is determined by one's cognitive appraisal of that event, but instead the cognitive appraisal is "an important aspect of emotion and is practically never disparate from nor linearly causative of affect" (p. 449).

At the same time, rational-emotive therapy emphasizes that individuals are born with the potential for rational thinking as well as irrational thinking. Thus they are capable of loving, happiness, growth, relating to others, and even self-actualization. They also have tendencies toward self-destruction, self-blame, superstition, intolerance, perfectionism, and avoidance of behavior that promotes growth and self-actualization.

FIGURE 5-1   Albert Ellis
(Courtesy of the Institute for
Rational Emotive Therapy)

Ellis (1989) emphasizes that people are self-taking, self-evaluating, and self-sustaining who create problems for themselves when they perceive simple preferences and desires as being essential needs. He lists some key assumptions about human nature:

> Individual's condition is to feel disturbed, rather than being conditioned by external sources.

> Humans are unique in that they create disturbing beliefs that they repeat to themselves, continuing the disturbance.

> Individuals have the capacity to change their cognitive, emotive, and behavioral processes by choosing to react differently from their usual patterns. This involves training themselves to refuse to allow themselves to become upset and to resist irrational thoughts by repeating rational thoughts to themselves.

By defining *rationality* as "the use of cognitions, emotions, and behaviors for human self-fulfillment and self-actualization," Ellis (1992) provides the basis for individuals to utilize rational thinking and behaving to free themselves from irrational thoughts and to make themselves far happier.

Key Concepts

Rational-emotive therapy emphasizes that "emotions" and "feelings of emotional disturbance" are largely the products of people's thoughts, ideas, or constructs. Ellis (1974) maintained that emotional disturbances are simply the result of an individual's mistaken, illogical ideas about a particular situation. Since almost all individuals do seem to want to be happy in their personal and vocational lives, emotions that interfere with their happiness are usually designated as "inappropriate" or "self-defeating."

Some emotions are "appropriate" in that they help people to get more of what they want and to avoid or eliminate what they do not want. Examples of appropriate emotions include pleasure, joy, love, curiosity, sorrow, regret, frustration, and displeasure. On the other hand, emotions such as rage, mania, depression, anxiety, self-pity, and feelings of worthlessness are inappropriate. These inappropriate emotions typically are not only unpleasant in themselves, but also tend to bring about poor results, such as inertia or alienation of other people (Ellis, 1973). Thus, RET counselors attempt to help people discriminate between "appropriate" and "inappropriate" feelings, as well as to intensify the appropriate while reducing or eliminating the inappropriate. This approach is based on the premise that there are a number of major illogical ideas held and perpetuated by individuals that invariably lead to self-defeat. These eleven ideas (Ellis, 1962) are summarized as follows:

It is absolutely essential for an individual to be loved or approved of by every significant person in his environment. This is irrational because it is an unattainable goal. If one strives for it, one becomes less self-directing and more insecure and self-defeating.

It is necessary that each individual be completely competent, adequate, and achieving in all areas if the individual is to be worthwhile. Again, an impossibility. To strive compulsively for such complete achievement results in a sense of inferiority, an inability to live one's own life, and a constant fear of failure; it also leads one to view every situation in competitive terms and to strive to beat others rather than to simply enjoy the activity.

Some people are bad, wicked, or villainous, and these people should be blamed and punished. This idea is irrational because there is no absolute standard of right or wrong and very little free will. Everyone makes mistakes as a result of stupidity, ignorance, or emotional unbalance. Blame and punishment do not usually lead to improved behavior since they do not result in less stupidity, more intelligence, or a better emotional state. Rather, they often lead to worse behavior and greater emotional disturbance.

It is terrible and catastrophic when things are not the way an individual wants them to be. The reality of life is that not all situations will be as we would like. To be frustrated is normal, but to be severely and prolongedly upset is illogical. It may be unpleasant or bothersome when things do not work out, but it is not a catastrophe. Treating an event as a catastrophe does not change the situation; it only makes us feel worse. If we don't like something we can try to change it. If we can't do anything about it, we should accept it.

Unhappiness is a function of events outside the control of the individual. Actually most outside events that we perceive as harmful are only psychologically harmful; we cannot be hurt unless we allow ourselves to be affected by our attitudes and reactions. A person disturbs himself by telling himself how horrible it is when someone is unkind, rejecting, or annoying. If he realized that disturbances consist of his own perceptions and internalized verbalizations, he could control or change these disturbances.

If something may be dangerous or harmful, an individual should constantly be concerned and think about it. This is irrational because simply thinking about something doesn't change it at all and may, in fact, lead to its occurrence or even make it worse than it actually is.

It is easier to run away from difficulties and self-responsibility than it is to face them. This is irrational because running away does not solve the difficulty. Usually the situation remains and must eventually be dealt with.

Individuals need to be dependent on others and have someone stronger than themselves to lean on. We are all dependent upon others to some extent, but there is no reason to maximize dependency, for it leads to loss of independence, individualism, and self-expression. Such dependency causes still greater dependency, failure to learn, and insecurity, since one is at the mercy of those on whom one depends.

Past events in an individual's life determine present behavior and cannot be changed. Although the past may influence the present, it does not necessarily determine it. Rather, the presumed influence of the past may be used as an excuse to avoid changing one's behavior. It may be difficult to overcome past leanings, but it is not impossible.

An individual should be very concerned and upset by others' problems. This is irrational because other people's problems often have nothing to do with us and therefore should not seriously concern us. Even if they do, it is our definition of the implication of the other's behavior that upsets us. Getting upset usually prevents us from helping others do anything about their problems.

There is always a correct and precise answer to every problem and it is catastrophic if it is not found. This is irrational because there is no perfect solution to any problem. The search for a perfect solution only produces continued anxiety. The individual is never satisfied and is always searching for the one lost solution.

Ellis formulated the ABC principle of emotional disturbance, which emphasizes the importance of cognitive control over emotional states. It is consistent with the phenomenological position that one's perception of an event determines one's behavioral response to that event. For Ellis, A is the existence of a fact or an event external to the person. B is generally the individual's attitude, beliefs, or interpretation of A. C is the emotional consequence of or reaction of the person. In this analysis, A is not the cause of C. Instead, B, the person's belief about A, causes C, the emotional response or reaction. For example, a counselor might explain to a client who is upset and is blaming her parents for it that it is not the behavior of her parents (A) that is upsetting her, but her own *beliefs* (B) about being a failure or being rejected that are upsetting (C) her. Thus the individual herself is responsible for her own emotional reactions and disturbances.

Process and Goals

The rational-emotive therapist helps clients acknowledge their inappropriate feelings and behavior, assume responsibility for these as self-created and self-perpetuated, accept themselves with their symptoms, and determine the philosophic sources of those symptoms. The first step in this process is to show the clients that they are illogical, to help them understand how and why they became so, and to demonstrate the relationship of their irrational ideas to their unhappiness and emotional disturbance. In doing so, clients become aware of the specific material to be dealt with in order to improve their emotional functioning. In addition, this insight tends to reduce feelings of powerlessness and despair by showing clients that they are not helpless victims of outside forces but have control over themselves. This insight also leads clients to understand the relationship between their values and attitudes and the "shoulds," "oughts," and "musts" they have incorporated into their lives.

The counselor must continually receive feedback to check whether the client is understanding what is being taught. In particular, clients must internalize the three basic insights of rational-emotive therapy: (1) individuals basically upset themselves through their beliefs; (2) present distress is not caused by previous distress, no matter how, when, or where the crooked thinking began; and (3) individuals will think rationally if they change their irrational thoughts through work and behavioral practice (Cottone, 1992).

The second step is to help clients believe that thoughts can be challenged and changed. This allows clients to explore logically their ideas to determine if they are appropriate—those that are pleasurable or that help them change conditions they find objectionable—or inappropriate—those that are unpleasant and do not help them to change obnoxious conditions. This is accompanied by direct disputing of client beliefs by the therapist. This disputing consists of questioning and challenging the validity of the ideas clients hold about themselves, others, and the world. In disputing, the therapist persistently and forcefully repeats this process, using the most direct, persuasive, and logical techniques available. Throughout this process, however, the therapist attempts to teach clients to dispute themselves in such a way that they reach the goal of thinking rationally on their own.

The final step involves helping the client go beyond disputing irrational/inappropriate ideas by encouraging them to continue their efforts toward more rational thinking by rational reindoctrination. This includes dealing with the main general irrational ideas, as well as developing a more rational philosophy of living, so that clients can avoid falling victim to other irrational ideas and beliefs. This rational philosophy of living involves the substitution of rational attitudes and beliefs for irrational ones and leads to the elimination of negative, disturbing emotions as well as self-defeating behaviors.

Although advocates of RET utilize relationship techniques, insight-interpretative techniques, and behavioral techniques, they are used primarily as preliminary strategies to gain the client's trust and confidence and thus increase the possibility of bringing about cognitive change. Ellis (1973) states that the RET counselor:

1. Is active-directive with most clients, doing a great deal of talking and explaining, especially in the early stages.
2. Confronts clients directly with their problems so as not to waste unnecessary time.
3. Takes a vigorous approach in getting clients first to think and then to get them to reeducate themselves.
4. Is persistent and repetitive in hammering away at the irrational ideas underlying clients' emotional disturbances.
5. Appeals to clients' reasoning powers, rather than their emotions.
6. Is didactic and philosophical in his approach.
7. Uses humor and shame exercises as a way of confronting the client's irrational thinking.

Implementation: Techniques and Procedures

RET allows for considerable flexibility. The counselor can be very eclectic in terms of techniques and procedures. Virtually all of the common behavioral techniques discussed in this chapter are mentioned by Ellis and used by various RET counselors. In addition, Ellis utilizes a variety of teaching devices—pamphlets, books, tape recordings, films, and filmstrips—as part of the process through which clients learn to recognize the irrational thoughts which are bringing about the disturbances that are upsetting their lives. Although Ellis recognizes many ways of facilitating change, there is essentially only one technique in RET: active, directive teaching.

Ellis feels that the techniques other counselors use are relatively indirect and inefficient. Techniques such as catharsis, dream analysis, free association, interpretation of resistance, and transference analysis are often successful, at least in bringing the client to recognize her illogical thinking. Even when these techniques are most successful, however, they are wasteful because they do not get at the illogical thinking soon enough and thus time is wasted. The counselor-client relationship and expressive-emotive, supportive, and insight methods, although used in rational-emotive therapy, are simply preliminary techniques to establish rapport, to enable clients to express themselves, and to show them that they are respected.

Soon after the counseling is initiated, the RET counselor assumes an active teaching role to reeducate the client. The counselor demonstrates the illogical origin of the client's disturbances and the self-verbalizations that perpetuate the disturbances in the client's life. Clients are shown that their internalized sentences are quite illogical and unrealistic. The effective counselor continually unmasks the clients' past and, especially, their present illogical thinking or self-defeating verbalizations. The counselor does this by bringing this illogical thinking forcefully to their attention or consciousness, by showing them how it is causing and maintaining their disturbance and unhappiness, by demonstrating exactly what the illogical links in their internalized sentences are, and by teaching them how to rethink, challenge, contradict, and reverbalize these sentences to make their internalized thoughts more logical and efficient.

Ellis has emphasized particularly the use of homework assignments as an essential part of RET. This homework generally involves giving clients specific assignments to "try out" behaviors that the clients fear (asking for a date or applying for a job), encouraging them to take risks, or having them intentionally fail at some effort to learn (1) that to fail is not catastrophic and (2) how to cope with feelings of failure. Homework assignments also include a great deal of cognitive work: reading specific materials or, more commonly, utilizing self-help forms to analyze their ABCs and to work toward disputing their irrational beliefs. The RET counselor counters their fear with logic and reason, teaching, suggestion, persuasion, confrontation, deindoctrination, indoctrination, and prescription of behavior to show the client the irrational philosophies, to demonstrate how these lead to emotionally disturbed behavior, to change thinking, and thus to change the client's emotions. As a result, the client is able to replace these irrational philosophies with rational, logical ones. In addition, the counselor instructs the client in the major irrational ideas of our culture and provides more effective rational ones, thus offering protection from future disturbances.

Contributions and Limitations

Rational-emotive therapy has made an outstanding contribution to counseling through its emphasis on the cognitive process in the development of emotional difficulties. The recognition of the existence and impact, as well as the identification, of commonly held irrational beliefs that are internalized by the individual is particularly worthwhile. Like the behavioral approaches, RET also emphasizes the idea of clients' actually trying out new behaviors and learning the specific desired change in behavior. Thus the stress is on extending change outside the counselor's office and encouraging an active involvement on the part of the counselor.

Probably the major limitation with the use of RET is that, with its emphasis upon persuasion, suggestion, and repetition, those who use this approach are in danger of imparting their own values and philosophies of life on their clients. This danger is particularly present when the counselor assumes the role of expert and acts in an authoritarian manner. At the same time, the almost total emphasis on cognitive and behavioral aspects leaves RET vulnerable to its own criticism—that of ignoring an important dimension of the individual. In this respect, of course, RET tends to shortchange the affective aspects. Also, RET places little emphasis on the need for "timing" when confronting a client, showing little concern for waiting until the client is ready to listen and respond.

Behavioral Counseling

Although behavioral counseling is a relatively new approach, its focus changed significantly in the late 1970s. Although still primarily concerned with behavior change, behavioral counselors have begun to emphasize processes that are more cognitive in nature, recognizing, for instance, that there is a cognitive element operating whenever behavior changes as the result of its consequences. Thus behavioral counseling has become less significant as a specific counseling approach but continues to make a major impact as its techniques, strategies, and scientific emphasis are integrated into other approaches.

Although not closely identified with any single person, behavioral counseling has several important proponents. Among these are Wolpe, Lazarus, Bandura, Krumboltz, and Thoresen. Important behavioral works include *Revolution in Counseling* (Krumboltz, 1966), *The Practice of Behavior Therapy* (Wolpe 1990), *Behavioral Counseling: Cases and Techniques* (Krumboltz and Thoresen, 1969), and *Action Counseling for Behavior Change* (Dustin and George, 1977).

View of Human Nature

To behavioral counselors, people are neither good nor bad; they are essentially neutral at birth with equal potential for good or evil. As a result behavioral theorists have not fully defined the basic nature of humanity that supports their theory. However, Dustin and George list four assumptions regarding the nature of humanity and how people change that are central to behavioral counseling:

1. People are viewed as being neither intrinsically good nor bad, but as experiencing organisms who have potential for all kinds of behavior.
2. People are able to conceptionalize and control their own behavior.
3. People are able to acquire new behaviors.
4. People are able to influence others' behavior as well as to be influenced by others in their own behavior (1977, p. 12).

For the behavioral counselor, individuals are a product of their experience. The behaviorist sees maladaptive behaviors as being learned behaviors; their development and maintenance are the same as those of any other behavior. One implication of this view is that no behaviors are maladaptive in and of themselves; rather a behavior becomes inappropriate because someone deems it so. Certain behaviors that may be considered appropriate at home are not considered appropriate in school and vice versa. A second implication of this view of maladaptive behaviors as learned is the idea that any behavior that brings a pleasant result or that helps to reduce unpleasant results is likely to be increased. Thus the behavioral view suggests that since maladaptive behavior is learned, it can also be unlearned. In dealing with such behaviors in therapy, the behaviorist generally considers the stimulus-response paradigm the basic pattern of all human learning. Each person reacts in a theoretically predictable way to any given stimulus, depending on his previous experiences and reinforcements. In this sense persons are no different from animals, except that their responses to stimuli are more complex and occur on a higher level of organization and conceptualization.

Behavior then is a function of a stimulus. This reduces considerably the complex factors influencing human reactions to situations and allows the behaviorist to focus on a specific problem as a reaction to a given set of stimuli. The key word underlying this behavioral view of humanity is *conditioning*. There are several types of conditioning, but two major parallel forms are usually discussed: *classical* (respondent) *conditioning* and *operant* (instrumental) *conditioning*. Classical conditioning occurs when a stimulus elicits a response; operant conditioning occurs when a response is emitted in order to obtain an outcome that reinforces the individual. Respondent behavior is controlled by its antecedent, whereas operant behavior is controlled by its consequences.

Respondent behavior includes such familiar behaviors as perspiration in response to heat, blinking the eyelids in response to the nearness of a foreign object, and salivation in response to food. A classic example of respondent conditioning is that reported by Watson and Rayner (1960). They elicited an emotional fear response in an infant by showing the infant a rat while a loud noise was produced; after several repetitions the fear response formerly caused by the loud noise was produced simply by presenting the rat.

In operant learning, the consequences that strengthen behavior are called *reinforcers*. A reinforcer is any event that, instead of eliciting a specific class of behaviors, increases the probability of any resulting behavior. For example, a hungry animal may behave in a wide variety of ways; any behaviors immediately followed by food will be strengthened. The activity or event is reinforcing simply because it has an effect on behavior. If a reinforcing stimulus is pleasant—for example, one that provides an individual the opportunity for some novel activity—then the event or stimulus is positive reinforcement; it increases the likelihood that the particular act it is associated with will be repeated. The initial act may have been learned as the result of previous consequences or it may be a random, somewhat spontaneous action. In either case, the action is more likely to recur because of the pleasant consequences that followed.

The process of eliminating an undesirable behavior is referred to as *extinction*. A behavior has been extinguished when it no longer occurs. Counselors must be aware of two important strategies of extinction. The first strategy is that of counterconditioning: A new, desirable behavior is substituted for the undesirable behavior. By way of example, in one of the articles by Jones (1960), originally reported in 1924, this incident is discussed: A three-year-old boy was afraid of rabbits, fur, white rats, and even cotton and wool. Jones treated the boy by desensitizing him to these fears. She introduced a rabbit during a play period, and gradually increased his toleration of the rabbit. At the beginning the rabbit was in a cage twelve feet away; gradually the cage was moved closer until the boy was able to fondle the rabbit affectionately. Jones also associated the rabbit with the presence of a pleasant stimulus (food), which aided in the elimination of the fear. She did this by bringing the rabbit into the room while the boy was eating dinner in his highchair. The rabbit was kept at the far end of the room and the boy was hungry, so the rabbit's presence did not interfere with the boy's pleasure from eating. As the rabbit was moved closer to him over a period of days the fear response gradually decreased until the boy was able to eat while petting the rabbit.

A second strategy of extinction is that of withdrawing the reinforcement that has previously followed a behavior. For example, many classroom teachers have the problem of students who blurt out questions and interrupt the class. The teacher often reinforces such behavior by answering the student quickly so that the lesson can continue. To extinguish this behavior, the teacher must ignore the student, denying him attention as well as preventing him from getting his question answered. This period of extinction is often difficult. The individual who controls the reinforcing events often fails to wait out the extinction period and gives the student the added attention. If this occurs too often, a partial reinforcement effect occurs. Reinforcement usually does not occur every time a correct response is made. Partial reinforcement is important not only because it explains resistance to extinction but also because it can be used to increase the permanence of an appropriate or desired behavior. New behaviors are more quickly learned when the behavior is reinforced each time it occurs. However, those behaviors are also easily unlearned. To bring about more permanent learning, the behavior should be reinforced every time it occurs, at the beginning. After the behavior is acquired, partial reinforcement builds a tendency to perform the behavior even when no reinforcement follows. The percentage of behaviors reinforced should be decreased gradually to prevent extinction.

Sometimes it is difficult to create conditions that elicit a desired behavior for the first time so that the behavior can be reinforced. If the probability of the desired behavior occurring is low or if the counselor does not wish to wait for the behavior, then the counselor must shape the response. Shaping is a procedure that reinforces successively closer approximations of the desired behavior. The way most normal children learn to talk illustrates the way shaping works. The first babbling sounds made by infants are certain to cause the parents to smile, speak warmly, and pay attention. Gradually, as the babbling sounds become more and more like words, only those sounds that parents find similar to their language are reinforced. Later, only closer approximations are reinforced, until the child learns to make sounds that are meaningful to adults.

Key Concepts

Behavior therapy differs from other therapy approaches in that the feelings of clients are secondary to client behavior. Rather, behavioral counselors focus on inappropriate learning as the reason for client problems (Meier and Davis, 1993). Dustin and George (1977) suggest that while many of the problems brought to the counselor seem to be emotional in nature, the problems are actually failures to deal successfully with problems in living. Thus the client who says, "I feel rejected" or "I feel lonely" is actually expressing a need for more successful behaviors that will enable him or her to relate more satisfactorily with other people.

As a result, behavior therapy is characterized by (1) a focus on specific, overt behavior, (2) very precise therapeutic goals, (3) the development of a specific treatment procedure appropriate to the client's problem, and (4) an objective assessment as to whether the therapeutic goals were accomplished (Corey, 1977). As such, behavior therapy is somewhat experimental in approach, concerned primarily with whether or not a desired effect occurs. This emphasis on specific counseling goals that are both observable and measurable means that both the client and the counselor will understand precisely the change that is desired. In addition, the specification of concrete, reachable goals provides greater opportunity for clients to see progress, which is a motivating force in itself.

Basically, then, behavior therapy attempts to help clients (1) alter maladaptive behavior, (2) learn the decision-making process, and (3) prevent problems by strengthening desirable behaviors. This is done by assessing the nature and extent of the problem, specifying counseling goals, choosing the most appropriate counseling strategies, and periodically reevaluating client progress to determine if the counseling has been successful, depending entirely on whether the goals have been accomplished.

Process and Coals

Behavioral counselors are generally less concerned about process per se than are most counselors. However, they place central importance on specific counseling goals. These goals are chosen by the client with help from the counselor. Once counseling goals are identified, then new conditions for learning are created. The rationale is that all behavior is learned, including maladaptive behavior: If neurosis is learned it can be unlearned, and more effective behaviors can be acquired. Thus behavioral counseling is essentially a process that focuses on changing clients' behavior by helping them to unlearn inappropriate behaviors and replace those with more desirable ones.

To increase the frequency or strength of a desired behavior, six steps are typically employed (Blackham and Silberman, 1975).

1. Identify and state the behavior to be changed in operational terms.
2. Obtain a base line of the desired target behavior.
3. Arrange the situation so that the target behavior will occur.
4. Identify potential reinforcing stimuli and events.
5. Reinforce the desired target behavior or successive approximations of it.
6. Evaluate the effects of the treatment procedure by maintaining records of change in the target behavior.

Although most behavioral counselors believe that counseling goals must be tailored to the individual client, behavioral therapy may be said to have five general goals: (1) altering the maladaptive behavior in the client under therapy, (2) helping the client learn a more efficient decision-making process, (3) preventing future problems, (4) solving the specific behavioral problem requested by the client, and (5) achieving behavioral changes that translate into action in life.

Implementation: Techniques and Procedures

Behavioral counselors typically use specific techniques, the results of which can be evaluated in terms of the client's progress toward goals. The techniques are employed in a systematic plan, although many of these same techniques can be used by counselors with other approaches.

Systematic Desensitization

A widely used technique in behavioral counseling, systematic desensitization is particularly useful with clients whose problem behavior is associated with a high level of anxiety. Such anxiety may be about dating, taking tests, speaking to groups, or engaging in various sexual activities. The anxiety may cause clients to be overly shy or overly aggressive, suffer from severe headaches or stomach distress, or have difficulty in performing various normal tasks of everyday living.

Desensitization is used to break down certain anxiety-response habits. During desensitization, the anxiety is unlearned or inhibited by an incompatible behavior, usually deep muscle relaxation. The term *desensitization* refers to the process of anxiety reduction. The person becomes desensitized—that is, gradually experiences more comfort in the presence of what formerly caused anxiety. This process of learning an incompatible behavior is sometimes called *counterconditioning* and is carried out on a step-by-step basis.

Counterconditioning became important as a technique after Wolpe (1955) devised a systematic procedure that increased the kinds of problems counterconditioning could deal with. Basically Wolpe contributed the idea of constructing the anxiety hierarchy, a rank list of situations to which the client reacts with increasing degrees of anxiety. By combining this anxiety hierarchy with training in muscular relaxation, the counselor is able to help the client gradually reduce anxiety to the various situations listed. The procedure usually involves three sets of operations: (1) relaxation training, (2) identifying anxiety producing situations, and (3) working through the anxiety hierarchy.

First, during the initial two or three sessions after desensitization has been decided on, the client is trained in the techniques of progressive muscular relaxation-alternately tensing and relaxing successive gross muscle groups—while the counselor makes verbal suggestions of warmth, calmness, and overall pleasant feelings. At this time the counselor focuses the client's attention on identifying the localized tension and relaxation. The counselor may suggest thoughts and create images of personally relaxing situations, such as lying under a hot sun or drifting on an inner tube on a warm day, to help the client reach a state of peacefulness. The counselor often uses the brief form of Jacobsen's (1935) progressive relaxation training to help the client relax all muscles. This training directs the client's attention to relaxing a particular set of muscles, then working throughout the body in the same way.

Ordinarily, the counselor devotes about thirty minutes to relaxation training and then encourages the client to practice between counseling sessions. When the client has learned to relax quickly and completely, the desensitization procedure itself will begin.

During these sessions in relaxation training, time is also spent identifying the anxiety-producing situations which will be part of the client's anxiety hierarchy. The client is first asked to state those situations that cause anxiety. Having identified the situations, the client then ranks them from slightly anxiety-producing to highly anxiety-producing. Ideally, the items in the hierarchy form subjectively equal intervals of noticeable differences in the degree of anxiety produced, but this is not always possible. For example, if a client has anxiety related to his fear of failing as a father, the list would begin with a situation that produces relatively little anxiety—perhaps a coworker criticizing fathers who "work too hard and don't spend time with their kids"—and would work up to a situation that produces high anxiety, such as his wife criticizing him for being too hard on the children. Between might be situations where he is criticized by a coworker, a close friend, and a relative.

When the client has learned relaxation and has constructed his anxiety hierarchy, the third step—simultaneously presenting the relaxation and the anxiety-eliciting stimuli from the hierarchy—begins. The client relaxes himself and then the counselor presents verbal instructions, having the client imagine the least disturbing item on his anxiety list. When the first item no longer evokes any anxiety, the client moves on to the second item on the list. The client progressively works through the entire hierarchy. During this process, the counselor moves slowly so that the feeling of relaxation is always greater than the feeling of anxiety. Whenever the client experiences a reduction in relaxation as he thinks about an item, he signals the counselor, who returns to the imagery of a personally relaxing situation or to a situation that elicits less anxiety. When the client can remain in a relaxed state while imagining the situation that previously produced the most anxiety, he is encouraged to expose himself to the anxiety-producing situations in his daily life.

Behavior Contract

The use of the behavior contract in counseling is one behavioral technique that has already been adopted by other counselors. The behavior contract is based on the idea that it is helpful to the client to specify the kind of behavior desired and the reinforcement contingencies. Such a contract enables individuals to anticipate changing their behavior on the basis of a promise or agreement that some positive consequence will be forthcoming.

Basically, a behavior contract is an agreement between at least two people in which the people involved try to change the behavior of at least one of the parties. Dustin and George (1977) suggest that such an approach helps to tell the client "what to do" without nagging. The agreement may be oral or written, but both parties must agree to the basic conditions. One aspect of the contract is the process of negotiating the acceptable terms, which are characterized by (1) reality, (2) specificity, (3) freedom from threat, and (4) flexibility (Dustin and George, 1977). Simply stated, this means that the client and counselor choose realistic goals that they can meet. Such goals are specifically stated, leaving no question as to what is expected of each. Generally, the contract employs positive reinforcement for reaching goals rather than punishment for undesirable behavior, thus eliminating threat. Lastly, the client and counselor agree that the terms of the contract may be changed by mutual consent, providing flexibility to change the goals and conditions whenever such change seems desirable.

Social Modeling

Based on the idea that a person will imitate the behavior of others, social modeling is used to help the client progressively modify his behavior toward that of an observed model. Bandura (1965) suggests that modeling procedures may be more effective than positive reinforcement in establishing new response patterns. In addition, behavior patterns acquired through imitation are often maintained without deliberate external reinforcement simply because individuals learn to reinforce themselves for certain behaviors.

Dustin and George (1977) suggest that social modeling can be used both to help the client learn new behaviors and to strengthen or weaken existing behaviors. The counselor uses audio models, filmed models, and live-models to enable the client to observe desirable behavior being reinforced and to lead the client to modify his behavior toward that of the model.

Assertion Training

A behavioral approach that has gained wide support, assertion training is particularly worthwhile for individuals who have difficulty asserting themselves in particular interpersonal situations. Although used primarily with individuals who are usually nonassertive, assertion training can be appropriate for most people, since almost all have difficulty asserting themselves in certain situations.

Assertion training is ordinarily practiced in a group setting. It emphasizes teaching clients to stand up for their own rights without violating the rights of others. Assertive behavior itself consists of expressing one's thoughts and feelings in direct, honest, and appropriate ways. It involves defending one's rights when one feels that he is being taken advantage of. It means expressing one's needs and wants to others without assuming whether or not the others will help meet those needs. Individuals who have learned to be assertive usually feel good about themselves, recognizing that they have "stood up" for themselves without humiliating or criticizing others. Increased self-respect results.

Contributions and Limitations

The behavioral counseling approach makes several important contributions to counseling effectiveness. By focusing on the specific behaviors that clients wish to change, the counselor can help clients to better understand what is to be accomplished as part of the counseling process. This focus also gives clients concrete information about their level of progress. Success is apparent and reinforces the whole counseling process. In addition, because the client's behavior changes are likely to be apparent to those around her, she receives positive feedback, further accelerating her progress. Focusing on specific behaviors also provides well-defined criteria for counseling outcomes. The behavioral counselor has the advantage of using a variety of specific counseling techniques that are well-tested in bringing about behavior change.

Major limitations of behavioral counseling include a lack of opportunity for the client to become creatively involved with the whole process of self-fulfillment or self-actualization. A second limitation rests in the possibility that the client may be "depersonalized" in his interaction with the counselor. Further, the whole process does not seem very applicable to clients whose difficulties are not directly related to overt behaviors. Clients who are functioning at relatively high levels but who are searching for meaning and purpose in their lives or who see themselves as failures or who recognize that they are not functioning up to their potential cannot expect much help from behavioral counseling.

Reality Therapy

Reality therapy was developed by William Glasser as a result of his dissatisfaction with the ineffectiveness of standard psychiatric treatment. Glasser changed the focus to present behavior, emphasizing the acceptance of personal responsibility, which he equated with mental health. Reality therapy is behavioral in approach in that the focus is on what the person does, not feels. Glasser's important works include *Reality Therapy* (1965), *Schools Without Failure* (1969), *The Identity Society* (1972), and *The Control Theory-Reality Therapy Workbook* (1986).

The reality therapist, like the behaviorist, views the individual largely in terms of his behavior. But rather than examining behavior in terms of the stimulus-response paradigm, as the behaviorist does, or looking at the individual's behavior phenomenologically, as the client-centered counselor does, the reality therapist measures behavior against an objective standard, which he calls reality. This reality may be a practical reality, a social reality, or a moral reality. The reality therapist sees the individual as functioning in consonance or dissonance with that reality.

Glasser himself believes that all human behavior is motivated by striving to meet basic needs—physiological and psychological—that are the same for all individuals. He suggests that people may label these needs differently but that all people, regardless of location or culture, have the same essential needs. Some of their needs are the traditionally defined physiological needs that maintain the organism. But beyond these basic needs, Glasser states that there are "two basic psychological needs: the need to love and to be loved and the need to feel that we are worthwhile to ourselves and to others" (1965, p. 9). These two basic psychological needs have been incorporated into one need, which Glasser calls *identity*. Glasser (1969) believes that identity is a person's most important psychological need, built into the biological system from birth. When individuals are frustrated in their attempts to satisfy their need to be loved and to feel worth while, they develop a "failure" identity and resort to other avenues such as delinquency and withdrawal. These alternative routes, however, still result in a failure identity. This failure identity can be changed to a success identity. but only when individuals change their behavior in such a way that their needs for love and self-worth are met. The process for bringing about this behavior change involves helping the client to do what is right, responsible. and realistic.

More recently, Glasser (1989) has changed his emphasis to control theory, which attempts to explain how individuals work to satisfy their needs. He has broadened needs to include belonging, power, freedom, and fun, as well as survival. By meeting these needs in a responsible way, individuals are able to develop an identity characterized by success and increased self-esteem. Part of this "responsible way" of acting is learning to make behavioral choices that are self-satisfying without infringing on the freedom of others to do the same.

Glasser (1989) also emphasizes the concept of total behavior, which includes *doing* (behavior), *thinking* (thoughts and self-statements), *feeling* (emotions) , and *physiology* (physical reactions to events, such as blushing, perspiring, etc.). He believes that all four of these components are part of total behavior, but that at any given time, one of the components is likely to be more prominent than the others.

Reality therapy emphasizes the idea of clients' making value judgments about their own behavior. Although Glasser does not suggest a universal code by which all individuals should live, he does believe that certain generally accepted moral principles should be encouraged by the therapist. More importantly the therapist forces clients to evaluate, or to make value judgments about, their own behavior in terms of whether it is helping or hurting themselves and others.

Once clients are able to make value judgments about their own behavior and to face reality squarely, they are ready to assume personal responsibility for their behavior. Glasser (1965) defines responsibility as "the ability to fulfill one's needs, and to do so in a way that does not deprive others of the ability to fulfill their needs" (p. 13). Glasser insists that change is impossible until individuals stop using conditions in the past, factors in the present, or the behavior of others as excuses for their own actions and start accepting responsibility for their own lives. In particular, Glasser relates responsibility to mental health—the more responsible people are, the healthier they are; the less responsible, the less healthy. Thus, the reality therapist attempts to teach clients an approach to life that involves living responsibly.

Glasser (1972) formulated an eight-step procedure as a guide for the counseling process. Although the order of the steps is sometimes flexible, they present a picture of the typical direction of reality therapy.

1. *Be involved.* Glasser emphasizes the need for the counselor to communicate concern to the client, along with warmth and understanding.

2. *Focus on behavior, not feelings.* The emphasis here is on making clients aware of what they are doing that makes them feel the way they do.

3. *Focus on the present.* The past is important only as it relates to present behavior.

4. *Making value judgments.* Clients must examine the quality of what they are doing and determine whether it is responsible behavior.

5. *Making a plan.* The counselor works with the client to develop a specific course of action that will change irresponsible behavior to responsible behavior.

6. *Getting a commitment.* Glasser believes that a plan is only worthwhile if the client makes a specific commitment to carry it out.

7. *Accept no excuses.* Since not all plans succeed, Glasser suggests that the emphasis be on developing a new plan rather than exploring why the old plan failed.

8. *Eliminate punishment.* Plan failures are not to be met with punishments, only with the natural consequence of the future to carry out the plan.

Transactional Analysis

Transactional analysis (TA) was developed by Eric Berne and stresses the interaction between individuals as both a symptom and a cause of psychological difficulties. Although TA can be used in individual counseling, it is particularly effective in group counseling, since the group setting allows the counselor to observe the individual interacting with others and thereby to analyze certain elements of personality structure and interpersonal relationships. Berne's most important books include *Transactional Analysis in Psychotherapy* (1961), *Games People Play* (1964), and *Principles of Group Treatment* (1966).

Transactional analysis focuses on the games people play to avoid intimacy in transactions with others. TA is based on a personality theory utilizing three distinct patterns of behavior or ego states: Parent, Adult, and Child. (Parent, Adult, and Child, capitalized, refer to ego states; whereas parent, adult, and child, written with small initial letters, refer to people.)

The Parent ego state is filled with values, injunctions, shoulds and oughts, and behaviors that the individual has internalized from significant others—parents and parent substitutes—during childhood. This influence leads persons to behave as they believe their parents would want them to behave and includes prohibitions as well as permissions and nurturing messages.

The Adult ego state is focused on data processing, probability estimating, and decision making. It deals with facts, not with feelings. In fact, the Adult state is seen as being devoid of feelings, although it can evaluate the emotional experiences of the Child and Parent ego states. It acts to regulate the activities of the Child and the Parent, mediating between them. The ultimate function of the Adult is to deal with presenting situations in an organized, adaptable, and intelligent way—that is, reality testing.

The Child ego state is conceptualized as the little boy or girl within us. As such, this ego state does not refer to childishness, but childlikeness; it is the fun loving part of most individuals. The Child is most likely to emerge in response to a communication from a Parent ego state. The Child functions in two distinct forms: the Natural Child and the Adapted Child. The Natural Child strives for total freedom

FIGURE 5-2   Playful behavior is a result of the child ego state
(Robert Harbison)

to do what it wants whenever it wants. This includes the natural impulses for love, affection, creativity, aggression, rebellion, and spontaneity. The Adapted Child, however, is influenced by the Parent and has discovered ways, usually compliance or procrastination, to deal with feelings in a way that will prevent Parent reprimand. As a result, the Adapted Child duplicates the original reactions individuals have toward their parents during childhood, including feelings like guilt, fear, anger, and frustration. The emerging adult in the Child is called the Little Professor and is the source of intuition, creativity, and manipulation; it serves as the negotiator between the Natural Child and the Adapted Child.

A central part of TA is learning to analyze one's relationships with others. One step in this is determining the predominant life position one has taken in making certain decisions with regard to compromise in satisfying needs or stimulus hunger. These decisions lead to this position toward self and others, which is ordinarily maintained against influences that question or threaten it. An individual may choose one of four basic life positions: (1) "I'm okay—you're okay"; (2) "I'm okay—you're not okay"; (3) "I'm not okay—you're okay"; (4) "I'm not okay—you're not okay."

TA also emphasizes the human need for emotional and physical strokes. Berne believed that all persons have a basic need for recognition from significant others.

This recognition comes in the form of strokes, which can be physical, verbal, or psychological. These strokes can be positive or negative, conditional or unconditional. Berne believed that individuals need to learn how to ask for the strokes they want.

Two kinds of analyses are fundamental to transactional analysis: structural analysis and transactional analysis. Structural analysis involves the analysis and recognition of the influence of the individual's ego states on thinking or behaving. Although the psychologically healthy individual can activate any one of the states whenever it's appropriate, it is possible to diagnose which ego state has the "executive," or controlling, power by observing an individual's overt behavior. By identifying which of her ego states is in power at any given time, the individual is better able to understand the nature of her behavior and the behavior of others within a social context: transactional analysis.

Since transactions are units of social action (Berne, 1963), transactional analysis, as process within the theory, is concerned with the diagnosis of the ego states from which a social interchange is emanating for the two persons involved and with the clarification of that exchange. When one person encounters another and speaks, this is called the *transactional stimulus*. The reply is called the *transactional response*.

Complementary transactions occur when both parties speak from their Adults, or when the vectors are parallel, as when Parent speaks to Child, and Child responds to Parent. The key to complementary transaction is that the response is appropriate and expected; it follows the natural order of healthy human relationships. Communication can proceed smoothly and indefinitely as long as transactions are complementary.

Crossed transactions occur when the vectors are not parallel and communication is broken off. The most common crossed transaction results from an Adult–Adult stimulus with a Parent–Child or Child–Parent response. Crossed transactions ordinarily end in a deadlock unless the respondent is able to mobilize her Adult to complement the Adult in the other person. Otherwise, the transaction is finished with one or both of the parties feeling hurt, angry, or misunderstood.

Ulterior transactions occur when more than two ego states are in operation simultaneously. In ulterior transactions, one message is usually sent on a social level, usually Adult–Adult, and an implied message is sent on a psychological level in another ego state.

One of the most important emphases in TA is the use of the contract, which includes a statement about what the client hopes to achieve in counseling, a statement about what the counselor will do to facilitate that process and some specific criteria for knowing when the goal has been achieved. This helps to avoid the client's shifting total responsibility to the counselor and establishes positive expectations.

The TA counselor acts very much like a "teacher, trainer, and resource person with heavy emphasis on involvement" (Harris, 1967, p. 239). She explains key concepts such as structural analysis, transactional analysis, script analysis, and game analysis. In addition, the counselor employs various techniques, particularly questioning about the client's earliest memories, to assist the client in understanding the various influences that led to their present life position. By helping clients free themselves from the constraints of those early decisions, TA counselors are attempting to help clients make full and effective use of all three ego states and to live game-free lives with intimate, rewarding relationships.

Thus the basic goal of transactional analysis is to help clients achieve autonomy (Berne, 1964). This autonomy is characterized by (1) awareness—a realistic understanding of one's world, (2) spontaneity—the ability to express emotion in an uninhibited, game-free fashion; and (3) intimacy—the capacity to share love and closeness with others. Related to this goal of autonomy is the attempt to enable the client to free his Adult from the influence of the Child and Parent so that the Adult is in control of decision making.

Other Emphases

Hypnotherapy

Clinical hypnosis has been used to treat various emotional and psychological problems for many decades, but its use has greatly increased in recent years. The work of Milton Erickson (1976; 1983) in particular has helped make the use of hypnosis acceptable to many counselors. In essence, hypnosis is a state of deep relaxation in which an altered state of consciousness is created. Clients under hypnosis focus their attention on their own functioning, become more aware of their bodies and sensations, their feelings and emotions, and their dreams and fantasies.

During the induction of this trance or altered state, the body and mind interact in such a way that as physical relaxation increases, the awareness of the inner self does also. Most induction methods combine three basic elements: relaxation, suggestion, and repetition. The induction is most effective if the counselor acts as a guide in leading clients in a process they do to themselves. This increases clients' acceptance of responsibility for the whole process and can be enhanced by having clients practice self-induced hypnosis at home through the use of a tape.

Hypnosis is used for many of the same kinds of problems that neurolinguistic programming is used for. It is a particularly effective tool for dealing with symptoms, including pain—real or imagined—tension, smoking, drinking, overeating, or phobias. The client, while in a trance, imagines the undesired situation, and therapeutic suggestions the counselor gives that will alleviate the problem.

Hypnosis is also used in helping clients to relive certain experiences and thus to deepen their awareness of themselves. This is particularly helpful in exploring and understanding feelings and memories that have long been repressed.

Neurolinguistic Programming (NLP)

Neurolinguistic programming has literally bounded into the field of counseling. The first important book, *The Structure of Magic I* (Bandler and Grinder, 1975), was followed in 1976 by *The Structure of Magic II* (Grinder and Bandler), and the professional enthusiasm for this approach was soon apparent.

Bandler and Grinder state that the following are a *few* of the specific things NLP practitioners can do: (1) cure phobias and other unpleasant feeling responses in less than an hour, (2) help children and adults with "learning disabilities" (spelling and reading problems, etc.) overcome these limitations, often in less than an hour, (3) eliminate most unwanted habits—smoking, drinking, overeating, insomnia—in a few sessions, (4) make changes in the interactions of couples, families, and organizations so that they function in ways that are more satisfying and productive, and (5) cure many physical problems—not only most of those recognized as "psychosomatic" but also some that are not—in a few sessions (1979, p. ii).

As might be expected from its name, NLP focuses on a linguistic model as a means to gain access to clients' "deep structure" from the "surface structure" statements they make. Clients are seen as presenting sentences that do not accurately represent their experiences by using *deletions* (leaving out important parts), *distortions* (assigning responsibilities to others that are within the clients' control), and *generalizations* (statements that fail to identify anything specific in their experience). These three elements are key to what is called the *meta-model* (Bandler and Grinder, 1975).

A fourth key element of the meta-model is that of the *representational systems*. The representational systems have to do with the pattern an individual uses in taking in and storing experiences, including seeing, hearing, and feeling. By identifying the client's favored representational system (the one most often used in dealing with stress or in solving problems), the counselor is able to respond out of the same system, which greatly increases trust and rapport. Assessing this system depends on the ability to listen for and identify the process words that are consistent with a particular system. Counselors may also watch eye movements in determining a client's representational system. For instance, NLP counselors believe that when individuals focus their eyes up and to the left, they are using a visual system.

Two major techniques utilized by NLP counselors are *anchoring* and *reframing*. Anchoring is the process by which the counselor attacks a desired emotional state with a specific stimulus, whether a touch, a sound, a facial expression, or a posture change. This process can be utilized to evoke new feelings and behaviors in situations in which the client previously experienced undesirable reactions. This anchoring can be done with or without the client's awareness. The specific steps that are followed in using anchors are outlined by Cameron-Bandler (1978).

Reframing is the process by which the counselor helps the client to see her behavior from a different perspective, thus placing a different valuation on that behavior. This may include learning to discriminate when the behavior is desirable and when it is undesirable, separating intention from behavior so that new behavior becomes desirable, or creating new ways of behaving in situations in which there had previously been only one alternative (Harmon and O'Neill, 1981).

Cognitive Therapy

Cognitive therapy is based on the idea that psychological problems result primarily from commonplace processes such as faulty learning, making incorrect inferences on the basis of inadequate information, and basing behavior on unreasonable attitudes. Thus the cognitive therapist helps clients sharpen discriminations, correct misconceptions, and learn more adaptive attitudes (Beck, 1976).

The cognitive perspective assumes that a person chooses the alternatives that appear to be in her own best interest, based upon a particular, although subjective, view of the situation. Thus, self-defeating behaviors are not the result of a desire to lose, as Freud might say, but instead result from the individual's inability either to conceive of, or to act upon and carry out, more constructive alternatives. In a 1988 interview with Weinrach, Beck stated that his focus is on thoughts, or cognitions, as well as on feelings. He emphasized that he believes that what individuals feel is influenced (but not totally controlled) by what they think, and that it is necessary to avoid "dysfunctional" thoughts in order to feel better. He also stated that he believed that cognitive therapy was developed primarily for the treatment of depression and anxiety and is now being found useful in the treatment of personality disorders, eating disorders, and other problems where he believes the individual's undesired affect and dysfunctional behavior is due to "excessive or inappropriate ways of interpreting their experiences" (Weinrach, 1988, p. 159).

Various techniques are used to accomplish the following objectives: (1) clients learn to gain insight into the views they take of various events, especially those that are upsetting, (2) clients learn to assess, reality test, and modify these views, so that the meanings they attribute to specific events are more congruent with objective reality, (3) clients learn to identify the conscious thoughts that occur between an external event and a particular emotional response, (4) clients then practice various cognitive and behavioral responses to anticipated and unexpected upsetting situations, and (5) clients generate new assumptions (or thought processes) and apply them to their lives (Rush, 1984).

Although the cognitive counselor acts as a guide, an empathic, objective relationship is stressed. The counselor is expected to think as the client does, to understand both the cognitive and the emotional responses, and to see the world as the client does, while remaining objective and logical about the client's thinking and situation.

Techniques of cognitive therapy include distancing (the ability to view one's thoughts more objectively, to draw a distinction between "I believe" and "I know"), decentering (learning to separate oneself from vicariously experiencing the adversities of others), changing the rules, reality testing, and authenticating the validity of one's thoughts, as well as many of the techniques used in RET. In addition, behavioral methods including activity schedules, graded task assignments, and homework provide a situational context and some behavioral data for testing the validity of the client's assertions, and thus provide a basis for cognitive reappraisal.

Family Systems Therapy

Although it is not within the scope of this text to deal with the subject of family therapy per se, a brief review of the family systems therapy model is appropriate because this approach is "among the counseling student's most basic choices for approaching individual as well as group and family counseling" (Mckenna, 1984,

p. 4). This approach is best understood by reading material by Becvar and Becvar (1982), Goldenberg and Goldenberg (1982),and Cottone (1992).

Family systems therapy represents a new paradigm, a new comprehensive philosophy which redefines many traditional concepts. Utilizing insights from such theorists as Harry Stack Sullivan (interpersonal psychology) and Kurt Lewin (field theory), systems theory emerged from the coalescing of five seemingly independent developments (Goldenberg and Goldenberg, 1982). These include (1) the extension of psychoanalytic treatment to a full range of emotional problems, including work with families, (2) the introduction of general systems theory, with its emphasis on exploring relationships between parts that compose an interrelated whole, (3) the investigation of the family's role in the development of schizophrenia in one of its members, (4) the evolvement of the fields of child guidance and marital counseling, and (5) the increased interest in the new clinical techniques such as group therapy and milieu therapy.

Of particular importance is the introduction of general systems theory with its emphasis on looking at any part of a whole in terms of its relationship with the other parts. Counselors working within a family systems framework stress the idea of circular causality, that a change in the behavior of one family member affects all other family members, as well as the family as a whole (Gladding, 1988). Such a perspective suggests that working with an individual's relationship with other family members is basic, since it focuses the therapist's attention on individuals only in the context of their relationships, consistent with a framework of contextual relativity (Becvar and Becvar, 1982).

As a result, individuals are understood in a relative sense, rather than in terms of diagnostic labels. In fact, family systems therapists tend to see diagnosis as detrimental to achieving therapeutic change, since diagnostic labels may trap people into roles rather than freeing them from role expectations and encouraging them to see themselves as alterable and adaptable.

The process of therapy in this approach is dependent upon the counselor's presenting new information to the system that will help the members of the family to look at themselves and the others differently, thus changing the patterns of interaction. The problem is defined as a family or context problem rather than as an individual's problem; the family system is viewed as consisting of family members but also of the relationships among them. The goal of the family counselor, in general, is to identify and understand the methods which various family members use in communicating with each other, in maintaining the family structure, and in helping, or hindering, the growth of family members (Meier and Davis, 1993).

From a systems perspective, neither intrapsychic labels—such as ego self-concept, drive, and self-awareness—nor labels assigning internal motivation—such as the concepts of discounting, selfishness, or rescuing—have any importance (Becvar and Becvar, 1982). Rather the emphasis is placed on labels that describe interpersonal processes, or the "observable dynamics which occur when elements of a system interface and when systems (as elements of a larger, supra-system) interface with other systems" (Becvar and Becvar, 1982, p. 9).

Among the concepts and constructs that have particular importance to systems theory are boundaries, communication/information processing, entropy, homeostatis, open and closed systems, positive and negative feedback, relationship, and wholeness. These concepts have definitions and explanations peculiar to a systems approach and are best understood in relationship with each other (Becvar and Becvar, 1982).

Since the goal of systems therapy is to help the family maintain itself without the use of maladaptive roles, the therapist tries to set the family's own resources into action in a different way. The precise direction this "different way" takes is determined by the family's particular style of adapting and maintaining stability.

Becvar and Becvar (1982) suggest one model of the healthy, functioning family. The six characteristics they include are as follows (p. 74):

1. A legitimate source of authority, established and supported over time.
2. A stable rule system established and consistently acted upon.
3. Stable and consistent shares of nurturing behavior.
4. Effective and stable child-rearing and marriage-maintenance practices.
5. A set of goals toward which the family and each individual works.
6. Sufficient flexibility and adaptability to accommodate normal developmental challenges as well as unexpected crises.

Counselors within this framework may employ a variety of styles—behavioral, cognitive, or affective—but do so within a particular understanding of the whole system. Allowing the counselor to use whatever means are deemed appropriate to the context, systems theory provides a unified framework within which techniques and strategies can be used. Some of these techniques are rooted in traditional approaches; some are unique to the individual therapist. Examples of the types of techniques frequently used are paradoxical intention, cognitive restructuring, behavioral reinforcement schedules, and homework assignments.

As a result, although family systems therapy can be viewed as eclectic in terms of technique and strategies, the approach is unique in its theoretical foundation, which recognizes that as an individual changes, her family or social system changes, thus requiring further change of the individual. When the entire system is worked with, the change within an individual becomes an integrated part of system changes and permits a more "holistic" approach to dealing with individual as well as family difficulties.

Summary

Cognitive-behavioral approaches focus *primarily on* the thinking process as it relates to those behaviors which relate to psychological and emotional difficulties. By helping clients change the way they think about their experiences, counselors induce behavior change, which leads to changes in the way clients feel about themselves.

Behavioral counseling is based on a learning theory called behaviorism. The focus is on overt and specific behavior, with a precise spelling out of goals and the formulation of a specific treatment procedure. The primary techniques include systematic desensitization, behavior contracts, social modeling, and assertion training.

Rational-emotive therapy stresses that what clients think about a particular fact or experience determines how they feel and what they do. Thus the focus is on replacing illogical thinking with logical thinking. In so doing, the counselor assumes an active teaching role.

Other cognitive-behavioral approaches that have contributed much to counseling include reality therapy, transactional analysis, neurolinguistic programming, and hypnotherapy.

References

Bandler, R. & Grinder, J. (1975). *The structure of magic I*. Palo Alto, CA: Science and Behavior Books.

Bandler, R. & Grinder, J. (1979). *Frogs into princes*. Moab, UT: Real People Press.

Bandura, A. (1965). Behavior modification through modeling procedures. In L. Krasner and L. Ullmann (Eds.). *Research in behavior modification*. New York: Holt, Rinehart & Winston.

Becvar, R. J., & Becvar, D. S. (1982). *Systems theory and family therapy*. Washington: University Press of America.

Beck, A. T. (1976). *Cognitive therapy and the emotional disorders*. New York: Meridian.

Berne, E. (1961). *Transactional analysis in psychotherapy*. New York: Grove Press.

Berne, E. (1963). *Structure and dynamics of groups and organizations*. Philadelphia: Lippincott.

Berne, E. (1964). *Games people play*. New York: Grove Press.

Berne, E. (1966). *Principles of group treatment*. New York: Oxford University Press.

Blackham, G. J., & Silberman, A. (1975). *Modification of child and adolescent behavior* (2nd ed.). Belmont, CA: Wadsworth.

Cameron-Bandler, L. (1978). *They lived happily ever after*. Cupertino, CA: Meta Publications.

Corey, G. (1977). *Theory and practice of counseling and psychotherapy*. Monterey, CA: Brooks/Cole.

Cottone, R. R. (1992). *Theories and paradigms of counseling and psychotherapy*. Boston: Allyn and Bacon.

Dustin, R. & George, R. (1977). *Action counseling for behavior change* (2nd ed.). Cranston, RI: Carroll Press.

Ellis, A. (1962). *Reason and emotion in psychotherapy*. New York: Lyle Stuart.

Ellis, A. (1973). *Humanistic psychotherapy: The rational-emotive approach*. New York: Julian Press.

Ellis, A. (1974). Rational-emotive theory. In A. Burton (Ed.). *Operational theories of personality*. New York: Brunner/Mazel.

Ellis, A. (1989). Rational-emotive therapy. In R. J. Corsini and D. Wedding (Eds.) *Current psychotherapies* (4th ed.). Itasca, NY: F. E. Peacock.

Ellis, A. (1992). First-order and second-order change in rational-emotive therapy: A reply to Lyddon. *Journal of Counseling and Development, 70,* 449–451.

Ellis, A., & Harper, R. (1961). *A guide to rational living*. Hollywood: Wilshire Books.

Erickson, M. H. (1983). *Healing in hypnosis*. New York: Irvington Press.

Erickson, M. H. , Rossi, E. L., & Rossi, S. I. (1976). *Hypnotic realities*. New York: Irvington Press.

Gladding, S. T. (1988). *Counseling: a comprehensive profession*. Columbus, OH: Merrill.

Glasser, W. (1965). *Reality therapy*. New York: Harper & Row.

Glasser, W. (1969). *Schools without failure.* New York: Harper & Row.

Glasser, W. (1972). *The identity society.* New York: Harper & Row.

Glasser, W. (1986). *The control theory-reality therapy workbook.* Canoga Park, CA: Institute for Reality Therapy.

Glasser, W. (1989). Control theory in the practice of reality therapy. In N. Glasser (Ed.), *Control theory in the practice of reality therapy: Case studies.* New York: Harper & Row.

Goldenberg, I., & Goldenberg, H. (1982). *Family therapy: An overview.* Monterey, CA: Brooks/Cole.

Grinder, J., & Bandler, R. (1976). *The structure of magic II.* Palo Alto, CA: Science and Behavior Books.

Harmon, R. L., & O'Neill, C. (1981). Neuro-linguistic programming for counselors. *Personnel and Guidance Journal, 59,* 449–453.

Harris, T. (1967). *I'm ok—you're ok.* New York: Avon.

Jacobsen, E. (1938). *Progressive relaxation.* Chicago: University of Chicago Press.

Jones, M. C. (1960). A laboratory study of fear: The case of Peter. In H. J. Eysenck (Ed.). *Behaviour therapy and the neuroses.* London: Pergamon Press.

Krumboltz, J. D. (Ed.). (1966). *Revolution in counseling.* Boston: Houghton Mifflin.

Krumboltz, J. D. & Thoresen, C. E. (1969). *Behavioral counseling: Cases and techniques.* New York: Holt, Rinehart & Winston.

Lange, A. J., & Jakubowski, P. (1976). *Responsible assertive behavior.* Champaign, IL: Research Press.

McKenna, K. R. (1984). *Family systems therapy: An introduction.* Unpublished manuscript, University of Missouri-St. Louis.

Meier, S. T., & Davis, S. R. (1993). *The elements of counseling* (2nd ed.). Pacific Grove, CA: Brooks/Cole.

Roberts, A. L. (1975). *Transactional analysis approach to counseling.* Boston: Houghton Mifflin.

Rush, A. J. (1984). Cognitive therapy. In L. Grinspoon (Ed.). *Psychiatry update. Vol. III* Washington: American Psychiatric Press.

Watson, J. B., & Rayner, R. (1960). Conditioned emotional reactions. In H. J. Eysenck (Ed.). *The hand book of abnormal psychology.* New York: Basic Books.

Weinrach, S. G. (1988). Cognitive therapist: A dialogue with Aaron Beck. *Journal of Counseling and Development, 67,* 159–164.

Wolpe, J. (1958). *Psychotherapy by reciprocal inhibition.* Stanford, CA: Stanford University Press.

Wolpe, J. (1990). *The practice of behavior therapy (4th ed.).* New York: Pergamon Press.

Chapter 6

Toward a Personal Theory of Counseling

The preceding chapters summarized some of the many approaches to counseling. Corsini (1981), in fact, has identified over 240 different forms of counseling and psychotherapy. The picture, at least on the surface, is one of diversity. The various counseling approaches appear to differ considerably, not only in their methods or techniques but also in their goals, their basic concepts, and their philosophical orientations. Wolberg (1987) pointedly states that "the problem with present-day models of psychotherapy is that they are too limited to deal with more than a few circumscribed areas of pathology" (p. 255).

These differences in conceptualization of the counseling process have been a source of uncertainty within the profession for some time. Counselor educators seem unsure as to whether such diversity should be seen as cause for despair or as a sign of the healthy growth of the profession. Those who see this diversity as healthy suggest that the diversity has come about because individuals have had different experiences and describe those experiences in different ways. Such a view might be compared to the fable of the blind men attempting to describe an elephant during their first encounter with one. One, touching the leg of the elephant, perceived the elephant as being like a big tree trunk. Another, touching the body of the elephant, described the elephant as being as big as a house. A third, touching the elephant's tail, believed that the elephant was something like a long rope. And the fourth, whose experience consisted of touching the elephant's trunk, described the elephant as being like a fire hose. Although each was accurate in describing his own experience with the elephant, a full understanding of the elephant requires all their experiences, as well as other aspects of the elephant.

Many see diversity as a positive direction for counseling: As different views of counseling are clarified and integrated, the counseling profession will gain a more thorough, comprehensive view of the total counseling experience. In 1980 Patterson pointed out that some progress had been made in reaching agreement on some common elements of psychotherapy, although he suggested that this progress had been limited mainly to approaches other than the cognitive-behavioral therapies. Marmor (1987) goes further and suggests that there are seven common factors found in all the major theoretical approaches. The most basic of these is the client-counselor relationship, which, although emphasized differently by different theorists, is still a major part of the therapeutic process. Other factors common to all theories are the release of emotional tension resulting from clients' expectancy of receiving the help they are seeking; the cognitive learning of an intelligible, meaningful, and rational framework for understanding the development of the problem that results; the impact of conditioning that occurs, including the corrective emotional experience; the identification with the counselor, in which clients tend to model themselves after the counselor and particularly model the values to which they are being exposed; the impact of suggestion and persuasion of the counselor as to more desirable or heathy patterns of behavior; and some amount of rehearsal and repetition that takes place.

Theorists may disagree with Marmor's conclusions; however, it is clear that research findings do not support any claims of overwhelming superiority of any one approach (Meier and Davis, 1993). Thus the task for any counselor is to search continually for improving the interaction of different approaches, as these work for the counselor with the kind of clients with whom the counselor works and in the setting in which counseling takes place. Clearly no one therapeutic approach—whether medical, cognitive-behavioral, sociological, psycho-dynamic, etc.—provides a complete model for understanding and helping individuals with the wide range of problems they have. Rather than arguing over which approach is the one to be used by all, counselor educators and counseling theorists are now interested in discerning the common elements and curative factors that are found in different counseling approaches that account for the theories' effectiveness.

Characteristics of Theories

If each of us possessed total recall of the past, we would probably have little need for theories. To solve a problem, we would only need to recall some facts from the past. But both our memories and the limitations of our previous experiences deny us a full comprehension of the problems and experiences we face in the present. As a result, we need theories to help us solve problems that we have not encountered before or that we do not recall. A theory provides a systematic approach to dealing with a problem.

Theories, by definition, are formulations of the relationships or the underlying principles of phenomena that have been observed and verified to some degree. Theories deal with principles rather than practice; however, they cannot be viewed as something removed from practice, as impractical formulations of ideas and principles with no relation to day-to-day reality. Rather, theory is an essential underpinning of effective practice.

Counselors baffled by a problem turn to theory to enlarge their perspective about the various alternatives. Since a theory's ability to explain what we are doing suggests the value of that theory, it follows that a theory would also suggest what needs to be done when we are faced with a problem.

This book takes the position that prospective counselors should familiarize themselves with the major approaches to counseling practice today to acquire a basis for developing their own personal style of counseling. Brammer and Shostrum (1982) point out that a counselor who lacks a solid foundation in the current thinking and research and who also lacks a solid set of assumptions on which to base counseling is doing nothing more than applying techniques to help clients solve their problems. Ford and Urban (1963) concur when they suggest that a counselor who lacks a systematic point of view is not only likely to be extremely inefficient in working with clients but may also do more harm than good. This tends to happen when a counselor works from some implicit rather than explicit theory. Such counselors are never really sure from which assumptions they are currently working. When a theory is made explicit, however, counselors have a better opportunity to test and evolve their own theories based on experiences and perhaps some of their own research efforts. Certainly a counseling theory is most useful when it has been tested to some degree by controlled evidence. Combs

(1989) suggests that a trustworthy theory of therapy must have six crucial characteristics. He states that an effective theory must be comprehensive, accurate, simple and orderly as possible, internally consistent, appropriate for problems confronted, and responsive to new information or conditions.

For the purposes of this chapter, however, theory will be viewed differently—as having four major functions:

First, it summarizes a body of information and draws appropriate generalizations; second, it makes complex phenomena more easily understood; third, it predicts the probable outcome of various sets of circumstances; and finally, it stimulates further fact finding to verify and expand its base.

These functions are directly applicable to the counselor confronted with a client. The counselor attempts to apply a theoretical approach by giving meaning and life to whatever is done in that situation. The counselor must somehow summarize the data provided by the client. Sometimes the data are both complex and confusing, forcing the counselor to make comparisons between the unique data supplied by the client and the larger body of generalizations that the counselor has made about human behavior.

All counselors stress understanding as fundamental to the counseling process; however, this understanding must go beyond merely comprehending the data to encompass a larger view of the client's whole life situation. A counselor's efforts and success at understanding this whole array of information—a client's self-perceptions, current feelings, past feelings, self-descriptive statements—are largely based on the particular theory that guides the counselor's behavior.

Although prediction does not seem on the surface to be a functional behavior on the part of the counselor, counselors do predict. The approach they decide to take is based on prediction of probable success. So too are the responses they choose to make to clients. Such predictions cannot be wild guesses, but must result from a systematic view (theory) about human behavior and about the effect of counseling on a client.

Counselors need to continually check out their effectiveness, as defined by their theory of counseling. To do so requires a theory that is explicit enough to enable the counselor to develop appropriate hypotheses.

Steps in Building a Personal Theory

Developing one's own view of the counseling process is a highly demanding, never-ending task. A personal theory must be continually reviewed and revised to include new experiences and insights that a counselor acquires during years of experience. At the beginning, however, new counselors must follow some particular steps to develop initial personal views. First they must familiarize themselves with the current major approaches to counseling practice. Although Corey (1991) recommends eclecticism as a framework for the professional education of counselors, he also points out the danger in an undisciplined and unsystematic approach—it can be an excuse either for failing to develop a sound rationale or for systematically adhering to certain concepts. Certainly there is the danger that counselors will pick and choose only those fragments from various counseling approaches that support their own biases and preconceived ideas.

This book takes the position that although beginning counselors need a firm understanding of all the major approaches, they must gain this familiarization after first grounding themselves in one theoretical approach to counseling. With experience, they can then judiciously integrate and assimilate techniques from other approaches that fit well within their theory and style; they will not be tempted to adopt every new and dramatic "in thing" just because everyone else seems to be doing so.

As a second step in developing a personal view of counseling, counselors must know their own assumptions about the nature of people. It is essential for counselors to attain a high level of awareness of their philosophical beliefs, values, needs, and attitudes regarding their expectations about what clients are like and what people should be (see Chapter 2). Soben (1962) suggests that it is not what the actual research tells us but rather our own psychological need structure that dictates what theory we will adapt as our primary approach. As a result, counselors who are about to develop their own theoretical approaches should look very closely at their own need structures to determine their real reasons for choosing one theory over another.

As a third step, new counselors must identify their own accepted models of the mature, well-functioning individual (see Chapter 2 for review). They can then relate such understandings to their goals for counseling, which they can in turn match with strategies and techniques to reach those goals most effectively. Every counselor borrows from other theorists in the sense that the counselor stands on their shoulders to reach higher levels of understanding and effectiveness in practice.

These pieces are then put together in a unified system that is comfortable and effective in a particular setting. Finally, the counselor tests this theory in practice and formulates new hypotheses that can be tested experimentally, and then incorporates the results of these tests into the counselor's own system.

Comparison of the Major Counseling Approaches

The various counseling viewpoints summarized in the preceding chapters have both similarities and differences. The following discussion will compare these theories on a point-by-point basis.

View of Human Nature

Some approaches emphasize human nature considerably more than others. The existentialists, for example, seem to write much more about human nature than the cognitive-behaviorists. Moreover, in each approach the concepts relating to human nature vary considerably. A view of human nature that sees the individual as determined by the environment or by internal needs and drives would seem to

FIGURE 6-1   Different theorists emphasize various traits and characteristics as being common to all newborn infants
(Color Image Inc., Jim Trotter)

have little in common with a view of the individual as capable of making choices and being free to do so.

Nevertheless, there are similarities. As a beginning, we can state that all agree that the individual is capable of changing or at least of being changed. The individual is not hopelessly predetermined, either by heredity or by early learning experiences, and may still change at any stage in life. Even the behaviorists base their approach on the belief that the individual is infinitely susceptible to change. The theories vary, of course, in their degree of optimism about the changeability of the individual, but all approaches assume change is possible. Otherwise, counseling would be pointless.

Patterson (1980) points out two other common elements among the various counseling approaches. All recognize that a disturbance or conflict or unsolved problem is undesirable and warrants attempts to change it. And all recognize the influence of the future—whether of anticipations, hopes, or expectations related to the future—on present behavior. This idea appears to tie together approaches as different as behavioral counseling and existential counseling, in that both accept the idea that behavior is not entirely caused by the past but is also influenced by future consequences or expectations of those consequences.

Certainly the affective approaches outlined in Chapter 4 tend to take a more positive view of human nature than the other approaches. Rogers, in particular, conceives of the individual as basically good, rational, and self-actualizing. In contrast, Freud viewed human nature as highly deterministic, with individuals being controlled by their biological drives and instincts. Though the behaviorists accept human nature as neither good nor bad, they see the individual's behavior not as self-actualizing but rather as resulting from reinforcements from the environment acting upon the individual. Ellis attempts to avoid the whole idea of potential for good or evil by suggesting that this premise has no empirical basis. Still, Ellis does see humans as being born with potentials for rational thinking, despite their tendencies toward crooked thinking. His view of human nature is somewhat less optimistic than that of either the affective or the behavioral approaches.

Key Concepts

Psychoanalytic Approaches

A major emphasis of the psychoanalytic approach is the interplay of the three systems of the personality—the id, ego, and superego—with the relative development of each of these as a major factor in the individual's emotional well-being.

Adler emphasized the social nature of humans, especially the need to feel a part of significant social groups, and suggested that an individual's life-style resulted from what the individual learned about behaviors necessary for becoming accepted by the group.

Horney and Sullivan also emphasized the social nature of humans, with Horney pointing out that children who are insecure in their primary social relationships handle these feelings by developing irrational solutions. Sullivan, on the other hand, believed that the self responds to anxiety resulting from one's interactions with others and acts to protect from anxiety and thus guard security.

Affective Approaches

In general, the affective approaches emphasize the internal focus of the individual—what is going on inside the individual, and particularly what feelings the individual is either experiencing or forcing out of the conscious.

Person-centered therapy views individuals as positive and emphasizes a counseling relationship in which certain "necessary and sufficient" conditions exist. These conditions apply to the counselor, the client, and the relationship.

Gestalt therapy emphasizes the need for clients to reach present awareness of what they are experiencing. Such awareness leads to increased responsibility and growth. The process is an active, confrontive one and results in clients gaining greater recognition of the strength they have and of how to use that strength in daily living.

**FIGURE 6-2   Children at play often reveal some of the most basic
emotions and needs of humanity**
(Photo by James T. Hurley)

Cognitive-Behavioral Approaches

The cognitive-behavioral processes emphasize thinking and doing rather than
feeling and experiencing. Rational-emotive therapy emphasizes that emotions are
the products of human thinking. Thus Ellis maintains that emotional disturbances
are simply the result of an individual's mistakes—illogical ideas about a particular
situation.

The behavioral approaches to therapy, on the other hand, place their major emphasis on the whole social-cultural conditioning process. In particular, behavioral counseling is characterized by (1) a focus on overt and specific behavior, (2) a precise delineation of treatment goals, (3) a formulation of a specific treatment procedure appropriate to the particular problem, and (4) an objective assessment of the outcome of therapy.

Process and Goals

In comparing the goals of the various counseling approaches, one finds a diverse group of objectives—finding meaning in life, curing an emotional disturbance, adjusting to society, attaining self-actualization, reducing anxiety, and unlearning maladaptive behavior and learning adaptive patterns. As diverse as these goals seem, they can be placed in perspective by viewing them as existing on a continuum from general, long-term objectives to specific, short-term objectives. The affective counseling approaches tend to stress the general, long-term objectives; the cognitive-behavioral approaches emphasize the specific, short-term objectives.

Psychoanalytic Approaches

The psychoanalytic view places a major focus on developing a transference relationship between the client and the counselor so that the client can relive unresolved conflicts, feelings, and experiences that have previously been denied or distorted. Thus the major therapeutic goal for Freudians is to enable clients to gain insight into their problems by uncovering material that was previously unconscious.

Adler suggested that the therapeutic process should include the establishment of a collaborative relationship, an assessment of the client's life style, the development of the client's problems, and the orientation of the client toward action.

Affective Approaches

In the person-centered view, the counseling process consists primarily of the counselor's establishing a therapeutic relationship with the client in which the counselor communicates minimally facilitative conditions, such as respect, congruence, and empathic understanding. The goals center around the individual's becoming more mature and reinstituting the process towards actualization by removing obstacles. Thus, from the person-centered standpoint, counseling is simply a process of releasing an already existing force in a potentially adequate individual.

Gestalt therapy, with its focus on the client's feelings, awareness of the moment, body messages, and blocks to awareness, emphasizes a process in which the counselor's role is to challenge clients to use all their senses fully. By encouraging clients to fully experience being stuck at an impasse, the counselor attempts to help clients through the impasse so that growth becomes possible, and clients move from external to internal support, discovering that they can do themselves what they have been manipulating others to do for them.

Cognitive-Behavioral Approaches

For the rational-emotive counselor, the process of counseling is the curing of un-reason by reason; that is, of helping clients avoid or eliminate most emotional dis-turbances by learning to think rationally, and of helping them to get rid of illogi-cal, irrational ideas and attitudes and to substitute logical, rational ideas and attitudes. The process results in the client's attaining rational behavior, happiness, and self-actualization. Although behavioral counselors are generally less con-cerned about process than most counselors, specific counseling goals occupy a place of central importance. Recent behaviorists have focused on the counselor-client relationship as simply a means of facilitating greater understanding of the client's view of the problem, which enables the counselor to develop a more suc-cessful behavioral plan for bringing about change in the client.

Counseling Techniques

Psychoanalytic Approaches

Therapists who subscribe to a psychoanalytic approach utilize several techniques in uncovering unconscious material. Interpretation involves the therapist's ex-plaining to the client the meanings of the newly uncovered material, thus leading to further insight. Dream interpretation permits the therapist to gain access to the unconscious, as does free association, in which clients are asked to share sponta-neously whatever thoughts, words, expressions, or feelings come to mind, without censorship.

Adler used various techniques to clarify the client's life-style and facilitate in-sight. He observed very carefully the client's position in birth order, associating characteristics with that position. He also used the adult's earliest memories to help in the understanding. In addition, he used confrontation, interpretation, and encouragement to help clients to take responsibility for their lives and to make new decisions that would enable them to reach their goals more effectively.

Affective Approaches

Person-centered therapy places little stress on technique; it emphasizes the coun-selor's person, beliefs, and attitudes, and the counseling relationship itself. The re-lationship is the critical variable, not what the counselor says or does. Thus, the "techniques" are expressing and communicating acceptance, respect, and under-standing, with an emphasis on the here and now of the individual's existence.

Counselors operating within a Gestalt therapy framework utilize confronta-tion techniques, establishing situations that will cause clients to experience their frustrations. The Gestalt counselor deliberately plays provocative games that are intended to force clients to confront and acknowledge the feelings that they have been so arduously trying to avoid. The Gestalt counselor also fosters a here-and-now orientation and utilizes a variety of experiential games with clients to increase their awareness of themselves and their impasses and then tries to help them rein-tegrate themselves.

Cognitive-Behavioral Approaches

The major technique of rational-emotive therapy is directive teaching. The counselor assumes an active teaching role to reeducate clients, enabling them to recognize that their internalized sentences are in many ways quite illogical and unrealistic. The effective RET counselor continually unmasks the past and especially the present illogical thinking and self-defeating verbalizations of the client. The counselor brings illogical thinking forcefully to the clients' attention, shows them how it is maintaining their unhappiness, demonstrates exactly the illogical links in their internalized sentences, and teaches them how to rethink and reverbalize these sentences to make them more logical and efficient. RET counselors also utilize homework assignments as an integral part of their practice.

Probably more than any other counselors, behavioral counselors use very specific techniques based on learning theory. Techniques utilized by behavioral counselors include systematic desensitization, behavior contracts, social modeling, and assertion training.

Desensitization is particularly useful with clients who are experiencing a high level of anxiety associated with a specific problem behavior, while behavior contracts permit the counselor and client to work together in gaining the client's commitment to specific behavior change. Social modeling is particularly useful in helping clients learn new behaviors and is often utilized in assertion training with individuals who have difficulty asserting themselves in interpersonal situations.

Building a Personal Theory of Counseling

Self-analysis

Those who wish to develop a personal theory of counseling should begin by thoroughly examining their own views of human nature. Such an analysis should include a thorough examination of ideas about what people are like and what their inherent tendencies are. The analysis should also include questions about choice making—Does each individual have freedom to make choices? Or are choices determined by previous events in the individual's life?—and about the trustworthiness of people, about their truthfulness, honesty, helpfulness, and selfishness. Those who wish to develop their own theory must consider how people are motivated to change and how such change can occur. Lastly, they must examine their views regarding the relationship between doing, feeling, and thinking in order to help clarify their philosophical orientation, which in turn will lead to a particular counseling approach.

Self-clarification

Along with examining views about the inherent nature of people, prospective counselors must develop a clear picture of *themselves* as people. They must achieve a thorough understanding of themselves since their own experiences, personality characteristics, and view of inherent human nature will influence their theoretical approach, which in turn will determine their behavior as counselors. One who attempts to accept and practice something that is incongruent with one's own personal makeup cannot function effectively as a counselor. This underlies the need to examine one's own values, beliefs, and ideas, realizing that only when one is clear about who one is can one be effective in facilitating growth in clients.

Integrating the Various Approaches

After they have clarified who they are, counselors in training need to examine the ideas regarding counseling processes, roles, and techniques that are most congruent with their ideas about people. Few individuals are likely to accept all aspects of any one theory. As we said early in this chapter, the prospective counselor must be able to commit to the fundamental tenets of one theoretical approach even while disagreeing with some of the specifics. This commitment to a counseling approach in the first few years of training is a highly tentative decision and subject to considerable modification. With experience and further study, the counselor can then examine the ideas and techniques of other theoretical approaches that seem congruent with the chosen approach. The integration of these techniques and goals within one's own counseling approach will lead to a systematic applicability in practice.

Counseling goals from various approaches can be integrated by recognizing that the behavioral and cognitive approaches have goals that stress specific, immediate change, and the affective approaches tend to stress broader or ultimate long-term goals. The counselor can employ specific short-term goals to deal with client problems that call for immediate change. These short-term, specific goals can also be intermediate steps toward achieving the long-term goals that may be the ultimate purpose of the total counseling process.

Bruce (1984) recommends the development of a framework in which several models can be utilized, depending on the needs and expectations of a particular client. He goes on to present one such framework, similar in concept to Maslow's hierarchy of needs in that more basic goals (such as self-preservation) take precedence over more abstract goals (like self-actualization). Likewise, Ward (1983) recommends the use of an affective-cognitive-behavioral, three-domain approach.

One current trend toward integrating aspects of different theories has developed as part of the emerging emphasis on a systems approach to counseling and psychotherapy. Wolberg (1987) calls for "a systems approach that recognizes that in any emotional or mental illness we are dealing with multiple variables requiring a broad eclectic orientation" (p. 256). Perhaps the most comprehensive systems approach that proposes a systemic theoretical framework for counseling in such a way as to present a "trans-paradigmatic" therapy is that of Cottone (1992). In his ground-breaking book, Cottone works toward developing a model that merges the traditional individual therapies described here with the various theories of marital and family therapy. In so doing, he proposes a counseling paradigm based on an analysis and integration of the major counseling theories, both individual and systemic.

View of the Counselor's Role

Those who would be counselors also need to examine their views of the counselor's role in facilitating therapeutic change. Is the counselor simply a good listener? an advice-giver? Should the counselor clarify, confront, provide alternatives, give information, or make decisions for the client? Does the counselor assume all these roles at various times? If so, what is the counselor's basic role in the overall helping process?

Frequently, beginning counselors see themselves as expert advice givers, expected to have answers for whatever problems clients bring to them. Such an attitude has built-in problems, suggesting as it does that counselors have expert knowledge about all fields. More important, however, even if counselors had such extraordinary overall knowledge, their providing all the answers would most likely reinforce the client's dependency rather than encourage the clients to learn to make their own decisions, to find their own information, and to solve their own problems.

A second role problem encountered by beginning counselors is deciding whether or not to give a client honest and direct feedback. Is the counselor's role one of an impartial observer who listens to the facts and the subjective feelings in the circumstance and then either provides answers or teaches the client how to find his own answers? Counseling theory for most counselors is not static; rather it is a dynamic, ever-changing process. As counselors function and interact with their clients they learn more about those counseling behaviors that are effective with particular clients in particular settings. As counselors integrate these insights into their counseling practice, their counseling theory is expanded and modified to more accurately reflect what they have come to believe to be the essential factors of their own counseling effectiveness. In the long run that is the purpose of counseling theory—to promote effective individual counseling on the part of every practicing counselor.

We agree with Blocher (1987), who takes a different approach to building one's own personal counseling model by proposing that each counselor must develop a "process model" for organizing the basic tasks of counseling. These tasks include:

Developing a facilitative relationship

Defining the client's life situation, including problems, concerns, and aspirations

Agreeing upon general goals and objectives

Restructuring the client's way of thinking

Specifying needed changes in the client's behavior

Providing for client change in real-life situations

Evaluating counseling outcomes and processes

Summary

All counselors interact with clients on the basis of a set of beliefs they have about people and how people change; therefore, the importance of counselors' clarifying those beliefs and developing them into a theoretical foundation is emphasized. To facilitate the development of a personal theory of counseling, the following points are emphasized: In developing an initial personal approach, counselors must become familiar with the current major approaches to counseling practice. They must develop a full understanding of their own assumptions about the nature of people and identify their own accepted models of the mature, well-functioning individual. They must clarify their goals and strategies in counseling and test their theory in practice, formulating new ideas based on their own experiences.

A comparison of the major counseling approaches with regard to their respective positions regarding view of human nature, key concepts in counseling, process and goals of counseling, and counseling techniques is presented to help identify similarities and differences among the various theories.

References

Blocher, D. H. (1987). *The professional counselor.* New York: Macmillan.

Brammer, L. M., & Shostrom, E. L. (1982). *Therapeutic psychology* (2nd ed.). Englewood Cliffs, NJ: Prentice-Hall.

Bruce, P. (1984). Continuum of counseling goals: A framework for differentiating counseling strategies. *Personnel and Guidance Journal, 62,* 259–263.

Combs A. W. (1989). *A theory of therapy.* Newbury Park, CA: Sage.

Corey, G. (1991). *Theory and practice of counseling and psychotherapy* (4th ed.). Pacific Grove, CA. Brooks/Cole.

Corsini R. J. (Ed.). (1981). *Handbook of innovative psychotherapies.* New York: Wiley.

Cottone R. R. (1992). *Theories and paradigms of counseling and psychotherapy.* Boston: Allyn and Bacon.

Ford, D. H. & Urban, H. B. (1963). *Systems of Psychotherapy: A comparative study.* New York: Wiley

Marmor, J. (1987). The psychotherapeutic process: Common denominators in diverse approaches. In J. K. Zeig (Ed.). *The evolution of psychotherapy.* New York: Brunner/Mazel

Meier, S. T., & Davis S. R. (1993). *The elements of counseling.* (2nd ed.) Pacific Grove, CA: Brooks/Cole.

Patterson, C. H. (1980). *Theories of counseling and psychotherapy* (3rd ed.). New York: Harper & Row.

Shoben, E. J., Jr. (1962). The counselor's theory as a personal trait. *Personnel and Guidance Journal, 40, 617–621.*

Ward, D. E. (1983). The trend toward eclecticism and the development of comprehensive models to guide counseling and psychotherapy. *Personnel and Guidance Journal, 62,* 154–157.

Wolberg, L. R. (1987). The evolution of psychotherapy: Future trends. In J. K. Zeig (Ed.). *The evolution of psychotherapy.* New York: Brunner/Mazel.

Part III

Counseling Processes and Methods

Characteristics of a Helping Relationship

The relationship established between the counselor and client is fundamental to the therapeutic process of counseling and psychotherapy. Through this relationship clients learn to examine their thoughts, feelings, attitudes, values, and behaviors, and as a result of this exploration they are able to grow and change. This exploration process is made possible because of the therapeutic climate established at the outset of the counseling experience. In this chapter we will explore the qualities and characteristics of a helping relationship; we will discuss the significance of trust and acceptance in the development of the therapeutic climate; we will review several responses that are barriers to the communication process; and we will examine the core conditions of effective counseling, including genuineness, empathy, positive regard, and concreteness.

The Helping Relationship: An Overview

The helping relationship has been discussed at length in the literature and has been defined by several authors and theorists.

Definition

Pepinsky and Pepinsky have defined the relationship "as a hypothetical construct to designate the inferred character of the observable interaction between two individuals" (1954, p. 171). Shertzer and Stone (1980) have described the helping relationship as "the endeavor, by interaction with others, to contribute in a facilitating, positive way to their improvement" (p. 5). Rogers defines the helping relationship as one "in which at least one of the parties has the intent of promoting the growth, development, maturity, improved functioning, improved coping with life of the other" (1961, p. 40).

From these definitions we glean that the helping relationship is a unique and dynamic process through which one individual assists another to use his or her inner resources to grow in a positive direction, actualizing the individual's potential for a meaningful life.

Characteristics

The above definition might describe various interpersonal relationships, including that between parent and child or teacher and student, but the helping relationship established between client and counselor is unique. A number of specific characteristics contribute to its uniqueness.

Affectiveness
The relationship established between counselor and client is more affective than cognitive. It involves the exploration of subjective feelings and perceptions. Because of the highly personal content of the discussions, the relationship can be

comforting and anxiety producing, intense and humorous, frightening and exhilarating.

Intensity

Because it is based on open direct, and honest communication, the relationship can be intense. Counselor and client are expected to share openly their perceptions and reactions to each other and to the process. This can result in intense communication.

Growth and Change

The relationship is *dynamic;* it is constantly changing as the counselor and client interact. As the client grows and changes, so does the relationship.

Privacy

All client disclosures are confidential, and counselors are obligated not to share what transpires in the interviews with others unless the client has given permission to do so. This protective aspect of the relationship is unique and frequently encourages client self-disclosure.

Support

Counselors, through the relationship, offer clients a system of support that often provides the necessary stability for taking risks and changing behavior.

Honesty

The helping relationship is based on honesty and open, direct communication between counselor and client.

The above list of characteristics of the helping relationship is not exhaustive. Many others could be added. These, however, should expand the reader's understanding of the relationship and help distinguish this relationship between counselor and client from other helping relationships.

Therapeutic Value

The above characteristics clarify what is meant by *helping relationship,* but they do not explain its therapeutic value. The effectiveness of the helping relationship in the remediation of emotional and psychological problems and in the growth, maturation, and self-actualization of individuals can be attributed to many factors.

One important factor is that the relationship established between the client and counselor is a microcosm of the client's world; it mirrors the client's patterns of relating to others. The relationship enables the counselor to observe the client's interpersonal style and also provides a vehicle for changing ineffective communication patterns. From this perspective the relationship is therapeutic, since the client and counselor encounter each other as two individuals working out the complexities of an intimate relationship.

Another factor in the effectiveness of the helping relationship is the establishment of a therapeutic climate based on trust and acceptance as well as the core conditions of genuineness, empathic understanding, positive regard, and specificity of expression.

The Therapeutic Climate

Trust

A prerequisite for establishing a therapeutic climate is trust. Clients entering the counseling relationship are often anxious and afraid. Their expectations for counseling may be unclear. They are seeking help with personal concerns and hope the counselor will respond with understanding. If, in the initial contact, they perceive the counselor as trustworthy, they will take increasingly greater emotional risks, sharing thoughts, feelings, anxieties, and fears that are difficult to discuss and that have sometimes been denied. As clients realize that the counselor is not finding fault with those aspects of themselves they dislike, they will become more accepting of themselves. As trust grows, so does the potential for growth and change. From the initial contact then, the counselor must be perceived as trustworthy.

Rogers emphasizes the importance of trust in establishing a helping relationship. In the following questions he not only clarifies the conditions that must be present, he also provides a challenge to counselors for their personal growth and development.

*Can I **be** in some way which will be perceived by the other person as trustworthy, as dependable or consistent in some deep sense?*

Can I be expressive enough as a person that what I am will be communicated unambiguously?

Can I let myself experience positive attitudes toward this other person—attitudes of warmth, caring, liking, interest, respect?

Can I be strong enough as a person to be separate from the other?

Am I secure enough within myself to permit him his separateness?

Can I let myself enter fully into the world of his feelings and personal meanings and see those as he does?

Can I receive him as he is? Can I communicate this attitude?

Can I act with sufficient sensitivity in the relationship that my behavior will not be perceived as a threat?

Can I free him from the threat of external evaluation?

Can I meet this other individual as a person who is in the process of becoming, or will I be bound by his past and by my past? (Rogers, 1961, pp. 50–55)*

The core dimensions of genuineness, empathy, and positive regard are also fundamental in establishing trust. These are explored later in the chapter.

Acceptance

The relationship between trust and acceptance has been alluded to in the above discussion of trust. An accepting attitude implies that the counselor can listen to the client's concerns without making judgments and can appreciate the client as a person regardless of the client's views, attitudes, and values. This accepting attitude communicates respect for the client as a person of dignity and worth. The client feels understood and valued in a very real sense.

Rogers discusses the impact of acceptance on client growth in the "if-then" hypothesis:

> *If I can create a relationship characterized on my part:*
>   *by a genuineness and transparency in which I am my real feelings;*
>   *by a warm acceptance of and prizing of the other person as a separate individual;*
>   *by a sensitive ability to see his work and himself as he sees them;*
>
> *Then the other individual in the relationship:*
>   *will experience and understand aspects of himself which previously he has repressed;*
>   *will find himself becoming better integrated, more able to function effectively;*
>   *will become more similar to the person he would like to be;*
>   *will be more self-directing and self-confident;*
>   *will become more of a person, more unique and more self-expressive;*
>   *will be more understanding, more acceptant of others;*
>   *will be more able to cope with the problems of life more adequately and more comfortably. (1961, p. 37–38)**

As summarized in the above hypothesis, the accepting attitude expressed by the counselor in the helping relationship frees clients to acknowledge those aspects of themselves that have previously been denied awareness. It is paradoxical that clients must accept themselves completely before they are free to move in the direction of positive growth and change (Rogers, 1961).

Barriers to Communication

As discussed above, acceptance is communicated through the counselor's responses to the client's expressed concerns. Unfortunately, counselors often confuse the communication of acceptance with responses that actually block communication and

---

*From *On Becoming a Person* by Carl R. Rogers. Copyright © 1961 by Carl R. Rogers. Reprinted by permission of Houghton Mifflin Co.

BOX 7-1   Some Barriers to Communication

1. Giving advice
2. Offering solutions
3. Moralizing and preaching
4. Analyzing and diagnosing

5. Judging or criticizing
6. Praising and agreeing; giving positive evaluations
7. Reassuring

---

that say to clients that they are not understood, are not valued and respected. The response patterns that communicate a lack of acceptance have been identified and explored by Gordon (1974) as they apply to parenting and teaching relationships. The impact of these barriers to communication on the counseling interview will now be discussed.

Giving Advice

Some novice counselors are anxious to help their clients by offering advice. They assume that it is their responsibility to guide clients in the right direction and to solve their problems. Because of their expertise in the areas of human development and behavior, they expect to help clients by instructing them regarding the right course of action. True, many clients want the counselor to give them advice, but this response places the counselor in the position of assuming responsibility for the client's life choices. For example, a client experiencing marriage difficulties is questioning whether to end the marriage. If the counselor recommends that the client ask for a divorce and the client acts on this advice, the client may later feel that divorce was a mistake and is likely to resent and blame the counselor for her role in the decision-making process. Offering clients advice only maintains their dependence on others and does not facilitate their movement to an internal locus of evaluation and control.

Offering Solutions

The difficulties with counselors offering solutions to client problems are several. First, the problems clients present in the initial interview may not be the concerns for which they need counseling. If the counselor begins solving these, the more basic problem may never surface. It is unrealistic and pretentious for counselors to assume they have solutions to the myriad concerns that clients face. This problem-solving approach reduces the complexities of living to simple problems that have solutions. Rogers (1961) suggests that a counselor who is willing to listen carefully to a client will become more respectful of life's complexities and much less willing to rush in and "fix" things. Rushing in with solutions communicates a lack of trust in clients as human beings who, with some support and understanding, are able to solve their own problems.

Moralizing and Preaching

When counselors moralize or preach, they evaluate the client's behavior and indicate what the client "ought" to do or how the client "should" feel. This type of response induces guilt, is judgmental, and attempts to change the client's behavior in the direction of the counselor's value system. Such counselors do not attempt to understand the client's world from the client's perspective. Examples of this type of response include: "You should not hate your mother." "You should not treat your sister that way." "I cannot believe you are smoking dope; don't you know it is illegal!" "You ought to be more assertive with your boss." "Abortions are murder!" "You shouldn't have gotten pregnant to begin with."

Analyzing and Diagnosing

Analyzing and diagnosing a client's problem is an example of ineffective and unaccepting communication because it puts the counselor in the position of viewing the client's problem from an external frame of reference. In other words, the counselor is removed and objective, seeking to identify the basic maladaptive behaviors and put them into a clinical framework. An example would be, "Your basic problem seems to be that you have an inferiority complex that prevents you from relating effectively to others."

Judging or Criticizing

When a counselor judges or criticizes a client's response, the client typically withdraws and withholds further information or feelings. Like moralizing or preaching, this response does not facilitate client self-disclosure but instead induces guilt. For example, a teacher refers a student to a counselor because the student consistently fails to complete homework assignments. If the counselor is judgmental and assumes that the student is irresponsible, playing after school rather than studying, the student may never feel comfortable enough to disclose the real source of the problem—poor concentration because she is worried about her parents' pending divorce.

Praising and Agreeing; Giving Positive Evaluations

The two responses of praising and agreeing and giving positive evaluations are somewhat more difficult to view in terms of their negative impact on the client. Acceptance implies a *neutral* stance toward the client's attitudes, values, and behaviors. At times it is appropriate for the counselor to respond to the client's growth or behavior change with genuine enthusiasm; however, the counselor must be careful that the seemingly positive response does not communicate a superficial attempt to make the client feel better, make the problem disappear, or to deny that the client really has a problem. An example of misused praise would be, "You're such a go-getter, I'm sure you can handle the pressures of next week without any problem."

Reassuring

Reassurance helps the client only on a superficial level. It stops interaction between the counselor and client and communicates to the client that many others have felt the same way. This type of statement prevents further discussion of the client's fears, anxieties, or concerns about particular issues. It says to the client, "Your feelings are not valid; don't feel the way you do." Rather than communicating understanding and acceptance of the client's world, the reassuring response attempts to gloss over problems.

Characteristics of an Effective Counseling Relationship

We have explored the importance of trust and acceptance in establishing a helping relationship and have discussed those counselor responses that serve as communication barriers. Next we will examine the core dimensions of effective counseling and their impact on the helping relationship.

Core Dimensions

As discussed in Chapter 2, extensive research efforts have sought to isolate those qualities or characteristics of the counselor that may be associated with positive outcomes in counseling and psychotherapy. Investigators have sought the answers to such questions as: What are the characteristics of an effective counseling relationship? Are there characteristics of counselors that can be associated with positive outcomes in counseling? Do these qualities transcend the theoretical orientation of the counselor? Some researchers have sought to identify lists of adjectives that describe effective counselors. These have included the following: empathic, sincere, warm, spontaneous, understanding, patient, friendly, calm, and stable. Many of the qualities that we intuitively associate with persons who are helpful in relationships with others have been objectively proven effective through extensive investigations (Belkin, 1975).

Various studies have demonstrated that a variety of qualities are associated with effective counseling, and a set of characteristics that consistently plays a central role in establishing and maintaining an effective therapeutic relationship has emerged. These characteristics have been delineated through various studies with a broad spectrum of clients:

> *An effective counselor*
> (1) *is not phony or defensive and comes across as an* authentic *and* genuine *person in the therapeutic relationship;*
> (2) *is able to provide a nonthreatening, safe, trusting and secure atmosphere, through his acceptance,* positive regard, *or* nonpossessive warmth *for the clients; and,*
> (3) *is able to understand, and have a high degree of* accurate empathic *understanding of, the client on a moment by moment basis. (Truax and Mitchell, 1971)*

Although these qualities have come to be closely associated with the client-centered approach, the research indicates that effective therapists, regardless of their theoretical orientation or training, exhibit high levels of the core conditions (Berenson and Carkhuff, 1967; Carkhuff, 1969a, 1969b; Rogers, Gendlin, Kiessler, and Truax, 1967; Truax and Carkhuff, 1967; Truax and Mitchell, 1971). Rogers

(1957) called these qualities of empathy, genuineness, and positive regard the necessary and sufficient conditions for therapeutic personality change.

These qualities of empathy, genuineness, and nonpossessive warmth seem to be present in most helping relationships and are not new to psychologists. Most of the phenomenologically oriented psychoanalysts, including Freud, Fromm-Reichmann, Otto Rank, and Alfred Adler as well as current behaviorally oriented psychologists, have agreed on the importance of these qualities (Truax and Mitchell, 1971). Each of these qualities will be explored and their therapeutic value in developing the helping relationship will be discussed.

Genuineness, or Congruence

Perhaps the most fundamental element in the development of the therapeutic climate is the counselor's genuineness, or congruence. Congruence refers to the ability of counselors to be themselves, without needing to present a professional front or facade. Counselors who are genuine do not hide behind a mask or play a role. They can communicate a "realness" in relationships because they are sensitively aware of their feelings and reactions as they are experiencing them and are honest and direct in their communication with their clients. Their verbal responses match their internal reactions and nonverbal communication and are characterized by their spontaneity. This type of interaction facilitates trust; the client does not have to wade through layers of defenses and facades to relate to the counselor. Counselors who are secure with themselves and open with their feelings, reactions, thoughts, and attitudes allow the client to feel safe and secure.

The counselor's genuineness can play an important part in the therapeutic process. As the counselor listens and responds to the content of what the client is saying, on another level the counselor is responding to the client as a person. The counselor who can be sensitively tuned into these internal reactions can promote client growth. For example, if a therapist is genuinely moved by the client's pain and struggle to find his own way, she can share these feelings. Likewise, if a counselor realizes that she is having difficulty listening and is, in fact, feeling very uninvolved and bored, she might try to identify the client behaviors to which she is reacting and share these feelings in a positive confrontation. This type of risk taking by the counselor can be highly facilitative, enabling the client to explore personal issues and behaviors that may be hindering other relationships. This risk taking can also promote intimacy and take communication to a new level. By disclosing reactions to a client as they are occurring, the counselor decreases distance in the relationship. Johnson has illustrated this process (Figure 7-1), which occurs in the therapeutic relationship as both counselor and client learn to trust themselves and each other and allow themselves to be authentic and transparent in the encounter.

Empathic Understanding

The ability to be empathic in a relationship requires that counselors respond sensitively and accurately to clients' feelings and experiences as if they were their own. Empathy is the ability to adopt the client's internal frame of reference so that the client's private world and meanings are accurately understood and clearly

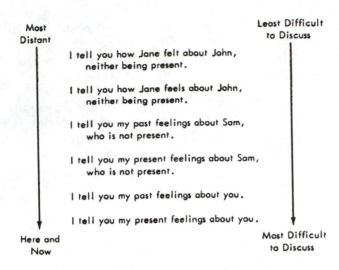

FIGURE 7-1   (Johnson 1972, p. 88)

communicated back. This process, called "trial identification," resembles the relationship a reader establishes with the main character of a novel. Truax and Mitchell have described this identification process:

> *As we come to know some of his wants, some of his needs, some of his achievements, and some of his failures, and some of his values, we find ourselves living with the other person much as we do the hero or heroine of a novel . . . we come to know the person from his own internal viewpoint and thus gain some understanding and flavor of his moment by moment experiences. (1971, p. 315)*

For counselors to respond empathically to the client's verbalizations, they must be sensitive to the client's communications, both verbal and nonverbal, and perceptive. Sensitivity in this context means an increased awareness of the other; perceptivity connotes the ability to understand. Sensitivity is an affective skill that allows the counselor to identify the client's feelings, and perceptivity is a cognitive skill that enables the counselor to identify the stimulus for the feeling. It is a combination of these two interpersonal skills that produces the advanced empathic response. The advanced empathic response is discussed in Chapter 9.

Empathy allows the therapist to hear and respond to the client's feelings—the client's anger, resentment, fear, hostility, depression, and joy. When the therapist can carefully listen to the client's world and accurately identify the feelings clients are experiencing, clients are more capable of listening to themselves. Empathy allows counselors to transcend themselves while maintaining their separateness and individuality.

Empathic understanding also involves the therapist's adopting the client's frame of reference. It implies listening to clients without making judgments. As clients share their thoughts, feelings, values, attitudes, hopes, and aspirations, the counselor listens without labeling right or wrong, good or bad. This nonevaluative attitude lets clients become more accepting of themselves.

Some risk is involved in allowing oneself to fully enter another's world. Rogers has described this risk:

> *If I am truly open to the way life is experienced by another person—if I can take his world into mine—then I run the risk of seeing life in his way, of being changed myself, and we all resist change. So we tend to view this other person's world only in our terms, not in his. We analyze and evaluate it. We do not understand it. But when someone understands how it feels and seems to be me, without wanting to analyze or judge me, then I can blossom and grow in that climate. (1961, p. 90)**

Rogers adds that when the counselor can grasp the client's inner world without losing his own identity in the process, then change is likely to occur.

Positive Regard or Respect

The literature refers to positive regard as the therapist's nonpossessive warmth or respect for the client. Rogers (1957) referred to this quality as "unconditionality of regard." By this, Rogers is suggesting the importance of the counselor's being able to genuinely prize the client as a person of worth and dignity. The counselor can reach out in a warm and caring way and accept the client unconditionally. In other words, the therapist does not pass judgment but accepts the client's attitudes, values, and behaviors in a nonevaluative fashion.

Carkhuff and Berenson (1977) have noted that positive regard or respect for others originates in self-respect. Counselors who do not respect their own experiences, thoughts, and feelings will have difficulty respecting other's thoughts and feelings. In many ways, communicating an attitude of caring, warmth, and regard for the client lays the foundation for empathy.

Positive regard is fundamental to the counseling process, and frequently leads counselors in training to wonder if they must like everyone who seeks counseling. Many counselors are able to respond positively to a variety of clients because the helping relationship allows them to move beyond behaviors, defenses, and facades that others find offensive. The counselor who cannot do this should refer the client to another counselor.

Respect or positive regard is somewhat related to the therapist's genuineness or congruence in the relationship. The therapist who does not respect the client's ability to cope with life, feelings, and reactions will find it difficult to share thoughts, feelings, and reactions to the client's behavior—a sharing that may be essential for client growth. In other words, without respect for the client, the therapist will have difficulty confronting the client in the relationship. Thus, the respect the counselor has for the client enables the counselor to be honest and congruent in the relationship.

Nonpossessive warmth and positive feeling for the client is communicated verbally and nonverbally. Verbal expressions of warmth include statements about the positive relationship: "I like you," "I care about you," "I am concerned about you," "I feel close to you," "I'm worried about you." Essentially these statements convey the speaker's feelings to the other person in a very direct and open manner. To be effective the content of the statement must be congruent with the voice and manner of the therapist. Such statements result in positive attitudes toward the person making them and are related to the trust, acceptance, and understanding that the receiver perceives in the sender (Johnson, 1971).

Warmth toward another person is also communicated nonverbally through eye contact, voice tone, facial expressions, physical position, and touch. Counselors should become aware of the nonverbal messages they send to clients; they should learn to communicate their warmth and regard nonverbally. Johnson (1990) has identified the nonverbal cues that express warmth and coldness.

They are listed in Box 7-2. The counselor can learn to act in ways that may be perceived as warm by the client, but these must be real and genuine.

Concreteness, or Specificity of Expression

In addition to the core conditions of genuineness, empathy and positive regard, Carkhuff and his associates have added the dimension of concreteness, or specificity of expression. According to Carkhuff and Berenson concreteness "involves the fluent, direct, and complete expression of specific feelings and experiences, regardless of their emotional content . . ." (1977, p. 13). They further describe the function of the dimension as follows:

1. Concreteness ensures that the counselor's response is close to the client's feelings and experiences.

2. Concreteness promotes accuracy and understanding of the client. Misunderstandings can be clarified when experiences and feelings are stated in specific terms.

BOX 7-2   Nonverbal Cues of Warmth and Coldness

Nonverbal Cue	Warmth	Coldness
1. Tone of Voice	soft	hard
2. Facial Expression	smiling, interested	poker-faced, frowning, disinterested
3. Posture	lean toward other; relaxed	lean away from other; tense
4. Eye Contact	look into other's eyes	avoid looking into other's eyes
5. Touching	touch other softly	avoid touching other
6. Gestures	open, welcoming	closed, guarding oneself and keeping other away
7. Spatial Distance	close	distant

From *Reaching Out: Interpersonal Effectiveness and Self-actualization,* by D. W. Johnson. Copyright (1990) by Prentice-Hall, Inc.

3. Concreteness forces the client to deal very specifically with problem areas and emotional conflicts. (1977, p. 13)

The importance of concreteness in the counseling relationship cannot be over-stated. This dimension perhaps more than empathy, genuineness, and positive regard, moves clients through the helping process by encouraging them to explore the problematic areas of their lives and their relationships to others. As Egan has stated, "The logic of the counseling process applies to concreteness: if the counselor is as concrete as possible in his responses to the client, the client will learn to be concrete in the exploration of his behavior" (1975, p. 101).

Quite frequently, clients are unable to express their feelings in concrete and specific terms. The counselor has the responsibility to help clients become more in touch with their feelings. The counselor does this by responding to the affect and the underlying stimulus for the feeling. If a client claims to be confused or frustrated, the counselor tries to identify more specifically the feeling the client is experiencing and also tries to identify a stimulus for the feeling.

Measurement of the Core Conditions

It can be argued that these core qualities of genuineness, empathy, positive regard, and concreteness are more than personality characteristics or qualities; rather they are skills that can be taught or composite responses that can be acquired through training. Research on the core conditions has been extensive and the accumulated evidence has been summarized in various volumes. These include: Rogers, et al. (1967), Truax and Carkhuff (1967), Carkhuff and Berenson (1977), Berenson and Carkhuff (1967), Carkhuff (1969a, 1969b), Carkhuff (1971), Truax and Mitchell (1971), and Berenson and Mitchell (1974).

Carkhuff and his associates have expanded the list of core conditions to include several process dimensions. Much of the evidence accumulated has been developed into a systematic model for human relations training. This model has been used to train lay persons and those in the helping professions. Much of the research by Carkhuff and his associates has focused on the development of five-point rating scales used to assess the counselor's level of functioning on each of the core dimensions. Rating scales have been developed for all four core dimensions.

Gazda and his associates (1977) have revised the Carkhuff rating scales, moving from the five-point structure to a four-point scale, and have also collapsed the scales for the core dimensions into a global rating of counselor effectiveness. Two of the rating scales as revised (Gazda, et al., 1977) are presented here as examples (see Tables 7-1, 7-2). On both the Carkhuff and Gazda scales a level of three is considered to be minimally facilitative. The Carkhuff rating scales have been widely used in counselor education to enable counselors in training to discriminate among levels of facilitative responses. Frequently trainees are asked to rate tapes of their own counseling sessions using the Carkhuff system.

TABLE 7-1   Empathy Scale

1.0 1.5	2.0 2.5	3.0 3.5	4.0
An irrelevant or hurtful response that does not appropriately attend to the surface feelings of the helpee. However, in instances where content is communicated accurately, it may raise the level of the response.	A response that only partially communicates an awareness of the surface feelings of the helpee. When content is communicated accurately it may raise the level of the response; conversely it may lower the level of the response when communicated inaccurately.	A response that conveys the helpee is understood at the level he is expressing himself; surface feelings are accurately reflected. Content is not essential, but when included it must be accurate. If it is inaccurate, the level of the response may be lowered.	A response that conveys the helpee is understood beyond his level of immediate awareness; underlying feelings are identified. Content is used to complement affect in adding deeper meaning. If content is inaccurate, the level of the response may be lowered.

> KEY WORDS
>
> Level 4— underlying feelings; additive
>
> Level 3— surface feelings reflected

Note: From *Human Relations Development: A Manual for Educators* (2nd ed.) by G. M. Gazda, F. R. Asbury, F. J. Balzer, W. C. Childers, R. P. Walters. Copyright 1977 by Allyn & Bacon, Inc., Boston. Reprinted with permission.

Summary

The helping relationship established between the counselor and client lies at the core of the helping process. Theoretical orientations may vary in the amount of emphasis placed on the relationship, but its significance in the therapeutic process has been widely acknowledged.

The helping relationship provides the opportunity for clients to examine patterns of relating under controlled conditions and with a person (counselor) who is skillful in interpersonal communication.

The qualities of trust and acceptance are fundamental to the therapeutic climate since they provide an atmosphere in which clients feel safe enough to examine those facets of themselves that have not previously been explored.

Several common response patterns inhibit therapeutic communications. These barriers to communication include giving advice, offering solutions, moralizing and preaching, analyzing and diagnosing, judging or criticizing, praising and agreeing, giving positive evaluations, and offering reassurance.

TABLE 7-2   Global Scale

1.0	1.5	2.0	2.5	3.0	3.5	4.0

1.0	2.0	3.0	4.0
A response in which the helper attends to neither the content nor the surface feelings of the helpee; discredits, devalues, ridicules, or scolds the helpee; shows a lack of caring for, or belief in, the helpee; is vague or deals with the helpee in general terms; tries to hide his feelings or uses them to punish the helpee; reveals nothing about himself or discloses himself exclusively to meet his own needs; passively accepts or ignores discrepancies in the helpee's behavior that are self-defeating; ignores all cues from the helpee regarding their immediate relationship.	A response in which the helper only partially attends to the surface feelings of the helpee or distorts what the helpee communicated; withholds himself from involvement with the helpee by declining to help, ignoring the helpee, responding in a casual way, or giving cheap advice before really understanding the situation; behaves in a manner congruent with some preconceived role he is taking, but is incongruent with his true feelings; is neutral in his nonverbal expressions and gestures; is specific in his verbal expressions (e.g., gives advice or own opinion) or solicits specificity from the helpee (e.g., asks questions) but does so prematurely; does not voluntarily reveal, but may briefly answer questions regarding his own feelings, thoughts, or experiences relevant to the helpee's concerns; does not accept discrepancies in the helpee's behavior but does not draw attention to them either; comments superficially on communications from the helpee regarding their relationship.	A response in which the helper reflects the surface feelings of the helpee and does not distort the content; communicates his openness to entering a helping relationship; recognizes the helpee as a person of worth, capable of thinking and expressing himself and acting constructively; communicates his attention and interest through his nonverbal expressions or gestures; shows that he is open to caring for and believing in the helpee; is specific in communicating his understanding but does not point out the directionality emerging for helpee action; shows no signs of phoniness but controls his expression of feeling so as to facilitate the development of the relationship; in a general manner, reveals his own feelings, thoughts, or experiences relevant to the helpee's concerns; makes tentative expressions of discrepancies in the helpee's behavior but does not point out the directions in which these lead; discusses his relationship with the helpee but in a general rather than a personal way.	A response in which the helper goes beyond reflection of the essence of the helpee's communication by identifying underlying feelings and meanings; is committed to the helpee's welfare; is intensely attentive; models and actively solicits specificity from the helpee; shows a genuine congruence between his feelings (whether they are positive or negative) and his overt behavior and communicates these feelings in a way that strengthens the relationship; freely volunteers specific feelings, thoughts, or experiences relevant to the helpee's concerns (these may involve a degree of risk taking for the helper); clearly points out discrepancies in the helpee's behavior and the specific directions in which these discrepancies lead; explicitly discusses their relationship in the immediate moment.

Research has isolated four core conditions of effective counseling that must be present if the relationship is to be therapeutic. These core conditions include genuineness, empathy, positive regard, and concreteness. Each plays a critical role in the establishment and maintenance of the therapeutic climate and must be exhibited by effective counselors. Counselors can be trained in response skills that will facilitate the communication of the core conditions. Persons who lack these basic qualities must seek personal counseling to grow in these areas if they are to be helpful to others.

References

Belkin, G. S. (1975). *Practical counseling in the schools*. Dubuque, IA: Wm. C. Brown.

Benjamin, A. (1969). *The helping interview* (2nd ed.). Boston: Houghton Mifflin.

Berenson, B. G., & Carkhuff, R. R. (1967). *Sources of gain in counseling and psychotherapy*. New York: Holt, Rienhart & Winston.

Berenson, B. G., & Mitchell, K. M. (1974). *Confrontation: For better or worse!* Amherst, Mass.: Human Resources Development Press.

Brammer, L., & Shostrom, E. (1982). *Therapeutic psycholoy: Fundamentals of counseling and psychotherapy* (4th ed.). Englwood Cliffs, N.J.: Prentice-Hall.

Carkhuff, R.R. (1969a). *Helping and human reltions: A primer for lay and professional helpers, Vol. I: selection and training*. New York: Holt, Rinehart & Winston.

Carkhuff, R.R. (1969b). *Helping and human relations: A primer for lay and professional helpers. Vol. 2: practice and research*. New York: Holt, Rinehart & Winston.

Carkhuff, R.R., (1971). *The development of human resources: Education, pychology, and social change*. New York: Holt, Rinehart & Winston.

Carkhuff, R.R., & Berenson, B.G. (1977). *Beyond counseling and therapy* (2nd ed.). New York: Holt, Rinehart & Winston.

Egan, G. (1975). *The skilled helper: A model for ststematic helping and interpersonal relating*. Monterey, Calif.: Brooks/Cole.

Gazda, G. M., Asbury, F.R., Balzer, F. J., Childers, W.C., & Walters, R.P. (1977). *Human relations development: A manual* (2nd ed.) Boston: Allyn and Bacon.

Gordon, T. (1974). *T.E.T.: Teacher effectiveness training*. New York: McKay.

Johnson, D. W. (1971). The effects of expressing warmth and anger upon the actor and listener. *Journal of Counseling Psychology, 18*, 571–578

Johnson, D. W. (1990). *Reaching out: Interpersonal effectiveness and self-actualization*. Englewood Cliffs, N.J.: Prentice-Hall.

Pepinsky, H. B., & Pepinsky, P. N. (1954). *Counseling theory and practice*. New York: Ronald Press.

Rogers, C. R. (1957). The necessary and sufficient conditions of therapeutic personality change. *Journal of Consulting Psychology, 22*, 95–103.

Rogers, C. R. (1961). *On becoming a person*. Boston: Houghton Mifflin.

Rogers, C. R., Gendlin, E. T., Kiessler, D., & Truax, C. B. (1967). *The therapeutic relationship and its impact: A study of psychotherapy with schizophrenics*. Madison: University of Wisconsin Press.

Rogers, C. R., & Stevens, B. (1971). *Person to person: The problem of being human*. New York: Pocket Books.

Shertzer, B., & Stone, S.C. (1980). *Fundamentals of counseling* (3rd ed.). Boston: Houghton Mifflin.

Truax, C. B., & Carkguff, R. R. (1967). *Toward effective counseling and psychotherapy*. Chicago: Aldine.

Truax, C. B., & Mitchell, K. M. (1971). Research on certain therapist interpersonal skills in relation to process and outcome. In A. E. Bergin and S. L. Garfield (Eds.). *Handbook of psychotherapy and behavior change: An empirical analysis*. New York: Wiley.

Chapter 8

Counseling Procedures/Skills: I

Initial Procedures

The Initial Counseling Interview

Counseling Skills

Summary

In this chapter, we will explore the counseling environment and the initial interview and review skills that are basic to the beginning stages of the counseling process. At the outset of the counseling experience, attention must be given to the specifics of organizing the first interview. Seating arrangements, intake procedures, opening the first session, structuring the interview, setting goals for the process, termination, and referral are all fairly simple procedures that must be dealt with regardless of the theoretical orientation of the counselor.

As counseling begins, the counselor's primary goal is to establish rapport with the client so that the therapeutic climate described in Chapter 7 will develop. In large measure, the establishment of the therapeutic climate will depend on the personality of the counselor and the extent to which the core conditions are communicated. There are some basic skills, however, such as observing nonverbal behaviors, and using attending behaviors, open-ended leads, silent listening, and summarization, that facilitate the initial stages of communication.

Initial Procedures

The Counseling Environment

Several investigations have focused on the importance of the setting and the relationship of such factors as chair arrangements and room size to the client's response to counseling. Haase and DiMattia (1976) studied room size and furniture arrangements to ascertain the degree to which these factors effected changes in the verbal behavior of the client. Their most significant finding was that room size does, in fact, affect the counseling process. In this particular investigation, a small room diminished the number of positive self-referent statements made by the client. In another study, Chaikin, Derlega and Miller (1976) found that client self-disclosure is significantly more intimate in a soft room environment than in a hard one. Client preference for seating arrangements was investigated by Brockmann and Moller (1973). They reported that subjects who were submissive and dependent tended to prefer greater distance between chairs; subjects who were dominant, self-assured, and independent preferred the closer seating arrangements.

Although these investigations lend support to the theory that the environment does affect the counseling interview, the counselor cannot always control environmental conditions. Some schools, for example, may not provide the counselor with an office, and interviews may have to be conducted wherever space is available.

In arranging an environment conducive to counseling, the privacy and sound-proofness of the room are possibly the most significant factors to consider (Sommers-Flanagan and Sommers-Flanagan, 1993). Counseling interviews can be anxiety producing; the clients should be able to discuss their concerns without fear that their personal self-disclosures will be heard by people walking by. Frequently, counselors prefer a casual environment as conducive to relaxation. Comfortable chairs, indirect lighting, and warm colors help develop a relaxed mood. Seating should be arranged so that the client is not threatened by the counselor's physical proximity. The counselor's freedom of movement toward the client is also important. Some counselors have found swivel chairs useful for keeping spatial distance directly under their control. Clients with high levels of anxiety may prefer the security of a desk between themselves and the counselor, but generally a desk is felt to be a barrier to communication.

The secretary plays a significant role in the counseling environment. Often the first person to greet the client, the secretary sets the tone and therefore should be a warm and friendly individual who relates well to others. The secretary needs to be hospitable, but should not assume the role of therapist by becoming emotionally involved in the clients' lives. Likewise, a secretary who has access to client records and files must understand that these are strictly confidential. The secretary can also ensure that the counselor is not interrupted during the session.

Intake Procedures

In private settings or community agencies the intake procedure includes clients filling out personal data sheets and often also taking a battery of psychological tests. In some settings an intake interview may be required. These interviews are conducted either by the counselor assigned to the case or by a paraprofessional who acts as an intake worker. Counselors in the public school setting may not follow formal intake procedures.

The purpose of the intake interview is to obtain a case history on the client. This case history is a collection of facts about the client's current and past life and may take many forms depending upon the style and preference of the counselor or therapist and the type of problem situation (Brammer and Shostrom, 1952). A career counselor, for example, would focus on factors influencing career choices; a psychoanalytically oriented therapist would want a detailed description of the client's early childhood experiences and affective development.

Confidentiality and Counselor Dependability

All that transpires in an interview is private, and counselors are obligated not to discuss client relationships with outside parties unless the client has given the counselor written permission to do so. The counseling relationship may be the only relationship in which the client can freely share the anxieties, fears, and feelings that have been harbored in many instances for a lifetime. As the client becomes confident that the counselor respects the privacy of the relationship, trust in the counselor grows. Because of the relationship between trust and confidentiality, counselors must respect at all times the client's right not to have information divulged to parties outside the relationship unless the client has given permission. The legal and ethical considerations involved here will be further explored in Chapter 14.

The dependability of the counselor affects the client's perception of trust in the relationship. As Benjamin has noted, it is more than a matter of courtesy for the counselor to meet scheduled appointments and to be on time. Counselors who are late or miss appointments can cause clients to wonder "whether we have forgotten him, whether he is of importance to us, whether we are keeping him waiting for some dark purpose unknown to him, whether we are being fair with him" (Benjamin, 1974, p. 16).

The Initial Counseling Interview

Counseling is a process that moves through predictable phases and stages. The process has a beginning, a middle, and an end, and counselors must be familiar with the appropriate procedures for opening the interview, for continuing the interview, and for terminating it.

How to Open the Session

After the client has been introduced to the counselor by name, the counselor may want to spend a few minutes in social conversation to relieve the tension and anxiety the client is probably experiencing; however, the counselor must be careful not to spend too much time in this fashion. Whether the client is self-referred or has been referred to counseling by another party will influence how the counselor opens the session. With a self-referred client, the counselor could begin the session by saying to the client any of the following: "We have about a half hour to talk and I'm wondering what brings you to counseling." We have an hour and I'd be interested in listening to anything you would like to share." "I thought we might begin today by your telling me about your expectations for counseling. We have an hour to talk." "How would you like to spend our time today? We have about forty-five minutes."

In the above examples, note that some structure is given in terms of time limits. Also, each statement communicates that the responsibility for the interview is the client's and that the client is to use the time in the most meaningful way.

Some clients come to counseling at the insistence of a third party. Teachers, parents, and the courts often require an individual to see a therapist for psychological counseling. Clients referred under such circumstances are frequently more anxious and resistant to the process. This situation requires careful thought and planning on the counselor's part. Regardless of the reason for the referral, the counselor must come across as warm and accepting. The counselor may want to discuss the reasons for the referral, but the client should not feel judged and the client should be allowed to choose the topic for the interview. Although the client may have been referred to the counselor for fighting on the school grounds, the client may need to discuss other personal concerns, such as the parents' divorce. Counselors must be careful not to allow their preconceived notions of the problems to interfere with their response to the client's immediate needs.

Structuring the Session

The counselor must give attention both to structuring the initial session and to establishing the long-term counseling relationship. Structuring the interview is essential because it clarifies for the client what can be expected of the counseling process. Clients frequently come to counseling with misconceptions. Some perceive counseling as a magical cure, as quick help, as problem solving or advice giving. Others often assume that the responsibility for success lies on the counselor's shoulders. These unrealistic expectations need to be clarified at the outset of the counseling process.

The counselor should open the first session by addressing the specific issues of client and counselor roles, client goals, and the confidentiality of the relationship. Such a statement should be as brief as possible. As noted above, the counselor could choose to begin by asking clients what brought them to counseling and what is expected of the process. After listening carefully to the client, the counselor reacts to the expectations expressed. Time permitting, the interview can then proceed with a topic of the client's choosing.

In this initial interview, the counselor must also deal with time limits as part of the structuring process. The length of the interview will vary, depending on the age of the client and the setting. An interview with a child between five and seven years old would be approximately twenty minutes long; between eight and twelve, approximately a half hour long; and for twelve and above, approximately an hour. Obviously, these are guidelines and cannot always be strictly adhered to. In the school setting, for example, the length of the interview will probably depend on the length of a class period.

The counselor should state at the beginning of the session how long the interview will be. This is important; clients need to understand how much time is available so that they can pace themselves accordingly and can bring up personally relevant material early enough in the session to allow discussion. Counselors who do not specify time limits frequently find that clients will hold on to a particularly painful concern until just before the end of the interview. This behavior can be very manipulative. To help prevent this situation, the counselor tells the client toward the end of the session how much time is left, giving the client an opportunity to raise any unfinished business before time runs out. A typical counselor statement might be, "John, we have about ten minutes left today; is there anything else you would like to discuss?" Clients are often so involved in their concern that they often lose track of the time and need a reminder from the counselor.

The duration of the counseling relationship can also be discussed in the initial interview, although the counselor will probably want one or two sessions with the client before estimating the duration. Most counseling will continue for at least a month and not longer than a year; the duration will depend on the severity of the problem and the effectiveness of the counseling.

Goals for the First Session

The initial counseling interview is in some ways the most important. The client begins to build trust in the counselor during this session, and many of the counselor's behaviors are being carefully scrutinized. The primary goal of the first session is establishing rapport. Eisenberg and Delaney have listed the following as appropriate process goals for the first session:

1. Stimulate open, honest, and full communication about the concerns needing to be discussed and the factors and background related to those concerns.

2. Work toward progressively deeper levels of understanding, respect, and trust between self and client.

3. Provide the client with the view that something useful can be gained from the counseling sessions.

4. Identify a problem or concern for subsequent attention and work.

5. Establish the "Gestalt" that counseling is a process in which both parties must work hard at exploring and understanding the client and his or her concerns.

6. Acquire information about the client that relates to his or her concerns and effective problem resolution. (1977, p. 75)

Termination of the Initial Interview

At the close of the initial counseling session, the client and counselor must make a decision regarding the continuation of their relationship. If the client and counselor both agree that another session is in order, then the next appointment must be scheduled. It should be reiterated that the client should be notified that the session is drawing to a close before the time period ends. The counselor may do this or may instruct the secretary to knock on the door or buzz the intercom at the appropriate time.

At the end of the initial interview, the counselor must decide whether or not to refer the client to another counselor or agency. The referral procedure requires some skill.

Referral Procedures

In many instances counselors cannot provide the counseling service needed by the client and must send the client elsewhere. Although referring a client may be viewed as a sign of inadequacy by some, a great deal of competency is needed to identify situations that require specialized services. It is unrealistic for counselors to assume that they can be of service to every person seeking assistance.

When to Refer

To make a good referral, the counselor must have information about the client and the nature of the client's concern. A brief interview may be conducted to gather this information, or as noted above, the referral can be made at the close of the initial interview.

It is appropriate to refer a client when

1. The client presents a concern that is beyond your level of competency.

2. You feel that personality differences between you and the client cannot be resolved and will interfere with the counseling process.

3. The client is a personal friend or relative, and the concern is going to require an ongoing relationship. Because of their basic skills in human relations, counselors are often the first persons sought out by friends and relatives in need of assistance, and it would be inhumane not to respond. However, it is difficult and in fact undesirable to maintain a counseling relationship over a period of time with a friend or relative. When it becomes obvious that the concern requires an ongoing therapeutic relationship, the individual should be referred to another counselor.

4. The client is reluctant to discuss problem with you for some reason.

5. After several sessions, you do not feel your relationship with the client is effective.

How to Refer

1. Rather than referring a client to an agency, whenever possible you should refer the client to a specific person in the agency. Become familiar with the services provided by local agencies and with the staff of each agency, so that you can match the client's needs with a specific counselor's competencies.

2. Provide the client with accurate and specific information, including the names, addresses, and phone numbers of the persons or agencies to whom you are referring him. The client may wish to place a call for an appointment from your office, but you should not make the appointment for the client. The client must assume responsibility for getting further help, and making the appointment reflects some commitment to the process.

3. Clients may ask you to share information about their concerns with the person to whom they have been referred. It is recommended that this information not be given in front of the client. Often this kind of contact relieves some of the client's anxiety about seeing a new counselor. It is preferable to get written permission from the client for this consultation.

4. Do not expect to be informed regarding the confidence shared by the client with the next counselor without the client's permission. If you continue to have a working relationship of a different nature with the client, you can request information regarding how to relate to the client in future interactions if such information is necessary.

5. Whenever possible, follow up the referral by checking with the client to see if the new relationship is satisfactorily meeting the client's needs. But avoid pressuring the client for information and accept whatever the client wishes to share.

Like the counseling process, referral procedures must be based on trust and respect for the individual seeking assistance. Counselors can only make clients aware of the alternatives that will provide the best means of assistance on the client's terms. The client may choose to ignore or accept the help available. The counselor's role is to create an awareness of the alternatives and to see that the client has the maximum opportunities to utilize them. Counselors should be aware of the legal issues surrounding the referral process and should be careful to take appropriate steps to prevent the possibility of legal action.

Counseling Skills

The following section will focus on specific counselor skills that are basic to the therapeutic process and are used by most counselors and therapists regardless of their particular theoretical orientation. We will define each skill, explore how it is performed, and attempt to assess the impact of the skill on the client.

Nonverbal Behavior

Mehrabian (1972) has stated that individuals are continuously transmitting information about themselves through their facial expressions, body movements, and proxemic behavior. In many ways, we cannot avoid communication. We send many messages about how we feel, what we think, and how we react to people and situations without uttering a word. Hence, nonverbal behavior plays a significant role in the communication process, and nonverbal channels are frequently less distorted (Haase, 1970; Hall, 1966).

The importance of nonverbal behavior in the counseling process has been acknowledged by counseling theorists and practitioners who assert that the complex interplay of verbal and nonverbal messages is an integral part of the counseling process. Counselors must be skillful at observing and responding to the nonverbal messages of clients, and they must be aware of the impact of their nonverbal behavior on the client during the counseling interview.

Modalities of Nonverbal Communication
This section will begin by examining nonverbal communication and its modalities in general terms, and then explore specific client and counselor nonverbal behavior and its impact on the counseling interview.

Gazda, Asbury, Balzer, Childers, and Walters (1984) have categorized nonverbal behaviors into four modalities, presented below as an aid in developing awareness and observation of nonverbal behaviors. It should be emphasized that nonverbal behaviors are highly idiosyncratic; interpretation of these clues must be tentative and based on the context in which they are sent.

1. NONVERBAL COMMUNICATION BEHAVIORS USING TIME
   Recognition
   Promptness or delay in recognizing the presence of another or in responding to his/her communication
   Priorities
   Amount of time another is willing to spend communicating with a person
   Relative amounts of time spent on various topics

2. NONVERBAL COMMUNICATION BEHAVIORS USING THE BODY
   Eye contact (important in regulating the relationship)
      Looking at a specific object
      Looking down
      Steady to helper
      Defiantly at helper ("hard" eyes), glaring
      Shifting eyes from object to object
      Looking at helper but looking away when looked at
      Covering eyes with hand(s)
      Frequency of looking at another
   Eyes
      "Sparkling"
      Tears
      "Wide-eyed"
      Position of eyelids
   Skin
      Pallor
      Perspiration
      Blushing
      "Goose bumps"
   Posture (often indicative of physical alertness or tiredness)
      "Eager," as if ready for activity
      Slouching, slovenly, tired looking, slumping
      Arms crossed in front as if to protect self
      Crossing legs
      Sit facing other person rather than sideways or away from
      Hanging head, looking at floor, head down
      Body positioned to exclude others from joining a group or dyad
   Facial expression (primary site for display of affects; thought by researchers
   to be subject to involuntary responses)
      No change
      Wrinkled forehead (lines of worry), frown
      Wrinkled nose
      Smiling, laughing
      ``Sad" mouth
      Biting lip
   Hand and arm gestures
      Symbolic hand and arm gestures
      Literal hand and arm gestures to indicate size or shape
      Demonstration of how something happened or how to do something
   Self-inflicting behaviors
      Nail biting
      Scratching
      Cracking knuckles

Tugging at hair
Rubbing or stroking
Repetitive behaviors (often interpreted as signs of nervousness or restlessness but may be organic in origin)
Tapping foot, drumming or thumping with fingers
Fidgeting, squirming
Trembling
Playing with button, hair, or clothing
Signals or commands
Snapping fingers
Holding finger to lips for silence
Pointing
Staring directly to indicate disapproval
Shrugging shoulders
Waving
Nodding in recognition
Winking
Nodding in agreement, shaking head in disagreement
Touching
To get attention, such as tapping on shoulder
Affectionate, tender
Sexual
Challenging, such as poking finger into chest
Symbols of camaraderie, such as slapping on back
Belittling, such as a pat on top of head
3. NONVERBAL COMMUNICATION BEHAVIORS USING VOCAL MEDIA
Tone of voice
Flat, monotone, absence of feelings
Bright, vivid changes of inflection
Strong, confident, firm
Weak, hesitant, shaky
Broken, faltering
Rate of speech
Fast
Medium
Slow
Loudness of voice
Loud
Medium
Soft
Diction
Precise versus careless
Regional (colloquial) differences
Consistency of diction

4. NONVERBAL COMMUNICATION BEHAVIORS USING THE ENVIRON-
MENT
   Distance
      Moves away when the other moves toward
      Moves toward when the other moves away
      Takes initiative in moving toward or away from
      Distance widens gradually
      Distance narrows gradually
   Arrangement of the physical setting
      Neat, well-ordered, organized
      Untidy, haphazard, careless
      Casual versus formal
      Warm versus cold colors
      Soft versus hard materials
      Slick versus varied textures
      Cheerful and lively versus dull and drab
      Discriminating" taste versus tawdry
      Expensive or luxurious versus shabby or spartan
   Clothing (often used to tell others what a person wants them to believe about
   him/her)
      Bold versus unobtrusive
      Stylish versus nondescript
   Position in the room
      Protects or fortifies self in position by having objects such as desk or table
         between self and other person.
      Takes an open or vulnerable position such as in the center of the room, side
         by side on a sofa, or in a simple chair. Nothing between self and other
         person.
      Takes an attacking or dominating position. May block exit from area or may
         maneuver other person into boxed-in position.
      Moves about the room.
      Moves in and out of other person's territory.
      Stands when other people sit, or gets in higher position than other person.
                                              (Gazda, et al., 1984, pp. 62–66)*

Interpretation of Nonverbal Behavior
As Gazda and his associates (1984) have noted, nonverbal behaviors must be
viewed simply as clues to the individual's underlying feelings and motives rather
than as proof of them. The counselor must interpret nonverbal messages tentatively and must realize that a given behavior may have opposite meanings for two
individuals or even for the same person on two different occasions (Gazda, et al.,

*From George M. Gazda et al., *Human Relations Development: A Manual for Educators,* 3rd ed. Copyright
© 1984 by Allyn and Bacon, Inc., Boston. Reprinted by permission.

1984). The meaning of nonverbal behaviors also varies among societies and cultures, and counselors should be sensitive to these differences.

The client's nonverbal behavior within the counseling interview is obviously important. It provides the counselor with additional information about the client's thoughts and feelings. Often an individual will communicate one message verbally and an entirely different message through voice tone, facial expression, or body posture. Such an interaction might sound like this:

Counselor: "How are you feeling today?"

Client: "Oh, fine. Everything's just fine."

Counselor: "You didn't look as though you felt good as you walked into the office. You were holding your head down and staring at the floor and now you seem to be avoiding my eye contact."

Client: "Well, I guess it's difficult for me to talk about how depressed I feel."

A common goal of the counseling process is to help the client openly express emotion (Loesch 1975); therefore, the counselor must be sensitive to nonverbal cues and, as illustrated in the above example, skillful at responding to discrepancies between the client's underlying feelings and verbal expressions of those feelings. Counselors' ability to be empathic is directly related to their ability to observe and respond to nonverbal communication.

In many instances it is sufficient for the counselor to bring the client's attention to the nonverbal behavior. For example:

Counselor: "Are you aware that you break out in a rash each time we discuss your relationship with your husband?"

Client: "I suppose I just get terribly anxious when we discuss my marriage because I feel guilty that I have been wanting a relationship with another man."

By bringing the nonverbal behavior to the client's awareness, the counselor encouraged the client to share more important and personally relevant unspoken feelings.

Frequently the ability to observe nonverbal behavior, and to respond on some level to the message being sent, enables the counselor to project an unusual warmth, sensitivity, and perceptiveness that enhances the intimacy of the relationship. Responding to a client's frown before the concern has been verbalized makes the client feel that the counselor is tuned in at a level that perhaps the client is not yet aware of experiencing. This type of interaction is possibly the source of the idea that counselors have a sixth sense and an almost mystical perceptiveness.

Counselor Nonverbal Behavior

The nonverbal behavior of the counselor also communicates unspoken feelings and thus has an impact on the client's perception of the relationship.

Attending Behaviors

The nonverbal behaviors of counselors that have received the most attention in the literature are referred to as physical attending behaviors. The physical presence of the counselor helps communicate to the client that the counselor is involved in what the client is sharing. The concept of physical attending may seem basic, yet in daily interactions we often fail to exhibit or experience basic attending.

How many times has someone said to you,

> *"You're not even listening to what I'm saying!" Or someone reads a magazine while you are talking to him, or it becomes obvious that the person at the other end of the telephone conversation is eating lunch, reading, or engaging in some clandestine activity that prevents him from giving his complete attention to you. (Egan, 1975, p. 61)**

These examples from daily interactions illustrate that, simple though the principles of basic attending are, we frequently find it difficult to apply them.

Among the physical attending behaviors, Egan (1986) lists eye contact, adopting an open posture, facing the person squarely, leaning slightly forward, and assuming a natural and relaxed position.

Eye Contact.   It is important that the counselor maintain good eye contact with the client. This does not imply that the eye contact should be uninterrupted. Rather, it should be as natural as possible.

Adopting an Open Posture.   As discussed previously, nonverbal behaviors are idiosyncratic. The same behavior by an individual can mean different things at different times. Crossed legs and arms are generally interpreted as signs of withdrawal. Although such an interpretation may not always be valid, the counselor should avoid communicating a lack of involvement through crossed leg and arm positions.

Facing the Person Squarely.   The physical environment should allow counselor and client to face each other without a table or desk between them. A posture directly facing the client promotes involvement.

Leaning Slightly Forward.   Physical proximity to the client is an important indicator of involvement. Some counselors begin an interview leaning back on their chairs, then lean forward as the level of interaction becomes more intense.

Assuming a Natural and Relaxed Position.   Since many clients are anxious as they enter a counseling session, it is important that the counselor act as normal and relaxed as possible. As the counselor becomes more and more comfortable with

---

*From *The Skilled Helper: A Model for Systematic Helping and Interpersonal Relating* by G. Egan. Copyright © 1975 by Wadsworth. Reprinted by permission of the publisher, Brooks/Cole, Monterey, Calif.

the basic attending posture, it will seem more natural without losing the sense of involvement.

Basic Communication Skills

Open-Ended Leads

An open-ended lead essentially says to the client, "Tell me about it." Unlike a closed question, the open-ended lead requires more than a yes or no; typically, it opens the door to a discussion of feelings rather than facts. Some examples of open and closed questions are as follows:

Open "Where would you like to begin today?"
        "How are you feeling about that?"
        "What kinds of things make you feel sad?"

Closed: "What time did you leave the room?"
          "Where did you go after that?"
          "Which way did you go?"
          "How many times did that happen?"

Open-ended leads encourage clients to share their concerns with the counselor. They place the responsibility for the interview on the client and allow the client to explore attitudes, feelings, values, and behaviors without being forced into the counselor's frame of reference. Closed questions, by comparison, elicit factual information that rarely has actual relevance to the client's concern and are asked out of the counselor's curiosity (Ivey and Simek-Downing, 1980).

Ivey (1971) has noted that open-ended leads can be used in several different counseling situations.

1. They help begin an interview.
   (What would you like to talk about today? How have things been since the last time we talked together?)
2. They help get the interviewee to elaborate on a point.
   (Could you tell me more about that? How did you feel when that happened?)
3. They help elicit examples of specific behavior so that the interviewer is better able to understand what the interviewee is describing.
   (Will you give me a specific example? What do you do when you get "depressed"? What do you mean when you say your father is out of his mind?)
4. They help focus the client's attention on his feelings.
   (What are you feeling as you're telling me this? How did you feel then?)
   (p. 151–152)

Despite the value of good, open questions in the counseling process, most beginning counselor trainees rely too heavily on questions simply because they have not mastered other, more productive responses. Excessive reliance on questions may lead to the following problems: (1) the interview digresses to a question-and-answer interrogation in which the client waits for the counselor to come up with the next topic; (2) the responsibility for the interview and the material to be discussed reverts to the counselor; (3) the discussion moves from affectively oriented topics to cognitively oriented topics; and (4) the interview loses a sense of flow and movement. For these reasons beginning counseling trainees are often instructed to avoid questions except as a way to open the counseling session.

Silence or Passive Listening

Possibly the most basic of all skills is using silence within the counseling interview. Clients need opportunities to explore their feelings, attitudes, values, and behaviors; initially they need someone to listen, even passively, to what they wish to share. New counselors are typically uncomfortable with time lapses during the interview, but if the counselor can become sensitive to the various meanings of silence and skillful at handling these pauses, these silences can prove very useful. First, silence lets clients know that the responsibility for the interview lies on their shoulders. Too often counselors rush in to fill up the space, thus assuming inappropriate responsibility for the session. Second, silence allows clients to delve further into thoughts and feelings and to ponder the implications of what has transpired during the session. Clients need this time to reflect and process without feeling pressured to verbalize every thought and feeling.

As Brammer and Shostrom (1982) have noted, silence during the interview can have other meanings. It can mean that the client feels uncomfortable and is anxious or embarrassed at having been sent to the counselor. It may also indicate client resistance to the process. In this instance the client may attempt to use it to manipulate the counselor. Silence can mean that the counselor and client have reached an impasse in the session and both are searching for direction. In each of these instances the question raised is whether or not the counselor should interrupt the pause. Counselors must learn to trust their own feelings in particular situations, which requires great sensitivity to the client's nonverbal communication. Often the most appropriate response a counselor can make to client-initiated silence is an accurate empathic statement such as, "You look very thoughtful; would you like to share what you're feeling?" or "You seem pretty quiet, and I'm wondering if you really are angry that you are here." As a rule of thumb it is wise to let the client assume responsibility for breaking the silence when the silence is client-initiated.

In summary, the therapeutic value of silence cannot be overstated. Silence communicates to the client a sincere and deep acceptance. It demonstrates the counselor's deep concern and willingness to let the client experience the relationship without sensing pressure to be verbal. Rogers has cited an excellent example of the therapeutic value of silence:

> I have just completed the strangest counseling case I've ever had. I think you might be interested in it.
> Joan was one of my very first clients when I started counseling one half-day each week at the local high school. She told the girls' adviser, "I feel so shy I couldn't even tell her what my problem is. Will you tell her for me?" So the ad-

viser told me before I saw Joan that she worried about having no friends. The adviser added that she had noticed that Joan seemed always to be so alone.

The first time I saw Joan she talked a little about her problem and quite a bit about her parents, of whom she seemed to be quite fond. There were, however, long pauses. The next four interviews could be recorded verbatim on this small piece of paper. By the middle of November Joan remarked that "things are going pretty good." No elaboration on that. Meanwhile, the adviser commented that the teachers had noticed that Joan was now smiling a friendly greeting when they met her in the halls. This was unheard of before. However, the adviser had seen little of Joan and could say nothing of her contacts with other students. In December there was one interview during which Joan talked freely; the others were characterized by silence while she sat, apparently in deep thought, occasionally looking up with a grin. More silence through the next two and one-half months. Then I received word that she had been elected "woman of the month" by the girls of the high school! The basis for that election is always sportsmanship and popularity with other girls. At the same time I got a message from Joan, "I don't think I need to see you any more." No, apparently she doesn't, but why? What happened in those hours of silence? My faith in the capacity of the client was sorely tested. I'm glad it did not waver. (1951, pp. 158–159)*

This example demonstrates Rogers's unfailing trust in clients' ability to help themselves if the therapeutic relationship is available.

Listening

The process of tuning in carefully to the client's messages and responding accurately to the meaning behind the message has been referred to simply as listening. Yet this type of listening moves a social conversation to different levels of communication, and it is the core of effective counseling. Listening at its simplest level calls on the counselor to feed back the content and feelings that the client has expressed. On another level, listening requires that the counselor decode the client's message. This decoding process is necessary because human communication is often indirect. When we speak, we have a tendency to encode our messages rather than communicating clearly and directly what we are thinking and feeling. This process is illustrated in Figure 8-1.

Listening, then, is a synthesis of the skills of restatement of content and reflection of feeling. It promotes within the client the feeling of being understood. It must be emphasized, however, that listening, as critical as it is to the counseling process, is not sufficient to produce the desired client growth and change. It must be implemented in conjunction with other counseling skills, described in detail in Chapter 9.

Rogers has spoken of the therapeutic value of listening in many of his writings. In the following excerpt Rogers describes the impact of being listened to.

---

*From *Client-Centered Therapy* by Carl R. Rogers. Copyright © 1951, renewed 1979 by Houghton Mifflin Co. Reprinted by permission.

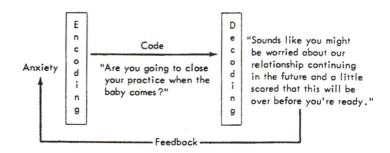

FIGURE 8-1   Process of decoding

A number of times in my life I have felt myself bursting with insoluble problems, or going round and round in tormented circles or, during one period, overcome by feelings of worthlessness and despair, sure I was sinking into psychosis. I think I have been more lucky than most in finding at these times individuals who have been able to hear me and thus to rescue me from the chaos of my feelings. I have been fortunate in finding individuals who have been able to hear my meanings a little more deeply than I have known them. These individuals have heard me without judging me, diagnosing me, appraising me, evaluating me. They have just listened and clarified and responded to me at all the levels at which I was communicating. I can testify that when you are in psychological distress and someone really hears you without passing judgment on you, without trying to take responsibility for you, without trying to mold you, it feels damn good. At these times, it has relaxed the tension in me. It has permitted me to bring out the frightening feelings, the guilts, the despair, the confusions that have been a part of my experience. When I have been listened to and when I have been heard, I am able to reperceive my world in a new way and to go on. It is amazing that feelings which were completely awful become bearable when someone listens. It is astonishing how elements which seem insoluble become soluble when someone hears, how confusions which seem irremediable turn into relatively clear flowing streams when one is understood. I have deeply appreciated the times that I have experienced this sensitivity, [and] empathic, concentrated listening. (1969, pp. 225–226)

As is evident from the above description, this kind of listening differs dramatically from the type of social interaction that typifies most of our daily experiences. Listening in on social conversations reveals that people rarely take the time or energy to be genuinely and sensitively involved in what someone else is sharing. Rather, they pretend to listen long enough to gain the floor so that they have the opportunity to share what is of importance to them. Perhaps this explains why listening, as described above, has such a powerful impact on clients— they rarely experience someone who is genuinely interested in understanding their world.

Restatement of Content

The ability to restate the content of the client's message or to paraphrase a client's statement is a beginning in the process of learning to listen. In restating the content of the client's message, the counselor feeds back to the client the content of the statement using different words. Restatement of content serves three purposes:

> *(a) to convey to the client that you are with him, that you are trying to understand what he is saying; (b) to crystallize a client's comments by repeating what he has said in a more concise manner; (c) to check the interviewer's own perception to make sure she/he really does understand what the client is describing. (Ivey, 1971, p. 156)*

In paraphrasing a client's statement, the counselor may respond to a feeling, but the focus of the restatement is on content. Some examples of paraphrasing are as follows:

Client: "I am so sick of school I can hardly get up in the morning to go to class."

Counselor: "You've just about reached your limits as far as school is concerned."

Client: "I don't know what to do with my life. Sometimes I think I should just go out and get a job for the experience, and then again sometimes I think I should just go on to graduate school, but I'm not sure what to major in."

Counselor: "You're struggling with a big decision about where to go from here with your life, and you're not sure which of the two choices makes the most sense."

In each of the above examples, the counselor responds to the content of the client's statement by paraphrasing the message in different words.

Paraphrasing is appropriate at the beginning of a counseling interview because it encourages the client to open up and elaborate upon the concern. However, paraphrasing does not lead to in-depth exploration and can result in circular discussion if the counselor does not bring in other skills as the interview proceeds.

Reflection of Feeling

The basic difference between restatement of content and reflection of feeling is one of emphasis. In reflecting a client's feeling, the counselor listens carefully to the client's statement and responds by paraphrasing the content of the message, but places the emphasis on the feeling the client expressed. By responding to the client's feelings, the counselor is attempting to perceive and understand the client accurately from the client's internal frame of reference. The counselor tries to identify the feeling accurately by listening not only to what the client says but also to how the client says it. Some examples:

Client: "I was happy to hear I've been selected for a scholarship to the university I want to attend."

Counselor: "What a thrill for you. You must be very excited and proud to know that you were selected for such an honor."

Client: "My mom and dad fight constantly. I never know what to expect when dad comes home from work."

Counselor: "It must be pretty scary for you to live with such uncertainty.

In both instances, the counselor's response reflects the basic feeling state of the client and thus communicates to the client the counselor's acceptance of her world.

Summarization of Content

Summarization enables the counselor to condense and crystallize the essence of the client's statements. It can further client exploration and can also serve as a perception check for the counselor. The summary of content differs from paraphrasing in that the summary typically responds to a greater amount of material. A paraphrase normally responds to the client's preceding statement; a summary can cover an entire phase of the session or even a total interview (Ivey, 1971).

Ivey has noted that a summarization of content is most frequently used in the following situations:

1. When the interviewer wishes to structure the beginning of a session by recalling the high points of a previous interview.
2. When the interviewee's presentation of a topic has been either very confusing or just plain lengthy and rambling.
3. When an interviewee has seemingly expressed everything of importance to him on a particular topic.
4. When plans for the next steps to be taken require mutual assessment and agreement on what has been learned so far.
5. When, at the end of a session, the interviewer wishes to emphasize what has been learned within it, perhaps in order to give an assignment for the interval until the next session. (1971, p. 159)

Summarization of Feeling

In a summarization of feeling the counselor attempts to identify and respond to the overriding feelings of the client, not only the expressed feelings but also the general feeling tone of the phase of the interview being summarized. Summarizing a client's feelings forces the counselor to synthesize the emotional aspects of the client's experience; as such it requires that the counselor respond in a deep and perceptive way to the emotional component of the client's experience (Ivey, 1971).

Ivey has suggested that the counselor:

1. Use reflections of feeling to indicate to the client that you are with him. Selective attention to feelings will assist him in exploring his emotional states.
2. Note consistent patterns of emotion as he (she) progresses through the interview. Also note his inconsistencies or polarities of feelings. Most clients have mixed feelings toward important love objects or situations and showing the client' how he has expressed his mixed feelings may be especially valuable to him.

3. At two or three points during the session and at the close of the session restate in your own words the feelings and perceptions that the client has been communicating. (1971, p. 158)

Summary

In this chapter we have explored the practical considerations involved in conducting a counseling interview and have discussed some basic skills that can facilitate initial communication.

Counselors should give special attention to the counseling environment. Room size, seating arrangements, privacy, lighting, and decor all have been found to have some impact on the counseling process and seem to affect the establishment of rapport.

The confidentiality of the counseling relationship enhances the growth of trust between counselor and client. Counselors should communicate in specific terms any circumstances under which a client disclosure will be shared with other parties.

The counseling process moves through somewhat predictable stages or phases. There are procedures and skills appropriate for each of the phases. Thus, counselors must be prepared to open the interview and establish rapport; to structure the session with reference to counselor and client roles, client goals confidentiality and time factors; to terminate the session; and to refer clients to other counselors or agencies when appropriate.

Nonverbal behavior plays an important role in the communication process. Counselors must be sensitive to the client's nonverbal behavior and must be aware of the impact of their nonverbal behavior on the client.

The counselor's primary goal during the initial stage of counseling is to establish rapport with the client. The development of the therapeutic climate will depend primarily on the personality of the therapist and the extent to which the core conditions are communicated; however, basic skills such as attending behaviors, open-ended leads, silence, listening, and summarization facilitate the initial stages of the process.

References

Benjamin, A. (1974). *The helping interview* (2nd ed.). Boston: Houghton Mifflin.

Brammer, L., & Shostrom, E. (1982). *Therapeutic psychology, Fundamentals of counseling and psychotherapy* (4th ed). Englewood Cliffs, N.J.: Prentice-Hall.

Brockmann, N.C., & Moller, A.T. (1973). Preferred seating position and distance in various situations. *Journal of Counseling Psychology, 20,* (6), 504–508

Chaikin, A.L., Derlega, V.J., & Miller, S.J. (1976). Effects of room environment on self-disclosure in a counseling analogue. *Journal of Counseling Psychology, 23,* (5), 479–481.

Egan, G. (1975). *The skilled helper: A model for systematic helping and interpersonal relating.* Monterey, Calif.: Brooks/Cole.

Egan, G. (1986). *The skilled helper: A systematic approach to effective helping* (3rd ed.). Monterey Calif. Brooks/Cole.

Eisenberg, D., & Delaney, S. (1977). *The counseling process.* Chicago: Rand McNally.

Gazda, G M., Asbury, F. R., Balzer, F. J., Childers, W. C., & Walters, R. P. (1984). *Human relations development: A manual for educators.* 3rd ed. Boston: Allyn and Bacon.

Haase, R.F. (1970). The relationship of sex and instructional set to the regulation of interpersonal interaction distance in a counseling analogue. *Journal of Counseling Psychology, 17,* 233–236.

Haase, R.F., & DiMattia, D.J. (1976). Spatial environments and verbal conditioning in quasi-counseling interview. *Journal of Counseling Psychology, 23,* (5), 414–421.

Hall, E.T. (1966). *The hidden dimension.* New York: Doubleday.

Ivey, A. (1971). *Microcounseling: Innovations in interviewing training.* Springfield, Ill.: Chas C. Thomas.

Loesch, L.C. (1975). Non-verbalized feelings and perceptions of the counseling relationship. *Counselor Education and Supervision, 15,* (2), 105–113.

Mehrabian, A. (1972). *Non-verbal communication.* Chicago: Aldine

Rogers, C. R. (1951). *Client-centered therapy.* Boston: Houghton Mifflin.

Rogers, C. R. (1969). *Freedom to learn.* Columbus, Ohio: Merrill.

Sommers-Flanagan, J. & Sommers-Flanagan, R. (1993). Boston: Allyn and Bacon.

Chapter 9

Counseling Procedures/Skills: II

Once the counseling process has begun and the therapeutic climate has been established, the counselor's task is to facilitate client self-exploration and to increase the level of client self-understanding so that effective and desired changes in behavior can occur. The counselor must employ more advanced skills to help clients reach this level of self-exploration and self-understanding. Such skills include advanced empathy, theme identification, self-disclosure, perception checks, interpretation, clarification, confrontation, and immediacy; they are discussed in this chapter. While these advanced skills will facilitate action in terms of behavior change in some clients, it is necessary for counselors to be prepared to implement action programs in the advanced stages of the counseling process with those clients who need specific help. This chapter will briefly explore the issue of facilitating action to achieve behavior change.

Advanced Empathy

The relationship of empathy to the helping process was discussed at some length in Chapter 7. Empathy was defined as the ability to tune in to the client's feelings and to be able to see the client's world as it truly seems to the client. Empathy, then, can be viewed as a skill as well as an attitude, and it can be employed at different levels. At its primary level, an empathic response communicates an understanding of the client's frame of reference and accurately identifies the client's feelings. In contrast, advanced empathy takes the client a step further into self-exploration by adding deeper feeling and meaning to the client's expression. Egan has illustrated the difference between primary and advanced accurate empathy in the following example:

Client: "I don't know what's going on. I study hard, but I just don't get good marks. I think I study as hard as anyone else, but all of my efforts seem to go down the drain. I don't know what else I can do."

Counselor A: "You feel frustrated because even when you try hard, you fail."

Counselor B: "It's depressing to put in as much effort as those who pass and still fail. It gets you down and maybe even makes you feel a little sorry for yourself."

> *Counselor A tries to understand the client from the client's frame of reference. He deals with the client's feelings and the experience underlying these feelings. Counselor B, however, probes a bit further. From the context, from past interchanges, from the client's manner and tone of voice, he picks up something that the client does not express overtly, that the client feels sorry for himself. The client is looking at himself as a victim, as the one who has failed, as the one who is depressed. This is "his" frame of reference, but in reality he is also beginning to say, "Poor me, I feel sorry for myself." This is a "different" perspective, but one that is also based on the data of the self-exploration process. (1975, p. 135)*

In the above example, the advanced empathy of counselor B takes the client to a new level of self-understanding. Because this counselor sees the situation from the client's perspective, but sees it more clearly and more fully, he can share the implications of the client's perspective for effective or ineffective living (Egan, 1975).

Theme Identification

The advanced empathic response also helps the counselor identify themes in the counseling session. Typically, clients express a variety of concerns during a session. At the outset these concerns may seem unrelated. The counselor who listens carefully and with a trained ear can begin to hear the relationship among various incidents, situations, problems, and feelings. For example, a client may bring up a concern such as his wife making most of the household decisions and then may express a concern that he doesn't feel very competent at work. As the session develops, the counselor may respond with the following statement: "It sounds to me like your inability to make decisions is beginning to have an impact on how you see yourself both at home and at the office."

Themes that might arise in a counseling situation could include the following:

The client's self-concept—a poor self-image
The client as a dependent person
The client's need for approval
The client's need to be loved and accepted by everyone
The client's lack of assertiveness
The client's need for control
The client's rebellion against authority
The client's insecurity with women (men)
The client's manipulative nature
The client's need for security
The client's inability to experience feelings in the here and now

As Egan (1975) has noted, by identifying themes the counselor takes clients beyond their expressed concerns and facilitates the self-exploration process by helping clients confront their interpersonal style. A counseling session may consist of several themes, but the central theme underlying the client's interpersonal style will be repeated throughout the interview. Often a theme will be signaled by what might be called a "red-flag" a word or phrase that stands out from the rest either through the voice tone used or the significance the word or phrase seems to have in the context of the discussion. Themes that are repeated throughout the session appear and reappear like a red thread woven into a cloth.

Consider the client who begins the session complaining about her teacher who caught her cheating, and progresses to talking of her difficulty relating to her fa-

*ther, and ends by complaining about how you confront her about the inconsisten-
cies she has stated. The red thread is the client's difficulty relating to authority figures in her world. (Pietrofesa, et al., 1978, pp. 289–290)*

This example illustrates the importance of theme identification in helping clients
come to new awareness regarding their interpersonal style. In this sense the identification of a central theme communicates an understanding of the client's frame
of reference beyond the present level of self-awareness and thus is related to the
advanced accurate empathic response.

A helpful description of how to make an advanced accurate empathic response is given by Means (1973).

Self-Disclosure

Self-disclosure involves revealing your feelings and reactions to events and people
as they occur. Within the counseling relationship, counselors may choose to reveal
themselves to the client to facilitate clients' openness. In one method of self-disclosure, the counselor might use immediacy to share reactions to the client or to
their relationship openly in the here and now. In another method the counselor
might respond to a client statement that is closely related to the counselor's own
experience by sharing the similar experience in feeling terms. This, however, can
be difficult, for two reasons: first, the counselor's experience must in fact closely resemble that of the client; and second, the counselor must make the self-disclosure
long enough to draw the similarity and brief enough so as not to take the focus of
the session off the client.

Self-disclosure, when properly implemented, can promote a client's feeling of
being understood. It can also enable the counselor to identify client feelings at a
deeper level than might otherwise be achieved. In this respect, self-disclosure can
facilitate an advanced empathic response. The following example illustrates how
this skill might be used in the counseling session:

Client: "I'm having difficulty with my father. He's getting older and he's very
lonely. He comes over and stays all day and I feel like I have to entertain him. I get
behind on all of my chores and my children are neglected. I want to be helpful to
him, but it's becoming more and more difficult."

Counselor: "I think I can understand how angry and resentful and yet guilty you
must feel. My mother-in-law is widowed and is lonely and bored. She keeps showing up at the most inconvenient times and stays for hours. I can hardly be pleasant
anymore, and I feel guilty for being so selfish."

In this statement the counselor bridges the gap between herself and the client first
by letting the client know something about her personal life and second by communicating an accepting and understanding attitude toward the client's guilt. In

essence, such a self-disclosure communicates to the client that the counselor is a real person with problems and concerns too.

Timing is very important in the success of self-disclosure. It cannot be overemphasized that the self-disclosure must be brief so as not to take the focus off the client.

Several investigators have examined the impact of counselor self-disclosure on the client. Studies by Jourard (1971), Powell (1968), and Truax and Carkhuff (1965) lend supporting evidence to the contention that therapist disclosures can facilitate client self-disclosures (Simonson, 1976).

Giannandrea and Murphy (1973) conducted an investigation using college males as subjects. They found that when the counselor employed an intermediate number of self-disclosures, significantly more students returned for a second interview than when the counselor used fewer or more self-disclosures. Thus, they surmised that an intermediate number of self-disclosures may increase the counselor's attractiveness as well as encourage the client to respond to the counselor.

Jourard and Jaffee (1970) found that when counselors increased the length of their self-disclosures before discussing a topic, the client responded with lengthier self-disclosures.

Drag (1969) found that counselors who themselves use self-disclosure elicit more self-disclosures from their clients and are also perceived as more trustworthy.

Perception Check

Counselor statements made in response to a client's feelings should be stated tentatively. Counselors must avoid coming across in an "I *know* how you feel" manner that will alienate the client. One alternative is, "I think I understand how you feel." Another alternative is for the counselor to use a perception check, which is an interpretation of the other's feelings stated in a tentative form. A perception check communicates to the client the counselor's interest in understanding exactly what the client is experiencing, especially when the client may not be expressing feelings directly. A counselor could check his or her perception with a tentative statement: "You seem to be really irritated with me for being late," or "Peggy, you seem rather removed from the discussion today, and I'm not sure if you're feeling bored or just tired." Still another example might be, "Diane, if I were you I might be feeling hurt that my feelings were not responded to. Is that what you're experiencing?"

Interpretation

Interpretive statements cover a broad range of counselor responses; their purpose is to add meaning to client's attitudes, feelings, and behavior. Interpretive responses draw causal relationships among these three areas. Because interpretations are a process of imposing meaning on behaviors, the interpretation will vary depending on one's theoretical orientation (Brammer and Shostrom, 1982).

Timing is important in making interpretive responses. In the early stages of the relationship, the counselor typically stays with the client and responds to the client's concerns from the client's frame of reference. As the relationship progresses, the counselor gains increasingly greater insight into the client's dynamics and is more able to suggest or infer relationships, perceive patterns of behavior and motives, and help the client integrate these understandings. It is of utmost importance that the client is at a point of readiness that will allow the counselor's response to facilitate growth and behavior change. If inappropriately timed, an interpretive response can cause the client to become defensive and resist the process. Because of the nature of the interpretive response, it should always be phrased tentatively, allowing the client to reject the comment if it is inaccurate or if the client is not ready to hear it.

How the counselor uses interpretive techniques will depend on his or her theoretical orientation. Traditionally, client-centered counselors have cautioned against the use of interpretive responses (Rogers, 1942). However, the classic client-centered technique, reflection of feeling, can be viewed as an interpretation.

Below we discuss three interpretive techniques: clarification, confrontation, and immediacy.

Clarification

In clarification, the counselor's response attempts to make a client's verbalization clearer to both the counselor and the client. A clarification can focus on cognitive information, or it can seek to highlight client meanings that are not initially clear. Clarification is related to both skill of interpretation and the core condition of concreteness. Some examples of clarification are: "I'm not sure if you got into a fight before or after you got to the school playground"; "Are you feeling angry or resentful?" and "Is the issue whether or not you can afford to quit your job or are you concerned about how others might respond to your unemployment?"

Confrontation

Confrontation holds the potential for promoting growth and change or for devastating the client. Because it is so powerful, counselors must implement a confrontive response with great skill. Here we will examine the various uses of confrontation, some guidelines in practicing the skill, and some cautions.

Confronting another's behavior is a delicate procedure requiring both a sense of timing and a sensitivity and awareness of the client's receptivity. When properly done, confrontation can help clients become more integrated and consistent in their behavior and in their relationships with others. A confrontive response should only be made in the context of trust and caring for the client and should not be used as a means of venting anger and frustration.

A confrontation may take several forms. It can be used to point to discrepancies

> between what we think and feel, and what we say and what we do, our views of ourselves and others' views of us, what we are and what we wish to be, what we really are and what we experience ourselves to be, our verbal and nonverbal expressions of ourselves. (Egan, 1975, pp. 159–161)

Some specific examples of these discrepancies adapted from Egan would be the following:

> "I'm depressed and lonely, but I say that everything's okay."
> "I believe that people need to make their own decisions, but I constantly give my children advice about their lives."
> "I see myself as witty and others perceive me to be sarcastic."
> "I would like to be a good student, but I'm a slow learner, yet I party every night and don't study."
> "I experience myself as overweight when in fact others see me as having a good build."
> "I say 'yes' with my behavior and dress, and yet hold others at a distance and am fearful of physical intimacy."
> "I say that I want to listen and be helpful to others, but I consistently dominate conversations."

Confrontation can also be used to help clients see things as they are rather than perceiving situations on the basis of their needs. In other words, counselors can help clients attain an alternative frame of reference, enabling them to clear up distortions in experience. An example of a distorted perception would be, "My husband has taken a job that requires him to travel because he doesn't love me." In a marriage counseling situation, the counselor could confront this message by responding to observations that indicate that the husband does love her, but that their financial situation requires that he take this better paying position, although it will require him to be away from home.

Still another use of confrontation is to help clients understand when they may be evading issues or ignoring feedback from others. When a client is evading an issue, the counselor might confront him with a statement such as this: "We've been meeting for two sessions, and you haven't raised the one issue you mentioned as a major concern—your sexual relationship with your wife. Every time we get close to the topic, you change the subject. I'm wondering what's going on."

When a client is ignoring feedback, the counselor might say: "I heard Joan saying that she has difficulty feeling close to you because you speak so cognitively about your experience, yet I haven't heard you even acknowledge her comment. What is your reaction to her statement?"

Because the question of when to confront so often arises, the following guidelines are offered: Confront when

1. You are willing to become more involved with the client.
2. The relationship has been built and the client's level of trust in you is high.
3. The confrontation can be done out of a genuine caring for the client's growth and change. Confrontation should not be used as a way to meet the counselor's needs.

Little research has been done on confrontation. Kaul, Kaul, and Bednar (1973) examined the relationship between client self-exploration and counselor confrontation. They found that confrontive counselors did not elicit more client self-exploration than speculative counselors, whether judged by raters or clients. When Berenson and Mitchell (1974) investigated confrontation they found it to be useful and concluded that confrontations help clients to see and experience problems rather than just understanding them. The research on confrontation is rather inconclusive, and it is recommended that confrontation be used discreetly and with care rather than as a *modus operandi.*

Immediacy

Of the myriad difficulties clients bring to counselors, most involve interpersonal relationships. The counselor-client relationship mirrors the client's behavior in the outside world, which makes it an ideal situation in which to explore the client's interpersonal skills. If counselors can be sensitive to the dynamics of their relationships with clients, they can help their clients explore interpersonal issues ranging from trust and dependency to manipulation. The skill of immediacy involves counselors' being sensitively tuned in to their interactions with and reactions to clients as they occur. They can respond to these feelings about either the client or the relationship in the here and now. Immediacy is closely related to the skills of self-disclosure and confrontation, as well as to counselor genuineness.

Immediacy requires that counselors trust their gut-level reactions and that they respect the client. The following example may help to illustrate this point.

Counselor: "I'm having difficulty staying tuned in today. It seems that we're rehashing old stuff, and I suppose that I'm getting tired of hearing the same things over again. How are you feeling about being here and what's transpired between us?"

Client: "Well, I suppose I'm avoiding talking about some issues that are very painful and that I'd like to ignore."

In this dialogue the counselor was able to share quite candidly a lack of involvement in the process, and this exchange led the client to explore more personally relevant material.

Action Strategies

Since the purpose of all counseling is to facilitate client change, counselors should be familiar with the basic principles underlying behavior change. As noted in the discussion on goal setting, internal processes and behavior are not viewed as separate entities; rather, they are intimately related to each other. Many clients are able to act on the insights and new understandings they gain through the therapeutic climate and through the various advanced skills employed by the counselor. However, at times counselors must facilitate the behavior change process by implementing specific action strategies or programs. The timing for implementation of these programs will depend on the theoretical orientation of the counselor and on the nature of the client's concern. In this section we will briefly review the behavioral techniques based on learning theory. We will then consider two approaches that facilitate action in counseling.

Behavioral Techniques

Based on the principles of learning theory described in Chapter 5, behavioral techniques are designed to alter maladaptive behaviors and to strengthen desirable ones. These techniques are the basis of behavior therapy and are often used as part of an action strategy by counselors who operate from other theoretical orientations.

Systematic Desensitization

Desensitization is appropriate when the client has a high level of anxiety associated with a problem behavior. Examples of such problems would include anxiety about test taking, fear of heights, fear of speaking to groups, and so on. Counterconditioning coupled with muscle relaxation procedures are used to desensitize the client to anxiety-producing situations. These procedures are discussed in detail in Chapter 5.

Behavior Contracts

A behavior contract is an agreement between two parties aimed at changing the behavior of one of the persons involved. The agreement specifies the reinforcement contingent on reaching the goal. The behavior contract obviously has many applications in facilitating client action and has been used with behaviors ranging from smoking and weight reduction to disruptive behavior and speech problems. An example of a behavior contract is shown on page 167.

Social Modeling

When the presenting concern of the client involves a problematic relationship with another, it is often useful for the client to practice new ways of relating to the other party with the counselor. The counselor is given instructions regarding how to act so that the situation will resemble real life, and then the client and counselor act out the situation. This gives the client the opportunity to get feedback from the

---

Behavioral Contract between (Son) and (Mother)

Son agrees to:
  Speak distinctly when talking, with no reminder

Mother agrees to:
  Give 1 cent to son each time he speaks distinctly

Both parties agree to the following conditions:
  1. Penalty for failing to speak distinctly will be reduction of 1 cent for each failure.
  2. Amount of payment or penalty will not exceed 45 cents per day.
  3. Account will be balanced at end of each day; payment will be each Friday.
  4. Mother must be present to hear speech.
  5. Reevaluation after a trial period of one week.

Signed: _____
                        Mother

Signed: _____
                         Son

Date: January, 1994

(Dustin and George, 1977, p. 77)

counselor regarding the effectiveness of the client's behavior. This technique is similar to the "empty chair" technique from the Gestalt approach.

Assertion Training

Used in conjunction with a therapeutic relationship, assertion training may supplement client growth and change when clients have difficulty saying no or expressing both their positive and negative feelings.

The above behavioral techniques, though typically associated with behavioral counseling, may be used in conjunction with the therapeutic relationship to facilitate client action.

In addition to the behavioral techniques described above, counselors should be familiar with two other approaches that facilitate client action: decision-making methodologies and problem-solving strategies.

Decision-Making Methodologies

The ability to make good decisions is an integral part of healthy personal functioning. We are constantly faced with situations that require effective decision-making skills. Many problems clients bring to counselors involve the inability to make good decisions. As discussed in the section on barriers to communication in Chapter 7, counselors are not interested in solving clients' concerns for them;

rather, they aim to give clients the skills to solve their own problems. This approach facilitates client independence.

Many authors have proposed that the decision-making process involves sequential steps. Stewart, Winborn, Johnson, Burks, and Engelkes (1978) list the following steps in their decision-making model:

1. *Identify the problem.* This step should include answers to problems such as: What is the problem? What prevents a solution? When and under what circumstances does the problem occur? and so on.

2. *Identification of values and goals.* During this phase the clients' values are examined so that the solution will be consistent with the clients' values and long-range goals.

3. *Identify alternative.* A list of possible alternatives is formulated.

4. *Examine alternatives.* At this stage the advantages and disadvantages of each proposal are weighed, based on factual information such as amount of time and money involved.

5. *Make a tentative decision.*

6. *Take action on the decision.* If the decision is critical and the client is unsure about the choice, the decision may be tested at this stage, then further information can be gained and fed back into the decision-making process.

7. *Evaluate outcomes.* Evaluation should be a continual part of the process.

It should again be emphasized that the role of the counselor is not to make clients' decisions for them. It is to give them the skills not only to deal with the present concern but also to deal effectively with future problems. Krumboltz's (1966) model emphasizes this important point by adding the step of generalizing the decision-making process to future problems. This model is presented below:

1. Generating a list of all possible courses of action

2. Gathering relevant information about each feasible alternative course of action

3. Estimating the probability of success in each alternative on the basis of the experience of others and projections of current trends

4. Considering the personal values which may be enhanced or diminished under each course of action

5. Deliberating and weighing the facts, probable outcomes and values for each alternative

6. Eliminating from consideration the least favorable courses of action

7. Formulating a tentative plan of action subject to new developments and opportunities

8. Generalizing the decision-making process to future problems (1966, p. 153–159)

Problem-Solving Strategies

Egan (1975) proposes a systematic problem-solving methodology that includes his approach to the decision-making process and incorporates forcefield analysis. The steps of the model are briefly summarized here.

1. *Identify and clarify the problem.* Clients often present counselors with rather vague problems that, as stated, are insolvable. Therefore, as a first step the problem must be stated in a solvable manner. Instead of accepting vague descriptions of feelings, such as "I'm so depressed," the counselor seeks the stimulus for the client's feelings: "I'm feeling sad and lonely because I've just moved into this new city and I don't have any friends." The counselor emphasizes that problems cannot be solved when stated vaguely, when they are not dealing with the present, and when they are attributed to outside forces.

2. *Establish priorities in choosing problems for attention.* After clients have a grasp of their problems as well as their resources, they must decide which problems to tackle first. Some criteria would include (a) problems directly under clients' control; (b) crisis situations; (c) a problem that is easily handled; (d) a problem that, when solved, will bring about some improvement; (e) move from lesser to greater severity (other than crises).

3. *Establish workable goals.* Problems reflect the way things are, and goals represent the future. In other words, problems equal "restraining" forces; goals equal "facilitating" forces. Goals should be workable and concrete and should be "owned" by the client.

4. *Take a census of available means for reaching the goal.* List restraining and facilitating forces related to goal achievement. List action steps that could reduce restraining forces and enhance facilitating forces.

5. *Choose the means that will most effectively achieve established goals.* The means must be consistent with client values, should have a high probability for success, and should help the client move systematically toward the goal.

6. *Establish criteria for the effectiveness of action programs.*

7. *Implementation.* Use chosen means to achieve the established goals.

Those who are interested in learning more about the model presented above are referred to Egan (1975) for an excellent discussion of the process with examples of each phase.

Goal Setting

Whether or not to set goals for the counseling process and what type of goals are considered acceptable will largely be determined by the counselor's theoretical orientation. Traditionally, behaviorists have been concerned with identification of specific counseling goals, stated as behaviors, that can be easily identified and measured. Counselors with a humanistic orientation, on the other hand, would be inclined to identify a few broad goals, such as improved self-concept or increased self-understanding, rather than to focus on behaviors. The difference here may be attributed to the value placed on observable behaviors, which can be measured, versus the value of unobservable feelings, attitudes, and values, which can only be inferred from clients' behavior and clients' self-report of their internal experiencing.

The broad goal of all counseling is one of change, whether in attitudes, values, beliefs, feelings, or behavior. Since internal processes and behavior walk hand in hand, many counselors feel it is appropriate to focus on both areas, if at different points in the process. Behavioral goals give the humanistic counselor a focus for action either during the session or between sessions. These action goals can be formulated throughout the process as they coincide with changes in the client's awareness. The basic difference between these approaches, then, becomes one of emphasis and the formality of the goal-setting procedure.

Most counselors find it useful to formulate both process and outcome goals for each client for each counseling session. Process goals refer to the goals that counselors set for their own behavior in the relationship. These goals will obviously change throughout the duration of the relationship. Examples of appropriate goals for a counseling session midway through the process would be: to confront the client's unwillingness to be assertive with his or her boss; to disclose instances when the counselor has experienced a similar difficulty; and to use advanced accurate emphatic responses. Some outcome goals might be to work on assertive responses through behavior rehearsal and to work on having the client become more direct and honest in the session.

Termination and Follow-Up

Counselors must learn how to bring a counseling session to a close effectively; they must also be familiar with issues and skills involved in terminating a counseling relationship.

In closing an individual session, the counselor must be aware of time and should let the client know when the session is near ending. These timing considerations were explored in Chapter 8. As the session draws to a close, the counselor may ask the client to summarize the main themes, feelings, or issues of the session. This helps clients crystallize in their own minds the important things that took place during the session. The counselor may prefer to do the summary as a means of tying themes, issues, and feelings together into a synthesized frame-work. A summary by the counselor is particularly useful since it recapitulates the entire session and serves as a stimulus to the formulation of goals for the client to work on between sessions.

Termination of the counseling relationship in most cases is a natural process in which both counselor and client decide that the relationship should draw to a close. In some instances, however, the counselor may feel that it is time to terminate, but the client may not feel ready. Then the counselor must explore and weigh the client's needs to continue against the counselor's feelings about ending the relationship. In other instances the client may wish to terminate the relationship, but the counselor may think that this is premature. When this happens the counselor can only confront the client's needs to terminate and express reservations about severing the relationship at that particular time. The counselor cannot, however, force their clients to continue against their wishes.

Once the relationship has been terminated, the counselor will want to keep in touch with the client to see how things are progressing. This communicates the counselor's genuine concern for the client's further growth and development.

Summary

Once the counseling process has been initiated and rapport between client and counselor has developed, the counselor begins to promote and facilitate client self-exploration and self-understanding.

To facilitate client self-exploration and self-understanding, advanced counseling skills are required. These skills include advanced empathy, theme identification, self-disclosure, perception checks, interpretation, clarification, confrontation, and immediacy.

The goal of all counseling is client change. Thus, counselors should be familiar with the learning principles that underlie changes in behavior.

Internal processes and behavior are viewed as interacting rather than as separate entities. Some clients are capable of translating new insights and perceptions into changes in their behavior with minimal help from the counselor. Other clients must be worked with more directly if behavior change is to occur. Thus, counselors should develop action strategies to help clients translate insight into behavior change.

Behavioral techniques such as desensitization, behavior contracts, social modeling, and assertion training may be implemented as action strategies by counselors from a variety of theoretical orientations as an adjunct to the therapeutic process.

Decision-making and problem-solving methodologies are particularly useful in working out action programs for clients.

References

Berenson, B. G., & Mitchell, K. M. (1974). *Confrontation: For better or worse!* Amherst: Human Resource Development Press.

Brammer, L., & Shostrom, E. (1982). *Therapeutic psychology: Fundamentals of counseling and psychotherapy* (4th ed.). Englewood Cliffs, N.J.: Prentice-Hall.

Drag, R. M. (1969). Self-disclosure as a function of group size and experimenter behavior. *Dissertation Abstracts International, 30*(5-B), 2416.

Dustin, R., & George, R. (1977). *Action counseling for behavior change* (2nd ed.). Cranston, R.I.: Carroll Press, p. 77.

Egan, G. (1975). *The skilled helper: A model for systematic helping and interpersonal relating.* Monterey, Calif.: Brooks/Cole.

Egan, G., & Cowan, M. (1979). *People in systems: A model for development in the human-service professions and education.* Monterey, Calif.: Brooks/Cole.

Giannandrea, V., & Murphy, K. C. (1973). Similarity self-disclosure and return for a second interview. *Journal of Counseling Psychology, 20* (6), 545–548.

Jourard, S. (1971). *Self-disclosure: An experimental analysis of the transparent self.* New York: Wiley Interscience.

Jourard, S. M., & Jaffee, P. E. (1970). Influence of an interviewer's self-disclosure on the self-disclosing behavior of interviewees. *Journal of Counseling Psychology, 17,* 252–257.

Kaul, T. T., Kaul, M. A., & Bednar, R. L. (1973). Counselor confrontation and client depth of self-exploration. *Journal of Counseling Psychology, 20*(2), 132–136.

Krumboltz, J. (1966). Behavioral goals for counseling. *Journal of Counseling Psychology, 13,* 153–159.

Means, R. (1973). Levels of empathic response. *Personnel and Guidance Journal, 52*(1), 23–28.

Pietrofesa, T. J., Hoffman, A., Splete, H. H., & Pinto, D. V. (1978). *Counseling: Theory, research, and practice.* Chicago: Rand McNally.

Powell, W. J. (1968). Differential effectiveness of interviewer interventions in an experimenter interview. *Journal of Counseling and Clinical Psychology, 32,* 210–215.

Rogers, C. R. (1942). *Counseling and psychotherapy.* Boston: Houghton Mifflin.

Simonson, N. R. (1976). The impact of therapist disclosure on patient disclosure. *Journal of Counseling Psychology, 23*(1) 3–6.

Stewart, N., Winborn, B., Johnson, R., Burks, H., & Engelkes, J. (1978). *Systematic counseling.* Englewood Cliffs, N.J.: Prentice-Hall.

Truax, C. B., & Carkhuff, R. R. (1965). Client and therapist transparency in the psychotherapeutic encounter. *Journal of Counseling Psychology, 12,* 3–9.

Chapter 10

Counseling Selected Special Populations

Brenda-Fay Glik, Ed.D.
Therese S. Christiani, Ed.D.

In this chapter we will explore relevant issues in counseling the following selected client populations: adult survivors of child sexual abuse, gay men and lesbians, HIV-infected clients, and older adults. We conclude with a discussion of gender-related issues in counseling. We have chosen these populations because they represent such a large percentage of clients and are receiving the most attention in current literature.

Adult Survivors of Child Sexual Abuse

As we have become a society of greater sexual openness, the prevalence of child sexual abuse has surfaced. Surveys conducted by Russell (1986) revealed that among 930 randomly selected women, 38 percent reported experiencing sexual abuse before reaching 18 years of age. And because men are usually less willing to admit being sexually victimized, many now believe that the incidence of sexual abuse among boys is closer to that of girls than once thought (Ratican, 1992).

What constitutes child sexual abuse (CSA)? According to Steele (1986), sexual abuse occurs "when a child of any age is exploited by an older person for his own satisfaction while disregarding the child's own developmental immaturity and inability to understand the sexual behavior" (p. 284). The child, in a less powerful, dependent status, is coerced or seduced to engage in sexual activity to fulfill the adult's needs without the ability to give informed consent.

CSA has been found to have serious, negative, and pervasive psychological effects on its victims (Courtois, 1988; Browne and Finkelhor, 1986; Russell, 1986). Indicators of extremes (i.e., the younger the victim, the closer the abuser, greater frequency, and if violence accompanied the abuse) may result in more serious psychological and relational consequences (Hutchinson and Brandt, 1987).

In order to cope, sexual abuse survivors may deny, repress, or minimize the abuse in their histories. Often consciously unaware of the abuse, survivors of child sexual abuse (CSA) tend to seek counseling for other concerns. Along with the prevalence of CSA, the often disguised presentation of issues makes it essential for counselors to be able to identify survivor symptoms and concerns (Ratican, 1992). Further, counselors who choose to continue working with their sexually abused clients (instead of making a referral) must understand the complex aftereffects of CSA and how to therapeutically facilitate the healing process. This section provides a brief overview of current information on the symptoms and specific issues of survivors of sexual abuse, treatment considerations, and implications for counselors in training.

Identifying Symptoms

From a review of recent research and personal clinical experience, Ratican (1992) summarized the symptoms she found frequently present among survivors of sexual abuse. Although the presence of one symptom may not indicate abuse in a client's history, several of them occurring together certainly indicates a need for further exploration (Biegen et al., 1988). The symptoms include:

1. Depression, Anxiety, and Somatization

Depression is the most common symptom experienced by sexual abuse survivors. Compared with depressed individuals who have not been abused, survivors tend to be more suicidal and self-destructive (Browne & Finkelhor, 1986).

Survivors also tend to experience chronic anxiety and tension. Their distress can result in sleep and eating disturbances, phobias, anxiety attacks, and physical ailments, such as gastrointestinal problems, headaches, and backaches (Briere and Runtz, 1988).

2. Guilt and Shame

Because victimized children tend to blame themselves for being abused, survivors often experience a pervasive sense of guilt. To overcompensate, adult survivors are often perfectionists (O'Hare and Taylor, 1983).

An even deeper wound is the intrinsic feeling of shame and worthlessness that develops from CSA (Bradshaw, 1989). Victims tend to believe that not only have they *done* something bad, but that they *are* bad. As Ratican (1992) states, "sexual abuse strikes at the very core of self-esteem" (p. 34).

Shame and low self-esteem are reflected in poor, distorted body image. Unable to integrate the traumatic sexual experience, survivors feel a sense of alienation, betrayal, and disgust toward their bodies. To punish themselves and their bodies, survivors may engage in self-destructive behaviors (e.g., drug abuse, eating disorders, and/or prostitution).

3. Relationship and Sexuality Issues

The scope of the impact that CSA has on its victims in the area of relationships and sexuality is tremendous. Having been betrayed and violated in a relationship, it is not surprising that survivors of CSA tend to play out their resulting psychological dysfunctions in a relational context. To thoroughly describe the aftereffects of CSA on survivors' relationships is beyond the scope of this section. What follows is a brief summary of some general relation and sexual themes. For more extensive descriptions, a variety of resources are available (Courtois, 1988; Herman-Lewis, 1981; Maltz and Holman, 1987; Russell, 1986; Westerlund, 1983).

Survivors generally do not trust others appropriately and tend to lack clear personal boundaries (Blume, 1990). They may swing from trusting too easily, allowing themselves to be revictimized, to fearing intimacy, keepings others at arm's length. Embarrassed by their shameful experience, sexual abuse survivors often feel different and isolated (Westerlund, 1983) and fear that others will discover how intrinsically *bad* they really are if they allow them to get too close.

The impact of CSA on relationships may differ between males and females. The female survivor tends to continue in the victim role, turning her anger inward against herself in the form of depression, powerlessness, and revictimization (Finkelhor et al., 1986; Wheeler & Walton, 1987). The male survivor, on the other hand, is more likely to express his anger by exploiting or abusing others (Vander Mey, 1988).

In sexual relationships, survivors tend to experience a range of difficulties. Sexual dysfunctions (e.g., fear of sex, desire and arousal inhibitions, and difficulties achieving orgasm), periods of sexual promiscuity, and conscious or unconscious flashbacks during sexual contact are all common among survivors of CSA.

4. Denial, Repression, and Dissociation

Because sexual abuse memories are typically repressed, survivors often report amnesia for parts of their childhood (O'Hare and Taylor, 1983). Poor memory and learning difficulties are not uncommon (Wheeler and Walton, 1987). Victims may also deny or minimize the trauma by discounting the importance and effects of the sexual abuse.

As a coping mechanism during the abuse, victims typically dissociated or split (Hutchinson and Brandt, 1987). That is, victims learned to split or wall off "emotions, body parts, and experiences which were too strong, too terrifying, too traumatizing to be incorporated into the self, the memory, and the conception of the family/perpetrator" (p. 2). The splitting continues and produces polarities in behavior that become ingrained coping defenses or roles. Therefore, victims often exhibit extreme bipolar and contradictory behavioral, emotional, and relational patterns (e.g., needy vs. grandiose independence).

Dissociation may also be seen in the form of confusion, disorientation, difficulty getting in touch with feelings, nightmares, flashbacks, and feeling cut off from parts of self (child stuck inside). In more severe cases, victims of CSA develop multiple personalities.

Treatment Issues

From their clinical experience, Biegen and her associates developed the following general guidelines to help counselors facilitate the healing process for victims of CSA (Biegen et al., 1988).

1. Belief in the client

Counselors must believe clients' reports of CSA and communicate this belief, even if their clients sometimes doubt it themselves. This helps them break their isolation, validate their reality, and build trust in the relationship.

2. Familiarity with CSA Literature

Counselors must be familiar with the intrapersonal and interpersonal symptoms and issues most frequently associated with sexual abuse. For more extensive descriptions, see the references.

3. Special Treatment Issues

Counselors working with adult survivors of CSA must acquaint themselves with the following special treatment issues: (a) the nature and management of flashbacks, (b) whether to confront the perpetrator and how, (c) the importance of education/counseling/support group experiences, and (d) procedures or techniques relevant to the symptomatology of sexual abuse survivors.

4. Education as Treatment
Survivors of CSA benefit from information about sexual abuse, its effects, and the therapeutic process. Such informations helps clients feel more in control, normalizes the frightening and complex symptoms, and provides assurance that the survivor is not to blame, bad, or crazy.

5. Control and boundary Issues
The process of therapy can revictimize the client if counselors are not sensitively attuned to the client's sense of control and personal boundaries. Counselors should allow the client to feel in control of the process at all times. Thus highly directive approaches are not recommended.

6. Integration
In order to heal, survivors of CSA must integrate their memories, emotions, and cognitions of their abusive childhood. A typically painful and terrifying experience, some suggest using the metaphor of an internal "child" to facilitate the healing process (Blake-White and Kline, 1985).

7. Sex of the counselor
Biegen and her associates point out that for many survivors, female counselors are the best choice because males have typically been the perpetrators. Courtois (1988) agrees, yet encourages counselors to help clients explore their own preference and what effect, if any, their counselor's gender may have on their healing process.

Deciding whether to work with survivors

Because of the prevalence and disguised nature of issues, many believe that counselors in this country cannot avoid working with survivors of sexual abuse (Ratican, 1992; Bass and Davis, 1988). However, for a variety of reasons, not all therapists feel they are able or wish to work with this population and develop a referral process in lieu of continuing the therapeutic relationship (Biegen et al., 1988).

What are some considerations when contemplating working with this population? First, counselors must be willing to witness great pain, often deep and wrenching, as clients share almost unbelievable stories and terrifying experiences. The arduous and emotionally draining process for facilitating the healing of sexual abuse survivors makes counselors' *self-care* an essential personal and professional requirement (Bass and Davis, 1988; Biegen et al, 1988; Courtois, 1988; Ratican, 1992). Emotionally "letting go" can take many forms (e.g., support groups, on-going supervision, visualization techniques, and/or 'fun and play'). Counselors must find what works best for them to maintain a vital, balanced personal life so they can assist their clients in their own quest for such a life (Bass and Davis, 1988).

Second, counselors must examine their own attitudes toward sexual abuse when considering working with survivors. In order to work effectively with sexually victimized clients, counselors need to be clear about their own perspective (e.g., personal philosophy or religion, areas of sexual confusion, etc.) to avoid imposing their own views on clients (Bass and Davis, 1988).

Another critical issue potential counselors of survivors must face is their own history and fears regarding sexual abuse. For counselors who have been abused themselves, it is imperative that they work through and resolve their own issues well enough to support their clients without confusing their issues. At a minimum, experienced supervision may be necessary to stay clear.

Overall, facilitating the healing of survivors of sexual abuse is one of the most intense and painful special populations with whom a counselor can work. Yet it can also be the most deeply fulfilling. To participate in relationships and witness individuals heal from the inside, feeling and experiencing themselves as they never have before; becoming whole and vital human beings when there once was nothing more than emptiness and rage can be a rare and special gift.

Gay Men and Lesbians

Coined as the "hidden minority," gay men and lesbian women comprise approximately 10 to 15 percent of the overall population (Fassinger, 1991). Their invisibility stems from our society's negative and repressive attitude toward same-sex behavior. This stigmatization has been sanctioned by our laws, our clergy, and until very recently within the mental health professions (Dworkin and Gutierrez, 1992).

With the classification of homosexuality as a mental illness—prior to the revised edition of DSM III (1986)—gay people have been diagnosed as sick, arrested in development, with immature relationship patterns (Klein, 1986). Thus, research literature and clinical treatment have focused on identifying causes of pathology in an effort to find a cure.

Although we have made considerable progress since the days of classifying homoerotic behavior as pathological, researchers and practitioners agree that gays remain a seriously understudied and underserved population (Dworkin and Gutierrez, 1989; Gelso and Fassinger, 1990). The historical unhealthy status of gays, coupled with their climate of secrecy, has left those in the helping professions feeling inadequately trained and lacking information to therapeutically relate with this population (Glenn and Russell, 1986). Yet despite their felt inadequacy, therapists are willing to treat gay, lesbian, and bisexual clients (Dworkin and Gutierrez, 1989). As Dworkin and Gutierrez (1989) point out, seeing clients without the proper training "is in direct violation of the *Ethical Standards* of the American Association of Counseling and Development (March, 1988)" (p. 7).

Gay/Lesbian-Affirmative Approach

In response to the growing visibility of the gay population and the violation of ethics occurring in the field, gay and lesbian counseling concerns have received considerable attention in recent counseling and psychology publications (Dworkin and Gutierrez, 1992; *Journal of Counseling and Development*, 1989; *The Counseling*

Psychologist, 1991). Helping professionals, many of whom are gays and lesbians, are reframing our society's conceptualization of lesbian and gay life experience. Rather than condemming same-sex relations as sick and unnatural, they are advocating the development and practice of therapy models that are *gay- and lesbian-affirmative*. Accepting homosexuality as a healthy lifestyle, gay-affirmative counselors address the myriad of issues that gays/lesbians present and refrain from making sexual orientation the problem. Moreover, gay/lesbian-affirmative models (1) are culturally relevant to the life experience of gay men and lesbian women; (2) can be applied to a full range of psychological adjustment; and (3) speak to the concerns and issues of well, though poorly functioning, individuals of the gay population (Gonsiorek, 1985).

Although gay-affirmative approaches to counseling discourage forcing the issue of sexual orientation, many gays and lesbians feel the effects of societal oppression in their lives and need to work through sexuality and identity issues in counseling (Clark, 1987). Research conducted by Miranda and Storms (1989) showed that the development of a positive lesbian and gay identity is related to psychological adjustment (i.e., greater ego strength and lower neurotic anxiety), pointing to the importance of integrating a positive gay identity for this population. Thus, many gay-affirmative researchers and practitioners follow a developmental approach to help lesbians and gays experience a positive gay identity.

Gay Identity Development

Often referred to as "coming out" (of the closet), the process of acquiring a positive gay identity can occur at any age and is generally difficult and ongoing. Since friends, family, and society at large are mostly unsupportive of developing a positive gay identity, counselors may serve as the only advocate for this population in their journey to find self-acceptance and self-actualization. This makes it essential for counselors to understand the process of gay identity development and the complexity of issues involved, and to help clients recognize, accept, and ultimately affirm their gay sexual orientation. A widely cited example of gay identity development is Cass's (1979) six-stage model (Fassinger, 1991; Dworkin and Gutierrez, 1992). Although presented here as linear, it is recommended to view this model from a process perspective, where every stage is free to be revisited again as clients face new thoughts, feelings, or experiences.

Stage 1: **Identity Confusion** Characterized by feelings of turmoil, in which one questions previously held assumptions about one's sexual orientation.

Stage 2: **Identity Comparison** Characterized by feelings of alienation, in which one accepts the possibility of being gay and becomes isolated from nongay others.

Stage 3: **Identity Tolerance** Characterized by feelings of ambivalence, in which one seeks out other gays, but remains separate public and private images.

Stage 4: **Identity Acceptance** Characterized by selective disclosure in which one begins the legitimization (publicly and privately) of one's sexual orientation.

Stage 5: **Identity Pride** Characterized by anger, pride, and activism, in which one becomes immersed in the gay subculture and rejects nongay people, institutions, and values.

Stage 6: **Identity Synthesis** Characterized by clarity and acceptance, in which one moves beyond a dichotomized worldview to an incorporation of one's sexual orientation as one aspect of a more integrated identity.

Bisexuality

Many individuals experience confusion and anxiety about their sexuality because they have adopted society's traditional dichotomous categorization of sexual orientation. As we expand our definition of sexuality to include not only sexual attraction and behavior, but also factors such as fantasy, emotional preference, social preference, self-identification, and lifestyle, our conceptualization of sexual preference is drastically shifting (Klein, Sepekoff, and Wolf 1985). In fact, researchers are now suggesting that sexuality and sexual preference are much more complex and certainly not as simplistic as the hetero- versus homosexual categories imply. Thus many more clients are finding themselves somewhere in the middle of the continuum, having intimate experiences with both sexes. These bisexual clients need assistance integrating an appropriate identity and lifestyle.

Counselor Role and Responsibilities

The American Counseling Association has recently reemphasized the counseling profession's undergirding values of development, prevention, and wellness (*Journal of Counseling & Development*, 1992). Consistent with this philosophy is the above-described therapeutic approach to working with gay men and lesbian women that frames their concerns in terms of normalcy and actualization rather than pathology and cure. Drawing from Fassinger (1991), House (1992), and Clark (1987), here are some specific recommendations for counselors aspiring to be in the forefront of affirmative therapy with the gay population:

1. Counselors must explore their feelings about their own sexuality so they are comfortable talking about sexual issues.

2. Whether gay or nongay, counselors must explore their own homophobic feelings to prevent blind spots when working with gay clients.

3. Counselors must reeducate themselves about homosexuality, exploring stereotypes and myths, to overcome communicating homophobic societal messages about same-sex relationships. This should include reading gay-affirmative books and periodicals (see the references) and staying abreast of professional associations and resources available to gays (Dworkin and Gutierrez, 1992).

4. Counselors must proactively create a gay-affirmative environment, communicating acceptance of same-sex relationships and desensitizing shame and guilt (e.g., have gay and lesbian books visible on shelves and encourage discussion along with empathy for clients' gay experiences).

5. Counselors must recognize, and help their clients recognize, the internal and external oppression faced by gay people and the impact on their own self-acceptance and self-regard.

6. Counselors must be familiar with the treatment of addictive behaviors (e.g., eating disorders and substance abuse), as they are common among the gay population.

7. Counselors must understand the range of diversity among the gay/lesbian population (depending on factors such as gender, race, religion, age, geographic location, etc.) and learn of the variation in the coming out process and in gay/lesbian experience overall (Dworkin and Gutierrez, 1992).

8. Counselors must be particularly sensitive to the inter- and intrapersonal conflict and stress clients often experience as they face the personal and social ramifications of "coming out." Despite the negative impact that secret feelings and perceptions about oneself have on personal integrity and self-worth, counselors must be patient and compassionate while clients struggle in their journey of positive gay identity.

9. Counselors may need to be prepared to help their gay clients "grieve gay." In the process of identifying a positive gay identity, clients typically experience a range of losses from losing a job because of their sexual orientation to never feeling the support and acceptance from friends and/or family.

In summary, although counselors need to understand the specific and unique developmental issues of the gay client population, gays, lesbians, and bisexuals struggle with the same fundamental concerns as all clients: self-acceptance, self-regard, and self-actualization. Gays and lesbians may have unique challenges to confront in their journey, yet their goal and their transformation process are no different than for any other client population. This makes a relationship characterized by genuineness, empathy, unconditional acceptance, and trust the most powerful and therapeutic vehicle of growth.

HIV-Infected Clients

Acquired Immune Deficiency Syndrome (Aids) was first identified as a specific disease in 1981. During the past decade it has become an epidemic of such magnitude that it is considered the nations major health and psychological crisis. It has even been predicted that as we begin the twenty-first century, one in ten U.S. residents will be HIV-positive (Cohen and Weisberg, 1990). Not only are counselors increasingly being called upon as a valuable source of assistance and support with HIV-infected clients (Hoffman, 1991), they must be more flexible and willing to take on a variety of new counseling roles (Gutierrez and Perlstein, 1992). Part of the complexity of the AIDS epidemic is that unlike other terminal illnesses such as cancer, AIDS doesn't just kill an individual, it infects and destroys entire social networks (Cochran and Mays, 1991).

In a special issue of the *Journal of Counseling and Development* on AIDS and HIV, Dworkin and Pincu (1993) have presented the issues that counselors will confront with this population. Counselors will increasingly be working with the medical profession, since they may be the first to recognize the early warning signs of HIV infection. They must know the symptoms and recognize the early warning signs so they can refer a client for medical help (Hoffman, 1991). As a case manager or consultant, counselors will have to move out of the confines of their office into the social systems that affect their clients lives (Dworkin and Pincu, 1993).

Working with an HIV-infected population may trigger many of the therapist's own issues regarding homophobia, drug use, sexuality, as well as death and dying (Gutierrez and Perlstein, 1992). Additionally, the counseling relationship may differ in several ways from a more traditional approach. Hoffman (1991), in her comprehensive model for working with the HIV-infected clients, discusses some of the variations that occur when counseling an HIV-infected patient.

Counseling Considerations

Rethinking Therapeutic Goals
Counseling the HIV-infected client differs from working with other clients. The focus shifts to day-to-day issues. Additionally, the counselor may become more directive as issues such as the client's and others' safety come up. The therapeutic goal of "seeking a cure" shifts to assisting with the client's concerns around death and dying (Hoffman, 1991).

Changing Boundaries of the Counseling Relationship
Working with an HIV-infected client may force the counselor to alter the traditional parameters of the relationship (e.g., setting, time frame for the session, duration of the relationship, payment schedules, insurance policies, etc).

Transference
Although transference may not occur in the classical sense, themes involving intimacy, trust, dependency, and death and dying may become more intense (Nichols, 1986). Clients may project rage onto the counselor or be fearful that the counselor will abandon them. Clients may worry that the counselor will be afraid of becoming infected by the client, or they may fear rejection due to their deteriorating physical appearance (Bartnof, 1988). Clients may become increasingly more dependent and more demanding of the counselor's time. Requests for extra sessions, non-office visits, and latitude with payments are common among HIV-infected clients (Hoffman, 1991).

Countertransference
Hoffman (1991) defines countertransference "to include feelings, attitudes, and reactions that arise from the counselor's life experiences as well as reactions to the here and now that arise in the context of the counseling relationship" (p. 525). As mentioned earlier, counselors may struggle with their own issues regarding (a)

death and disease, (b) sexuality and intimacy, and (c) caretaking or being taken care of (McKusick, 1988).

Counselor Helplessness, Stress, and Burnout

Counseling HIV-positive clients may be the most demanding clientele a counselor will face. Counseling these clients will place extraordinary demands on the counselor's energy as well as on their skills (Winiarski, 1991). These unusual demands easily result in counselor burnout. It seems particularly important for the AIDS counselor to receive some form of supportive therapy.

Ethical Dilemmas

The ethical dilemmas posed by working with HIV-infected persons are unusually complex (Harding, Gray, and Neal, 1993). As Gray and Harding (1988) have noted, "the recent development of this disease and the resulting deaths raise the following professional question: At what point, if any, do counselors breach a confidential relationship with a client who has the AIDS virus to preserve society's goals of health and safety" (p.219)? The issue around confidentiality and duty to warn partners of HIV-infected clients must be fully explored by any counselor working with this population, especially since research (Kegeles et al., 1988 and Elias, 1988) has indicated that dishonesty towards sexual partners regarding sexual history and infectious state appears to be common (Hoffman, 1991).

Client Issues

The issues faced by the client who is HIV-infected are extremely complex and multileveled. These issues may be further complicated by the clients' developmental phase or his/her specific population (Dworkin and Pincu, 1993; Hoffman, 1991). By specific population, we mean gender, gender-role identity, race, ethnicity, social class, etc. In addition to the multiplicity of psychosocial issues clients face, a very prominent theme is anticipatory grief (Hoffman, 1991). Counselors working with HIV-infected clients should find Hoffman's model (1991) and the special issue of the *Journal of Counseling and Development* (Vol. 71, 1993) invaluable resources. Keeling's article (1993) also contains current information on the epidemiologic, clinical, and virologic aspects of the disease.

Training Needs

Hoffman (1991) has noted the importance of training counselors to work with AIDS clients. He recommends that all counseling psychology curricula include a course on counseling HIV-infected clients. At the very least, workshops should be available to train counselors for this population.

In addition to the topics covered above from the Hoffman (1991) model, counselors will see an increasing number of persons with a fear of AIDS. Bruhn (1989) has stated that "AIDS has created panic, fear, and hysteria as it spreads to the heterosexual population, affecting persons of all ages, ethnicity, and social status"

(p. 455). According to Bruhn (1989), three groups of persons are most likely to experience heightened anxiety over the fear of contracting the AIDS virus. These groups include: (a) persons in high-risks groups who fear both AIDS and the disclosure of belonging to a risk group, (b) persons not in a high-risk group but who are prone to hypochondriacal concerns and (c) AIDS patients who face additional and significant psychological burdens. Bruhn (1989) proposes guidelines for counseling persons with a fear of AIDS.

Partners, families, and spouses of persons with AIDS are possibly the most in need of counseling services. Sadly, few social supports are available for this group, which increases geometrically as the number of persons with AIDS grows (Williams and Stafford, 1991). Peer groups are most often suggested as the best forms of intervention for this group although traditional forms of treatment such as individual, group, and family counseling are also recommended.

In summary, the HIV-infected person, their partners, families, and spouses, as well as persons who are fearful of contracting the HIV virus, are a rapidly growing population of clients who not only need counseling but who will require that all counselors be personally and professionally prepared to respond to one of the greatest health crises in history. While we can consider at this moment in time the HIV-infected client to be a special population in counseling, it seems likely that within a few years, all counselors will be working with clients whose lives have been touched by the disease.

Older Adults

The number of adults in the United States age 65 and older is increasing. In 1975 an estimated twenty million persons, approximately 10 percent of the population, were over age 65 (Butler, 1975; Lombana, 1976). It has been projected that by the year 2000, thirty million (12 percent) of the population will be over age 65. And by the year 2030, fifty-seven million (18.3 percent) of the population will be over the age of 65 (Allan and Brotman, 1981). With the increasing number of persons in the 65 and older age bracket, counselors must be prepared to work with this population.

Successful Aging

The counseling skills necessary for working with older adults are no different than those for other developmental stages. What counselors must have is some sensitivity to the issues that are specific to working with older adults. Generally, working with older adults can be viewed more broadly than assisting with late-life transitions, which usually include retirement (decreased finances and increased leisure); relocation; ageist attitudes; loss and separation; terminal illness; sexuality; physical decline and chronic ailments; and isolation. Although many older adults need counseling to deal with these transitions, counselors of the future could be instrumental in promoting "successful aging" (Ponzo, 1992). This approach is consistent with the wellness philosophy adopted by the American Counseling Association (Myers, 1992).

Successful aging does not imply staying young. It focuses on assisting people to stay vital longer. The emphasis shifts their expectations from what is typical to what is possible. In other words, successful aging involves a shift in our vision of aging by helping people see that they can exercise some control over their aging process (Ponzo, 1992). Thus many problems associated with aging can be prevented or ameloriated. For example, preretirement counseling can help a retiree plan for all areas of retirement from health and insurance needs to avocational and leisure interests. Health education over the life span can supply information on all aspects of good physical and mental health, including nutrition, exercise, and regular medical checkups. Additionally, as mentioned earlier, counselors can educate the general public about successful aging, thus dispelling the myths that surround the senior citizen. Stereotypical views can be diffused in an attempt to create a more useful and helpful view of the aging adult (Lombana, 1976).

Remedial Services

To work effectively in providing remedial services to the older adult, counselors may need to make some adaptations in their skills and approaches. Gross and Capuzzi (1991) suggest the following:

1. Due to ageist attitudes, counselors may need to restore clients' self-esteem.
2. Efforts must be made to convince the client of the positive benefits of counseling.
3. Increased attention to environmental factors must be made to ensure that the client is comfortable and able to benefit from the session. Counselors must be sensitive to factors such as noise distractions, counselor voice levels due to hearing loss, adequate lighting for the visually impaired, furniture that is both accessible and comfortable, and office accessibility. The length of the sessions may be an additional factor if the client cannot sit for increased amounts of time.
4. The counselor's role may involve advocacy with regard to accessing other services such as transportation, home health care, and vocational rehabilitation.
5. Rather than focusing on in-depth psychological issues, the counselor may stay focused in the present, dealing with coping strategies for daily living situations.
6. In dealing with the client's loss of independence, the counselor may need to be supportive of the client's dependence on others due to changes in physical health, finances, or loss of a spouse or other family.
7. The counselor should be sensitive to the probable age differential as well as the differing values in delicate areas such as finances or sexual concerns.
8. The use of diagnostic tools should be used with caution.

Training

The National Board for Counselor Certification (NBCC) has approved a specialty certification entitled National Certified Gerontological Counselor (NCGC). Receiving this certification requires a review of training, experience, and supervisory evaluations (Myers, 1992). More specifically, the criteria include: "(a) two

years of professional counseling experience; (b) three graduate courses in geron-
tology (or the equivalent in 120 hours of related gerontological continuing education), and a 600-hour internship or supervised experience in a gerontological setting; (c) completion of a self-assessment of competence; and (d) two professional
assessments of competence" (Myers, 1992, p. 38). In addition to the above specialty
certification, CACREP (1992) has developed gerontological counseling standards
as a specialty within community counseling.

Due to the demographics of the U. S. population, it is clear that counselors will
increasingly be working with older adults. As Walz, Gazda, and Shertzer (1991)
have stated: "Clearly, adult development must become a major component of all
counselor education programs . . . Preserving the self-esteem of adults, empowering adults, wellness in later life, the needs of parents of adult children, and gerontological counseling are topics that generally receive scant attention in counselor
education today, but will become major considerations in the emerging future"
(p. 48).

Gender Issues in Counseling

Although gender is a rather broad categorization, an awareness of the potential
impact of being male or female in American society can be a valuable addition as
we conceptualize clients' concerns and engage ourselves in a relationship with
them. What follows is a brief overview of current thinking on women's and men's
issues in counseling.

Women's issues

Consistent with the perspective that we must consider individuals within their social context (Enns, 1993), the women's movement has encouraged us to think about
how women see themselves, and the world, based on their role in society. Since the
human rights movement of the 1960s and early 1970s, the psychology of women
has received considerable attention in the mental health profession. Resulting in
feminist therapy, a major focus has been on remediating the negative impact of
being a woman living in a male-dominated society, where women are victims of
discrimination, oppression, and devaluation. The high rate of women seeking
therapy for concerns such as depression, anxiety, eating disorders, and unhealthy
self-esteem can be explained by the oppressive nature of their gender role stereotypes (Lerner, 1988). And since mental health professionals have been brought up
through the same patriarchal institutions that have promoted sex bias, they too
have been criticized for continuing and deepening the very attitudes from which
women are trying to escape.

Approaches to women's issues in counseling have experienced rapid growth
and transformation over the past two decades [See Enns (1993) for a thorough
summary and historical review]. The most recent force in the field reaches to the
roots of mainstream theory and calls for a paradigm shift. Because most writers

about therapy in the past have been men writing about women, the male point of view has become "the" point, never allowing women to see themselves through their own eyes. The male representation of the world and human development has created a serious sex bias in therapy, leaving the female experience not only invalidated but often pathologized.

Women such as Gilligan (1982), Josselson (1987), Miller (1986), Belenky et al. (1986), and Jordan et al. (1986) have recognized the need to describe women's life experience, perception of reality, and identity development in their own terms and from a healthy, positive perspective. Although a work in progress, their intensive research on women's daily experiences has resulted in identity models that frame women's relational characteristics as strengths rather than weaknesses. In other words, rather than punishing women for centralizing the role of affiliations in their lives, these models recognize women's relational tendency as a valid process for healthy identity development. Although criticized for not addressing the complexity and diversity of women's lives, Enns (1991) concludes that the new relationship theories "help counselors think more flexibly and positively about the nature of women's psychological maturation" (p. 216). Moreover, these models speak directly to the importance of a mutually enhancing, emotionally empowering relationship between client and therapist.

In addition to understanding the nature of women's identity from this relational and more positive perspective, counselors must prepare themselves for the myriad of issues women face today. Sex discrimination and sex-role stereotyping are still real for many women. As more women enter and reenter the work force, they face issues such as career choice, balancing professional life with family roles, and sexual harrassment. Counselors may also find their female clients with therapeutic needs such as parenting concerns, sexual and reproductive choices, and childhood sexual abuse.

Men's Issues

More recently, the women's movement has sparked the realization among men that they, too, "are victims of the gender roles to which they are socialized" (Scher, 1990, p. 322). In contrast to the oppressive nature of women's societal roles, male gender roles tend to have a suppressive and constraining impact on men. For example, men are socialized to be in control (of themselves and their environment) and to stay clear from qualities that approach feminity (O'Neil, 1981). These roles restrain men from exhibiting the more emotional and vulnerable attitudes and behaviors, causing them to be generally more rigid, distant, and stoic (Scher, 1990). In an effort to more specifically describe the negative consequences of the male gender role, O'Neil et al. (1986) conceptualized four factors of the male role that lead to conflict. They include (a) success, power, and competition; (b) restrictive emotionality; (c) restrictive affection between men; and (d) conflict between work and family relations. Good and Mintz (1990) found that these conflicts inherent in the male gender role are directly related to depression in men. In other words, men who have internalized the success and power male role, for example, tend to define their personal value by their career success and are more likely to deny their interpersonal needs; hence these men were found more likely to be depressed.

Despite the increasing symptomology among men, they are less likely to seek counseling than women. And for those males who do enter a therapeutic relationship, many are resistant to the process and the relational bond that is traditionally required for therapeutic movement. As a result, there has been a growing recognition for the need to understand the meaning of being a man in our society, and more particularly, of being a man in therapy (Osherson and Krugman, 1990; Pollack, 1990; Levant, 1990; Scher, 1990; and Robertson and Fitzgerald, 1992). Levant (1990) describes four factors related to the norms of the traditional male role that stand in the way for men in therapy. According to Levant, men tend to:

1. Have difficulty in admitting the existence of a problem
2. Avoid asking for help
3. Have difficulty processing emotional states
4. Experience discomfort with and often fear intimacy.

Just as women in the field are developing models of theory and practice that reflect the female perspective, men are now in the process of generating approaches and alternatives to therapy which are based on a more accurate understanding of male growth and identity development. For example, Levant (1990) and Robertson and Fitzgerald (1992) found that men prefer psychological services described as workshops and seminars emphasizing self-help and problem-solving approaches.

Because male clients tend to experience the same conflicts engendered by the sex role that brings them to therapy in the first place (Scher, 1990), counselors need to be aware of the restraints and expectations of the male gender role as they work with male clients. Men have the opportunity to transcend their gender role and nurture their natural male strengths with a counselor who is patient, resilient, and sensitive to the world of their male clients.

In summary, writers of men's and women's issues support joining together in a cooperative movement to overcome sex-role discrimination. Since change and transformation are central to any counselor's work, we have the opportunity and responsibility to help free society from gender bias.

Summary

This chapter has focused on several selected client populations and the relevant issues in working with each. It is hoped that readers will use the references as a resource for further research and practice. Although there are obviously other populations that deserve attention, we selected populations representing a large number of clients and whose issues are important for counselors to understand.

References

Adult Survivors of CSA

Bass, E., & Davis, L. (1988). *The courage to heal: A guide for women survivors of child sexual abuse.* New York: Harper & Row.

Biegen, S., Pierce, L., & Van Diggelen, M. (1988). *Guidelines for assessment and treatment of women who are survivors of child sexual abuse.* St. Louis, MO: Women's Issues Committee of the Missouri Psychological Association.

Blake-White, J., & Kline, C. M. (1985). Treating the dissociative process in adult victims of incest. *Social Casework. 66*(17), 394–405.

Blume, E. S. (1990). *Secret survivors: Uncovering incest and its aftereffects in women.* New York: Wiley.

Bradshaw, J. (speaker).(1989) *Healing the shame that binds you* (Cassette recording No. 1-55874-043-0). Deerfield Beach, FL: Health Communications.

Briere, J., & Runtz, M. (1988). Symptomatology associated with childhood sexual victimization in a nonclinical adult sample. *Child Abuse and Neglect, 12,* 51–59.

Browne, A., & Finkelhor, D. (1986). Impact of child sexual abuse: A review of the research. *Psychological Bulletin, 99,* 66–77.

Courtois, C. A. (1988). *Healing the incest wound: Adult survivors in therapy.* New York: Norton.

Finkelhor, D., Araji, S., Baron, L. Browne, A., Peters, S., & Wyatt, G. (1986). *Sourcebook on child sexual abuse.* Newbury Park, CA: Sage.

Herman-Lewis, J. (1981). *Father-daughter incest.* Boston: Harvard.

Hutchinson, M., & Brandt, S. (1987). *Survivors of childhood sexual abuse.* Paper presented at Spring 1987 Missouri Psychological Association Convention, Springfield, MO.

Maltz, W., & Holman, B. (1987). *Incest and Sexuality.* Lexington, MA: Lexington Books.

O'Hare, J., & Taylor, K. (1983). The reality of incest. *Women and Therapy, 2*(2–3), 214–229.

Ratican, K. L. (1992). Sexual abuse survivors: Identifying symptoms and special treatment considerations. *Journal of Counseling and Development, 71,* 33–38.

Russell, D. E. (1986). *The secret trauma: Incest in the lives of girls and women.* New York: Basic Books.

Steele, B. F. (1986). Notes on the lasting effects of early child abuse throughout the lifecycle. *Child Abuse and Neglect, 10,* 283–291.

Vander Mey, B. J. (1988). The sexual victimization of male children: A review of previous research. *Child Abuse and Neglect, 12,* 61–72.

Westerlund, E. (1983). Counseling women with histories of incest. *Women and Therapy, 2*(4), 17–31.

Wheeler, B.R., & Walton, E. (1987). Personality disturbances of adult incest victims. *Social Casework, 68,* 597–602.

Gay Men and Lesbians

American Association for Counseling and Development. (1988, March). *Ethical Standards.* Alexandria, VA: Author.

American Psychiatric Association. (1986). *Diagnostic and Statistical manual of mental disorders.* (3rd ed. revised). Washington: Author.

Cass, V. C. (1979). Homosexual identity formation: A theoretical model. *Journal of Homosexuality, 4,* 219–235.

Clark, D. (1987). *The new loving someone gay.* Berkeley, CA: Celestial Arts.

Dworkin, S., & Gutierrez, F. (1989). Introduction to special issue: Counselors be aware: Clients come in every size, shape, color, and sexual orientation. *Journal of Counseling and Development, 68,* 6–8.

Dworkin, S., & Gutierrez, F. (1992). *Counseling gay men and lesbians: Journey to the end of the rainbow.* Alexandria, VA: American Association for Counseling and Development.

Fassinger, R. (1991). The hidden minority: Issues and challenges in working with lesbian women and gay men. *The Counseling Psychologist, 19*(2), 157–176.

Gelso, C. & Fassinger, R. (1990). Counseling Psychology: Theory and research on interventions. *Annual Review of Psychology, 41,* 355–386.

Glenn, A. A., & Russell, R. K. (1986). Heterosexual bias among counselor trainees. *Counselor Education and Supervision, 26*, 222–229.

Gonsiorek, J. (1985). Introduction: Present and future direction in gay/lesbian mental health. In J.C. Gonsiorek (Ed.), *A guide to psychotherapy with gay and lesbian clients* (pp. 5–7). New York: Harrington Park Press.

Goodyear, R. K. (Ed.). (1989). Special Issue: Gay, lesbian, and bisexual issues in counseling. *Journal of Counseling and Development, 68*(1).

House, R. M. (1992). Counseling gay and lesbian clients. In Capuzzi, D. & Gross, D. (Eds.). *Introduction to counseling: Perspective for the l990s.* (pp. 353–387). Boston: Allyn and Bacon.

Klein, C. (1986). *Counseling our own.* Renton, WA: Publication Service Inc.

Klein, F., Sepekoff, B., & Wolf, T. (1985). Sexual orientation: A multivariate dynamic process. In F. Klein & T. Wolf (Eds.). *Bisexuality: Theory and Research.* New York: Haworth.

Miranda, J., & Storms, M. (1989). Psychological adjustment of lesbians and gay men. *Journal of Counseling and Development, 68*, 41–45.

Meyers, J., Emmerling, D., & Leafgren, F. (Eds.). (1992). Special Issue Wellness throughout the lifespan *Journal of Counseling and Development,* (71) 2.

Stone, G. L. (Ed.). (1991). Counseling lesbian women and gay men [Special Issue]. *The Counseling Psychologist, 19*(2).

HIV-Infected Clients

Bartnof, H.S. (1988). Health care professional education and AIDS [Special issue: AIDS: Principles, practices, and politics]. *Death Studies,* (12), 547–562.

Bruhn, J.G. (1989). Counseling persons with a fear of AIDS. *Journal of Counseling and Development,* (67), 445–457.

Cochran, S.D., and Mays, U.M. (1988). Psychosocial HIV Interventions in the second decade: A note on social support and social networks. *The Counseling Psychologist, 19*, 551–557.

Cohen, R., & Weisberg, L.S. (1990). *Double Jeopardy-thrust to life and human rights: Discrimination against persons with AIDS.* Cambridge, MA: Human Rights Internet.

Dworkin, S.H., & Pincu, L. (1993). Counseling in the era of AIDS. *Journal of Counseling and Development,* (71), 275–281.

Elias, M. (1988, August 15). Many lie about AIDS risk. *USA Today* p. D-1.

Gray, L.A., and Harding, A.K. (1988). Confidentiality limits with clients who have the AIDS virus. *Journal of Counseling and Development 66,* 219–223.

Gutierrez, F.J., & Perlstein, M. (1992). Helping someone to Die. In S.H. Dworkin and F.J. Gutierrez (Eds.). *Counseling gay men and lesbians: Journey to the end of the rainbow* (pp. 259–275). Alexandria, VA.: American Association of Counseling & Development.

Harding, A.K., Gray L.A., & Neal, M. (1993). Confidentiality limits with clients who have HIV: A review of ethical & legal guidelines and professional policies. *Journal of Counseling and Development,* (71), 297–305.

Hoffman, M.S. (1991). Counseling the HIV-Infected Client: A psychosocial model for assessment and intervention, *The Counseling Psychologist,* (19). 467–542.

Keeling, R.P. (1993). HIV Disease: Current Concepts. *Journal of Counseling and Development,* (71), 261–274.

Kegeles, T., Catania, I., & Coates, T. (1988). Intentions to communicate positive HIV status to sex partners [letter to the editor]. *Journal of the American Medical Association,* (259), 216–217.

McKusick, L. (1988). The impact of AIDS on practitioner and client. *American Psychologist,* (43), 935–950.

Nichols, S.E. (1986). Psychotherapy and AIDS. In T.S. Stein & C.J. Cohen (Eds.). *Contemporary perspective on psychotherapy with lesbians and gay men* (pp. 202–239). N.Y: Plenum.

Williams, R.F., and Stafford, W.B. (1991). Silent casualties: Partners, families, and spouses of persons with AIDS. *Journal of Counseling and Development,* (69), 423–427.

Winiarski, M.G. (1991). *AIDS-related psychotherapy.* NY: Pergamon.

Older Adults

Allan, C. & Brotman, H. (1981). *Chartbook on aging in America.* Washington, DC: 1981 White House Conference on Aging.

Butler, R. N. (1975). *Why survive? Being old in America.* New York: Harper & Row.

Council for Accreditation of Counseling and Related Educational Programs. (1992). Minutes of CACREP board meeting. Alexandria, VA: Author.

Gross, D. R., & Capuzzi, D. (1991). Counseling the older adult. In D. Capuzzi and D. Gross (Eds.). *Introduction to counseling: Perspectives for the 1990s.* Boston: Allyn & Bacon.

Lombana, J. H. (1976). Counseling the elderly: Remediation plus prevention. *Personnel and Guidance Journal, 55,* 143–144.

Myers, J. E. (1992). Competencies, credentialing, and standards for gerontological counselors: Implications for counselor education. *Counselor Education and Supervision, 32,* 34–42.

Myers, J. E. (1992). Wellness, prevention, "development:" The cornerstone of the profession. *Journal of Counseling and Development, 71,* 136–138.

Ponzo, Z. (1992). Promoting successful aging: Problems, opportunities, and counseling guidelines. *Journal of Counseling and Development, 71,* 210–213.

Walz, G.R., Gazda, G., and Shertzer, B. (1991). *Counseling futures.* Ann Arbor: ERIC Counseling and Personnel Services Clearinghouse.

Women's Issues

Belenky, M., Clinchy, B., Goldberger, N., & Tarule, J. (1986). *Women's way of knowing.* New York: Basic Books.

Enns, C. Z. (1991). The "new" relationship models of women's identity: A review and critique for counselors. *Journal of Counseling and Development, 69,* 209–217.

Enns, C. Z. (1993). Twenty years of feminist counseling and therapy: From naming biases to implementing multifaceted practice. *The Counseling Psychologist, 21*(1), 3–87.

Gilligan, C. (1992). *In a different voice.* Cambridge, MA: Harvard.

Jordan, J. , Kaplan, A., Miller, J. Stiver, I., Surrey, J. (1991). *Women's growth in connection: The writings from the stone center.* New York: Guilford Press.

Josselson, R. (1987). *Finding herself: Pathways to identity development in women.* San Francisco: Jossey-Bass.

Lerner, H. G. (1988). *Women in therapy.* Northvale, NJ: Jason Aronson.

Miller, J. B. (1986). *Toward a new psychology of women* (2nd ed.). Boston: Beacon.

Men's Issues

Good, G., Mintz, L. (1990). Gender role conflict and depression in college men: Evidence for compounded risk. *Journal of Counseling and Development, 69,* 17–21.

Levant, R. F. (1990). Psychological services designed for men: A psychoeducational approach. *Psychotherapy, 27*(3), 309–315.

O'Neil, J. M. (1981). Patterns of gender role conflict and strain: Sexism and fear of femininity in men's lives. *Personnel and Guidance Journal 60,* 203–210.

O'Neil, J. M., Jelms, N. Gable, R., David, L., & Wrightsman, L. (1986). Gender-role conflict scale: College men's fear of femininity. *Sex Roles, 14,* 335–350.

Osherson, S., & Krugman, S. (1990). Men, shame, and psychotherapy. *Psychotherapy, 27*(3), 327–339.

Pollack, W. S. (1990). Men's development and psychotherapy: A psychoanalytic perspective. *Psychotherapy, 27*(3), 316–321.

Robertson, J., & Fitzgerald, L. (1992). Overcoming the masculine mystique: Preferences for alternative forms of assistance among men who avoid counseling. *Journal of Counseling Psychology, 39*(2), 240–245.

Scher, M. (1990). Effect of gender incongruities on men's experience as clients in psychotherapy. *Psychotherapy, 27*(3), 322–326.

C h a p t e r **11**

Models of Helping

This chapter will focus on three models of helping: the counselor as consultant; group counseling; and crisis intervention.

Counselor As Consultant

The counselor's role as a consultant to other human service professionals, such as teachers and nurses, and to organizations in the not-for-profit sector or business and industry, is rapidly growing. Counseling and consulting are slightly different processes involving similar skills. Students who are interested in learning more about consultation are referred to the July/August 1993 and November/December 1993 issues of the *Journal of Counseling and Development* for a more in-depth view of the consultation process.

In an effort to define consultation, most authors agree that it is a triadic relationship. That is, it involves a consultee who works with a client or a client system (Kurpius and Fuqua, 1993). Thus, three distinct roles are maintained, and the consultant does not interfere with the relationship between the consultee and the client. Other more general aspects of consultation include the fact that the consultant does not assume professional or ethical responsibility for the final outcome with the client and the consulting relationship is not either supervisory (involving performance judgment about people) or therapeutic (focused on the person rather than the work situation) (Kurpius and Fuqua, 1993).

Counselors may consult within the organization in which they are employed as an "internal consultant," or they may consult with other social or business units as external consultants. For example, school counselors who are consulting with teachers are internal consultants. A counselor working in private practice or in academia might consult in a business and industry setting, and some counselors might be employed in the area of organization development or in an employee assistance program. Either of these positions could emphasize consultation as a primary role responsibility. This is another "internal" consulting position. The application of consulting skills in community agencies or in business and industry has broadened the scope of employment opportunities for counselors.

Consultant Roles

Kurpius and Robinson (1978) note that consultants may assume a variety of roles because of the variety of purposes of consulting activity. Consultant roles are frequently delineated according to the particular model of consultation followed. Four broad consultant roles have been identified (Kurpius and Robinson, 1978) and are briefly outlined here.

Trainer/Educator
Under some circumstances the consultant may be hired to teach the staff a set of skills. For example, a school district might employ a counselor-educator to train its teachers in basic communication skills; a corporation might hire a consultant to teach its managers performance appraisal skills.

Expert/Prescriptive

In this approach to consultation the consultee buys the expertise of the consultant. The relationship resembles that of the medical model in that the consultant diagnoses the problem and prescribes a solution.

Negotiator

When a client system is experiencing difficulty, a consultant may be hired to mediate the conflict between parties. In this instance, the consultant works as a facilitator of communication and gives the system objective feedback regarding the processes that are blocking change.

Collaborator

The consultant may choose to form egalitarian relationships with consultees, resulting in joint diagnosis with the consultant working as a facilitator in the problem-solving process. This collaborative relationship has the advantage of teaching clients methods for solving their own problems. In the collaborative model the consultant must possess good relationship skills.

Consultant Skills

Many writers have discussed the skills and qualities that characterize an effective consultant. Dinkmeyer and Carlson (1973) have suggested the following counselor competencies:

1. He must be empathic and be able to understand how others feel and experience their world.
2. He must be able to relate to children and adults in a purposeful manner. While he should be effective in developing rapport and working relationships, he must be judicious in the use of this time. This necessitates the capacity to establish relationships with his clientele which are in line with the purposes of this program.
3. He must be sensitive to human needs. He would understand Maslow's hierarchy of needs, but more than that, it is vital that he be able to perceive a need and be available as a facilitator to help the person meet that need.
4. He must be aware of psychological dynamics, motivations, and purpose of human behavior. His training qualifies him not only to talk about psychological dynamics, but actually to deal with them in the here and now.
5. He must be perceptive of group dynamics and its significance for the educational establishment. This suggests that he is aware of the impact of group forces upon the teacher, that he sees the teacher in the context of forces from *without* (such as administration and parents) and forces from *within* (such as his own goals and purposes).
6. He must be capable of establishing relationships which are characterized by mutual trust and mutual respect. His appearance as a consultant to either a group or an individual should inspire confidence. His personal approach to people should make it apparent that they are collaborators with him.

7. He must be personally free from anxiety to the extent that he is capable of taking a risk on an important issue. He must be able to take a stand on significant issues that affect human development. The consultant's role requires a courageous approach to life. He has the courage to be imperfect, recognizing that he will make mistakes, but realizing mistakes are learning experiences and he must not be immobilized by the fear of making one. This courage is developed through group experiences and in the supervised practical experience.

8. Perhaps the most important of all, assuming he is able to establish the necessary and sufficient conditions for a helping relationship, the consultant should be creative, spontaneous, and imaginative. The consultant position, by its very nature, demands flexibility and the ability to deal with a variety of expectations—on one hand, the principal's need for order and structure; on the other, the child's need for participation, care, and concern. Thus, the consultant will find his creativity continuously challenged.

9. He should be capable of inspiring leadership at a number of levels from educational administrators who look to him as a specialist in understanding human relations and human behavior to parents who see him as a specialist in child psychology. Teachers would see him as a resource in connection with pupil personnel problems. He would be available to children who see him as a resource in helping them to understand self and others. (pp. 24–25)

The above competencies, while written for use in an educational environment, are appropriate for consultants in all settings. These nine competencies emphasize relationship building and counseling/communication skills which are essential to the consultant role.

Problem assessment skills are also fundamental in the counseling/consultant role. Consultants should be able to identify the focal issue in a given situation. Blake and Mouton (1978) state that the focal issue is that aspect of a situation which is causing the client difficulty. Blake and Mouton further suggest four basic focal issues: (1) the exercise of power and authority, (2) morale and cohesion, (3) problems that arise from standards or norms of conduct, and (4) issues in the area of goals and objectives. In assessing the consultee's problem, the consultant may discover that any one of the above issues or a combination of them could be the source of the problem. The ability to accurately assess the client problem and prescribe an appropriate intervention may be the determinant of consultant effectiveness (Blake and Mouton, 1978).

Bargaining, negotiating, and mediating abilities are basic consulting skills since the consulting role may require the consultant to negotiate conflicts or to use problem-solving methods in a small-group situation (Kurpius and Robinson, 1978).

As a trainer/educator the consultant must possess effective human relations skills. She should be able to teach communication skills and organize and plan workshop activities. Perhaps most important, the trainer/educator should understand group dynamics and small-group process. The consultant/trainer must not only understand a wide range of skills but must also be able to teach these skills to others. The literature has emphasized the necessity for counselors to "give away" their skills. The trainer role is therefore essential in the consultant's skill development process.

The Consulting Process

As a consultant enters into a relationship with a client, group, or institution, the consulting process should be organized around recognizable stages or phases. All consultants will not organize their work in an identical fashion; however, their approaches will have some similarities. Here we will examine some approaches that describe the phases and stages of the consulting process.

Kurpius, Fuqua, and Rozecki (1993) divide the consulting process into six steps: (1) pre-entry; (2) entry, problem exploration, and contracting; (3) information gathering, problem confirmation, and goal setting; (4) solution searching and intervention selection; (5) evaluation; and (6) termination. Usually, these stages occur in this order; however, recycling may occur between any of the above stages. Recycling will typically occur between entry and contracting or after evaluation (p. 601).

Pre-Entry

Before engaging in a consulting relationship, consultants must make a careful self-assessment to determine their beliefs and values so that they can understand "how individuals, families, programs, organizations or systems cause, solve, or avoid problems" (p. 601). During this stage consultants should explore their own professional competencies as well as their conceptual model of the consultation process.

Entry, Problem Exploration, and Contracting

This phase has to do with the initial contact made with the consultee and also involves the problem exploration and decision regarding a contract. During this stage the consultant may use two models, the "cycles of change" and the "forces for change" so they can better understand the problem and culture surrounding the problem. A contract including a statement of fees should be drawn up.

Information Gathering, Problem Confirmation, and Goal Setting

Problem definition is a critical component of successful consultation, and good data should be used to accurately define the problem. Typically the data is gathered by both the consultant and consultee. Once the data has been collected, analyzed, and synthesized, agreement on ownership of the problem must be reached. The problem then becomes the goal of the consultation process.

Solution Searching and Intervention Selection

This stage of the process requires that the consultant choose an intervention from several different types. The choice of an intervention may be determined by the setting. For example, a school or mental health clinic might require an intervention that focuses on human development, while a business might require a structural intervention to change policies or technology.

Evaluation

The evaluation phase involves the importance of assessing the success or failure of the intervention.

Termination

At this stage both parties agree to terminate the consulting process either because it has been successful or because success is unlikely. Kurpius, Fuqua, and Rozecki recommend that the following are considered: "Inform all appropriate members that termination is forthcoming and say when and why; explain the effect of the interventions and the objectives which have been met; recognize numbers and processes that contributed to the success; and reflect on how the work culture may have been improved as a result of the consultation" (p. 606).

Group Counseling

Group therapy has been recognized as a therapeutic procedure for many years, but only recently have group methods gained popularity. Groups of all varieties are now available to those seeking help for serious psychological problems, to those experiencing a situational crisis such as divorce, and to healthy individuals who wish to expand their self-awareness and increase their level of interpersonal functioning. There are rehabilitation groups for alcoholics and those with other drug-related problems; there are women's groups, divorce adjustment groups, conjoint family therapy groups, children's groups, and assertiveness training groups. There are also groups characterized by the theoretical orientation of the leader—transactional analysis groups, Gestalt groups, bioenergetics groups, and so on. In this chapter we will introduce group counseling by examining (1) a definition of group counseling; (2) the terminology associated with the group movement; (3) the advantages and goals of working in groups; (4) the limitations of group work.

Definition of Group Counseling

While the term *group counseling* has become very popular and is used to identify a variety of practices, there is still some variation in what the term means to different individuals. Beyond an acceptance that a group consists of three or more members who influence each other and are influenced by others, little else about groups is accepted as consensus. For the purpose of this chapter, we will rely on George and Dustin (1988) in which they define group counseling as the *use of group interaction to facilitate self-understanding as well as individual behavior change* (p. 5).

Terminology of the Group Movement

The group movement has generated its own terminology. Such terms as group guidance, group counseling, group therapy, T-groups, sensitivity groups, and so on have been misused in the literature and by practitioners. To help eliminate this confusion over terminology, we will attempt here to distinguish among the various types of groups and to define such group terminology as group process, norms, and cohesion. Our discussion will be restricted to those groups in which the focus and content are primarily personal and psychological as contrasted with groups organized to reach a goal or to complete a task, such as committees.

Types of Groups

Guidance Groups.   Guidance groups are group discussion sessions in which the content of the discussion is affective or psychological. These groups may also be used to distribute information relevant to the student's personal needs and interests, such as educational, vocational, or social information. Guidance groups are most often found in the educational setting and are typically conducted with a class. They range in size from twelve to forty participants. One characteristic that distinguishes a guidance group from a counseling or therapeutic group is that a guidance group is relatively structured and the topic to be discussed is generally chosen by the group leader. Another distinguishing feature is that a guidance group is concerned with preventing problems rather than remediating psychological difficulties.

There is disagreement in the literature about what constitutes a guidance group. Perhaps the term *guidance* has become outdated and a broader term such as *psychological education* should be substituted. The new psychological education or affective education curricula typically rely on group process within the classroom setting and meet other criteria of guidance groups.

Counseling Groups.   Counseling groups, as contrasted with guidance groups, focus on the individual rather than on the topic (Mahler, 1969). A counseling group is smaller (five to ten participants), and less structure is provided by the counselor. The counselor's role is to create a safe and secure environment where group members feel comfortable sharing personal concerns related to their families, interpersonal relationships, self-concepts, or other personal, social or educational difficulties. The content of the discussions is affective and personal; each member has the opportunity to discuss developmental and interpersonal concerns, and these concerns are ultimately related to desired behavior change.

Therapy Groups.   Therapy groups were the first groups to be used for therapeutic purposes. Group therapy procedures were developed during World War II in response to the high rate of psychiatric problems and the concurrent shortage of personnel to provide individual therapy (Lifton, 1972; Corey and Corey, 1977). Unlike those in counseling groups, the participants in therapy groups need intensive psychological help. Their problems are typically deep-seated and involve personality disorganization. Group therapy, then, most often involves persons who are unable to function "normally." Therapy groups would be of longer duration than counseling groups and would require a leader with more training and expertise.

Encounter or Sensitivity Groups.   Encounter groups, sensitivity groups, or personal growth groups are part of the larger human potential movement, which focuses on expanding personal self-awareness and developing individual potential. These groups are at the opposite end of the continuum from therapy groups and obviously serve an entirely different population. The purpose of an encounter group is to provide the opportunity for healthy, well-functioning individuals to explore and to actualize their potential in the areas of self-awareness and interpersonal relationships.

Encounter groups typically provide participants with an intense, very personal, and intimate experience that grows out of trust, openness, sharing, and risk-taking. Nonverbal exercises emphasizing touch and other sensory awareness experiences are frequently used to facilitate this intimacy (Corey and Corey, 1977). An encounter group can be highly structured, with the leader guiding the participants through a series of structured exercises. These experiences are often referred to as *microlabs*. Encounter groups are sometimes conducted over a weekend. In essence, participants go on a retreat for an intensive group experience. These weekend growth groups are frequently referred to as *marathons*. The group meets for unusually long periods of time and capitalizes on fatigue to facilitate letting go of roles and facades to promote directness and honesty in communication.

T-Groups.   Human relations training began in the 1950s with the development of the first training center at Bethel, Maine. The National Training Laboratories, or NTL, were founded by Leland Bradford, Ronald Lippitt, and Kenneth Benne. The "T-Group," or Training Group, first gained acceptance in industry as a method for studying the process by which a group functions in an attempt to improve the efficiency and effectiveness of the team. T-groups emphasize member roles within the group and focus on the relationship of each group member to what is going on in the group at the time (Lifton, 1972). As contrasted with guidance, counseling, therapy, or encounter groups, the T-group is more task-oriented and concerned with how the group functions and with educating participants to become better group members.

Group Terminology

Group Process.   *Group process* can be distinguished from *group content* in that *content* refers to what the group is discussing, whereas *process* refers to how the discussion is being conducted (Johnson and Johnson, 1982). To be an effective group leader or member, one must be able to both participate in the discussion and observe what is going on. In a counseling group, the counselor must be able not only to listen carefully and intently to each speaker but also to observe patterns in communication, roles assumed by each member, nonverbal communication, and so on.

Group Cohesion.   *Group cohesion* refers to the interacting forces that keep the group together. A group is cohesive to the extent that the positive aspects of group membership outweigh the negative ones. However, since group cohesion is de-

FIGURE 11-1   **The counseling group brings together several individuals to form one group for the purpose of mutual growth and support**
(Robert Harbison)

pendent on the attractiveness of the group for each member at any given time, the cohesiveness of the groups is always changing (Johnson and Johnson, 1982).

A cohesive group is dependent on group members' sharing similar goals for group membership. Group cohesiveness can be evaluated by such factors as whether or not members attend regularly, whether the participants arrive promptly, and the level of affection, trust, and mutual support that members express toward each other (Johnson and Johnson, 1982).

Group Norms.   Group norms are closely related to group cohesiveness. *Group norms* refer to the formal and informal rules that govern what is considered to be appropriate behavior within the group (Corey and Corey, 1977). For example, an important norm when working with children in groups would be that only one person talks at a time. Another common group norm is that of maintaining the confidentiality of what is discussed in the group. Giving and accepting feedback and sharing personally relevant and meaningful material might also be appropriate group norms. It is important that groups establish their formal norms at the outset of the group experience. The informal norms arise as members try out various behaviors and experience the positive and negative consequences of their actions.

Why Counsel in Groups?

Group counseling has many advantages, but it is not appropriate as an intervention strategy for all clients. What are the advantages of counseling clients in groups? When is group counseling the most effective therapeutic approach with a client? What limitations are associated with group counseling? When should one recommend group as opposed to individual counseling? These questions have been addressed by many practitioners and theoreticians. This section will summarize their opinions and offer some guidelines regarding the use of group counseling as a therapeutic intervention.

Advantages

In citing the advantages of counseling in groups, the first and most obvious is its practicality. Counselors in most settings are overloaded with clients. Group counseling is viewed as a preferred mode of treatment not only because it is efficient but also because it is more effective than individual counseling with certain client concerns. When working in groups, counselors can meet with as many as eight clients in the same amount of time that they spend with a single client in individual counseling. Group counseling offers other distinct advantages and is based on a sound theoretical rationale.

One argument for counseling individuals in groups is that many psychological problems are of an interpersonal nature, and group counseling provides the individual with the opportunity to work through these interpersonal problems in a social context. For example, feedback about behavior is much more influential in group therapy since it comes from the client's peers rather than from the counselor. Clients in the group setting, then, have the opportunity to grow through the process of receiving honest feedback from members of their own peer group. As George and Dustin (1988) point out, the counseling group acts as a microcosm of society and provides an opportunity for the individual to experience peer pressure, social influence, and conformity as part of the counseling experience.

Clients also have the opportunity to practice new behaviors and to receive support for and feedback on their experimentation. Personal growth, change, and exploration can thus take place in a safe, secure environment before new and risky behaviors are tried out in the world in which the client lives.

Group counseling enables clients to explore their problems and also exposes them to the feelings, concerns, and experiences of others. Clients are often experiencing their difficulties in isolation; they find it hard to put their problems in perspective. The group setting gives clients the opportunity to learn that others also have problems. As clients share themselves in the group, a level of trust develops that results in close, intimate contact among the group members. The group experience develops into a support system and as such becomes an important source of security and strength to the participants.

While clients in groups are focusing on resolving their own interpersonal or intrapersonal difficulties, they are also exposed to interpersonal relationship skills being modeled by both the group leader and the other group members. As such skills as empathy, active listening, feedback, and confrontation are modeled within the group, group members observe and have the opportunity to practice them within the group. Learning these skills and behaviors, which are essential to effective interpersonal relationships, enables clients to improve their interpersonal functioning.

A final benefit of group counseling is that clients have not only the opportunity to receive help from the counselor and other group members but also the opportunity to give help to others. Responding in a helpful way to others redirects the client's attention outside himself and helps build a more positive self-concept as the helping behavior is reinforced by other group participants.

Limitations

Despite its many advantages, as with any therapeutic approach group counseling has its limitations. Shertzer and Stone (1974) have identified the following:

1. Some clients need individual help before they can function in a group. The client may be insecure and incapable of entering the group environment without first experiencing the counseling process on a one-to-one basis. After working through some basic issues, however, many clients are able to enter a group smoothly, if the nature of their concerns fits the goals of the group process.

2. The counselor's role in group counseling tends to be much more diffused and therefore more complex. The counselor must be simultaneously able to focus on the concerns of each client, respond to the interaction among group members, and observe the dynamics of the group.

3. The group can become bogged down in "group process" issues that are time-consuming and may detract from individual concerns of group members.

4. Some clients may find it difficult to develop trust with a group of individuals; therefore, feelings, attitudes, values, and behaviors that are considered unacceptable may not be brought out for discussion.

5. There is still some disagreement and lack of information about which client concerns can better be dealt with in a group than on a one-to-one basis.

Corey and Corey (1977) add the following limitations of groups:

1. Some counselors and clients expect too much from the group experience and view group therapy as a "cure-all."

2. Pressure to conform to group norms can cause clients to inappropriately substitute the group's norms for their own.

3. For some clients the group experience becomes an end in itself rather than an experience that is used to improve their functioning in daily interactions.

4. Some clients misuse the understanding and acceptance of the group experience. They vent their problems to the group and do not attempt to change their behavior.

5. There is a danger of inadequate leadership in groups as persons with no training other than involvement in a group experience decide to organize and lead groups.

6. The potential for psychological destruction is as great as the potential for psychological growth. Group participants can make themselves very vulnerable and

---

BOX 11-1 Advantages of Counseling in Groups

1. It is efficient. Counselors can provide services to many more clients.
2. Group counseling provides a social interpersonal context in which to work on interpersonal problems.
3. Clients have the opportunity to practice new behaviors.
4. It enables clients to put their problems in perspective and to understand how they are similar to and different from others.
5. Clients form a support system for each other.
6. Clients learn interpersonal communication skills.
7. Clients are given the opportunity to give as well as to receive help.

---

can experience extreme pain when confronted by group members. Because of the number of group participants, the leader can lose control of the situation, resulting in psychological harm to the group members.

Therapeutic Elements in Group Counseling

A number of researchers/theorists (Corsini and Rosenberg, 1955; Hill, 1957; Ohlson, 1977; Yalom, 1970; Bloch, Reibstein, and Crouch, 1979) have identified factors or elements that are shared by group counselors with various leadership styles. These individuals proposed a variety of therapeutic elements and developed classification systems for organizing them. George and Dustin (1988) attempted to build on the work of these individuals, as well as their own experiences, and proposed a somewhat simpler model for identifying those therapeutic elements that they believed to be necessary and sufficient for effective group counseling.

They proposed that therapeutic effectiveness in group counseling results from these essential elements:

1. Installation of hope
2. Sense of safety and support
3. Cohesiveness
4. Universality
5. Vicarious learning
6. Interpersonal learning

They also suggested that other, more process-oriented elements are also important, including catharsis, imparting of information, and humor.

Group Goals

Closely related to the advantages and limitations of group counseling as outlined above are the appropriate goals for clients entering a group counseling experience. These goals, which have been identified by Corey and Corey (1977), are illustrated

BOX 11-2

1. To become more open and honest with selected others
2. To decrease game-playing and manipulating, which prevent intimacy
3. To learn how to trust oneself and others
4. To move toward authenticity and genuineness
5. To become freer and less bound by external "shoulds," "oughts," and "musts"
6. To grow in self-acceptance and learn not to demand perfection of oneself
7. To recognize and accept certain polarities within oneself
8. To lessen one's fears of intimacy and to learn to reach out to those one would like to be closer to
9. To move away from merely meeting other's expectations and decide for oneself the standards that will guide one
10. To learn how to confront others with care, concern, honesty, and directness
11. To learn how to ask directly for what one wants
12. To increase self-awareness and thereby increase the possibilities for choice and action
13. To learn the distinction between having feelings and acting on them
14. To free oneself from the inappropriate early decisions that keep one less than the person one could or would like to be
15. To recognize that others struggle too
16. To clarify the values one has and to decide whether and how to modify them
17. To be able to tolerate more ambiguity—to learn to make choices in a world where nothing is guaranteed
18. To find ways of resolving personal problems
19. To explore hidden potentials and creativity
20. To increase one's capacity to care for others
21. To learn how to give to others

in Box 11-2. The goals outlined by Corey and Corey in Box 11-2 are related to self-concept development. The group counseling experience is possibly most beneficial to clients when the major issues or concerns to be dealt with reside in the client's feeling about self. In other words, the group experience seems to be of particular value in helping the client find answers to questions such as "Who am I?" "Am I lovable and capable?" "How do others respond to me?" "How am I similar to and yet different from my peers?"

When to Recommend Group Counseling
Since group counseling is very effective in self-concept development, clients with poor self-concepts, with a lack of self-confidence and self-esteem, should be carefully considered as participants in group counseling. The goals of group counseling as listed in Box 11-2 should serve as a guideline in determining whether group counseling should be recommended. When is group counseling unwise?

Mahler (1969) has suggested that one-to-one counseling is indicated in the following situations:

1 When the client is in a state of crisis
2. When confidentiality is essential to protect the client
3. When interpreting tests related to self-concept
4. When the client has an unusual fear of speaking
5. When the client is grossly ineffective in the area of interpersonal relationship skills
6. When the client has very limited awareness or his or her own feelings, motivations, and behaviors
7. When deviant sexual behavior is involved
8. When the client's need for attention is too great to be managed in a group

Considerations in Group Formation

Counselors must give careful consideration to the group formation process. There are several steps to follow to insure that the group will be able to function effectively. Here we will examine such specific issues as the presentation, intake interview, the screening and selection process, and group size and composition.

The Presentation

Ohlsen has defined the presentation as a "description of the treatment process for prospective group counseling clients" (1977, p. 21). The presentation includes both counselor and client expectations of the process. It can either be given to clients as individuals or to a group of prospective clients, such as a class. The presentation provides the counselor with the opportunity to explain the group process to prospective clients. Ohlsen (1977) notes that it serves two other purposes: (1) The presentation encourages clients to accept responsibility for their participation in the group and emphasizes the counselor's expectation that client concerns be discussed openly and honestly; and (2) it increases the attractiveness of group counseling.

During the presentation the counselor specifies what occurs in a group counseling session and enumerates the benefits of participating in a group. The counselor has an opportunity to clarify the distinction between a counseling session and a class discussion or rap session with one's peers. The counselor may choose to give specific examples of client problems that have been dealt with in the group context or may have former group clients describe their experience. Clients are given the opportunity to ask questions about the process, including such issues as confidentiality, frequency and duration of sessions, and attendance requirements (Ohlsen, 1977). Following the presentation the counselor will ask for volunteers and will set up screening interviews.

The Intake Interview

The intake interview, a critical part of the group formation process, enables the counselor to screen clients. The dynamics of a counseling group are such that client selection greatly influences the outcome of the group experience.

During the intake interview the counselor uses listening skills to help the prospective client identify specific issues or concerns that might be discussed in the counseling group. A primary function of the intake interview is to secure a commitment from the prospective client to openly discuss any concerns that are identified.

Following the intake interviews the counselor works on group composition and structure. The counselor should consider age, sex, and personality distribution; size of the group; length, frequency, and duration of sessions; whether the group will be open or closed, and voluntary versus involuntary participation (Mahler, 1969).

Selection of Group Members

Lowrey and Slavson (1943) and Gazda (1978) concur that skill and insight in grouping is the most essential element in group; the counselor's personality is the second most important factor.

Age

Age is perhaps more important in forming groups of children and adolescents than groups of adults. Counselors should select clients of approximately the same age, but even more important is the social maturity of the client. For example, a socially immature sixth grader may not be ready to discuss problems related to sexuality with other eleven-year-olds.

Sex

The client's sex is also an important factor to consider when forming a counseling group. However, opinions differ on whether or not to treat boys and girls together during the latency period. Ohlsen and Gazda (1965) found differences in the way girls and boys in the fifth grade participated in group discussions and in their interest in the opposite sex; these authors disagree as to whether or not fifth graders should be grouped by sex. Ohlsen contends that treating boys and girls together at this stage provides an opportunity for them to deal with their differing psychosocial development; Gazda prefers to treat them separately.

Personality Composition

Perhaps the most significant factor in client selection has to do with grouping clients by their personality types. The research on homogeneous versus heterogeneous personality types seems to support grouping clients with mixed personality types and problems (Peck and Stewart, 1964). When clients with similar problems—such as drug addicts, alcoholics, children from divorced families, or gifted underachievers—are grouped together most researchers and theoreticians agree on the importance of including in the group peers who have successfully coped with the problem or who can serve as role models (Gazda, 1978). When models are not included, homogeneously grouped clients have difficulty helping each other work through their problems; in many instances clients with similar personal and social characteristics reinforce each other's ineffective behaviors.

To summarize briefly, the guidelines for organizing a counseling group would recommend homogeneous grouping by age or social maturity and sex for children and early adolescent clients and heterogeneous grouping of personality types. Counseling groups composed of adult clients can be heterogeneously grouped on all factors.

Size of Group

The size of the group will vary depending on the age of the clients, the amount of involvement expected and the personalities of the group members. Ideally, a counseling group has from six to eight participants. This number allows for some variation in personality types and for adequate member participation. With young children a successful group can be run with fewer participants.

When a group of adults has more than eight members, a couple of problems may arise. First, each client may not have the opportunity to explore personal issues, and second, the leader may have difficulty following the interaction of so many participants. If a group must have more than ten participants, coleaders are advisable.

Length and Frequency of Meetings

The length of a group counseling session varies widely depending on the age of the clients and the restrictions of the setting. With elementary school children expecting a concentration span of more than twenty to thirty minutes at a sitting is unrealistic. Group sessions for adolescents should probably last about an hour. Sessions for adults are most beneficial when they are between two and three hours long. This amount of time allows group members to become involved and for important issues to surface and be dealt with. In order for the momentum of the group to be maintained not more than a week should elapse between sessions. With young children the sessions should not only be shorter, as noted above, but also more frequent, perhaps twice a week.

Duration of the Group

Although some groups have met over a period of years, a span of more than a year is not recommended. After a year's time most personal issues have been dealt with, and the group will have served its purpose. In a school setting the semester serves as a natural beginning and ending point.

Open versus Closed Membership

The membership of a group may be open or closed. In a closed group those persons present at the outset stay in the group for its duration; no new members are allowed. In an open group members are allowed to join at different points in the group's life. Open group membership can create problems of trust, acceptance, and support within the group.

Guidelines for Forming Groups

The following questions will serve as a checklist for group organization, facilitating the group formation procedure and helping to ensure a successful group counseling experience.

1. What type of group will it be? A personal-growth type group or a group designed to treat people with certain disorders? Long-term or short-term?
2. Whom is the group for? For a specific population, such as college students or married couples? For people seeking a certain thing, such as personal growth or help with a personal problem?
3. What are your goals for this group? That is, what will members gain from participating in it?
4. Why do you feel that there's a need for such a group?
5. What are the basic assumptions underlying this project?
6. Who will lead the group? What are his or her qualifications?
7. What kind of screening and selection procedures will be used? What is the rationale for using these particular procedures?
8. How many members will be in the group? Where will the group meet? How often? How long will each meeting last? Will new people be allowed to join the group once it has started?
9. How will the group members be prepared for the group experience? What ground rules will be established by the leader at the outset?
10. What kind of structure will the group have? What techniques will be used? Why are these techniques appropriate?
11. How will you handle the fact that people will be taking some risks by participating in the group? What will you tell the members about this, and what will you do about it? Will you take any special precautions with participants who are minors?
12. What evaluation procedures do you plan? What follow-up procedures.
13. What kinds of topics will be explored in this group? To what degree will this be determined by the group members and to what degree by the leader?
14. What do you expect to be the characteristics of the various stages of the group? What is the function of the leader at each stage? What might the problems be at each stage, and how will the leader cope with them (Corey and Corey, 1977, p. 88)?

Effective Group Leader Behaviors

The counselor's role in a group is diffused and complex. The counselor must be able to respond sensitively and empathically to each individual while observing other members' reactions to the communication. The counselor must also be able to observe group dynamics and have the skills to process the complex interaction that occurs in the group. What behaviors or communication skills are essential? The following section will outline effective group leadership skills and, through examples, explore their application in the group counseling setting.

Listening

Effective listening is composed of two basic skills: restatement of content (or paraphrasing) and reflection of feeling. These skills, fundamental in individual counseling, are also fundamental to the group counseling process. The effective group leader fully tunes in to the client's message and responds to much more than the spoken word. The counselor responds to the client's nonverbal communication and notes any apparent incongruence between body posture, voice tone, and what the person is saying. The counselor can accurately identify the client's feelings, perhaps before the client is aware of them.

Listening builds trust and communicates the counselor's acceptance of the client. For example, a fifth-grade boy involved in a custody suit comes to group and expresses anger at another student who sits in his chair. The counselor might respond with, "It sounds like you're pretty angry with Jim because he took your seat. I noticed that you seemed pretty wound up as you came into group; maybe you're just a little nervous and scared because you have to go to court today and are taking some of your feelings out on Jim."

Perception Check

Perception checks are also facilitative in the group setting. A perception check conveys that the counselor wants to understand the clients' feelings and is literally checking out his or her perception of the clients' experience. In a perception check the counselor accurately labels the clients' feeling and then asks whether or not the perception is accurate. For example, the counselor might ask, "Did you feel angry about what John just said?" or "I get the impression you are annoyed with me. Are you?" or "I'm not sure from your facial expression if my remark made you angry, confused, or exasperated."

Feedback

Since a therapeutic goal of group counseling is to learn how one comes across to others, the counselor must give feedback to group members. Feedback should be descriptive rather than evaluative; it must identify the specific behaviors. Examples of good feedback would include statements such as:

"I noticed that you waited until Sue was finished before you began talking."
"When you described your feelings in such detail (so openly), I was able to feel very close to you."
"Are you aware that every time John speaks you stare at the floor?"
"I have a lot of difficulty tuning in to you because the smile on your face seems so inconsistent with the anger you are expressing."
"I'd like to be your friend, but when I learn that you've broken a confidence I feel I cannot trust you.

Linking

Through the skill of linking the leader relates the concerns or statement of one group member to those of another in the group (Corey and Corey, 1977). In essence, linking points out the commonalities of experience among group members in an attempt to encourage member-to-member communication. For instance, Joe may communicate an uneasiness, and the leader may relate this to the unhappiness Jane expressed earlier.

Open-ended Leads

Using open-ended leads or questions in groups can force the members to be very specific about feelings and the sources of these feelings. They also enable the counselor to focus on events or experiences that bring the discussion into the here and now. What and how questions are more useful than why questions.

Some examples of the use of open-ended questions in group counseling are:

"How are you feeling now?"
"How are you feeling about Joan?"
"What is your reaction to the present discussion?"
"How would you like for me to respond to you?"
"How would you like Mike to perceive you?"
"What is the source of your anger?"
"What is the group experiencing now?"
"What is the relationship between what you've just related to us and how you're feeling now?"

Confrontation

Confrontation can be the most powerful leader skill when used with sensitivity and care. The counselor might choose to confront discrepancies in an individual's verbal and nonverbal behavior; he or she might confront behavior that disrupts the group's functioning (Corey and Corey, 1977). The counselor may also choose to confront the group as a whole. Examples of confrontive responses include, "I've noticed that you smile while you express anger toward Paul"; "I'm angry and frustrated that you take up group time discussing the baseball game"; and "I'm con-

fused about where this group is going. You made a commitment to wor
lems or concerns and no one seems willing to share."

Process Skills

An effective group leader must have the ability to observe the process by which the
group is functioning and be prepared to comment on it as it relates to the group
goals. The counselor can begin by asking group members what has happened during a session and then might comment on the dynamics of the session. For example, following a particularly slow session the group leader might say "I've noticed
that it's been rather difficult for us to get started today. I wonder if this is related
to the fact that Susan received a lot of negative feedback last week and each of us
is somewhat afraid that the same thing will happen to us if we open up. Perhaps
the level of trust in the group has been damaged. What do you think?" This type
of comment forces the group to examine itself and its functioning.

Summarization

As in individual counseling, summaries have an important place in the group
process. The group leader listens carefully to all the interaction in the group and
uses a summary to help the group move to a different level of interaction. A summary is also useful when the group becomes bogged down. If, for example, members begin disagreeing on a specific group interaction, the leader may need to summarize the basic arguments so that the process can proceed.

Overall Responsibilities

The role of the group leader is much more comprehensive than a listing of essential skills might suggest. The group leader may find it necessary to share information regarding effective and ineffective communication. He or she has the responsibility to be sure everyone owns their own feelings and asks for feedback from
other members. Possibly the most important requirement of the group leader role
is to model effective communication skills and appropriate group behaviors. As
group members observe the leader's use of effective communication skills, they
will be able to assume more responsibility for the group. This pattern, once established, will increase member-to-member behavior and decrease leader-to-member
interaction, freeing the group leader to spend more time observing group process.

BOX 11-3   Effective Group Leadership Skills

1. Active listening
2. Perception check
3. Feedback
4. Confrontation
5. Process Skills
6. Linking
7. Open-ended leads
8. Summarization

ortant that the group leader enable group members to receive
urately. To do so the group leader may (1) have the receiver re-
f what is said; (2) rephrase the sender's message so that the re-
urately; (3) encourage the receiver to question the speaker if
r.

oup leader is complex and diffused. Group counselors must have
nce in their counseling skills. Those interested in leading counseling
groups should consider working with an experienced therapist as a coleader to observe appropriate group counseling skills and behaviors.

Effective Group Member Behaviors

As noted, the counselor must model those behaviors that promote effective interaction in the group. Given the opportunity to observe the leader's behavior, group
members become actively involved in the interactive group process. What roles do
group members typically perform in a group? Johnson and Johnson (1982) in a discussion of the distributed functions theory of leadership have outlined twenty task
and maintenance functions that are performed in most groups by members and
leaders alike. These task and maintenance functions appear below.

Task Functions:

1. Information and Opinion Giver: Offers facts, opinions, ideas, suggestions, and
relevant information to help group discussions.
2. Information and Opinion Seeker: Asks for facts, information, opinions, ideas,
and feelings from other members to help group discussion.
3. Starter: Proposes goals and tasks to initiate action within the group.
4. Direction Giver: Develops plans on how to proceed and focuses attention on
the task to be done.
5. Summarizer: Pulls together related ideas or suggestions and restates and summarizes major points discussed.
6. Coordinator: Shows relationships among various ideas by pulling them together and harmonizes activities of various subgroups and members.
7. Diagnoser: Figures out sources of difficulties the group has in working effectively and the blocks to progress in accomplishing the groups goals.
8. Energizer: Stimulates a higher quality of work from the group.
9. Reality Tester: Examines the practicality and workability of ideas, evaluates alternative solutions, and applies them to real situations to see how they will work.
10. Evaluator: Compares group decisions and accomplishments with group standards and goals.

Maintenance Functions:

11. Encourager of Participation: Warmly encourages everyone to participate, giving recognition for contributions, demonstrating acceptance and openness to ideas
of others, is friendly and responsive to group members.

12. Harmonizer and Compromiser: Persuades members to analyze constructively their differences in opinions, searches for common elements in conflicts, and tries to reconcile disagreements.
13. Tension Reliever: Eases tensions and increases the enjoyment of group members by joking, suggesting breaks, and proposing fun approaches to group work.
14. Communication Helper: Shows good communication skills and makes sure that each group member understands what other members are saying.
15. Evaluator of Emotional Climate: Asks members how they feel about the way in which the group is working and about each other, and shares own feelings about both.
16. Process Observer: Watches the process by which the group is working and uses the observations to help examine group effectiveness.
17. Standard Setter: Expresses group standards and goals to make members aware of the direction of the work and the progress being made toward the goal and to get open acceptance of group norms and procedures.
18. Active Listener: Listens and serves as an interested audience for other members, is receptive to others' ideas, goes along with the group when not in disagreement.
19. Trust Builder: Accepts and supports openness of other group members, reinforcing risk taking and encouraging individuality.
20. Interpersonal Problem Solver: Promotes open discussion of conflicts between group members in order to resolve conflicts and increase group togetherness (Johnson and Johnson, 1975 pp. 26–27).

Stages and Phases of Group Process

Most authors and researchers agree that groups go through somewhat predictable stages. Despite different labels in the literature, these stages generally seem to consist of (1) an initial or involvement stage; (2) a transition phase; (3) a working stage; and (4) a termination stage. Group leaders should be familiar with the phases and stages of group process and should be able to accurately identify stages of any group they are leading. An in-depth understanding of group stages enables the group leader to make perceptive observations about group process and to serve as a guide as to particular skills and behaviors necessary at a given point to move the group toward its goal. In this section we will briefly explore the characteristics of the four stages as summarized by Mahler (1969).

Involvement

During the involvement stage several tasks need to be accomplished. First, the counselor must *clarify* the clients' purposes for their participation in the group. Each client must be able to identify personal goals and explore his or her expectations for the group experience. Then the group members and group leaders begin the process of getting acquainted. Initially this may take the form of group members sharing specific information or personal data about themselves; on an informal level members observe each other's interpersonal style and assess the trustworthiness of other participants and the group leader. A critical process of the involvement phase is development of a trusting and accepting relationship among participants. At this point the group's activity should focus on exploring ideas and feelings. To begin problem solving at this early stage is inappropriate. The tasks of the involvement stage may be accomplished in one session or may require five or six sessions, depending on the group.

Transition

The transition stage is characterized by some tension and resistance among the group participants. Typically group members begin to experience ambivalence as the expectations of leaders and other members become clear. Mahler (1969) suggests that the following might characterize some of the feelings of group members during the phase:

> *"I didn't realize that we were going to talk so personally."*
> *"I didn't intend to get really involved, or to share any of my real feelings."*
> *"I am not at all sure about this idea of sharing our feelings; it seems pretty dangerous to me."*
> *"I want very much to learn about myself, but what will other people think when they really get to know me?"*
> *"I have lots of feelings, but maybe it will sound silly if I talk about them."*
> *"I doubt that anyone is really interested in me anyway"* (p. 14).

In the transition phase the leader's skills are of utmost importance. Mahler has identified three skills that are essential during this stage: (1) a sense of timing, of when to intervene in the discussion, (2) the ability to pick up patterns of behavior; and (3) skill in assessing the emotional climate of the group. These leadership skills should be added to the list presented in Box 11–3. A cogent discussion of these skills can be found in Mahler (1969).

Working

The working stage takes up the majority of the group's life. During the working stage group members bring their concerns to the group and welcome other group members' understanding support, and help. The working stage is characterized by a high level of morale and sense of belonging. As members open up and choose to use the group as a place to sort through their concerns, they also begin to focus on changing undesirable behaviors. During this stage leader-to-member interaction decreases, and member-to-member interaction increases. The group leader has more opportunity to act as an observer and facilitator of participants' interactions.

Termination

As the group draws to a close, the leader must prepare the group for its termination. Individual group members should be encouraged to assess their own growth during the group experience and formulate future goals. The basic issue during termination is dealing with group members' feelings and reactions to the experience as a whole and with termination.

Crisis Intervention Counseling

Overview of the Crisis Situation

Counselors in all settings, as well as those engaged in a wide variety of helping professions, encounter crisis situations as an incidental development in their work. These situations are frequently explosive in nature and often involve a threat to the survival of the individual or to the family unit to which the individual belongs.

Puryear (1979) indicates that a crisis state is characterized by (1) symptoms of stress, primarily psychological and physiological, always with extreme discomfort, (2) an attitude of panic or defeat, wherein the individual feels overwhelmed, inadequate, and helpless, but may exhibit either agitation or withdrawal, (3) a focus on relief, with little interest in the initial problem, (4) lowered efficiency, and (5) limited duration.

Crisis intervention is an approach to helping people in crisis. As such, it consists of intensive work over a short period of time, with emphasis on the concrete facts of the current situation and on the client's own efforts at changing it. While crisis intervention is clearly a "helping" strategy, it is not counseling; it has a narrower and more superficial focus, more modest goals, and briefer duration.

Since most of counselor training focuses on therapeutic intervention over a period of time, crisis situations typically create an intense sense of frustration and inadequacy for the counselor who is unsure of exactly which direction should be taken. Resorting to normal counseling strategies may be inadequate since the crisis could be ended by disaster—suicide, homicide, chronic psychosis, or a permanent disintegration of the family unit—before the next counseling session can take place.

Thus the primary goal of crisis intervention is to avoid catastrophe. In addition, one must distinguish the unresolved initial problem from the coping efforts, the stress symptoms, and the relief efforts. The individual or family must be prevented from dangerous action until a state of equilibrium can be reached, creating a situation in which therapeutic intervention can be effective.

A Model for Crisis Intervention

There are three stages in crisis intervention which are similar to the counseling process, but which recognize the nature of the crisis situation. Emphasis in each stage is given to the special needs of the individual in crisis. During the first

FIGURE 11-2   Teenagers experimenting with alcohol and other drugs often become a crisis situation for counselors
(Photo by James T. Hurley)

stage, the counselor is particularly concerned about establishing that she genuinely understands what the individual is going through—the fears, dangers, feelings, and hopelessness. This involves getting into the client's world. By doing so, the counselor establishes that she is not only a professional who *may* be able to help, but one who *can* help, since the individual knows that the counselor recognizes the desperateness of the situation. The three important processes of the first stage are establishing rapport, assessing the situation, and clarifying the problem. To establish rapport, the counselor creates an environment that allows the client to discuss his crisis. Roadblocks may occur here, preventing the intervention from continuing. The client may test the helper with questions like, "Are you married? Divorced? How old are you? What are your qualifications?" It is important to remember that the client is really asking "Can you help me?" Also, clients often communicate a problem that is only an introduction to the underlying problem as the reason for seeing the counselor. Counselors must remain sensitive to the possibility that the presenting problem may just be a way of mustering enough courage to discuss a more serious problem. Thus, as in typical counseling situations, the counselor's emphasis should be on communicating genuine warmth and empathic understanding.

Once a crisis situation has been identified, the counselor should immediately assess the urgency of the situation. If there is no reason to believe that an immediate emergency exists—if, for example, the client has already taken steps that would be of severe danger to self or others—the counselor may begin assessing the overall problem, including some judgment as to the severity of the crisis, a formulation of the series of events that led up to the crisis, and an identification of the problem that lies behind the crisis. At this point, counselor behaviors that may lead to further problem clarification can be utilized.

The transition from the first stage to the second stage of crisis intervention can be made most smoothly if the counselor, believing that the problem has been sufficiently explored for the moment, summarizes and reviews her perceptions with the client. This serves two functions: First, it reassures the client and the counselor that the counselor has a reasonably clear perception of the crisis as the client perceives it, and second, it helps in determining whether the client is ready to move into the second stage. During the second stage, the counselor and the client agree on the possibility and direction of change. This can be initiated by either, but both must be in agreement to ensure the best possibility of crisis resolution.

Once the client and counselor agree on the possibility and direction of change, they are ready to enter the third stage of the process, in which possible alternatives are considered and a plan of action is eventually determined. The first set of variables to explore during this stage are the resources and support immediately available to the client. Information to discuss at this point includes prior methods of coping with crisis situations, the client's ability to help himself, related support groups (both from within the client's immediate world and from social agencies), and facts needed to locate an appropriate agency or private practitioner who might provide the kind of services necessary to resolve the current crisis; these facts include age, sex, religious affiliation, finances, insurance coverage, location, and occupation. After alternatives have been discussed and the client seems in agreement, the alternatives should be reviewed and the client should commit himself to following through. The task to which the client agrees should be simple and clear. If many tasks are necessary, it may be helpful to focus on those that are immediately necessary, making additional agreements during follow-up sessions. During the follow-up sessions, once the crisis has been resolved, the counselor may return to the usual methods of counseling.

Cavanagh (1982) identifies five factors that are particularly relevant for the counselor to be aware of in dealing with a crisis situation: (1) *dealing with reality,* thus helping the individual to broaden her perspective and see beyond the negative aspects; (2) *emphasizing beneficial effects,* allowing the person to utilize crisis reactions as a healing process until effective steps can be taken to counteract that situation; (3) *attempting to help,* which may lead to frustration and withdrawal for the counselor and the significant others within the client's life and thus leaving the client feeling even more alone, alienated, and hopeless; (4) *avoiding further anxiety,* recognizing that the crisis reaction may create a new set of anxieties or a new, separate crisis; and (5) *anticipating delayed reactions,* which may occur weeks or even months after the precipitating event.

While crisis counseling is usually anxiety producing for the counselor, it is potentially highly rewarding, since even a minimal amount of intervention can often bring relief for the client. The satisfaction resulting from being there when needed and from helping someone through what is often a life-saving process makes the counselor's fear and anxiety worthwhile. In addition, a crisis frequently presents an excellent opportunity for change, because individuals are usually more willing and more motivated to change during crisis than they are at other times.

Summary

In this chapter we have focused on three models of counseling that expand the counselor's role and require additional knowledge or advanced skill. In the first section we examined the counselor's role as a consultant to organizations and explored the various roles, skills, and processes that might be used.

Because counselors often work with clients in groups, we discussed the pros and cons of groups, the therapeutic elements of groups, and the considerations in group formation and the stages and phases of group process.

The last section presented crisis intervention counseling and discussed a specific model for crisis counseling.

References

Counselor as Consultant

Blake, R., & Mouton, J. (1978). Toward a general theory of consultation. *Personnel and Guidance Journal, 56 (6),* 328–334.

Dinkmeyer, D., & Carlson, J. (1973). *Consulting: Facilitating human potential and change processes.* Columbus, OH: Chas. E. Merrill.

Kurpius, D., & Fuqua, D. (1993). Fundamental issues in defining consultation. *Journal of Counseling and Development, 71,* 598–600.

Kurpius, D., Fuqua, D., & Rozecki, T. (1993). The consulting process: A multidimensional approach. *Journal of Counseling and Development, 71,* 601–606.

Kurpius, D., & Robinson, S. (1978). Overview of consultation. *Personnel and Guidance Journal, 56 (6),* 321–323.

Group Counseling

Bloch, S., Reibstein, J., & Crouch, E. (1979). A method for the study of therapeutic factors in group psychotherapy. *British Journal of Psychiatry, 134,* 257–263.

Corey, G., & Corey, M. S. (1977). *Groups: Process and practice.* Monterey, CA: Brooks/Cole.

Corsini, R., & Rosenberg, B. (1955). Mechanisms of group psychotherapy: Processes and dynamics. *Journal of Abnormal and Social Psychology, 51,* 406–411.

Gazda, G. (1978). *Group Counseling: A Developmental Approach.* Boston: Allyn and Bacon.

George, R. L., & Dustin, D. (1988). *Group counseling: Theory and practice.* Englewood Cliffs, NJ: Prentice-Hall.

Hill, W. F. (1957). Analysis of interviews of group therapists' papers. *Provo Papers, 1,* 1.

Johnson, D. W., & Johnson, F. P. (1982). *Joining together: Group theory and group skills,* 2nd ed. Englewood Cliffs, NJ: Prentice-Hall.

Lifton, W. M. (1972). *Groups: Facilitating individual growth and societal change.* New York: John Wiley.

Lowrey, L. G., & Slavson, S. R. (1943). Group therapy special action meeting. *American Journal of Orthopsychiatry, 13,* 648–690

Mahler, C. A. (1969). *Group counseling in the schools.* Boston: Houghton Mifflin.

Ohlsen, M. M. (1977). *Group counseling* (2nd ed.). New York: Holt, Rinehart & Winston.

Ohlsen, M., & Gazda, G. (1965). Counseling underachieving bright pupils. *Education, 86,* 78–81.

Peck, M. L., & Stewart, R. H. (1964). Current practices in selection of criteria for group play therapy. *Journal of Clinical Psychology, 20,* 146.

Shertzer, B., & Stone, S. (1974). *Fundamentals of counseling.* Boston: Houghton Mifflin.

Yalom, I. D. (1970). *The theory and practice of group psychotherapy.* New York: Basic Books.

Crisis Intervention

Cavanaugh, M. E. (1982). *The counseling experience.* Monterey, CA Brooks/Cole.

Puryear, D. A. (1979). *Helping people in crisis.* San Francisco: Jossey-Bass.

C h a p t e r *12*

Career Counseling

In the late twentieth century, as during most of history, work is still one of our most important life activities, occupying almost half of our adult lives. When enjoyed, work can be a source of need satisfaction, self-esteem, and healthy adjustment. When disliked or dreaded, it can cause worry, stress, frustration—even physical illness and psychological and social maladjustment. To a large extent, work determines our social status, level of income, and standard of living. Work influences our self-concept and feelings of value, worth, and personal identity. As Cook (1991) points out, work is a vehicle by which adults connect with the world around them.

Most individuals can fulfill their need to work and be happy at any of several jobs. They may have no great desire for career assistance from a counselor. Most people view getting and holding a job as a simple procedure, never recognizing that they might be able to find a more meaningful and relevant job with counseling assistance.

The need for guidance in career development has long been an accepted function of counseling. The whole counseling movement, as outlined in Chapter 1, sprung largely from the career guidance movements. Yet there is a rising awareness that this one aspect of counseling services—career planning and related elements—is not being provided as effectively as the current circumstances facing youth and adults require. Too often the client has not understood the need for assistance or the potential value of seeking help from a counselor.

Hansen, Stevic, and Warner (1977) have pointed out four potential benefits of counseling. First, clients improve their prospects for job placement since counselors may have information about potential employment opportunities. Second, the counselor can aid the client in the process of job adjustment, which may well make the difference between job advancement or stagnation. Third, the counselor can provide assistance in the area of job satisfaction by helping the client understand the good and bad aspects of the job prior to job entry. Finally, the counselor can help the individual who either is forced to or decides to change a current position. In short, the skilled career counselor can provide assistance to individuals as they develop vocationally, seek and choose a job, advance in a job, and change or leave employment.

In a nationwide study of student career development involving over 28,000 students, Prediger, Roth, and Noeth (1973) found that three-fourths of the eleventh-grade students in the study wanted help with career planning. The proportion of eighth graders wanting such help was almost as high. Still, although 84 percent of the eleventh-grade students indicated that they could almost always see a counselor when they wanted to, only 13 percent felt that they had received "a lot of help" with career planning from this school; another 37 percent felt they had received "some help." In addition, approximately 40 percent were uncertain whether their educational plans were appropriate for the occupations they were considering, and approximately one-fourth were not sure if they would be able to complete the steps necessary for entering those occupations.

The results of this study are consistent with those of other studies that have indicated that students want help with career planning yet receive far less help than they wish. The students' apparent lack of knowledge about work options and the career-planning process suggest that much time and energy is lost through floundering and indecision and that this loss has a direct impact on society itself in terms of work loss, diminished productivity, and individual alienation.

Few comprehensive surveys of adult needs for career counseling are available, but there is every reason to believe that the career-counseling needs of this group are also very high. Conger (1992) points out that most serious research in counseling involves university students as a sample and that more research in career counseling needs to take place with ordinary people who are being served by a variety of social agencies. For example, the services provided by our vocational rehabilitation agencies and our employment services have made a major impact on the careers of those who have sought help. But these agencies typically deal with very visible or very severe problems of career choice or adjustment, and as a result such agencies frequently have little time or assistance for the individual experiencing job alienation in subtle, agonizing ways—the woman who has been out of the labor force for many years, or the veteran who simply cannot find a satisfying role in the work world.

The Changing World of Work

One of the most profound changes in the past few decades has been in the area of attitudes toward work. An increasing number of people no longer view work as toil and drudgery; rather, they see it as a means of personal expression, of growing and of building self-esteem, and of satisfying personal needs. In the past individuals typically remained in a particular occupation throughout most of their lives. Today more are changing their occupations many times in their lives. In addition, more and more people are questioning the validity of yearly income as the sole criterion of occupational success and are changing from higher-paying jobs to lower-paying jobs simply because they find the lower-paying jobs more desirable in other respects. Such individuals have determined that such criteria as personal need fulfillment, living where they want to, and having time to spend with their family are more important indicators of success to them than high income. And as the drastically increased earning power of blue-collar workers continues to undermine the idea that only people with college degrees can find suitable, well-paying jobs, attitudes about the importance of college are also changing.

Several striking changes have also occurred in the American occupational structure during the past quarter century. The number of workers involved in industries providing services has dramatically increased, while the number of workers in goods-producing industries has remained relatively constant. The number of employees in blue-collar occupations has increased relatively little, while the number in white-collar occupations has grown markedly. The average educational attainment of those in the labor force has also risen appreciably; more than 75 percent of workers now have at least a high school education. The proportion of American women in the labor force has increased significantly.

These trends in the work world are readily apparent. Determining what will happen in the future is a much more complex problem. Many of today's occupations did not exist 15 years ago; still more new occupations will surface in the next 15 years, making it difficult to project specific occupational categories that will be in demand in the future.

Career counseling parallels other kinds of counseling, but it focuses on planning and making decisions about occupations and education. As in all counseling, the personal relationship between the counselor and the client is critical. Values and attitudes are explored in career counseling, but more information and factual data are required than in personal counseling. Career counselors also recognize that they cannot help someone with a career problem while ignoring such other aspects of the person's life as needs, conflicts, and relations with others.

Morrill and Forrest (1970) have identified four types of vocational counseling events in terms of the width of focus that the counseling situation has on the kinds of situations for which the counseling has relevance. Type 1 is counseling that aids the client with a specific decision by providing information and clarifying issues. Type 2 is counseling that aids the client with a specific decision by focusing on decision-making skills rather than on only the decision at hand, applying these skills to the specific situation as well as later choice points. Type 3 counseling views the career as a process rather than an end-point toward which all decisions lead; thus, it changes the focus from the objective of making a correct ultimate choice and a once-and-for-all pronouncement of identity to a process of making a continual series of choices. Type 4 counseling focuses on giving individuals the ability to utilize their personal attributes to achieve self-determined objectives and to influence the nature of future choices rather than merely adapting to external pressures.

A number of considerations determine the level or focus of counseling. First are the expectations of the client, the immediacy of the client's needs, and the client's level of development. Career counseling involves counseling the whole person; an effort must be made to avoid compartmentalizing personal and vocational counseling. The developmental nature of career counseling is recognized today and is placed in perspective as an aspect of the growth of the whole person. A career-counseling process that provides individuals with only the information and self-knowledge to select a single vocational direction or job does little to provide them with the developmental skills and abilities necessary to make continual progress and to shape their own destiny.

Theories of Career Development

Professional interest in the process of how an individual selects an occupation is relatively new. With industrialization and urbanization, vocational choices were no longer limited to what a person's father or mother did or to the types of work that existed within a particular community. The ever-increasing range of occupational alternatives and the accompanying uncertainties and confusion created the need for professional assistance in selecting a career. As the field of career counseling has attempted to meet the need, various theoretical rationales have been developed to provide a framework for the practice of career counseling.

A theory of career development must account for the fluid, changing process of vocational awareness and feelings. The value of any particular theory to counselors lies in its ability to help them organize and integrate client data simply, logically, and usefully. A theory should provide a counselor with the expertise necessary to help a client make decisions that will lead to personal growth and attainment of specific objectives. A theory should also allow a counselor to predict client behavior more successfully, thus helping clients accurately anticipate the consequences of their decision. Most of all, career development is intimately related to the factors that motivate or impede decisions.

Just as the way in which the counselor proceeds with a counseling session depends to a large degree on that counselor's personal counseling theory, so the career counselor's conduct during a career-counseling session depends on the counselor's career-counseling theory. The numerous theories of career development postulated over the past few decades can be classified into four areas: trait-factor theories, structural theories, developmental theories, and decision-making theories.

Trait-Factor Theories

From a historical standpoint, the first theory that attempted to explain the process of occupational choice was the trait-factor theory, essentially a theory of individual differences (Williamson, 1965). This approach is based on the assumption that each person possesses a uniquely organized pattern of personal traits (interests, abilities, and personality characteristics) that are fairly stable and seldom change after late adolescence. The process of career counseling that evolves from this theory includes (1) gaining self-understanding, including information about aptitude, achievement, interests, values, and personality characteristics; (2) obtaining knowledge about the world of work, including information about various occupations; and (3) integrating information about self and the world of work (Sharf, 1992). The personal traits can be identified through objective means, usually psychological tests or inventories, and then profiled to represent the individual's potential. Occupations can also be profiled by analyzing them in terms of the amounts of the various individual traits they require. By matching one profile to the other, the probable degree of fit between person and job can be identified.

A more recent approach has developed out of the use of the Myers-Briggs Type Indicator as many career counselors have found it applicable to counseling with clients. Myers-Briggs theory pertains to the way that individuals perceive their world and make decisions based on that perception. Thus the key mental activities are perceiving and judging. According to Myers (1980), the two contrasting ways of perceiving are *sensing*, or taking in information through the senses, and *intuition*, or using the unconscious for input by perceiving meanings and relationships in events. Judging, on the other hand, also involves two types: *thinking*, which refers to analyzing and being objective about perceived event or thought, and *feeling*, which is a subjective reaction in which the event or thought is related to one's own value system. The styles which a particular individual uses—and eight Myers-Briggs types are identified—are then related to career decision-making and work adjustment.

Essentially, then, the trait-factor approach is a rigorous, scientific, and highly personalized method of matching individuals with occupations. Without such assistance, individuals may or may not choose occupations that will agree with their profile of abilities, interests, and personality. If an appropriate choice is made, the individual may waste much time and energy before eventually gravitating toward a more satisfying occupation. A major task of the career counselor who is oriented toward trait factor theory is to assist people in making better career decisions by helping them become more knowledgeable about their own traits, learn about job requirements, and match those personal characteristics with the job requirements. Such a process is highly cognitive in nature.

Structural Theories

The first structural theory to be examined is the one proposed by Roe (1956). She theorized and researched the concept that there are definite personality differences between members of various occupations and that these differences are attributable to early parent-child relationships. Basing her theory upon Maslow's ideas of the integrated unity of the individual as a bond of interacting levels of needs, Roe specifically postulates three psychological climates in the home that are a function of parent-child relations: (1) emotional concentration on the child—either overprotecting or overdemanding climate; (2) avoidance of the child—either neglecting or rejecting climate; and (3) acceptance of the child—either casual or loving climate.

Since career choices reflect the desire to satisfy needs not met by parents in childhood, deficiencies during childhood can be compensated for, by, and through work. Thus, individuals who did not receive sufficient praise and respect from their parents may attempt to elicit these through their work and, consequently, may seek jobs that can bring them praise and respect. The same holds true for other needs that were unmet at earlier stages of development: The individual turns to work to gratify these needs.

Roe's concerns with specific child-rearing practices, the manner in which the parents interact with the child, the resulting need structure, and the ensuing orientation toward or away from persons were then translated into a useful classification of occupations by field and level.

Although Roe's system has received a number of valid criticisms, it does have a number of strong points. Her theory allows an integrative role to the job function and relates occupational choice to the entire structure of the personality. From a counseling point of view, Roe's insights help the counselor to better understand the variety of factors that play a part in the individual's decision to pursue or avoid certain jobs, as well as to understand why a job does or does not meet an individual's needs. This is supported by evidence that shows about two-thirds of job changes occur within the same occupational group (Roe and Lunneborg, 1990).

Hoppock (1976) has developed a composite view of personality approaches to career development. His theory is basically a summary of other theories. Hoppock proposes a series of straightforward points about career choice that give prominence to need satisfaction:

1. Occupations are chosen to meet needs.

2. The occupation that we choose is the one that we believe would best meet the needs that most concern us.

3. Needs may be intellectually perceived, or they may be only vaguely felt as attractions that draw us in certain directions. In either case, they may influence choices.

4. Occupational choice begins when we first become aware that an occupation can help to meet our personal needs.

5. Career choice improves as we become better able to anticipate how well a prospective career will meet our needs. Our capacity to anticipate depends on our knowledge about ourselves, our knowledge about occupations, and our ability to think clearly.

6. Information about ourselves affects career choice by helping us to discover the careers that may meet our needs and by helping us to anticipate how well satisfied we may hope to be in one career as compared with another.

7. Information about occupations affects career choice by helping us to discover the occupation that may meet our needs.

8. Job satisfaction depends on the extent to which the job we hold meets the needs we feel it should meet. The degree of satisfaction is determined by the ratio between what we have and what we want.

9. Satisfaction can result from a job that meets our needs today or from a job that promises to meet those needs in the future.

10. Career choice is always subject to change when we believe that a change will better meet our needs.

The last structural theory to be examined in this chapter is the one proposed by Holland (1985). He has stated that his theory is a theory of personality structure as well as of vocational choice. It focuses primarily upon vocational choice, but it is also concerned with emotional functioning, creativity, and personal development. Sometimes described as a "differential" approach, Holland's theory emphasizes that the typology of the individual and the typology of the working environment are essential factors in work satisfaction (Gladding, 1988).

Four assumptions constitute the heart of Holland's theory: First, in our culture most persons can be categorized as one of six types—realistic, investigative, artistic, social, enterprising, or conventional. Second, most environments can also be categorized as realistic, investigative, artistic, social, enterprising, or conventional. Third, people search for environments that will let them exercise their skills and abilities, express their attitudes and values, and take on agreeable problems and roles. And finally, individuals' behavior is determined by an interaction between their personalities and the characteristics of their environments.

To emphasize this person-situation correspondence, Holland has classified work environments into the six categories analogous to the six personal orientations and has coded more than 12,000 careers into Holland codes (Gottfredson and Holland, 1989). By doing so, Holland makes explicit that occupations are ways of life, helping to define social status, life-style, and standard of living. He postulates that stereotypes of occupations have important psychological and sociological significance. Thus, he suggests that a person's occupational choice can have limited but useful value as a projective device in revealing motivations, insight, and self-understanding (Holland, 1985).

Since behavior is determined by the interaction between personality and the characteristics of the environment, Holland believes that vocational satisfaction, stability, and mobility are a function of the extent to which a person's personality and occupational environment are congruent. Such congruent interactions of people and their environments lead to more stable vocational choice, higher vocational achievement, higher academic achievement, better maintenance of personal stability, and greater satisfaction.

Since the theories of Roe, Hoppock, and Holland all stress the importance of need satisfaction in choosing an occupation, it becomes highly important for a structurally oriented counselor to assess clients' cognitive, affective, and social needs. Counselors are then able to provide clients with enough career information to allow them to choose a career that will satisfy their needs and be congruent with their personality structure.

Developmental Theories

Developmental theories of career behavior and decision making differ from the trait-factor and the structural theories in that they are typically more inclusive, more concerned with longitudinal expressions of career behavior, and more inclined to highlight the importance of the self-concept (Herr and Cramer, 1979).

Ginzberg and his associates (1951) were early leaders in theorizing about career development as a process that culminates in an occupational choice in one's early twenties. In their early work they stressed that occupational choice is an irreversible development process involving a series of decisions that extend over many years. That is, as each occupationally relevant decision is made, other choices are eliminated. They identified four sets of factors that interact to influence the ultimate career choice: individual values, emotional factors, amount and kind of education, and impact of reality through environmental pressures.

Ginzberg and his associates also identified three phases in the period of career choice development: fantasy (from birth to age 11) tentative (from ages 11 to 17) and realistic (between ages 17 and early twenties). With the exception of the fantasy stage, each period is broken into subaspects. The tentative period is divided into stages of interest, capacity, value, and transition. The realistic period is broken into exploration and crystallization stages. During these life stages individuals are faced with certain tasks. As they confront these tasks, they make compromises between wishes and possibilities, and each compromise contributes to the irreversibility of the unfolding process.

In his reformulation of the theory, Ginzberg (1972) suggested some modifications. First, he believes that the process of career choice making is not limited to the period up to and including young adulthood but is likely to occur throughout the individual's working life. Second, he has reduced his emphasis on the irreversibility of occupational choice, emphasizing the cumulative effect on occupational prospects of the educational and occupational decisions that the young person makes between childhood and the twenty-first or twenty-fifth year. Third, he has substituted the word *optimization* for the earlier term *compromise*. This change suggests that rather than emphasizing the compromises individuals make between wishes and possibilities, he is emphasizing the individual's search to find the best occupational fit between changing desires and changing circumstances, a continuing search.

Probably the theoretical approach that has received the most continuous attention and is most widely used in career development is the one proposed by Super (1953). His theory of career choice is based on the idea that individual's self-concepts influence their occupational choice and their ultimate satisfaction or dissatisfaction with their choice. This vocational choice is the result of a developmental process that puts the individual's self-concept into practice. In addition, Super (1990) pointed out that individual roles that include study, community service, leisure, work, and family are important. Although his initial statement of theory was a response to the theory proposed by Ginzberg and associates, Super attempted to integrate several approaches to career development theory, including aspects of differential, social, developmental, and phenomenological psychology. His position, however, is primarily developmental.

Super has made some refinements to his original proposal, but his theory remains substantially the same as originally proposed. The original ten propositions that characterize his theory include the following:

1. People differ in their abilities, interests, and personalities.

2. They are qualified, by virtue of these characteristics, each for a number of occupations.

3. Each of these occupations requires a characteristic pattern of abilities, interests, and personality traits, with tolerances wide enough, however, to allow both some variety of occupations for each individual and some variety of individuals in each occupation.

4. Vocational preferences and competencies, the situations in which people live and work, and hence their self-concepts, change with time and experience (although self-concepts are generally fairly stable from late adolescence until late maturity), making choice and adjustment a continuous process.

5. This process may be summed up in a series of life stages characterized as those of growth, exploration, establishment, maintenance, and decline, and these stages may in turn be subdivided into (a) the fantasy, tentative, and realistic phases of the exploratory stage, and (b) the trial and stable phases of the establishment stage.

6. The nature of the career pattern (that is, the occupational level attained and the sequence, frequency, and duration of trial and stable jobs) is determined by the individual's parental socioeconomic level, mental ability, and personality characteristics, and by the opportunities to which he is exposed.

7. Development through the life stages can be guided, partly by facilitating the process of maturation of abilities and interests and partly by aiding in reality testing and in the development of the self-concept.

8. The process of vocational development is essentially that of developing and implementing a self-concept: it is a compromise process in which the self-concept is a product of the interaction of inherited aptitudes, neural and endocrine make-up, opportunity to play various roles, and evaluations of the extent to which the results of role playing meet with the approval of superiors and fellows.

9. The process of compromise between individual and social factors, between self-concept and reality, is one of role playing, whether the role is played in fantasy, in the counseling interview, or in real life activities such as school classes, clubs, part-time work, and entry jobs.

10. Work satisfactions and life satisfactions depend upon the extent to which the individual finds adequate outlets for his abilities, interests, personality traits, and values; they depend upon his establishment in a type of work, a work situation, and a way of life in which he can play the kind of role which his growth and exploratory experiences have led him to consider congenial and appropriate. (1953, pp. 189–190)

As these ten propositions clearly point out, Super's developmental approach is comprehensive. It is a theory of career development rather than of occupational choice. His attempts to synthesize various approaches seem apparent as he emphasizes the various factors that contribute to a career pattern. The jobs individuals hold over a lifetime represent the development of their self concepts as expressed in the world of work. For Super, then, work is a way of life as well as an expression of selfhood and a means of support.

Decision-making Theories

The most recent trend in career development theory has resulted from attempts to theorize about educational and occupational choice through the use of decision models. The major concept in decision-making theory is that each individual has several possible alternatives from which to choose. Each alternative has identifiable results or consequences. Each of the anticipated results has a specific value for the individual, a value that can be estimated through some method of psychological scaling. Therefore, if the resulting values of the alternatives can be determined and arranged in a hierarchy, the probable occurrence of each outcome can also be determined. Then the value of each event can be multiplied by the probability of its occurrence to determine the sound decision for the particular individual (Hills, 1964).

Bergland (1974) has identified a sequence of events that occur in decision making, including the following steps:

1. Defining the problem
2. Generating alternatives
3. Gathering information
4. Processing information
5. Making plans and selecting goals
6. Implementing and evaluating plans

Kalder and Zytowski (1969) take still another approach to the application of decision-making theory to career choice. In their model, the elements consist of inputs (personal resources such as intellectual and physical characteristics), alternatives, and outputs. Again, the inputs are priced in terms of what the decision maker forgoes in using them in a particular occupational alternative. The alternative to be chosen is the one offering the greatest net value—the highest value in input costs are balanced against output gains. Implicit in such a model is the assumption that the decision maker has sufficient information about personal characteristics and the alternatives available to rank the values, utilities, and sacrifices associated with each possible action.

Krumboltz (1979) has proposed a social learning theory of career decision making. His theory attempts to explain how educational and career preferences and skills are acquired and how selections of courses and careers are made. It identifies the interactions of genetic factors, environmental conditions, learning experiences, cognitive and emotional responses, and performance skills that produce movement along one career path or another. Krumboltz points out that combinations of these factors interact in different ways to produce different decisions.

Three types of influence and their interactions lead to several types of outcomes:

1. Self-observation generalizations (SOGs), which include overt or covert statements evaluating one's own actual or vicarious performance in relation to learned standards.
2. Task approach skills (TASs), which are cognitive and performance abilities and emotional predispositions for coping with the environment, interpreting it in relation to SOGs, and making covert or overt predictions about future events.
3. Actions, which include entry behaviors that indicate overt steps in career progression.

The Krumboltz model accents the importance of learning experiences as well as task approach skills as instrumental in producing preferences for activities. Such a model, however, suggests that becoming a particular kind of worker is not a simple function of preference or choice but is the result of complex environmental factors, many beyond the control of any single individual. These factors, however, can be recognized by the individual, and career decision-making skills can be systematically learned. Sharf (1992) summarizes these skills (DECIDES) and shows how they can be used to facilitate the career counseling process.

The Career-Counseling Process

In the several approaches covered in this chapter, career development has been described as a process shaped by an interaction of self-references, self-knowledge., knowledge about training and occupations, educational and occupational opportunities, genetic and early childhood influences, personality styles, and patterns of traits that individuals express in their choice of behavior and career identity. This suggests that career development is no different from all human behavior in that it is complex and part of the total fabric of personality development.

Herr and Cramer (1979) have suggested a number of career development implications that provide a conceptual base for those planning career-counseling activities. First is the recognition that work provides a means for meeting needs of social interaction, dignity, self-esteem, self-identification, and other forms of psychological gratification. Each individual's personal, educational, occupational, or career maturation is reached through a complex of learning processes that began in early childhood and continue throughout life. The actual choice occurs not at a particular point in time but in relation to antecedent experiences and future alternatives. It is a continuous, tentative, and often more psychological than logical process of decision making. Value systems, both individual and cultural, are important in shaping career development.

Herr and Cramer also include the need for adequate information. Career information must include not only the objective facts, such as earning possibilities, training requirements, and numbers of positions available, but also the social and psychological aspects of careers. Moreover, since occupational and career choices are methods of implementing an individual's self-concept, information about self-characteristics—attitudes, aptitudes, and values—is as necessary as career or occupational information.

Career development theory indicates that decision making involves action. Therefore, another implication is that ways must be found to help persons take responsibility for their own learning and for their own direction. They need to be helped to develop a conscious awareness that they do have choices, to determine at any given time what kind of decision is involved, and to recognize the factors inherent in the decision that make a personal difference.

Occupational choices and career patterns are basic to one's lifestyle and reflect developmental experiences, personality, goals, and so on. As Herr and Cramer state, career choice can be an essentially rational process if the person knows how to select and obtain appropriate information and then apply the decision-making process to it.

During the past few decades career counseling had been in the somewhat paradoxical position of being seen as less exciting and meaningful than personal counseling. Yet career counseling remains a major area of need for those individuals who seek help from a counselor. Career counseling is not a totally unique version or variety of counseling. It requires many of the skills necessary to conduct any form of counseling dealing with the individual's intellectual and emotional being. Still, there are some notable differences. Leigh (1977) has identified three differences between career counseling and other counseling specialties. First, the prime focus of career counseling is to assist a person in choosing and adjusting to the world of work. Second, career counseling requires that a counselor be familiar with current occupational information and is, therefore, more concrete than other counseling specialties. Last, career problems are often seen by clients as a safe and socially acceptable way into psychotherapy. Thus, a career counselor must be able to determine the actual nature of the client's complaint in the early stages of counseling by conducting a thorough assessment during the initial counseling contacts.

Career counseling generally follows an orderly process, beginning with the development of the relationship and ending with follow-up and potential change of plans. Between these two steps the counselor helps clients to develop an understanding of their problems or concerns. Data from several sources are presented to clients so that they better understand themselves and their vocational decisions and alternatives. The counselor and client then work to synthesize the appraisal process and individual client profile into a plan of action or choice.

A counselor should help clients examine their personal characteristics. A counselor should determine a client's level of intelligence, interests, special abilities, aspirations, needs, and values, among other qualities. Various methods—including checklists, inventories, tests, previous records, and interview data—can aid the counselor in assessing this information. Counselors may wish to focus the attention of the client on such areas as special aptitudes, personality traits, and educational attainment.

While clients are learning more about themselves, they must also learn about the environment in which they will eventually be seeking employment. The environment includes all the facets within which the individual functions. Such information can be gathered from a number of sources, including publications, audiovisual aids, programmed instruction materials, computer-based systems, interviews with experts, and direct observation of work experiences. Obviously, such information should be accurate, current, usable, and thorough.

Once clients have had adequate opportunity to explore career possibilities, they need to thoroughly understand the various possibilities available. Thus the counselor participates in the clarification and integration phases, by helping clients gain factual information which promotes full understanding and integrates this material into career decisions. By this point, clients have accumulated a great deal of data about themselves and have information about various occupations. Clients need to understand that this is not the end point and should be invited back for further discussions regarding the actual job chosen. As clients then begin to act on their choices, the counselor provides supportive assistance in implementing the choice. If the client is not ready to make the decision, the counselor may have to spend more time helping the client understand what has occurred, perhaps even dealing with the client's inability to make such a decision.

Thus, as Peterson and Nisenholz (1987) point out, "All career counseling is personal. All personal counseling is not career" (p. 239). Manuele-Adkins (1992) ar-

FIGURE 12-1   **A counselor provides feedback regarding
personal data related to a career decision**
(Color Image Inc., JimTrotter)

gues that career counseling is personal counseling, and that career counselors must go beyond an emphasis on the rational, informational aspects of career decision-making to include the affective, psychological issues confronting clients with career concerns. She identifies these psychological variables as developmental stages and tasks, identity formation and status, self-concept, psychological needs, and internal barriers. Likewise, C. H. Patterson (Freeman, 1990), long identified with client-centered counseling, has clearly indicated that he also believes that career counseling is personal counseling, emphasizing that in career counseling, it is essential to get the clients themselves involved in obtaining information. He states that the information is more meaningful if the client helps select the information needed and finds the information with some direction from the counselor.

Of particular importance is the career counseling experiences afforded women and minorities. As will be pointed out in Chapter 14, counselors must take into account the total experience of a client which often includes the client's gender and ethnic background. Career counselors must stay in touch which occupational sex stereotyping and recognize societal changes in career opportunities for various groups. Hoyt (1989) summarizes some of these changes and makes recommendations for enhancing equity of opportunity for career development. D'Andrea and Daniels (1992) clarify the need for different experiences in preparing inner-city black youth for the U. S. labor market.

An emerging trend is that of providing career counseling for couples instead of individuals. Based on family and systemic counseling principles, career counseling for couples recognizes the dynamics of the couple as a key factor in individual career choice-making. In this context, career counseling often involves an extensive career intake interview, the administration of appropriate tests (with an interest inventory taken twice by each—once conventionally and once anticipating how each would expect her/his partner to complete the items), individual feedback sessions, and joint evaluation and summary sessions (Benjamin, 1992).

Career-Counseling Tools

Almost all of the career-counseling theorists assume that the greater the degree of accurate self-understanding one has, the more likely one is to make realistic, satisfying educational and career choices. Certainly, accurate self-understanding does not *guarantee* good decision making, but good decisions only rarely occur without a realistic picture of one's abilities and interests. Thus, career counselors typically utilize assessment devices as a vehicle for helping the client gain greater self-understanding.

Individuals facing educational and career decisions also require accurate information about their choices. Individuals must possess and be able to use information about occupational outlook, entry, education and training required, social and psychological factors, and salary. Career counselors must be able to identify and utilize sources of this information.

Career Testing

Assessment in career counseling usually involves the use of aptitude tests and interest inventories, which measure abilities and interests. Since no one aptitude test provides enough information for most individuals, career counselors usually employ a test battery to provide a multiscore summary of the various strengths and weaknesses. Some of the most widely used aptitude test batteries include:

> *The Differential Aptitude Tests* (DAT). Published by the Psychological Corporation, the DAT requires approximately four hours to complete and provides scores in eight areas: verbal reasoning, numerical reasoning, abstract reasoning, space relations, mechanical reasoning, clerical speed and accuracy, spelling, and language usage. The DAT also provides a verbal score and a numerical score, which combine for a general intelligence measure.
>
> *The General Aptitude Test Battery* (GATB). Published by the United States Employment Service, the GATB requires two and one-half hours to complete and provides nine scores: intelligence, verbal aptitude, numerical aptitude, spatial aptitude, form perception, clerical perception, motor coordination, finger dexterity, and manual dexterity.

Flanagan Aptitude Classification Tests (FACT). Published by Science Research Associates, the FACT requires approximately five to six hours to complete and provides fourteen scores related to thirty occupations.

Interest inventories attempt to measure an individual's interest in various careers by determining the pattern of interest from his responses to lists of occupations and activities. Some of the widely used interest inventories include the following:

Strong-Campbell Interest Inventory (SCII). Published by Stanford University Press, the SCII requires about thirty to forty-five minutes to complete and provides scores for the six theme areas of Holland, as well as for twenty-three basic interests and one hundred twenty-four occupations.

Kuder Preference Records and Interest Surveys. Published by Science Research Associates, these include a total of five instruments that can be used for different age groups and different purposes. The information provided ranges from scores on ten interest scales (Form E) to scores on seventy-seven occupational scales and twenty-nine college major scales (Form DD).

Ohio Vocational Interest Inventory (OVII). Published by Harcourt Brace Jovanovich, the OVII requires about one and one-half hours to complete and provides scores for twenty-four interest scales.

Occupational Interests Inventory (OII). Published by the California Test Bureau, the OII requires approximately forty minutes to complete and provides scores in six fields of interest: personal-social, natural, mechanical, business, arts, and sciences; and in three types of interest: verbal, manipulative, and computational.

One other instrument that is in wide use is the *Self-Directed Search* (SDS), Form E. Broader in scope than interest inventories, the SDS utilizes self-reports and estimates regarding occupational daydreams, preference for activities, competencies, preferences for kinds of occupations, and abilities in various occupational areas. This information then provides for summary codes according to Holland's career scales.

Career Information

Most counselors have in-depth information on only a few occupations. Thus, career counseling typically requires the use of career information sources that will give clients a complete, accurate picture of various occupations. Certainly, the two best-known of the published materials are the *Dictionary of Occupational Titles* (DOT) and the *Occupational Outlook Handbook* (OOH).

The DOT is published periodically (most recent was the fourth edition, published in 1978 and revised in 1991) by the U.S. Department of Labor. Information relating to approximately twenty thousand jobs is provided alphabetically by occupational categories, by worker traits, and by industries. Each job entry includes alternate job titles, summary of the occupation, and the specific tasks performed.

The OOH is also published periodically by the U.S. Department of Labor. Used with the *Occupational Outlook Quarterly,* the OOH provides information regarding trends and outlook for eight hundred occupations and industries.

There are a number of other sources of career systems (for example, Occupational Library, Careerdex, Career Information Kit, and Mini-briefs). There are also various printed series of occupational booklets as well as career guidance media that use audio and visual means of disseminating information. In addition, a number of career guidance simulations and games have been developed to give individuals the opportunity to explore careers vicariously.

Use of Computer Technology in Career Counseling

With the increasing work load of career counselors, the use of computer technology in career counseling has proved to be an important tool in providing services for more clients effectively and efficiently. A variety of computer-assisted career guidance systems have been developed. Sampson (1990) analyzed five trends in computer applications in testing and assessment in relation to five goals of counseling psychology. These included computer-based test interpretation and computer-assisted instruction, both of which are essential aspects of career counseling. In considering which computer-based career guidance system to use, Sampson and Reardon (1990) pointed out that the key to choosing a system is identifying the client population, the organizational structure, financial resources, staff time and skills, and one's theoretical approach and then choosing the system that provides the features needed for those clients under those working conditions at an acceptable cost.

Summary

A major function of counseling is that of helping clients develop vocationally as they choose, seek, advance in, and change jobs. This vocational guidance function, an early emphasis of counseling, is frequently undervalued today by counselors, but it is still highly important to individuals who seek help in planning and making decisions about their jobs and education.

Career counseling is based on a positive, personal relationship between client and counselor; it includes exploration of values and attitudes as well as gathering and assessment of information and factual data. The major career development theories include trait-factor theories, structural theories, developmental theories, and decision-making theories.

Generally, career counselors help clients explore, clarify, and integrate various vocational possibilities to enable them to choose among the available alternatives. In doing so career counselors use a number of career-counseling tools, including career-testing materials, career information sources, and computer technology.

References

Benjamin, B. A. (1992). Career counseling with couples. *Journal of Counseling and Development, 70,* 544–549.

Bergland, B. (1974). Career planning: The use of sequential evaluated experience. In E. L. Herr (Ed.). *Vocational guidance and human development.* Boston: Houghton Mifflin.

Conger, D. S. (1992). Whereto career development and counseling. *The Career Development Quarterly, 40,* 376–377.

Cook, E. P. (1991). Annual review: Practice and research in career counseling and development, 1990. *The Career Development Quarterly, 40,* 99–131.

D'Andrea, M., & Daniels, J. (1992). A career development program for inner-city black youth. *The Career Development Quarterly, 40,* 272–280.

Freeman, C. (1990). C. H. Patterson on client-centered career counseling: An interview. *The Career Development Quarterly, 38,* 291–301.

Ginzberg, E. (1972). Restatement of the theory of occupational choice. *Vocational Guidance Quarterly, 20,* 169–176.

Ginzberg, E., Ginzberg, S. W., Axelrad, S., & Herma, J. R. (1951). *Occupational choice: an approach to a general theory.* New York: Columbia.

Gladding, S. T. (1988). *Counseling: A comprehensive profession.* Columbus, OH: Merrill.

Gottfredson, G. D., & Holland, J. L. (1989). *Dictionary of Holland occupational codes* (2nd ed.). Odessa, FL: Psychological Assessment Resources.

Hansen, J. C., Stevic, R. R., & Warner, R. W., Jr. (1977). *Counseling: Theory and process* (2nd ed.). Boston: Allyn and Bacon.

Herr, E. L., & Cramer, S. H. (1979). Career guidance through life span. Boston: Little, Brown.

Hills, J. R. (1964). Decision theory and college choice. *Personnel and Guidance Journal, 43,* 17–22.

Holland, J. L. (1985). *Making vocational choices* (2nd ed.). Englewood Cliffs, NJ: Prentice-Hall.

Hoppock, R. (1976). *Occupational information* (4th ed.). New York: McGraw-Hill.

Hoyt, K. B. (1989). The career status of women and minority persons: A 20-year perspective. *The Career Development Quarterly, 37,* 202–212.

Kalder, D. R., & Zytowski, D. G. (1969). A maximizing model of occupational decision-making. *Personnel and Guidance Journal, 47,* 781–788.

Krumboltz, J. D. (1979). A social learning theory of career decision making. In A. M. Mitchell, G. B. Jones, & J.D. Krumboltz (Eds.). *Social learning and career decisionmaking.* Cranston, RI: Carroll Press.

Leigh, K. B. (1977). Career counseling. In G. J. Blackham. *Counseling: Theory, process, and practice.* Belmont, CA: Wadsworth.

Manuele-Adkins, C. (1992). Career counseling is personal counseling. *The Career Development Quarterly, 40,* 313–323.

Morrill, W. H. , & Forrest, D. J. (1970). Dimensions of counseling for career development. *Personnel and Guidance Journal, 49,* 299–305.

Myers, I. B. (1980). *Gifts Differing.* Palo Alto, CA: Consulting Psychologists Press.

Peterson, J. V., & Nisenholz, B. (1987). *Orientation to counseling.* Boston: Allyn and Bacon.

Prediger, D. J., Roth, J. D., & Noeth, R. J. (1973). *Nationwide study of student career development.* Iowa city, IA: The American College Testing Program.

Roe, A. (1956). *The psychology of occupations.* New York: Wiley.

Roe, A., & Lunneborg, P. W. (1990). Personality development and career choice. In D. Brown, L. Brooks, and Associates (Eds.). *Career choice and development* (2nd ed.). San Francisco: Jossey-Bass.

Simpson, J. P., Jr. (1990). Computer-assisted testing and the goals of counseling psychology. *The Counseling Psychologist, 18,* 227–239.

Sampson, J. P., Jr., & Reardon, R. C. (1990). Evaluating computer-assisted career guidance systems: Synthesis and implications. *Journal of Career Development, 17,* 143–149.

Sharf, R. S. (1992). *Applying career development theory to counseling.* Pacific Grove, CA: Brooks/Cole.

Super, D. E. (1953). A theory of vocational development. *American Psychologist, 8,* 185–190.

Super, D. E. (1990). A life-span, life-space approach to career development. In D. Brown, L. Brooks, and Associates (Eds.) *Career choice and development* (2nd ed.). San Francisco: Jossey-Bass.

Williamson, E. G. (1965). *Vocational counseling: Some historical, philosophical, and theoretical perspectives.* New York: McGraw-Hill.

Chapter 13

Diagnosis and Assessment

James T. Hurley, Ed.D., AABM

This chapter focuses on two significant issues in the field of counseling—diagnosis and assessment. Diagnosis is a new issue that may face practitioners in the counseling profession. With more states licensing counselors, and with the potential for third-party reimbursement to counselors, these professionals will find themselves in a new role—that of diagnosing their clients.

Assessment, to many counselors, is not new. Many techniques and strategies have changed, however, making assessment a viable tool for counselors and other mental health professionals.

Diagnosis

Although few counselors go through the formal process of making diagnostic decisions, most informally diagnose in order to formulate a plan of treatment for a client. Hansen, Stevic, and Warner, Jr. (1982) indicate that the concept of diagnosis was brought into counseling via psychiatry, which, as a branch of medicine, was already accustomed to diagnosing. The art of diagnosing is alien to most counseling professionals, however, since most graduate curricula do not teach counselors to diagnose.

Purposes

What are the uses of diagnosis in counseling? With the trend toward employment of counselors in nonschool settings such as mental health centers, hospitals, and drug and alcohol abuse programs, many counselors have encountered new responsibilities, one of which is the need to diagnose emotional difficulties (Seligman, 1983). Seligman also points out that the growing trend toward licensure for counselors has brought along the potential to establish private practices and to receive health insurance reimbursement. She also concludes that diagnosis had become a vehicle for human service agencies to classify the clients they serve in order to demonstrate accountability and to justify their role in the community. In addition, the need for school counselors to be knowledgeable of the diagnostic procedures and categories continues to increase in importance if those counselors are to communicate effectively with psychiatrists and mental health agencies. This knowledge is also essential in providing special education and school psychological services.

Hansen, et al. (1982) explain that the purpose of diagnosis is to identify the client's life-style of functioning, or the disruption of the lifestyle. Diagnosis can help to identify the problem area, label it, and establish goals for the client.

Hersen, Kazdin, and Bellack (1983) suggest that establishing a diagnosis enables the counselor to predict the symptoms that are likely to be seen. Thus, in reviewing a file on a client diagnosed as having a generalized anxiety disorder, we would expect this client to have a certain group of symptoms based on the diagnostic category.

Weiner (1959) suggests that diagnosis

1. Allows the counselor to make a prediction about the client's behavior.
2. Allows the counselor to determine whether he will be able to provide appropriate treatment for the client.
3. Aids the counselor in determining what the client needs most.

As suggested by Weiner and others, there seem to be plausible reasons for diagnosing clients; this is probably more true today than ever before. Most likely, diagnosing will become a routine practice for counselors out of necessity, dictated by the demands of others, rather than out of what counselors themselves see as necessary.

Classification

Today there are basically two systems of diagnostic classification used by mental health professionals. One is the third edition of the *Diagnostic and Statistical Manual of Mental Disorders* (DSM-III-R), published in 1987; the other is the *Manual of the International Statistical Classification of Diseases, Injuries, and Causes of Death*, Volume I (1977), also known as the *ICD-9*.

The DSM-III-R is the current standard nosology for the United States. It was preceded by the DSM in 1952, the DSM-II in 1958, and the DSM-III in 1980. A major innovation of the DSM-III was the use of a multiaxial system of diagnosis.

A multiaxial evaluation requires that every case be assessed on several "axes," each of which refers to a different class of information. In order for the system to have maximal clinical usefulness, there must be a limited number of axes; there are five in the DSM-III-R multiaxial classification system. The first three axes constitute the official diagnostic assessment.

> AXIS I   Clinical Syndromes
>   Conditions Not Attributable to a Mental Disorder That Are a
>   Focus of Attention or Treatment (V. Codes)
>   Additional Codes
> AXIS II   Personality Disorders
>   Specific Developmental Disorders
> AXIS III Physical Disorders and Conditions

Axes IV and V are available for use in special clinical and research settings and provide information supplementing the official DSM-III-R diagnoses (Axes I, II, and III) that may be useful for planning treatment and predicting outcome:

> AXIS IV   Severity of Psychosocial Stressors
> AXIS V   Highest Level of Adaptive Functioning Past Year (1987, p. 20)

The following example of a multiaxial diagnosis illustrates how this system works:

> AXIS I—296.23; Major depression, single episode, without psychotic features 303.90; Alcohol dependence

AXIS II—301.60; Dependent personality disorder
AXIS III—Headaches
AXIS IV—Psychosocial stressor: marital separation. Severity: 5—severe
AXIS V—Highest level of adaptive functioning in past year: 4—fair.

The DSM-III-R is longer and includes 340 categories, compared to 108 in the DSM-I, 182 in the DSM-II; and 265 in the DSM-III. For each of the 340 categories of disorders, the DSM-III-R provides a description of each illness, including the diagnostic criteria required. Seligman (1983) reports that for each disorder, the diagnostic description generally contains the following:

1. A list of its essential features and a clinical sketch
2. A summary of characteristics usually associated with the disorder
3. Information on the typical onset and course of the disorder, the impairment caused and potential complications
4. Information on known predisposing factors and frequency of occurrence of the disorder
5. Information on similar disorders, to facilitate differential diagnosis
6. Diagnostic criteria

To many, the DSM-III-R classification system is overwhelming at first glance. Like any other system, proficiency in using it comes with practice. Some additional sources of help in understanding and using the DSM-III-R are *The New Language of Psychiatry* (Levy, 1982), *DSM-III-R Casebook* (Spitzer, et al., 1989), and the *DSM-III Training Guide* (Webb, et al., 1981). Additionally, there are workshops offered through the American Psychological Association's group of approved continuing education programs and through independent groups throughout the country. Today, the DSM-III-R is accepted as an approved diagnostic model by most insurance companies for third-party reimbursement.

Originally expected to be published by December 1992, a new version of the DSM—the DSM-IV—is now expected by early 1994 (Hohenshil, 1992). This new edition will be the result of the work of hundreds of experts with diverse clinical and research expertise. Advance information regarding the DSM-IV suggests that there will be some probable organization changes (e.g., a new section called "schizophrenia and other psychotic disorders"), as well as up to thirty new mental disorders, including such categories as self-defeating personality disorder, substance use disorders, gender identity disorder, and eating disorders.

Cautions

While there are advantages for using diagnosis, there are those who oppose its use. Sundberg, Taplin, and Tyler (1983) point out that many notable professionals, including Carl Rogers, argue that categorizing people dehumanizes and deindividualizes them and prevents proper attention to therapy. Attaching a label may stereotype an individual and may bias others toward him.

Sundberg further indicates that one of the most significant problems with diagnosing is the reliability of agreement between diagnosticians. The most common examples are the multitude of professional opinions expressed in evaluating individuals who are on trial for various crimes, and the studies of individuals who are readmitted to hospitals for various mental conditions and are seen by different psychiatrists or psychologists. The diagnostic reliability among professionals in these cases seems to be lacking.

Another consideration is that the individual's ability to change may be affected by the diagnostic labeling process. Clients may be too eager to accept a label as proof of limitations in their psychological structure. Monahan (1977) did an interesting study on the effects of labels on expectations for clients' change and recovery. The use of preliminary labels, such as in a hospital or clinic, may affect the way staff members behave with clients. Monahan used thirty-nine staff members, who were given a description of a client and asked to predict (1) the length of stay in the hospital, (2) the chance of readmission, (3) the chances of leading a normal life, and (4) the overall prognosis. The results showed the staff members who worked in acute treatment areas were significantly negatively affected by the diagnosis when rendering a prognosis. This evidences one of the hazards in using diagnostic labels and should serve as a caution to those who diagnose.

Some further cautions in diagnosing have been brought about by the modern age of technology. Hersen, et al. (1983) indicate that by the beginning of the twenty-first century, many mental health professionals will have computers in their offices to perform billing, record keeping, communication, and other functions—including diagnosing. This modern technology already exists. More and more mental health professionals are using computers for assessment and for record keeping. Some programs already exist to help the professional to make diagnostic decisions based on the DSM-III-R.

Hersen explains that the major advantage to using a computer for diagnosis is that computers are almost perfectly consistent; when given the same information, the computer program will always formulate the same diagnosis. Human decision makers, on the other hand, lack consistency. The hazard is that computers are not flexible and lack the skills of the trained clinician to make exceptions based upon data that may not be in the computer program. As is the case with computer assessment, the trained mental health professional cannot accept on face value the diagnostic decision made by a computer. It should only be used to help the professional make the decision.

Assessment

Assessment has long been a function in the mental health professions. However, there has been a long-running debate among these professionals about its value. Specifically, assessment is more widely used among those in the practice of psychology than among counseling professionals. Many counseling professionals feel that assessment relies too heavily on complex concepts, overlooking a true understanding of the individual. Despite these criticisms, assessment does have a role in the practice of counseling as it exists today, and the following information is provided as an aid in understanding the uses of this tool.

Anastasi (1992) points out that the key to effective assessment is the choice of appropriate assessment measures for the specific individual and problem under consideration, as well as the proper interpretation of the assessment data within the total assessment process.

Purposes

Why do we use assessment as a counseling tool? Assessment can be a positive factor in counseling. Of course, there are specific reasons for assessment—it is not done just for fun or to occupy time. A. D'Augelli, J. D'Augelli, and Danish (1981) suggest that assessment helps address two questions: (1) What is the problem? and (2) Why did the problem occur and what causes the problem to continue?

Certainly few could argue that many clients enter a counseling situation not knowing specifically what the problem is that brought them to counseling. General statements dealing with feelings of anxiety, confused thoughts or a general depressed mood do not specifically define the problem area. Thus, assessment may help to further clarify for the client the specific nature of the problem.

Hansen, et al. (1982) suggest four basic functions of assessment: (1) *Prediction*—Tests can help predict an individual's success or degree of success in a course of study, job, or career. (2) *Diagnosis*—Tests can help both the client and the professional gain insight into strengths and weaknesses. (3) *Monitoring*—Tests can serve a useful function of monitoring the progress, or lack of progress, the client is making. (4) *Evaluation*—Tests can be used to evaluate the client's growth, the counselor's success, or the achievement of certain goals.

Sundberg, et al. (1983) discuss three important functions of assessment. The first is decision making, which usually takes place during the initial contacts with the client. Decisions have to be made regarding whether the counselor can work with the client, or whether an appropriate referral should be made.

The second function of assessment in this framework is image forming. The counselor and all who are involved with the client need a working image of the person seeking assistance. As Sundberg points out, dangers exist here, and the clinician must always attempt to keep the working image tentative and open to modification.

The third factor, that of hypothesis checking, basically refers to the checking and rechecking by the clinician of tentative informed guesses or diagnoses in an attempt to confirm or disconfirm them. Checking also keeps the other two functions in perspective so that quick decisions and distorted images are prevented.

Assessment has distinct purposes and functions. It is not an all-inclusive tool, but is merely one aid in the professional's repertoire of skills. A look now at specific types of assessment should prove useful to further understanding the benefits of assessment.

Types

There are basically two categories of assessment—testing and nontesting. Within each are many techniques, and all can be useful to the professional in counseling. The relative value of one technique or test over another depends in part on the situation, the specific client and her needs, and the training and skill level of the professional.

Nontesting

This type of testing refers to the use of techniques that do not involve standard psychological tests. Most of these techniques have been used for years by counselors and other mental health professionals; in most cases, they have preceded the development of standardized formal testing.

Belkin (1981) discusses the use of some nontest forms of assessment. *Observation*, he reports, is the basis of all science. From the psychologist's studying animals in the laboratory to the counselor's observing a student's behavior in the classroom, observation has long been one of the most useful clinical techniques. The problem with observation is the potential for subjective biases and poor insight, which may prevent an accurate evaluation.

Belkin further lists *anecdotal records*—the recording of observations—as a form of nontest assessment. He sees the anecdotal record as playing a positive role in the counseling process by providing the counselor with a developmental and longitudinal portrait of the client.

The *cumulative record* is another technique Belkin discusses. He describes it as a progressive, coordinated record. Certainly this information can be valuable to the counselor not only as factual data but also for predictive purposes.

Other techniques described by Belkin are the *autobiography*, which gives the counselor insight into the clients' self-perceptions, and *rating scales*, which are used to quantify and categorize the client according to the rating categories.

One approach to nontesting assessment is that of Goldman (1992), who discusses qualitative assessment as a means of helping clients develop a better understanding of themselves. He describes a variety of assessment methods, other than standardized tests, that may offer more information related to the client, depending on the purpose of the assessment. These include diverse methods such as card sorts, simulations, exercises and games, work examples, and others.

Perhaps the most important nontest assessment technique is the *diagnostic interview*. The diagnostic interview is the first and most important skill that the new clinician must learn (Sundberg, et al., 1983). Hersen, et al. (1983) describe the diagnostic interview as the cornerstone of psychodiagnosis. Methods of conducting the interview vary widely from informal to formal structured situations. The diagnostic interview relies heavily on the skill of the professional. A skilled professional can obtain essential information from this technique. The *Psychiatric Diagnostic Interview* (PDI) (1981) published by Western Psychological Services is an excellent example of a structured diagnostic interview.

Testing

The majority of assessment techniques fall into the category of testing. Sundberg, et al. (1983) define a test as a method for acquiring a sample of a person's behavior in a standard situation. The counseling approach to the use of tests involves five emphases (Duckworth, 1990): a method of enhancing short-term therapy; an aid to focusing on developmental issues; an aid to problem-solving; an aid in decision-making; and a role in the psychoeducational function of counseling.

There are many types of tests, some of which will be discussed shortly. In fact, the *Eleventh Mental Measurements Yearbook* (Kramer and Conoley, 1992) reviews some 1184 tests. It is somewhat overwhelming to look at the number of tests available to mental health professionals. Deciding which test or tests to use requires an assessment of validity and reliability, two important constructs in the field of test development.

Validity.   Validity refers to whether the test accurately measures what it purports to measure. To what extent does a personality test really measure personality? Sundberg, et al. (1983) list four kinds of validity.

1. Concurrent Validity—Correlating scores with outcomes on other tests or current real life conditions
2. Predictive Validity—Correlating scores with outcomes on later achievements
3. Content Validity—Analyzing the nature and sampling of items in the test
4. Construct Validity—Ascertaining how scores link up with many variables that theory suggests should be related to them

Validity is an important factor to consider in choosing a test and having faith in the ability to relate valid results to the client.

Reliability.   Reliability refers to the ability of the test to produce the same or similar results again and again. Correlations help determine whether tests are reliable. Tests can be given to subjects on two separate occasions and a correlation run to check for reliability.

It is important to choose a test with a high degree of reliability to be certain that the test is measuring the same concept each time. The higher the correlation coefficient in reliability, the better the test.

Types of Tests

There are many tests available to counseling professionals. These tests measure different concepts and therefore can be divided into several categories. Belkin (1981) divides tests into the following categories:

1. Achievement Tests—basically measure what a person has learned
2. Aptitude Tests—are used to measure a person's potential in a particular area

3. Interest Inventories—are used to help individuals make career decisions

4. Intelligence Tests—are used to measure the general aptitude for intellectual performance, known as IQ

5. Personality Tests—are used to formulate the absence or presence of psychopathology and to determine personality characteristics

Most authors seem to agree with this classification of tests. Within these categories there are many individual and group instruments to measure a specific construct. A closer look at some of the more popular test instruments may give the reader insight into what is available and what is currently being used by practitioners.

Intelligence Tests

Intelligence tests can be administered to individuals or to groups. By far, group testing has been used most commonly by the school systems. In terms of individual instruments, the two most widely used are the Stanford-Binet, which was adapted by Dr. Lewis Terman in 1916 from a version developed in France by Alfred Binet and Theodore Simon, and the Wechsler series of tests, developed by David Wechsler. This series consists of the Wechsler Pre-School and Primary Scale of Intelligence-Revised (WPPSI-R), the Wechsler Intelligence Scale for Children-III (WISC-III) and the Wechsler Adult Intelligence Scale-Revised (WAIS-R). The different versions are available for different age groups. The Wechsler series of tests has been more widely used in recent years and is considered to be the most sophisticated measure of intelligence available today. Unlike the Stanford-Binet, the Wechsler series gives scores of intelligence in verbal, performance, and full-scale measures.

Group intelligence testing is not regarded as an equal to individual testing because valuable clinical information is lost in group administration. With an individually administered intelligence test, the clinician gains valuable information from observing how the individual performs while taking the test.

Group testing today is mostly confined to large organizations such as schools. Two frequently used group tests are the Otis-Lennon Mental Ability Test and the California Test of Mental Maturity.

Achievement Tests

Achievement tests have been widely used by our educational systems for years. Even the advanced sections of the Graduate Record Examination (GRE) are measures of what one has learned. Some popular achievement tests include the Iowa Tests of Basic Skills and the Wide Range Achievement Test. Achievement testing may be seen as more the function of a counselor in a school setting than the function of one in a mental-health setting, although many professionals in private practice do include some type of achievement test in a standard battery of psychologi-

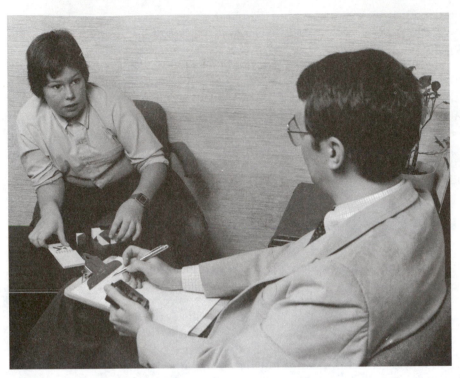

FIGURE 13-1   **Individualized intelligence testing provides essential clinical data**
(Color Image, Inc., Jim Trotter)

cal tests. Today many school psychologists compare achievement test scores to intelligence test scores as a tool in assessing learning disabilities.

Aptitude Tests

The focus of aptitude tests is on potential, not on what has been learned. Aptitude tests are used to predict potential success. The verbal and quantitative parts of the Graduate Record Examination are one such type of aptitude test. Another type of aptitude test that is used by many counselors and psychologists is the Differential Aptitude Test (DAT).

Interest Inventories

Interest inventories, such as the Career Assessment Inventory the Strong-Campbell Interest Inventory, and the Kuder Preference Record, usually are designed to put the client in a position of having to make a formal choice of items. The way the client responds, and the pattern of responses, give an indication of the type of occupation in which the client would be successful. Of course, as with many psychological tests, the data obtained is only as good as the client's honesty in answering the questions.

Personality Tests

Personality testing seems more identified with the mental health profession than any other type of testing. There are a wide variety and a large volume of personality tests from which to choose. We can categorize personality tests into two subcategories, objective and projective.

The most widely used objective measure of personality assessment is the Minnesota Multiphasic Personality Inventory (MMPI). The MMPI was developed in the late 1930s by Hathaway and McKinley who were working on a set of personality scales. A revised version of the MMPI was completed in 1989. The new version revised or eliminated some items that were outdated or considered offensive, as well as developing some items, resulting in a total of 567 test items. However, the MMPI-2 requires an eighth-grade reading level, which is often a problem. In addition, there is a new adolescent version of the MMPI-2, which utilizes additional norms for adolescent interpretation.

Years of research and work have been done on and with the MMPI, yielding many additional scoring scales. This, combined with the ease of administration and scoring, makes the MMPI-2 one of the most significant and respected objective measures of personality.

Of course, here are many other objective measures of personality; they are too numerous to mention here. Two of the most widely used are the California Psychological Inventory (CPI) and the Sixteen Personality Factors Questionnaire (16PF). New tests are always being developed and must undergo rigid clinical trials before being accepted.

The other type of personality testing is projective assessment. These types of assessment usually require that the clinician have more formal training and experience in order to derive clinical judgments from them. Projective techniques require a client to project his own perceptions onto stimuli that are ambiguous, such as inkblots or making up stories from pictures.

The most commonly used projective techniques are the Rorschach, the Thematic Apperception Test (TAT), the Draw-A-Person or House-Tree-Person tests, and the various forms of sentence completion tests (Sundberg et al., 1983).

The Rorschach technique was developed by Hermann Rorschach, a Swiss psychiatrist, in 1921 (Klopfer and Davidson, 1962). Probably more than any other projective technique, the Rorschach has been used both by researchers and practitioners, and today there are a variety of scoring systems and interpretation systems available for use.

Levitt (1980) describes the widespread use of the Rorschach as following the trend of most projective techniques—it has had its ups and downs. He describes the period from 1960 to 1970 as one of disenchantment with psychological testing, and particularly with the projective techniques, including the Rorschach. Today, however, the Rorschach and other projective techniques have regained a high degree of use in clinical practice. Numerous workshops are offered around the country on the administration, scoring, and interpretation of the Rorschach and other instruments.

The TAT, another popular projective instrument, was developed around 1935 by Morgan and Murray. Today much research and many articles have been written about the TAT. The basic premise is that the client is given a series of pictures to look at and is asked to formulate a story based upon what is happening in the picture, who the characters are, and what the outcome of the situation will be. The individual must rely on her own perceptions and personality structure to formulate a story based on an ambiguous picture.

There are many other forms of projective techniques that utilize such activities as drawing and sentence completion. There are also many critics of projective techniques who base their criticisms on the vagueness and complexity of interpretation of these instruments. The question of lack of reliability and validity of the instruments also presents problems for some clinicians. Taken in conjunction with other measures of personality and with clinical observation, projective techniques can offer the clinician additional information to use in assessment.

Computerized Testing

With the availability and decline in price of the small office computer, there has been a rapid growth in the use of computers among mental health professionals. Office management systems, billing systems, and word processing are just a few of the popular uses that clinicians find for their computers. But perhaps most important, the computer for the counselor, psychologist, and psychiatrist can serve the function of administering, scoring, and interpreting the many clinical instruments that are now available for the office microcomputer and that once required processing by larger computer test-scoring services.

Turkington (1984) discusses some advantages and disadvantages of computerized assessment. For example, test scores are available faster—within minutes rather than within the days or weeks needed for the scores to return from a test-scoring service. Other advantages are that computerized testing in the office can be less expensive, and clients seem to like it better because they feel less intimidated by the computer than traditional testing procedures.

There are both simple and sophisticated systems. Several companies sell complete programs including the computer terminals and testing software. Or practitioners can purchase a microcomputer and then choose various kinds of programs that best suit their needs. Most software companies that sell psychological test programs for computers have standardized the programs for the most popular computers such as the Apple and the IBM PC. Such programs may include WISC-III and WAIS-R interpretations, MMPI-2 scoring and interpretations, Beck Depression Inventory, Bender-Gestalt interpretations, the Self-Directed Search and other career interest inventories, and many others. Even Rorschach interpretive programs are available.

FIGURE 13-2   Computerized testing is expedient for the counselor and fun for the client
(Photo by James T. Hurley)

Of course in many cases, such as with the WISC-R, the WAIS-R, and the Rorschach, the computer does not actually administer the test. Administration still requires a skilled examiner. But it can provide some consistency in interpretation, especially if the examiner gives a large number of tests.

There are disadvantages and dangers to be considered with computerized assessment. Many psychologists question the accuracy of the interpretations made by computerized assessment. If the tests are carried out by a well-trained clinician, the results can be useful. But there seems to be a fear that many of these instruments may be used by individuals who are not well trained, especially since there are so many companies now selling these products. Most reputable testing companies will only sell to qualified individuals. Usually only licensed psychologists or those showing evidence of advanced training in testing courses at the graduate level are considered qualified. Many companies require the potential purchaser to complete a qualifications form. Not all companies require this, however, and there is no law mandating it.

Turkington further points out that as the use of computerized assessment grows, guidelines will need to be developed to protect the public from inadequate users of this form of testing. The Colorado Psychological Association in 1982 developed such guidelines, and two committees of the American Psychological Association are currently working on similar guidelines for their membership.

In the hands of a well-qualified mental health professional, computerized assessment can be a valuable tool. However, the clinician should not accept and feed back the results verbatim from the computer. Skilled judgment in reviewing the results should always be the rule.

Communicating Results

Perhaps as important as obtaining test data is interpreting or presenting the findings of such data to various individuals. Whether the results are reported to the client, teachers, other counselors, or psychologists and other professionals, the responsibility of presenting accurate and understandable information is crucial.

As Hansen et al. (1982) indicate, counselors sometimes face a dilemma when presenting test results. The task can be a pleasant one if the client has scored well and has shown no significant problem areas, but counselors must avoid displaying a negative reaction to the test results if they are not pleasant, since this attitude can easily be detected by the client. Objectivity is the key element to maintain.

Some types of test information are easier to interpret to clients than others. Achievement, aptitude, and interest tests are less threatening than intelligence and personality tests. Many clinicians would argue that there are inherent dangers in giving clients too much information, especially if there are severe psychopathological problems present. Sometimes these interpretations are best left among professionals; they may be too complex for the client to comprehend.

Keeping the information to be communicated simple and free of technical jargon appears to be a rule agreed upon by many professionals. Parents sitting in on a conference during which test results concerning their child or adolescent are presented are sometimes overwhelmed by the technical nature of the discussion. They often leave such a conference wondering if they really understood what had taken place. It is the responsibility of the examiner to be able to convey the results to persons with any and all levels of expertise. The counselor or clinician faces a great responsibility in providing not only an expertise in assessing but also an expertise in interpreting and communicating assessment results.

Summary

This chapter has focused on two issues of vital importance in counseling today. Diagnosis, although not a new tool in the mental health professions, will be a new and challenging tool for many counseling professionals. Although many counselors have used informal diagnosis, the trend is toward using more specific and detailed approaches that will be required as counselors take on new roles outside the school environment.

Assessment, the other issue featured in this chapter, is more familiar to counselors. Counselors have used assessment for years but modern trends and concepts have brought new importance to this area. The need for better and more accurate assessment is indicated, and new advances with the use of computers have made assessment easier, more accurate, and more useful.

Reference

American Psychiatric Association (1987). *Diagnostic and statistical manual of mental disorders*, (3rd ed., revised). Washington, DC: Author.

Anastasi, A. (1992). What counselors should know about the use and interpretation of psychological tests. *Journal of Counseling and Development, 70,* 610–615

Belkin, G. S. (1981). *Practical counseling on the schools*. Dubuque, IA: Wm. C. Brown.

D'Augelli, A. R D'Augelli J. F., & Danish, S. J. (1981). *Helping others*. Monterey CA: Brooks\Cole.

Duckworth, J. (1990). The counseling approach to the use of testing. *The Counseling Psychologist, 18,* 198–204.

Goldman, L. (1992). Qualitative assessment: An approach for counselors. *Journal of Counseling and Development, 70,* 616–623.

Hansen, J. C., Stevic, R. R., & Warner, R. W., Jr. (1982). *Counseling: Theory and process* (3rd ed.). Boston : Allyn and Bacon.

Hersen, M. Kazdin, A., & Bellack, A. S. (1983). *The clinical psychology handbook*. New York: Pergamon Press

Hohenshil, T. H. (1992). DSM-IV progress report. *Journal of Counseling and Development, 71,* 249–251.

Klopfer, B., & Davidson, H. H. (1962). *The Rorschach technique: An introductory manual*. New York: Harcourt Brace Jovanovich.

Kramer, J. J. & Conoley, J. C. (Eds). (1992). *The eleventh mental measurements yearbook*. Lincoln, NE: University of Nebraska Press.

Levitt, E. E. (1980). *Primer on the Rorschach technique: A method of administration, scoring, and interpretation*. Springfield, IL: Charles C. Thomas.

Levy, R. (1982). *The new language of psychiatry: Learning and using DSM-III*. Boston: Little, Brown.

Monahan, L. (1977). Diagnosis and expectations for change: An inverse relationship? *Journal of Nervous and Mental Disease, 164,* 214–217.

Seligman, L. (1983). An introduction to the new DSM-III. *Personnel and Guidance Journal, 61,* 601–605.

Spitzer, R. L., Skodol, A. E., Gibbon, M., & Williams, J. B. W. (1989). *Dsm-III-r-case book*. Washington D.C. American Psychiatric Press.

Sundberg, N. D., Taplin, J. R., & Tyler, L. E. (1983). *Introduction to clinical psychology*. Englewood Cliffs, NJ: Prentice-Hall.

Turkington, C. (1984). The growing use, and abuse, of computer testing. *APA Monitor, 15,* 7 & 26.

Webb, L. J., DiClemente, C. C., Johnstone, E. E., Sanders, J. L., & Perley, R. A. (1981). *Dsm-III training guide*. New York: Brunner-Mazel.

Weiner, I. B. (1959). The role of diagnosis in a university counseling center. *Journal of Counseling Psychology, 6,* 110–115.

Chapter *14*

Professional Issues

Counseling as a profession entails more than facilitative skills and attitudes. Counselors must respond to the complex legal and ethical considerations that have a direct impact on both the delivery of counseling services and the attitude of the public toward those services. Public acceptance of counseling as a valued service and of counselors as respected professionals depends in large measure on an adherence to a high level of ethical and legal behavior. In addition, professional behavior calls for a continuing evaluation of the service being provided as a means of improving that service.

In this chapter these issues of ethics, laws, future trends and evaluation as they apply to counselors are reviewed.

Ethical Considerations in Counseling

Counselors, like all professionals, have ethical responsibilities and obligations. The counseling literature contains numerous references to ethics and the legal status of the counselor, but for a number of reasons ethical problems pose particularly difficult situations for people in the various helping professions. First, clear-cut, specific ethical codes that provide adequate guidelines for ethical behavior in the very wide range of situations encountered in counseling relationships have yet to be evolved. Second, most counseling professionals work within the context of institutions such as schools, colleges, hospitals, churches, and private agencies whose institutional value systems may be quite different from those of the counseling profession itself. Finally, counselors are particularly likely to encounter situations where their ethical obligations overlap or conflict. Often a counselor is working simultaneously with several people who are involved in their own close interpersonal relationships, whether in the family, the school, or other institutions. In such situations, ethical obligations become exceedingly complex.

The principal rule supporting ethical obligations is that the counselor must act with full recognition of the importance of client rights, the ethics of the profession, and the relationship of moral standards and values, individual or cultural, in the life of that client.

The Nature of Ethical Obligations

Ethics are suggested standards of conduct based on a consensus value set. When an aspiring professional group undertakes an activity that involves a considerable element of public trust and confidence, it must translate prevailing values into a set of ethical standards that can serve to structure expectations for the behavior of its members in their relationships with the public and with each other. As the group emerges in its development toward professionalization, ethical standards are generally formalized in terms of a code of ethics. National professional organizations, such as the American Counseling Association (ACA) and the American Psychological Association, have developed ethical standards which they have made available to practitioners. In each case members who were directly involved in writing the code reviewed and examined a wide range of ethical behavior and problems of professional practice that were of concern to a broadly based membership. Both codes stress adherence to rigorous professional standards and to exemplary behavior, integrity, and objectivity toward clients.

The ACA ethical code, revised in 1988, consists of a preamble and eight sections: general, counseling relationship, measurement and evaluation, research and publication, counseling, private practice, personnel administration, and preparation standards. This code, which is found in Appendix A, does not contain any classification of misbehavior, nor does it attach penalties to the violation of the standards. Rather, the standards focus on guidelines for professional conduct by which specific actions of a counselor may be evaluated. The fundamental rule is that the human being must be respected and protected at all times, which can be done only by counselors who manifest honesty, integrity, and objectivity in their behavior toward their clients.

Unethical behavior usually occurs when the counselor communicates in a way that establishes one set of expectations and then behaves in a way that is inconsistent with those expectations. For example, the counselor structures the counseling situation verbally or nonverbally to imply mutual trust, concern, and confidentiality. The counselor then behaves in a way that upsets these expectations, because the counselor then assigns greater value to another societal role. Clients may see such inconsistent behavior as unethical, although the inconsistency may stem from the lack of professional identity on the part of the counselor.

In a fairly recent report of the ACA Ethics Committee (1992) information was presented regarding the actual ethical complaints received during 1991–92. Recognizing that most ethical complaints are handled long before they reach the ACA committee and that many cases included complaints of a violation of more than one standard, it is still important to note that of the nineteen complaints received, twelve violations of confidentiality were cited; eleven violations of the counseling relationship were cited, including five for dual relationships with clients, three for sexual intimacy, and three for dual or multiple roles with students; six complaints for an inaccurate representation of professional qualifications; two complaints for unethical research procedures; and twelve other, miscellaneous complaints. These do seem to be fairly representative of the complaints of unethical behavior overall.

Dual role relationships, whether they involve sexual contact, seem to be particularly troublesome. Kitchener (1988) suggests three guidelines in differentiating between relationships that are likely to be harmful and those that are not. First, as the incompatibility of expectations increases between roles, the potential for harm also increases. Second, as the obligations associated with different roles diverge, the potential for reduced objectivity and divided loyalties increases too. Third, as the power and prestige between the roles of the professional and the consumer (client or student) increase, so does the potential for exploitation and the ability of the consumer to look at the relationship objectively. Thus any relationship other than professional must be entered into very carefully and with the welfare of the consumer foremost in priority.

Confidentiality

The greatest source of ethical dilemma in counseling results from questions of confidentiality. As Gibson and Mitchell (1990) point out, "Trust is an important cornerstone in the counseling relationship and central to the development and maintenance of trust is the principle of confidentiality" (p. 453). However, issues related to confidentiality are not always easily resolved. In particular, confidentiality brings into sharp focus the issue of the counselor's responsibilities to the profession, to the institution or agency that employs the counselor, to the society, and, most of all, to the individual seeking help.

Principles of Confidentiality

Schneiders (1963) terms the information revealed in counseling an "entrusted secret," information revealed with the condition that it be kept secret. Schneiders suggests seven general principles that govern confidentiality and communication:

1. The obligation of confidentiality is relative rather than absolute since there are conditions which can alter it.
2. Confidentiality depends on the nature of the material, so that material which is already public or can easily become so is not bound by confidentiality in the same way as is the entrusted secret.
3. Material that is harmless does not bind the counselor to confidentiality.
4. The material that is necessary for a counselor or an agency to function effectively is often released from the bonds of confidentiality.
5. Confidentiality is always conditioned by the intrinsic right of the counselee to his integrity and reputation, to be secret, and to resist aggression. Such rights can be protected by the counselor even against the law.
6. Confidentiality is limited also by the rights of the counselor to preserve his own reputation and integrity, to resist harm or aggression, and to preserve privileged communication.
7. Confidentiality is determined and limited by the rights of an innocent third party and by the rights of the community. (1963, p. 263)

Schneiders goes on to state that the obligation of secrecy is no longer relevant when (1) the common welfare demands revelation, (2) the secret is invalid, (3) there is unjust aggression, (4) the client gives consent, or (5) there is publication of the secret.

Questions of confidentiality, however, are clearer when they are examined in terms of "levels of confidentiality" (Blocher, 1966). Confidentiality involves a commitment that is always relative rather than absolute. For example, it is hard to conceive of any counselor withholding the information that a client had put a time bomb in a crowded auditorium.

Levels of Confidentiality

Three rather distinct levels of confidentiality can be established in counseling. The first level of confidentiality involves the professional *use* of information. Every counselor has the obligation to handle information about clients or potential clients only in professional ways. Such information, no matter how it is acquired or how trivial it may seem, should never be used loosely in social conversation or in nonprofessional settings. This includes not only information obtained in counseling interviews, but also the fact of the client *being a client*. All sources of information should be handled in ways that insure that they do not fall into the hands of persons who might handle the information in nonprofessional ways.

The second level of confidentiality relates to information that arises out of a counseling relationship. In all such situations, clients have a right to expect that information will only be used for their welfare. The very nature of the counseling relationship implies this, whether or not the counselor verbally communicates it. This sharing of information obtained during the counseling session can pose a particularly difficult ethical dilemma when the counselor wishes to share the information with others—for example, other counselors, teachers, social workers, psychologists, parents, or a spouse—who may have a primary concern for the client's welfare. Blocher (1966) points out that the ideal solution to this kind of problem is to clearly communicate to the client this level of confidentiality before confidences are accepted. If clients understand in advance that the counselor will use information only for professional purposes and only in the client's best interest, then many of the resulting decisions will be professional judgments rather than ethical decisions.

A third level of confidentiality occurs when it is obvious that the client will not communicate in complete confidence, except in cases of clear and immediate danger to human life. In such a case the counselor is providing the client with an opportunity for sharing some disturbing and shocking confidences in order to provide that client a helping, confidential relationship. The key to the whole matter rests in the counselor's ability to structure in advance the level of confidentiality at which she operates. Keeping that confidence once it is accepted at a particular level is an ethical matter. The counselor who does not keep confidences in an ethical manner will soon have no confidences to keep.

Denkowski and Denkowski (1982) review the historical rationale for confidentiality and argue for a limited and qualified standard. They analyze the need for balance between the rights of the individual and the safety of society with specific attention to the importance of counselors keeping up-to-date with the legal status of confidentiality in their states. Knapp and Vandecreek (1983) give further clarification to this issue, pointing out that judicial courts do not always interpret privileged communication laws the way counselors would like them to. Arthur and Swanson (1993, pp. 19–20) summarize a variety of situations in which exceptions to confidentiality exist. Among these are:

1. The client is a danger to self or others.
2. The client requests the release of information.
3. A court orders release of information.

4. Legal and clinical consultation are needed.

5. Clients raise the issue of their mental health in a legal proceeding. This is particularly true if the welfare of a child is involved.

6. Clients are below the age of 18.

7. Intra-agency or institutional sharing of information is part of the treatment process.

8. The counselor has reason to suspect child abuse.

The case of *Tarasoff v. Board of Regents of the University of Calfornia,* which occurred in 1969, highlighted this particularly sticky problem. In this instance, the California Supreme Court ruled that the University and its employees acted in an irresponsible manner when they failed to notify an intended victim of a threat, resulting in the victim's murder. Knapp and Vandecreek (1983) point out that differences in state laws make the legal aspects of the "duty to warn" difficult to interpret; however, they suggest that if counselors follow reasonable standards in predicting violence and in providing proper warning, the counselors will have acted properly. (As may be seen, the principle of confidentiality is complex and requires continuous updating. Corey et al. (1984), however, provide an excellent overview of the issue.)

Legal Considerations for Counselors

Counselors are ordinarily governed by the laws of their particular states with regard to the profession of counseling; there is wide diversity among the states in terms of the specific application of the law to counselors. Actually, relatively few court cases and even fewer pertinent statutes deal directly with the counselor. In most instances the examination of the legal status of the counselor must be based on the law as it applies to everyone. The law is generally supportive or neutral toward codes of ethics and standards such as those discussed in the previous section (Stude and McKelvey, 1979). The law is supportive in that it enforces minimum standards for counselors through licensing requirements and generally protects the confidentiality of statements and records provided by clients during counseling. It is neutral in that it allows the counseling profession to police itself and to govern counselors' relations with their clients and other counselors. The law intervenes and overrides professional codes of ethics only when necessary to protect the public health, safety, and welfare. This happens primarily when the counseling profession's standards of confidentiality require the suppression of information, when the necessity of preventing harm overrides the necessity to insure effective treatment.

Buckley-Pell Amendment

McGuire and Borowy (1978) have reviewed the issues relating to confidentiality and the Buckley-Pell Amendment of Public Law 93–380 passed in 1974. Although this amendment was seen by some counselors as undermining the confidentiality codes of their ethical standards, McGuire and Borowy suggest that the Buckley-Pell Amendment may be interpreted to be supportive rather than in conflict with these ethical standards. As a result, they recommend that counselors critically examine their own record-keeping practices, limit their use of technical language, diagnostic labels, and such, and maintain only information considered critical to the counseling situation. Information that is accessible only to counselors and to the support personnel who are directly related to the treatment of the client is excluded from the definition of the kind of records that must be made available to students and their parents. However, psychologically relevant materials obtained or utilized for purposes other than counseling treatment, or materials that are maintained in files accessible to other officials or staff at the institution or agency, would be defined as part of the student's educational records and would be available to the student or parent.

Privileged Communication

The legal support for privileged communication is also unclear. Privileged communication is simply anything said by a client to a counselor in a counseling interview with the understanding that the counselor will not be called upon to divulge the information, regardless of its nature. Privileged communication has long existed for ministers, for lawyers, for spouses, and for medical doctors. It is not always clear whether counselors have privileged communication, since there is little consistency in the law across states.

Types of Privileged Communication

There are two types of privileged communication: absolute and qualified. The best that most counselors can expect is qualified, which means that exceptions are possible and in some cases specific. Thus some conditions should be made clear before any exchange of privileged communication. First, there must be an understanding that the communications will not be disclosed. The counselor may need to indicate at times during the interactions that the material being discussed may be outside his or her protected area of privilege.

Second, confidentiality must be deemed necessary to the maintenance of the relationship. This creates difficulties in that the counselor may not know until after some portion of the communication has occurred that confidentiality is essential. Thus the counselor needs to be sensitive to the intensity of the interaction so that any potential problem area can be anticipated and a satisfactory method devised for dealing with it.

Third, the relationship between the privileged parties must have support or be fostered by the community. Although society frequently places enough value in the counseling service to include it in this category, there is often sufficient doubt in people's minds to render this condition ambiguous.

Fourth, there is concern over the extent to which disclosure would harm the individual. The benefit to the client by maintaining confidentiality must be greater than the benefit to society by disposition of the case.

FIGURE 14-1 **Attending professional meetings is one way of keeping up-to-date on legal considerations**
(Guy Gillette/Photo Researchers, Inc.)

Counselor Alternatives

Since privileged communication does not occur in many states, counselors must take action to protect their clients.Counselors should inform clients, at an appropriate time, what the status of privileged communication is as the counselor understands it. This suggests that the counselor is alert to various statements of the client that may need to be discussed later with others. Examples might be statements concerning a client's inclinations toward violence, an abhorrence of what the client has done, and similar statements. The counselor may eventually be asked to repeat, under oath, the statements made by the client.

Since the counselor may have to produce whatever records he may have on the client, he needs to keep very careful records, purging them from time to time to eliminate any material that is no longer relevant. In addition, counselors may wish to keep records that require their interpretation, in this way maintaining some control over interpretations by people who have not interacted with the client. Clearly some method of insuring the highest degree of confidentiality is necessary.

Even with such precautions, a counselor may be called upon to testify in a court case involving the client. In those situations the counselor has several alternatives. The counselor may give testimony, which has the effect of saying that the issue is best settled by due process rather than by an individual decision. Or the counselor may refuse to testify, claiming violation of confidence and conscience. Such counselors may find themselves held in contempt of court and may face a lawsuit. The counselor may feel compelled to refuse to testify despite the potentially damaging consequences.

Other alternatives are sometimes available. The counselor may develop a compromise kind of activity for this court appearance. If the counselor relies on memory, it is usually difficult to remember specifics well enough to be of value in any court of law. Or the material which the court is interested in is frequently hearsay from the counselor's point of view, since the counselor did not actually observe the activities reported by the client. The counselor knows only what she was told, and this is usually not admissible evidence. Such suggestions should not be misinterpreted to suggest that counselors play games with client data and the serious problem of courtroom appearance; rather, these ideas are intended to show the difficulty and possibility of conflict in this area. Counselors should check out their rights as established by their own local laws.

Competence and Malpractice

An important aspect of legal considerations for counselors, related to the credentialing issues discussed in Chapter 1 and to the ethical standards discussed earlier in this chapter, is that of counselors practicing within the limits of their professional expertise. With the dramatic increase in malpractice suits over the past decade, it is clear that the competence of counselors is under legal scrutiny and that counselors need to be aware of the limits of their knowledge and skills in order to avoid creating harm for their clients. Such areas as giving birth control advice, legal advice, abortion-related advice, and prescribing drugs are the most common situations in which legal problems are likely to occur. Put more simply, counselors must practice as "counselors" and not as physicians or attorneys.

Current and Future Trends in Counseling

As the counseling profession moves toward the twenty-first century, it is important to summarize where counseling is and where the profession is headed. Two recent, major analyses of trends in counseling have been published. One is the work of Daniel and Weikel (1983), which resulted from a survey of counselor educators and identified various trends as being "highly probable" or "probable." The second was a study sponsored by Chi Sigma Iota (a national professional fraternity of counselors) in which some leading counselor educators were asked to share their ideas about future trends, resulting in a monograph (Walz, Gazda, & Shertzer, 1991). Combining the ideas of these two major contributions with other information, and taking the dates of these publications into account, it is possible to summarize the most likely trends that are occurring at this point in time and/or which are likely to be significant in the future.

Issues in Providing Counseling Services for Older Adults Will Gain in Prominence. Although this area has been identified as a trend that would emerge, there is little evidence that this had occurred. It is clear that this "sleeping giant" will soon awaken. The proportion of older adults over the age of 65 in the United States has risen significantly and will continue to do so. The American Counseling Association has already recognized a national division, the Association for Adult Development and Aging, which focuses on matters related to the development and needs of adults of all ages, but has become the major group for studying the needs of the elderly.

As more federal and state funds are allocated for services to be provided to older adults, counselors are expected to assume a major role in meeting the psychological and sociological needs of this group. Preserving the self-esteem of older adults who can no longer tie their sense of self-worth to their careers, helping older adults develop new avocational activities appropriate for any physical limitations they may have, facilitating older adults in their working through issues of loss resulting from the death of family and peers, providing experiences that will enable them to gain a sense of empowerment, and promoting wellness in later life are just a part of the issues which will become important for counselors.

Counselors Will Continue to Be in the Forefront in Facilitating Cultural Diversity in Our Society. As the proportion of minorities increases to the point where white Americans will be a plurality and not a majority in this society, understanding and acceptance of the characteristics and needs of non-whites will become even more essential.

As a result, counselors will require sensitivity and specialized knowledge in promoting cultural diversity in a society where diversity is often punished. Ivey, Ivey, and Simek-Morgan (1993) have identified three basic needs in cultural expertise:

> *The ability to generate a maximum number of thoughts, words, and behaviors to communicate with self and others within a given culture.*
>
> *The ability to generate the thoughts, words, and behaviors necessary to communicate with a variety of diverse groups and individuals. Both clients and counselors need to communicate within their own culture and learn the ability to understand other cultures as well.*
>
> *The ability to formulate plans, act on many possibilities existing in a culture, and reflect on these actions.*

Thus counselors of the future will need expanding knowledge about various minority groups. In addition, the counseling profession will take (as it must) steps to attract individuals of diverse backgrounds to become counselors in all settings if the kind of cultural diversity desired for American society is to be attained.

The Importance of Counselors Developing an Awareness of the Use and Misuse of Various Mood-Altering Chemicals will Continue to Increase. Although educational efforts have helped a greater number of individuals, both professionals and society at large, become familiar with the dangers of drug misuse, the impact on much of American society has been minimal. Counselors will need to develop a far greater insight into the relationship between various emotional/social/psychological aspects of an individual's life and drug abuse. Learning to identify individuals who are at-risk for drug abuse and to develop strategies for helping those individuals adopt less dangerous means of coping with those at-risk circumstances will become major concerns in training future counselors.

Counselors Will Have a New Emphasis on "Career Change" as Opposed to "Career Choice." With the rapid change in job requirements as technological advancements change or eliminate many jobs, the counselor will have an even greater need to be able to work with individuals who have worked at a particular job for many years and are no longer needed for that job. Assessing transferability of skills, identifying emotional/psychological needs being met by work, and helping the individual prepare for a new career will be a major focus of career counseling, eventually requiring more time than helping individuals make their first career decision. In addition, working with older adults who have chosen early retirement or who wish to continue as part of the work force after normal retirement will be a challenge.

The Issue of Counselor Accountability Will Gain Emphasis, Requiring More Counseling Outcomes Research. With societal changes, the demand for demonstrating the contribution of various social services will grow. Counselors will be required to provide evidence on a continuing basis that what they are doing makes a difference for the individual clients and/or agencies they serve. The professional counselor must have the skill to conduct the kind of counseling outcome studies that will document the value of counseling services in language and measures acceptable to the public. Related to this will be the need for counselor training programs to document that their graduates have developed the skills and gained the knowledge needed to be effective as counselors.

The Use of Computers and Other Technology Will Become an Integral Part of the Counseling Profession. Recognition that computers will not replace counselors but will help them so that clients can receive maximum benefit, will be the first step in changing the counseling profession's use of technology. The rapidly changing world, with information that is often out-of-date within a few years, means that counselors must rely on sources of information that can be easily updated. The use of computers and other technology can result in the counselor having the most recent information about careers, sources of social services, test data, and even counseling knowledge itself. The increased sophistication of technology will free the counselor from using time to provide information and thus provide more time for helping the client in determining how to use that information.

The Focus on Prevention Activities of Counselors Will Become a Growing Emphasis. The currently growing strength of the holistic approaches to counseling, in which the total person of the client has become of importance to the counselor, means that an emphasis on preventive measures will develop. Counselors have long recognized that it is easier to prevent a problem than to remediate it. As knowledge about various emotional/psychological problems increases, counselors will have greater information about steps that can be taken to prevent the problems from developing. A major role of the counselor will become that of acting as a preventive consultant to parents, teachers, and specialized groups to educate them in preventive measures.

The Need for Comprehensive, Systematic Plans for Professional Growth and Development Will Become Necessary for All Counselors in All Settings. Continuing education of counselors is, and will continue to be, important to keep counselors abreast of new developments in counseling knowledge and skills. Both the needs of clients and emerging developments in counseling knowledge are changing rapidly. Counselors who rely on what they learned in their counselor training program even a few years earlier will become ineffective in a short time.

Research and Evaluation in Counseling

Need for Research

Remer points out that "a person cannot be a counselor, ethically or morally, without many of the skills and competencies engendered in learning about research, statistics, and testing . . . " (1981, p. 567). He goes on to suggest that counselors have an ethical responsibility to both their clients and the public to know the effects and limits of the tools and techniques they use.

Research efforts are necessary to determine the effects that counselors have on clients during counseling, to ascertain the value of various specialized programs on the behavior of clients (for example, drug education programs, and assertion training groups), to assess the needs of those with whom counselors work, and to provide information that will meet accountability requirements in schools and agencies. The ACA Code of Ethics states that counselors have a responsibility to gather data on their effectiveness and use that data to improve their services.

Purposes of Evaluation

Measuring the effectiveness of counseling continues to be a source of difficulty. Part of the problem is that many counselors see evaluation as a threatening process. The purpose of evaluation, however, is to provide new insights that will help counselors perform at higher and more professional levels. The counseling experience makes heavy demands on staff members, clients, and the community, in both financial and emotional terms. Consequently, it is necessary to determine the value of those counseling services by applying standards, and this process is evaluation. Thus, the major aim of evaluation is to ascertain the current status of the counseling service within some frame of reference, and then on the basis of this knowledge to improve its quality and its efficacy. Evaluation is the vehicle through which one learns whether counseling is doing what is expected of it.

Difficulties in Evaluation

Certainly, most counselors accept that evaluation is one approach to bringing about self-improvement. Yet good evaluation studies in counseling effectiveness are relatively rare, for a number of reasons. The first and most fundamental problem is the difficulty of obtaining agreement on definitions of process and outcome that permit meaningful evaluations. Basically, counseling has no generally accepted goals or objectives. Instead, there are almost as many goals as there are researchers in the field. Some of these goals are almost completely nonoperational, in that they cannot be easily converted into measurable behaviors. Goals such as developing self-actualization, improving the client's self-concept, or reorganizing the client's self-structure are a bit difficult to translate into measurable behaviors. Traditionally, client self-reports, counselor judgments of improvement, improved grades, changes in test scores, and indices of behavioral change have been used as criteria for measuring client improvement. Each of these criteria, however, has definite weaknesses, either in terms of validity or in terms of showing long-term changes.

The weaknesses of these traditional criteria, along with the current emphasis on accountability, have placed a greater emphasis on behavioral criteria. Such an emphasis, while highly acceptable to behaviorally oriented counselors, is frequently rejected by counselors who believe that such emphasis on the specific behaviors is only a limited aspect of counseling and does not get at the important focus of the whole counseling process.

A second important problem encountered in measuring or evaluating counseling centers on the use of control groups. In any experimental design an attempt must be made to isolate the effects of the treatment by designating a control group of subjects who are like the experimental group in every way except that they do not receive the treatment. Such control groups are best established by randomly dividing a single population into control and experimental groups. The presumption is that if change occurs in the group receiving treatment and not in the control group, the change can be attributed to the treatment. Control and experimental groups are generally selected to be as similar as possible on a large number of variables; they are matched in characteristics such as age, sex, IQ, and socioeconomic status.

In counseling research, however, the most relevant characteristics are the hardest to match. The most obvious relevant characteristic is motivation to enter counseling. Obviously a well-matched control group must contain individuals who also want and need the counselors' services. A serious ethical issue comes into play at this point. An individual who expresses a need for counseling does not wish to be assigned to a control group where no counseling help is provided. Such an assignment could well have a negative impact on the client and perhaps affect the validity of the results. In counseling evaluation, this issue is often resolved by utilizing a delaying tactic, keeping the control group subjects on a waiting list while providing the experimental subjects with counseling. After both groups are assessed for change, the control subjects receive counseling. Sometimes subjects in the control group receive very limited noncounseling contact to assure them that help will be received and to permit the counselor to determine if the need for counseling help is urgent.

Maintaining minimal noncounseling contact with the control group may also help eliminate the placebo effect. Some evidence indicates that some clients begin to show progress simply because they are in counseling, rather than because of what is happening during the counseling process. Providing limited noncounseling contact to the control group may help researchers distinguish between the improvement clients show as a result of the counseling and the improvement that occurs simply because they feel optimistic about being in counseling.

Another major problem in counseling evaluation is contamination of treatment effects. If a group of individuals who want counseling services are identified and half are selected to be a treatment group and half a control group, little can be done to prevent either of these groups from obtaining other outside assistance. This is particularly true if counseling is viewed primarily as a relationship; the therapeutic qualities of a counseling relationship are not necessarily confined to relationships that originate in professional settings. The control group, which presumably is receiving no counseling help, may also show improvement as a result of relationships established outside the counseling setting, thereby undermining the evaluative significance of the help the treatment group has received through counseling.

Criteria for Evaluation

Blocher (1966) has identified four major types of criteria by which client improvement can be measured. These criteria include (1) social adjustment criteria, (2) personality criteria, (3) vocational adjustment criteria, and (4) educational criteria, along with other miscellaneous criteria.

Social adjustment criteria include changes in "adjustment" measures made by significant others in the client's life, such as parents or teachers. Sometimes more objective measures are used, such as increased participation in group activities or reduction in disciplinary offenses.

Personality criteria include subjective measures, such as changes in the kinds of self-descriptive adjectives the client uses in reference to himself over a period of time. Personality criteria also include changes in the scores attained on various personality tests, such as the Stevenson Q-sort or various personality inventories.

Vocational adjustment criteria may include improvements in the specificity of vocational plans as well as persistence or promotions on the job. In addition, vocational adjustment criteria may include clients' self-reports of job satisfaction or supervisors' reports of client performance on the job.

The most traditional educational criterion is increase in grade point averages of clients. Other measures that are sometimes used include a reduction in truancy or in the dropout rate and the correlation between grades and measured aptitudes.

Clients themselves provide a major source of information regarding counseling effectiveness. These reports may consist of subjective evaluations of improvement—statements such as, "I seem to be getting along better with my friends" or "I'm not as uptight about taking exams as I was before." Although the client's subjective evaluation has limitations, often much can be learned from the client's perception of change. Unless the client is experiencing some satisfaction in the results of the counseling process, the likelihood of the client's continuing the process is very small.

The counselor's subjective report about the effectiveness of the counseling process is also important, although not ordinarily sufficient as the only means of evaluating counseling effectiveness. Experienced counselors learn to trust their own judgments about client growth during the counseling process, and such subjective evaluation can help them determine future courses of action during the counseling relationship.

In setting up an evaluation program counselors must develop some sort of systematic approach that will give full recognition to those aspects they wish to emphasize. To do so, they must conceptualize three sets of experimental variables considered relevant in any comprehensive evaluation of counseling.

The first set of variables to be considered are those involved in the counseling situation, which can be categorized in terms of three subsets: counselor variables, client variables, and situational variables. *Counselor variables* include such factors as the counselor's age, sex, socioeconomic background, training, theoretical orientation, and institutional role. *Client variables* include the client's age, sex, socioeconomic background, nature of presenting problem, and expectations for counseling. *Situational variables* include the nature of referral and the institution or agency in which counseling occurs. Each of these input variables must be considered and controlled to determine if some individual counselors are helpful to some clients but are either useless or even harmful to others. The setting in which counseling occurs, the way in which clients are referred, and the clients' expectations are all extremely relevant. Failure to sort out these important variables could well mask the most important results.

The intermediate or process variables are also extremely important. What actually happens in the counseling situation—the kind of relationship established, the number of contacts, and the approaches used—provides valuable insights into the relationship that occurs during the process. Although these process variables are less important to the behavioral counselors, the process by which behavioral change is facilitated is an important variable for evaluation.

The third set of experimental variables are outcome variables. These include changes that have occurred in the client during the counseling process presumably as a result of counseling intervention. These changes must be relevant to the counseling goals established in the counseling situation. Such outcome variables may very well include differences in how clients feel, think, or behave; however, such outcomes must be evaluated to determine whether the counseling situation has succeeded in bringing about the desired change in the client.

Summary

Counselors must respond to the complex legal and ethical considerations that directly affect both the delivery of counseling services and the attitude of the public toward these services. As professionals, counselors must insist on a high level of ethical and legal behavior, on respected credentials of its practitioners, and on continuing evaluation.

Ethical obligations of counselors are stated in the ethical standards developed by the American Association for Counseling and Development and by the American Psychological Association. Both codes stress adherence to rigorous professional standards and to exemplary behavior, integrity, and objectivity toward clients.

Counselors are obligated to maintain professional levels of confidentiality, with three levels clearly differentiated. There is a wide diversity among states as to the status of privileged communication for counselors, but few states provide the same degree of privileged communication for counselors that they do for ministers, lawyers, and medical doctors.

Despite the difficulties in measuring counseling effectiveness, research and evaluation are extremely important and a necessary part of ethical behavior for counselors.

References

ACA Ethics Committee. (1992). Report of the ACA ethics committee: 1991–92. *Journal of Counseling and Development, 71,* 252–253

American Counseling Association. (1988). *Ethical Standards.* Alexandria, VA: Author.

Arthur, G. L., Jr., & Swanson, C. D. (1993). *Confidentiality and Privileged Communication.* Alexandria, VA: American Counseling Association.

American Psychological Association. (1992). *Ethical Principles of Psychologist and Code of Conduct.* Washington, DC: Author

Blocher, D. H. (1966). *Developmental Counseling.* New York: Ronald Press

Corey, G., Corey, M. S., & Callahan, P. (1984). *Issues and Ethics in the Helping Professions,* 2nd ed. Monterey, CA: Brooks/Cole.

Daniel, R. W., & Weikel, W. J. (1983). Trends in Counseling: A Delphi Study. *Personnel and Guidance Journal, 61,* 327–331.

Davis, J. W. (1981). Counselor licensure: Overkill? *Personnel and Guidance Journal, 60,* 83–85.

Denkowski, K. M., & Denkowski, G. C. (1982). Client-counselor confidentiality: An update of rationale, legal status, and implications. *Personnel and Guidance Journal, 60,* 371–375.

Gibson, R., & Mitchell, M. (1990). *Introduction to guidance,* 2nd ed. New York: Macmillan.

Ivey, A. E., Ivey, M. B., & Simek-Morgan, L. (1993). *Counseling and psychotherapy: A multicultural perspective,* 3rd ed. Boston: Allyn and Bacon.

Kitchener, K. S. (1988). Dual role relationships: What makes them so problematic? *Journal of Counseling and Development, 67,* 217–221.

Knapp, S., & Vandecreek, L. (1983). Communications and the counselor. *Personnel and Guidance Journal, 62,* 83–85.

McGuire, J. M., & Borowy, T. D. (1978). Confidentiality and the Buckley-Pell Amendment: Ethical and legal considerations for counselors. *Personnel and Guidance Journal, 56,* 554–557.

Remer, R. (1981). The counselor and research: Introduction. *Personnel and Guidance Journal, 59,* 567–571.

Schneiders, A. A. (1963). The limits of confidentiality. *Personnel and Guidance Journal, 42,* 252–253.

Stude, E. W., & McKelvey, J. (1979). Ethics and the law: Friend or foe? *Personnel and Guidance Journal, 57,* 453–456.

Walz, G. R., Gazda, G. M., & Shertzer, B. (1991). *Counseling futures.* Ann Arbor, MI: ERIC.

Wittmer, J. (1988). CACREP or APA: A counselor educator's personal view. *Counselor Educational Supervision, 27,* 291–294.

Appendix *A*

Ethical Standards of the American Counseling Association*

Preamble

The association is an educational, scientific, and professional organization whose members are dedicated to the enhancement of the worth, dignity, potential, and uniqueness of each individual and thus to the service of society.

The Association recognizes that the role definitions and work settings of its members include a wide variety of academic disciplines, levels of academic preparation, and agency services. This diversity reflects the breadth of the Association's interest and influence. It also poses challenging complexities in efforts to set standards for the performance of members, desired requisite preparation or practice, and supporting social, legal, and ethical controls.

The specification of ethical standards enables the Association to clarify to present and future members and to those served by members the nature of ethical responsibilities held in common by its members.

The existence of such standards serves to stimulate greater concern by members for their own professional functioning and for the conduct of fellow professionals such as counselors, guidance and student personnel workers, and others in the helping professions. As the ethical code of the Association, this document establishes principles that define the ethical behavior of Association members. Additional ethical guidelines developed by the Association's Divisions for their specialty areas may further define a member's ethical behavior.

*(Formerly the American Association for Counseling and Development). As revised by AACD Governing Council, March 1988. Copyright ACA. Reprinted with permission. No further reproduction authorized without written permission of the American Counseling Association.

Section A: General

1. The member influences the development of the profession by continuous efforts to improve professional practices, teaching, services, and research. Professional growth is continuous throughout the member's career and is exemplified by the development of a philosophy that explains why and how a member functions in the helping relationship. Members must gather data on their effectiveness and be guided by the findings. Members recognize the need for continuing education to ensure competent service

2. The member has a responsibility both to the individual who is served and to the institution within which the service is performed to maintain high standards of professional conduct. The member strives to maintain the highest levels of professional services offered to the individuals to be served. The member also strives to assist the agency, organization, or institution in providing the highest caliber of professional services. The acceptance of employment in an institution implies that the member is in agreement with the general policies and principles of the institution. Therefore the professional activities of the member are also in accord with the objectives of the institution. If, despite concerted efforts, the member cannot reach agreement with the employer as to acceptable standards of conduct that allow for changes in institutional policy conducive to the positive growth and development of clients, then terminating the affiliation should be seriously considered.

3. Ethical behavior among professional associates, both members and nonmembers, must be expected at all times. When information is possessed that raises doubt as to the ethical behavior of professional colleagues, whether Association members or not, the member must take action to attempt to rectify such a condition. Such action shall use the institution's channels first and then use procedures established by the Association.

4. The member neither claims nor implies professional qualifications exceeding those possessed and is responsible for correcting any misrepresentations of these qualifications by others.

5. In established fees for professional counseling services, members must consider the financial status of clients and locality. In the event that the established fee structure is inappropriate for a client, assistance must be provided in finding comparable services of acceptable cost.

6. When members provide information to the public or to subordinates, peers, or supervisors, they have a responsibility to ensure that the content is general, unidentified client information that is accurate, unbiased, and consists of objective, factual data.

7. Members recognize their boundaries of competence and provide only those services and use only those techniques for which they are qualified by training or experience. Members should only accept those positions for which they are professionally qualified.

8. In the counseling relationship, the counselor is aware of the intimacy of the relationship and maintains respect for the client and avoids engaging in activities that seek to meet the counselor's personal needs at the expense of that client.

9. Members do not condone or engage in sexual harassment which is defined as deliberate or repeated comments, gestures, or physical contacts of a sexual nature.

10. The member avoids bringing personal issues into the counseling relationship, especially if the potential for harm is present. Through awareness of the negative impact of both racial and sexual stereotyping and discrimination, the counselor guards the individual rights and personal dignity of the client in the counseling relationship.

11. Products or services provided by the member by means of classroom instruction, public lectures, demonstrations, written articles, radio or television programs, or other types of media must meet the criteria cited in these standards.

Section B: Counseling Relationships

This section refers to practices and procedures of individual and/or group counseling relationships.

The member must recognize the need for client freedom of choice. Under those circumstances where this is not possible, the member must apprise clients of restrictions that may limit their freedom of choice.

1. The member's primary obligation is to respect the integrity and promote the welfare of the client(s), whether the client(s) is (are) assisted in-

dividually or in a group relationship. In a group setting, the member is also responsible for taking reasonable precautions to protect individuals from physical and/or psychological trauma resulting from interaction within the group.

2. Members make provisions for maintaining confidentiality in the storage and disposal of records and follow an established record retention and disposition policy. The counseling relationship and information resulting there-from must be kept confidential, consistent with the obligations of the member as a professional person. In a group counseling setting, the counselor must set a norm of confidentiality regarding all group participants' disclosures.

3. If an individual is already in a counseling relationship with another professional person, the member does not enter into a counseling relationship without first contacting and receiving the approval of that other professional. If the member discovers that the client is in another counseling relationship after the counseling relationship begins, the member must gain the consent of the other professional or terminate the relationship, unless the client elects to terminate the other relationship.

4. When the client's condition indicates that there is clear and imminent danger to the client or others, the member must take reasonable personal action or inform responsible authorities. Consultation with other professionals must be used where possible. The assumption of responsibility for the client's(s') behavior must be taken only after careful deliberation. The client must be involved in the resumption of responsibility as quickly as possible.

5. Records of the counseling relationship, including interview notes, test data, correspondence, tape recordings, electronic data storage, and other documents are to be considered professional information for use in counseling, and they should not be considered a part of the records of the institution or agency in which the counselor is employed unless specified by state statute or regulation. Revelation to others of counseling material must occur only upon the expressed consent of the client.

6. In view of the extensive data storage and processing capacities of the computer, the member must ensure that data maintained on a computer is: (a) limited to information that is appropriate and necessary for the services being provided; (b) destroyed after it is determined that the information is no longer of any value in providing services; and (c) restricted in terms of access to appropriate staff members involved in the provision of services by using the best computer security methods available.

7. Use of data derived from a counseling relationship for purposes of counselor training or research shall be confined to content that can be disguised to ensure full protection of the identity of the subject client.

8. The member must inform the client of the purposes, goals, techniques, rules of procedure, and limitations that may affect the relationship at or before the time that the counseling relationship is entered. When working with minors or persons who are unable to give consent, the member protects these clients' best interests.

9. In view of common misconceptions related to the perceived inherent validity of computer-generated data and narrative reports, the member must ensure that the client is provided with information as part of the counseling relationship that adequately explains the limitations of computer technology.

10. The member must screen prospective group participants, especially when the emphasis is on self-understanding and growth through self-disclosure. The member must maintain an awareness of the group participants' compatibility throughout the life of the group.

11. The member may choose to consult with any other professionally competent person about a client. In choosing a consultant, the member must avoid placing the consultant in a conflict of interest situation that would preclude the consultant's being a proper party to the member's efforts to help the client.

12. If the member determines an inability to be of professional assistance to the client, the member must either avoid initiating the counseling relationship or immediately terminate that relationship. In either event, the member must suggest appropriate alternatives. (The member must be knowledgeable about referral resources so that a satisfactory referral can be initiated.) In the

event the client declines the suggested referral, the member is not obligated to continue the relationship.

13. When the member has other relationships, particularly of an administrative, supervisory, and/or evaluative nature with an individual seeking counseling services, the member must not serve as the counselor but should refer the individual to another professional. Only in instances where such an alternative is unavailable and where the individual's situation warrants counseling intervention should the member enter into and/or maintain a counseling relationship. Dual relationships with clients that might impair the member's objectivity and professional judgement (e.g., as with close friends or relatives), must be avoided and/or the counseling relationship terminated through referral to another competent professional.

14. The member will avoid any type of sexual intimacies with clients. Sexual relationships with clients are unethical.

15. All experimental methods of treatment must be clearly indicated to prospective recipients, and safety precautions are to be adhered to by the member.

16. When computer applications are used as a component of counseling services, the member must ensure that: (a) the client is intellectually, emotionally, and physically capable of using the computer application; (b) the computer application is appropriate for the needs of the client; (c) the client understands the purpose and operation of the computer application; and (d) a followup of client use of a computer application is provided to both correct possible problems (misconceptions or inappropriate use) and assess subsequent needs.

17. When the member is engaged in short-term group treatment/training programs (e.g., marathons and other encountertype or growth groups), the member ensures that there is professional assistance available during and following the group experience.

18. Should the member be engaged in a work setting that calls for any variation from the above statements, the member is obligated to consult with other professionals whenever possible to consider justifiable alternatives.

19. The member must ensure that members of various ethnic, racial, religious, disability, and socioeconomic groups have equal access to computer applications used to support counseling services and that the content of available computer applications does not discriminate against the groups described above.

20. When computer applications are developed by the member for use by the general public as self-help/stand-alone computer software the member must ensure that: (a) self-help computer applications are designed from the beginning to function in a stand-alone manner, as opposed to modifying software that was originally designed to require support from a counselor, (b) self-help computer applications will include within the program statements regarding intended user outcomes, suggestions for using the software, a description of the conditions under which self-help computer applications might not be appropriate, and a description of when and how counseling services might be beneficial; and (c) the manual for such applications will include the qualifications of the developer, the development process, validation data, and operating procedures.

Section C: Measurement & Evaluation

The primary purpose of educational and psychological testing is to provide descriptive measures that are objective and interpretable in either comparative or absolute terms. The member must recognize the need to interpret the statements that follow as applying to the whole range of appraisal techniques including test and nontest data. Test results constitute only one of a variety of pertinent sources of information for personnel, guidance, and counseling decisions.

1. The member must provide specific orientation or information to the examinee(s) prior to and following the test administration so that the results of testing may be placed in proper perspective with other relevant factors. In so doing, the member must recognize the effects of socioeconomic, ethnic, and cultural factors on test scores. It is the member's professional responsibility to use additional unvalidated information carefully in modifying interpretation of the test results.

2. In selecting tests for use in a given situation or with a particular client, the member must consider carefully the specific validity, reliability, and appropriateness of the test(s). General validity, reliability, and related issues may be questioned legally as well as ethically when tests are used for vocational and educational selection, placement, or counseling.

3. When making any statements to the public about tests and testing, the member must give accurate information and avoid false claims or misconceptions. Special efforts are often required to avoid unwarranted connotations of such terms as IQ and grade equivalent scores.

4. Different tests demand different levels of competence for administration scoring and interpretation. Members must recognize the limits of their competence and perform only those functions for which they are prepared. In particular, members using computer-based test interpretations must be trained in the construct being measured and the specific instrument being used prior to using this type of computer application.

5. In situations where a computer is used for test administration and scoring, the member is responsible for ensuring that administration and scoring programs function properly to provide clients with accurate test results.

6. Tests must be administered under the same conditions that were established in their standardization. When tests are not administered under standard conditions or when unusual behavior or irregularities occur during the testing session, those conditions must be noted and the results designated as invalid or of questionable validity. Unsupervised or inadequately supervised test-taking, such as the use of tests through the mails, is considered unethical. On the other hand, the use of instruments that are so designed or standardized to be self-administered and self-scored, such as interest inventories, is to be encouraged.

7. The meaningfulness of test results used in personnel, guidance, and counseling functions generally depends on the examinee's unfamiliarity with the specific items on the test. Any prior coaching or dissemination of the test materials can invalidate test results. Therefore, test security is one of the professional obligations of the member.

Conditions that produce most favorable test results must be made known to the examinee.

8. The purpose of testing and the explicit use of the results must be made known to the examinee prior to testing. The counselor must ensure that instrument limitations are not exceeded and that periodic review and/or retesting are made to prevent client stereotyping.

9. The examinee's welfare and explicit prior understanding must be the criteria for determining the recipients of the test results. The member must see that specific interpretation accompanies any release of individual or group test data. The interpretation of test data must be related to the examinee's particular concerns.

10. Members responsible for making decisions based on test results have an understanding of educational and psychological measurement, validation criteria, and test research.

11. The member must be cautious when interpreting the results of research instruments possessing insufficient technical data. The specific purposes for the use of such instruments must be stated explicitly to examinees.

12. The member must proceed with caution when attempting to evaluate and interpret the performance of minority group members or other persons who are not represented in the norm group on which the instrument was standardized.

13. When computer-based test interpretations are developed by the member to support the assessment process, the member must ensure that the validity of such interpretations is established prior to the commercial distribution of such a computer application.

14. The member recognizes that test results may become obsolete. The member will avoid and prevent the misuse of obsolete test results.

15. The member must guard against the appropriation, reproduction, or modification of published tests or parts thereof without acknowledgment and permission from the previous publisher.

16. Regarding the preparation, publication, and distribution of tests, reference should be made to:

    a. "Standards for Educational and Psychological Testing," revised edition, 1985, published by the American Psychological Association on behalf of itself, the American Educational Research Association and the National Council of Measurement in Education.

b. "The Responsible Use of Tests: A Position Paper of AMEG, APGA and NCME," *Measurement and Evaluation in Guidance,* 1972, 5, 385–388.

c. "Responsibilities of Users of Standardized Tests," APGA, *Guidepost,* October 5, 1978, pp. 5–8.

Section D: Research and Publication

1. Guidelines on research with human subjects should be adhered to, such as:

a. *Ethical Principles in the conduct of Research with Human Participants* Washington, D.C.: American Psychological Association, Inc., 1982.

b. Code of Federal Regulation, Title 45, Subtitle A, Pan 46, as currently issued.

c. *Ethical Principles of Psychologists,* American Psychological Association, Principle #9: Research with Human Participants.

d. Family Educational Rights and Privacy Act (the Buckley Amendment).

e. Current federal regulations and various state rights privacy acts.

2. In planning any research activity dealing with human subjects, the member must be aware of and responsive to all pertinent ethical principles and ensure that the research problem, design, and execution are in full compliance with them.

3. Responsibility for ethical research practice lies with the principal researcher while others involved in the research activities share ethical obligation and full responsibility for their own actions.

4. In research with human subjects, researchers are responsible for the subjects' welfare throughout the experiment, and they must take all reasonable precautions to avoid causing injurious psychological, physical, or social effects on their subjects.

5. All research subjects must be informed of the purpose of the study except when withholding information or providing misinformation to them is essential to the investigation. In such research the member must be responsible for corrective action as soon as possible following completion of the research.

6. Participation in research must be voluntary. Involuntary participation is appropriate only when it can be demonstrated that participation will have no harmful effects on subjects and is essential to the investigation.

7. When reporting research results, explicit mention must be made of all variables and conditions known to the investigator that might affect the outcome of the investigation or the interpretation of the data.

8. The member must be responsible for conducting and reporting investigations in a manner that minimizes the possibility that results will be misleading.

9. The member has an obligation to make available sufficient original research data to qualified others who may wish to replicate the study.

10. When supplying data, aiding in the research of another person, reporting research results, or making original data available, due care must be taken to disguise the identity of the subjects in the absence of specific authorization from such subjects to do otherwise.

11. When conducting and reporting research, the member must be familiar with and give recognition to previous work on the topic, as well as to observe all copyright laws and follow the principles of giving full credit to all to whom credit is due.

12. The member must give due credit through joint authorship, acknowledgments, footnote statements, or other appropriate means to those who have contributed significantly to the research and/or publication, in accordance with such contributions.

13. The member must communicate to other members the results of any research judged to be of professional or scientific value. Results reflecting unfavorably on institutions, programs, services, or vested interests must not be withheld for such reasons.

14. If members agree to cooperate with another individual in research and/or publication,

they incur an obligation to cooperate as promised in terms of punctuality of performance and with full regard to the completeness and accuracy of the information required.

15. Ethical practice requires that authors not submit the same manuscript or one essentially similar in content for simultaneous publication consideration by two or more journals. In addition, manuscripts published in whole or in substantial part in another journal or published work should not be submitted for publication without acknowledgment and permission from the previous publication.

Section E: Consulting

Consultation refers to a voluntary relationship between a professional helper and help-needing individual, group, or social unit in which the consultant is providing help to the client(s) in defining and solving a work-related problem or potential problem with a client or client system.

1. The member acting as consultant must have a high degree of self-awareness of his/her own values, knowledge, skills, limitations, and needs in entering a helping relationship that involves human and/or organizational change and that the focus of the relationship be on the issues to be resolved and not on the person(s) presenting the problem.

2. There must be understanding and agreement between member and client for the problem definition, change of goals, and prediction of consequences of interventions selected.

3. The member must be reasonably certain that she/he or the organization represented has the necessary competencies and resources for giving the kind of help that is needed now or may be needed later and that appropriate referral resources are available to the consultant.

4. The consulting relationship must be one in which client adaptability and growth toward self-direction are encouraged and cultivated. The member must maintain this role consistently and not become a decision maker for the client or create a future dependency on the consultant.

5. When announcing consultant availability for services, the member conscientiously adheres to the Association's Ethical Standards.

6. The member must refuse a private fee or other remuneration for consultation with persons who are entitled to these services through the member's employing institution or agency. The policies of a particular agency may make explicit provisions for private practice with agency clients by members of its staff. In such instances, the clients must be apprised of other options open to them should they seek private counseling services.

Section F: Private Practice

1. The member should assist the profession by facilitating the availability of counseling services in private as well as public settings.

2. In advertising services as a private practitioner, the member must advertise the services in a manner that accurately informs the public of professional services, expertise and techniques of counseling available. A member who assumes an executive leadership role in the organization shall not permit his/her name to be used in professional notices during periods when he/she is not actively engaged in the private practice of counseling.

3. The member may list the following: highest relevant degree, type and level of certification and/or license, address, telephone number, office hours, type and/or description of services and other relevant information. Such information must not contain false, inaccurate, misleading, partial, out-of-context, or deceptive material or statements.

4. Members do not present their affiliation with any organization in such a way that would imply inaccurate sponsorship certification by that organization.

5. Members may join in partnership/corporation with other members and/or other professionals provided that each member of the partnership or corporation makes clear the separate specialties by name in compliance with the regulations of the locality.

6. A member has an obligation to withdraw from a counseling relationship if it is believed that employment will result in violation of the Ethical Standards. If the mental or physical condition of the member renders it difficult to carry out an ef-

fective professional relationship or if the member is discharged by the client because the counseling relationship is no longer productive for the client, then the member is obligated to terminate the counseling relationship.

7. A member must adhere to the regulations for private practice of the locality where the services are offered.

8. It is unethical to use one's institutional affiliation to recruit clients for one's private practice.

Section G: Personnel Administration

It is recognized that most members are employed in public or quasi-public institutions. The functioning of a member within an institution must contribute to the goals of the institution and vice versa if either is to accomplish their respective goals or objectives. It is therefore essential that the member and the institution function in ways to: (a) make the institutional goals specific; and public; (b) make the member's contribution to institutional goals specific; and (c) foster mutual accountability for goal achievement.

To accomplish these objectives, it is recognized that the member and the employer must share responsibilities in the formulation and implementation of personnel policies.

1. Members must define and describe the parameters and levels of their professional competency.

2. Members must establish interpersonal relations and working agreements with supervisors and subordinates regarding counseling or clinical relationships, confidentiality, distinction between public and private material, maintenance and dissemination of recorded information, work load, and accountability. Working agreements in each instance must be specified and made known to those concerned.

3. Members must alert their employers to conditions that may be potentially disruptive or damaging.

4. Members must inform employers of conditions that may limit their effectiveness.

5. Members must submit regularly to professional review and evaluation.

6. Members must be responsible for inservice development of self and/or staff.

7. Members must inform their staff of goals and programs.

8. Members must provide personnel practices that guarantee and enhance the rights and welfare of each recipient of their service.

9. Members must select competent persons and assign responsibilities compatible with their skills and experiences.

10. The member, at the onset of a counseling relationship, will inform the client of the member's intended use of supervisors regarding the disclosure of information concerning this case. The member will clearly inform the client of the limits of confidentiality in the relationship.

11. Members, as either employers or employees, do not engage in or condone practices that are inhumane, illegal, or unjustifiable (such as considerations based on sex, handicap, age, race) in hiring, promotion, or training.

Section H: Preparation Standards

Members who are responsible for training others must be guided by the preparation standards of the Association and relevant Division(s). The member who functions in the capacity of trainer assumes unique ethical responsibilities that frequently go beyond that of the member who does not function in a training capacity. These ethical responsibilities are outlined as follows:

1. Members must orient students to program expectations, basic skills development, and employment prospects prior to admission to the program.

2. Members in charge of learning experiences must establish programs that integrate academic study and supervised practice.

3. Members must establish a program directed toward developing students' skills, knowledge, and self-understanding stated whenever possible in competency or performance terms.

4. Members must identify the levels of competencies of their students in compliance with relevant Division standards. These competencies must accommodate the paraprofessional as well as the professional.

5. Members, through continual student evaluation and appraisal, must be aware of the personal limitations of the learner that might impede future

performance. The instructor must not only assist the learner in securing remedial assistance but also screen from the program those individuals who are unable to provide competent services.

6. Members must provide a program that includes training in research commensurate with levels of role functioning. Paraprofessional and technician-level personnel must be trained as consumers of research. In addition, personnel must learn how to evaluate their own and their program's effectiveness. Graduate training, especially at the doctoral level, would include preparation for original research by the member.

7. Members must make students aware of the ethical responsibilities and standards of the profession.

8. Preparatory programs must encourage students to value the ideals of service to individuals and to society. In this regard, direct financial remuneration or lack thereof must not be allowed to overshadow professional and humanitarian needs.

9. Members responsible for educational programs must be skilled as teachers and practitioners.

10. Members must present thoroughly varied theoretical positions so that students may make comparisons and have the opportunity to select a position.

11. Members must develop clear policies within their educational institutions regarding field placement and the roles of the student and the instructor in such placement.

12. Members must ensure that forms of learning focusing on self-understanding or growth are voluntary, or if required as part of the educational program, are made known to prospective students prior to entering the program. When the educational program offers a growth experience with an emphasis on self-disclosure or other relatively intimate or personal involvement, the member must have no administrative, supervisory, or evaluating authority regarding the participant.

13. The member will at all times provide students with clear and equally acceptable alternatives for self-understanding or growth experiences. The member will assure students that they have a right to accept these alternatives without prejudice or penalty.

14. Members must conduct an educational program in keeping with the current relevant guidelines of the Association.

Policies and Procedures for Processing Complaints of Ethical Violations*

Section A: General

1. The American Counseling Association, hereinafter referred to as the "Association" or "ACA", as an educational, scientific, and charitable organization, is dedicated to enhancing the worth, dignity, potential, and uniqueness of each individual and rendering service to society.

2. The Association, in furthering its objectives, administers Ethical Standards that have been developed and approved by the ACA Governing Council.

3. The purpose of this document is to facilitate the work of the ACA Ethics Committee by specifying the procedures for processing cases of alleged violations of the ACA Ethical Standards, codifying options for sanctioning members, and stating appeal procedures. The intent of the Association is to monitor the professional conduct of its members to ensure sound ethical practices.

Section B: Ethics Committee Members

1. The Ethics Committee is a standing committee of the Association. The Committee consists of six (6) appointed members, including the Chairperson. The editor of the *Ethical Standards Casebook* serves as an *ex officio* member of this Committee without vote. Two members are appointed annually for a three (3) year term by the President-Elect; appointments are subject to confirmation by the ACA Governing Council. Any vacancy occurring

*Approved March, 1990-Amended December, 1991

on the Committee will be filled by the President in the same manner, and the person appointed shall serve the unexpired term of the member whose place he or she took. Committee members may be reappointed to not more than one (1) additional consecutive term.

2. The Chairperson of the Committee is appointed annually by the incumbent President-Elect, subject to confirmation by the ACA Governing Council. A Chairperson may be reappointed to one additional term during any three (3) year period.

Section C: Role and Function

1. The role of the Ethics Committee of the Association is to assist in the arbitration and conciliation of conflicts among members of the Association except where appropriate client concerns may be expressed. The Committee also is responsible for:

A. Educating the membership as to the Association's Ethical Standards,
B. Periodically reviewing and recommending changes in the Ethical Standards of the Association as well as the Policies and Procedures for Processing Complaints of Ethical Violations,
C. Receiving and processing complaints of alleged violations of the Ethical Standards of the Association, and
D. Receiving and processing questions.

2. In processing complaints about alleged ethical misconduct, the Committee will compile an objective, factual account of the dispute in question and make the best possible recommendation for the resolution of the case. The Committee, in taking any action, shall do so only for cause, shall only take the degree of disciplinary action that is reasonable, shall utilize these procedures with objectivity and fairness, and in general shall act only to further the interests and objectives of the Association and its membership.

3. The ACA Ethics Committee itself will not initiate any ethical violation charges against an ACA member.

4. Of the six (6) voting members of the Committee, a vote of four (4) is necessary to conduct business. In the event the Chair or any other member of the Committee has a personal interest in the case, he or she shall withdraw from reviewing the case. A unanimous vote of those members of the Committee who reviewed the case is necessary to expel a member from the Association.

5. The Chairperson of the ACA Ethics Committee and/or the ACA Executive Director (or his/her designee) may consult with ACA legal counsel at any time.

Section D: Responsibilities of Committee Members

1. The members of the Ethics Committee must be conscious that their position is extremely important and sensitive and that their decisions involve the rights of many individuals, the reputation of the counseling and human development community, and the careers of the members. The Committee members have an obligation to act in an unbiased manner, to work expeditiously, to safeguard the confidentiality of the Committee's activities, and to follow procedures that protect the rights of all individuals involved.

Section E: Responsibilities of the Chairperson

1. In addition to the above guidelines for members of the Committee, the Chairperson, in conjunction with Headquarters staff, has the responsibilities of:

A. Receiving (via ACA Headquarters) complaints that have been certified for membership status of the accused,
B. Notifying the complainant and the accused of receipt of the case,
C. Notifying the members of the Ethics Committee of the case,
D. Presiding over the meetings of the Committee,
E. Preparing and sending (by certified mail) communications to the complainant and accused member on the recommendations and decisions of the Committee, and
F. Arranging for legal advice with assistance and financial approval of the ACA Executive Director.

Section F: Complaints

1. All correspondence, records, and activities of the ACA Ethics Committee will remain confidential.

2. The ACA Ethics Committee will not act on anonymous complaints, nor will it act on complaints currently under civil or criminal litigation.

3. The ACA Ethics Committee will act only on those cases where the accused is a current member of ACA or was a member of ACA at the time of the alleged violation. State Division and State Branch Ethics Committees may act only on those cases where the accused is a member of the State Division or State Branch and not a member of ACA.

Section G: Submitting Complaints — Procedures for ACA Members

1. The procedures for submission of complaints to the Ethics Committee are as follows:

A. If feasible, the complainant should discuss with utmost confidentiality the nature of the complaint with a colleague to see if he or she views the situation as an ethical violation.

B. Whenever feasible, the complainant is to approach the accused directly to discuss and resolve the complaint.

C. In cases where a resolution is not forthcoming at the personal level, the complainant shall prepare a formal written statement of the complaint and shall submit it to the ACA Ethics Committee. Action or consideration by the ACA Ethics Committee may not be initiated until this requirement is satisfied.

D. Formal written complaints must include a statement indicating the behavior(s) that constituted the alleged violations(s), and the date(s) of the alleged violation(s). The written statement must also contain the accused member's full name and complete address. Any relevant supporting documentation may be included with the complaint.

E. All complaints that are directed to the ACA Ethics Committee should be mailed to the Ethics Committee, c/o The Executive Director, American Counseling Association, 5999 Stevenson Avenue, Alexandria, Virginia 22304. The envelope must be marked "CONFIDENTIAL." This procedure is necessary to ensure the confidentiality of the person submitting the complaint and the person accused in the complaint.

Section H: Submitting Complaints— Procedures for Non-members

1. The ACA Ethics Committee recognizes the rights of non-ACA members to file grievances concerning a member. Ordinarily this non-member will be a client or student of an ACA member who believes that the ACA member has acted unethically.

2. In such cases, the complainant shall contact the ACA Executive Director (or his/her designee) and outline, in writing, those behaviors he or she feels were unethical in nature. Headquarters staff will delineate the complaint process to the complainant.

Section I: Processing Complaints

1. When complaints are received at Headquarters, the ACA Executive Director (or his/her designee) shall: (a) check on the membership status of the accused, (b) acknowledge receipt of the complaint within ten (10) working days after it is received in ACA Headquarters, and (c) consult with the Chairperson of the ACA Ethics Committee within (10) working days after the complaint is received in ACA Headquarters to determine whether it is appropriate to proceed with the complaint. If the Director (or designee) and Chairperson determine it is inappropriate to proceed, the complainant shall be so notified. If the Director (or designee) and Chairperson determine it is appropriate to proceed with the complaint, they will identify which Ethical Standard(s) are applicable to the alleged violation. A formal statement containing the Ethical Standard(s) that were allegedly violated will be forwarded to the complainant for his/her signature. This signed formal statement will then become a part of the formal complaint.

2. Once the formal complaint has been compiled (as indicated above), the Chairperson of the ACA Ethics Committee shall do the following:

A. Inform the complainant in writing that the accused member has been notified of the charges,

B. Direct a letter to the accused member informing the member of accusations lodged against him or her, including copies of all materials submitted by the complainant, asking for a response, and requesting that relevant information be submitted to the Chairperson within thirty (30) working days.

3. The accused is under no duty to respond to the allegations, but the Committee will not be obligated to delay or postpone its review of the case unless the accused so requests, with good cause, in advance. Failure of the accused to respond should not be viewed by the Committee as sufficient ground for taking disciplinary action.

4. Once the Chairperson has received the accused member's response or the thirty (30) days have elapsed, then the Chairperson shall forward to the members of the ACA Ethics Committee legal counsel's opinion (if applicable), staff verification of membership status, allegations, and responses, and direct the Committee to review the case and make recommendations for its disposition within two (2) weeks of receipt of the case.

5. The ACA Ethics Committee will review the case and make recommendations for its disposition and/or resolution within two hundred (200) working days following its receipt.

6. The ACA Ethics Committee Chairperson may ask the President of ACA to appoint an investigating committee at the local or state level to gather and submit relevant information concerning the case to the Committee.

Section J: Options Available to the Ethics Committee

1. After reviewing the information forwarded by the Chairperson, the Ethics Committee shall have the power to:

A. Dismiss the charges, find that no violation has occurred, and dismiss the complaint, or

B. Find that the practice(s) in which the member engages that is (are) the subject

of the complaint, is (are) unethical, notify the accused of this determination, and request the member to voluntarily cease and desist in the practice(s) without impositions of further sanctions, or

C. Find that the practice(s) in which the member engages, that is (are) the subject of the complaint, is (are) unethical, notify the accused of this determination, and impose sanctions.

Section K: Appropriate Sanctions

1. The committee may consider extenuating circumstances before deciding on the penalty to be imposed. If the Committee finds the accused has violated the Ethical Standards and decides to impose sanctions, the Committee may take any of the following actions:

A. Issue a reprimand with recommendations for corrective action, subject to review by the Committee, or

B. Place the member on probation for a specified period of time, subject to review by the Committee, or

C. Suspend eligibility for membership in ACA for a specified period of time, subject to review by the Committee, or

D. Expel the member from ACA permanently.

Section L: Consequences of Sanctions

1. Both a reprimand and probation carry with it no loss of membership rights or privileges.

2. A suspended member forfeits the rights and privileges of membership only for the period of his or her suspension.

3. In the event a member is expelled from ACA membership, he or she shall lose all rights and privileges of membership in ACA and its divisions permanently. The expelled member shall not be entitled to a refund of dues already paid.

4. If the member is suspended or expelled, and after any right to appeal has been exhausted, the Committee will notify the appropriate state licensing board(s) of the disciplined member's status with ACA. Notice also will be given to the National Board for Certified Counselors, the ACA Divisions of which the disciplined party is a mem-

ber, the State Branch of ACA in which the member resides, the members of ACA, the complainant, and other organizations as the Committee deems necessary. Such notice shall only state the sanctions imposed and the sections of the ACA Ethical Standards that were violated. Further elaboration shall not be disclosed.

5. Should a member resign from the Association after a complaint has been brought against him or her and before the Ethics Committee has completed its deliberations, that member is considered to have been expelled from the Association for failure to respond in a timely and complete manner to the Ethics Committee.

Section M: Hearings

1. At the discretion of the Ethics Committee, a hearing may be conducted when the results of the Ethics Committee's preliminary determination indicate that additional information is needed. The Chairperson shall schedule a formal hearing on the case and notify both the complainant and the accused of their right to attend.

2. The hearing will be held before a panel made up of the Ethics Committee and, if the accused member chooses, a representative of the accused member's primary Division. This representative will be identified by the Division President and will have voting privileges.

Section N: Recommended Hearing Procedures

1. Purposes of Hearings. The purposes for which hearings shall be conducted are: a) to determine whether a breach of the Ethical Standards of ACA has occurred, and (b) if so, to determine what disciplinary action should be taken by the ACA. If a hearing is held, no disciplinary action will be taken by ACA until after the accused member has been given reasonable notice of the hearing and the specific charges raised against him or her and has had the opportunity to be heard and to present evidence in his or her behalf. The hearings will be formally conducted. The Committee will be guided in its deliberations by principles of basic fairness and professionalism, and will keep its deliberations as confidential as possible, except as provided herein.

2. Notice. At least forty-five (45) working days before the hearing, the accused member should be advised in writing of the time and place of the hearing and of the charges involved. Notice shall be given either personally or by certified or registered mail and shall be signed by the Committee Chair. The notice should be addressed to the accused member at his or her address as it appears in the membership records of the ACA. The notice should include a brief statement of the complaints lodged against him or her, and should be supported by the evidence. The accused is under no duty to respond to the notice, but the Committee will not be obligated to delay or postpone its hearing unless the accused so requests in writing, with good cause, in advance. Failure of the accused to appear at the hearing should not be viewed by the Committee as sufficient ground for taking disciplinary action.

3. Conduct of the Hearing.

A. Accommodations. The Committee shall provide a private room to conduct the hearings, and no observers shall be permitted. The location of the hearing shall be determined at the discretion of the Committee, taking into consideration the convenience of the Committee and the parties involved.

B. Presiding Officer. The Chair of the Ethics Committee shall preside over the hearing and deliberations of the Committee. In the event the Chair or any other member of the Committee has a personal interest in the case, he or she shall withdraw from the hearing and deliberations and shall not participate therein. The Committee shall select from among its members a presiding officer for any case where the Chair has excused himself or herself. At the conclusion of the hearing and deliberation of the Committee, the Chair shall promptly notify the accused and complainant of the Committee's decision in writing.

C. Record. A record of the hearing shall be made and preserved, together with any documents presented as evidence, at the ACA Headquarters for a period of three (3) years following the hearing decision.

The record may consist of a summary of testimony received, or a verbatim transcript, at the discretion of the Committee.

D. Right to Counsel. The parties shall be entitled to have counsel present to advise them throughout the hearing, but they may not participate beyond advising. Legal Counsel for ACA shall also be present at the hearing to advise the Committee and shall have the privilege of the floor.

E. Witnesses. Either party shall have the right to call witnesses to substantiate his or her version of the case. The Committee shall also have the right to call witnesses it believes may provide further insight into the matter before the Committee. Witnesses shall not be present during the hearings except when they are called upon to testify. The presiding officer shall allow questions to be asked of any witness by the opposition or members of the Committee and shall ensure that questions and testimony are relevant to the issues in the case. Should the hearing be disturbed by disparaging or irrelevant testimony or by the flareup of tempers, the presiding officer shall call a brief recess until order can be restored. Witnesses shall be excused upon completion of their testimony. All expenses associated with witnesses or counsel on behalf of the parties shall be borne by the respective parties.

F. Presentation of Evidence.

(1) A member of the Committee shall be called upon first to present the charge(s) made against the accused and to briefly describe the evidence supporting the charge(s).

(2) The complainant or a member of the Committee shall then be called upon to present the case against the accused. Witnesses who can substantiate the case shall be called upon to testify and answer questions of the accused and the Committee.

(3) If the accused has exercised the right to be present at the hearing, he or she shall be called upon last to present any evidence which refutes the charges against him or her. This includes the presentation of witnesses as in Subsection (E) above. The accused member has the right to refuse to make a statement in his or her behalf. The accused will not be found guilty simply for refusing to testify. Once the accused chooses to testify, however, he or she may be cross-examined by members of the Committee or the complainant.

(4) The Committee will endeavor to conclude the hearing within a period of approximately three (3) hours. The parties will be requested to be considerate of this time frame in planning their testimony. Testimony that is merely cumulative or repetitious may, at the discretion of the presiding officer, be excluded.

(5) The accused has the right to be present at all times during the hearing and to challenge all of the evidence presented against him or her.

G. Relevancy of Evidence. The Hearing Committee is not a court of law and is not required to observe the rules of evidence that apply in the trial of lawsuits. Consequently, evidence that would be inadmissible in a court of law may be admissible in the hearing before the Committee, if it is relevant to the case. That is, if the evidence offered tends to explain, clarify, or refute any of the important facts of the case, it should generally be considered. The Committee will not receive evidence or testimony for the purpose of supporting any charge that was not set forth in the notice of the hearing or that is not relevant to the issues of the case.

4. Burden of Proof. The burden of proving a violation of the Ethical Standards if on the complainant and/or the Committee. It is not up to the accused to prove his or her innocence of any wrong-doing. Although the charge(s) need not be proved "beyond a reasonable doubt," the Commit-

tee will not find the accused guilty in the absence of substantial, objective, and believable evidence to sustain the charge(s).

5. Deliberation of the Committee. After the hearing with the parties is completed, the Committee shall meet in a closed session to review the evidence presented and reach a conclusion. The Committee shall be the sole trier of fact and shall weigh the evidence presented and judge the credibility of the witnesses. The act of a majority of the members of the Committee shall be the decision of the Committee and only those members of the Committee who were present throughout the entire hearing shall be eligible to vote.

6. Decision of the Committee. The Committee will first resolve the issue of the guilt or innocence of the accused. Applying the burden of proof in paragraph 4 above, the Committee will vote by secret ballot, unless the members of the Committee consent to an oral vote. In the event a majority of the members of the Committee do not find the accused guilty, the charges shall be dismissed and the parties notified. If the Committee finds the accused has violated the Ethical Standards, it must then determine what sanctions to impose in accord with Section K: Appropriate Sanctions.

Section O: Appeal Procedures

1. Appeals will be heard only in such cases wherein the appellant presents evidence that the sanction imposed by the Committee has been arbitrary or capricious or that the procedures outlined in the "Policy Document" have not been followed.

2. The complainant and accused shall be advised of the appeal procedure by the Chairperson of the ACA Ethics Committee. The following procedures shall govern appeals:

A. A three (3) member review committee composed of the Executive Director of the ACA, the President of the ACA Division with which the accused member is most closely identified, and the immediate Past President of ACA. The ACA attorney shall serve as legal advisor and have the privilege of the floor.

B. The appeal with supporting documentation must be made in writing within sixty

(60) working days by certified mail to the ACA Executive Director and indicate the basis upon which it is made. If the member requires a time extension, he or she must request it in writing by certified mail within thirty (30) working days of receiving the decision by the ACA Ethics Committee. The extension will consist of ninety (90) working days be ginning from that request.

C. The review committee shall review all materials considered by the ACA Ethics Committee.

D. Within thirty (30) working days of this review, the members on the review committee shall submit to the President of the ACA a written statement giving their opinion regarding the decision of the Ethics Committee. Each member shall concur with or dissent from the decision of the Ethics Committee.

E. Within fifteen (15) working days of receiving this opinion, the President of ACA will reach a decision based on the considered opinions of the review committee from the following alternatives:

(1) support the decision of the Ethics Committee, or

(2) reverse the decision of the Ethics Committee.

3. The parties to the appeal shall be advised of the action in writing.

Section P: Records

1. Records of the ACA Ethics Committee and the review committee shall remain at the ACA Headquarters.

Section Q: Procedures for Submitting and Interpreting Questions of Ethical Conduct

1. The procedures for submitting questions to the Ethics Committee are as follows:

A. Whenever possible, the questioner is first advised to consult other colleagues seeking interpretation of questions.

B. If a national level resolution is deemed appropriate, the questioner shall prepare a written statement, which details the conduct in question. Statements should include the section or sections of the Ethical Standards to be interpreted relative to the conduct in question. All questions that are directed to the Ethics Committee should be mailed to: Ethics Committee, c/o ACA Executive Director.

C. The ACA Ethics Committee Chairperson or his/her designee:

(1) may confer with legal counsel, and

(2) shall direct a letter to the questioner acknowledging receipt of the question, informing the member that the questions will be interpreted by the Committee, and outlining the procedures to be involved in the interpretation.

D. The Ethics Committee will review and interpret the question and, if requested by the questioner, make recommendations for conduct.

Appendix B

Ethical Principles of Psychologists and Code of Conduct

CONTENTS

Introduction

The American Psychological Association's (APA's) Ethical Principles of Psychologists and Code of Conduct (hereinafter referred to as the Ethics Code) consists of an Introduction, a Preamble, six General Principles (A-F), and specific Ethical Standards. The Introduction discusses the intent, organization, procedural considerations, and scope of application of the Ethics Code. The Preamble and General Principles are *aspirational* goals to guide psychologists toward the highest ideals of psychology. Although the Preamble and General Principles are not themselves enforceable rules, they should be considered by psychologists in arriving at an ethical course of action and may be considered by ethics bodies in interpreting the Ethical Standards. The Ethical Standards set forth *enforceable* rules for conduct as psychologists. Most of the Ethical Standards are written broadly, in order to apply to psychologists in varied roles, although the application of an Ethical Standard may vary depending on the context. The Ethical Standards are not exhaustive. The fact that a given conduct is not specifically addressed by the Ethics Code does not mean that it is necessarily either ethical or unethical.

Membership in the APA commits members to adhere to the APA Ethics Code and to the rules and procedures used to implement it. Psychologists and students, whether or not they are APA members, should be aware that the Ethics Code may be applied to them by state psychology boards, courts, or other public bodies.

This Ethics Code applies only to psychologists' work-related activities, that is, activities that are part of the psychologists' scientific and professional functions or that are psychological in nature. It includes the clinical or counseling practice of psychology, research, teaching, supervision of trainees, development of assessment instruments, conducting assessments, educational counseling, organizational consulting, social intervention, administration, and other activities as well. These work-related activities can be distinguished from the purely private conduct of a psychologist, which ordinarily is not within the purview of the Ethics Code.

The Ethics Code is intended to provide standards of professional conduct that can be applied by the APA and by other bodies that choose to adopt them. Whether or not a psychologist has violated the Ethics Code does not by itself determine whether he or she is legally liable in a court action, whether a contract is enforceable, or whether other legal consequences occur. These results are based on legal rather than ethical rules. However, compliance with or violation of the Ethics Code may be admissible as evidence in some legal proceedings, depending on the circumstances.

In the process of making decisions regarding their professional behavior, psychologists must consider this Ethics Code, in addition to applicable laws and psychology board regulations. If the Ethics Code establishes a higher standard of conduct than is required by law, psychologists must meet the higher ethical standard. If the Ethics Code standard appears to conflict with the requirements of law, then psychologists make known their commitment to the Ethics Code and take steps to resolve the conflict in a responsible manner. If neither law nor the Ethics Code resolves an issue, psychologists should consider other professional materials[1] and the dictates of their own conscience, as well as seek consultation with others within the field when this is practical.The procedures for filing, investigating, and resolving complaints of unethical conduct are described in the current Rules and Procedures of the APA Ethics Committee. The actions that APA may take for violations of the Ethics Code include actions such as reprimand, censure, termination of APA membership, and referral of the matter to other bodies. Complainants who seek remedies such as monetary damages in alleging ethical violations by a psychologist must resort to private negotiation, administrative bodies, or the courts. Actions that violate the Ethics Code may lead to the imposition of sanctions on a psychologist by bodies other than APA, including

---

This version of the APA Ethics Code was adopted by the American Psychological Association's Council of Representatives during its meeting, August 13 and 16, 1992, and is effective beginning December 1, 1992. Inquiries concerning the substance or interpretation of the APA Ethics Code should be addressed to the Director, Office of Ethics, American Psychological Association, 750 First Street, NE, Washington, DC 20002–4242.

This Code will be used to adjudicate complaints brought concerning alleged conduct occurring on or after the effective date. Complaints regarding conduct occurring prior to the effective date will be adjudicated on the basis of the version of the Code that was in effect at the time the conduct occurred, except that no provisions repealed in June 1989, will be enforced even if an earlier version contains the provision. The Ethics Code will undergo continuing review and study for future revisions; comments on the Code may be sent to the above address.

The APA has previously published its Ethical Standards as follows:

American Psychological Association. (1953). *Ethical standards of psychologists.* Washington, DC: Author.
American Psychological Association. (1958). Standards of ethical behavior for psychologists. *American Psychologist, 13,* 268–271.
American Psychological Association. (1963). Ethical standards of psychologists. *American Psychologist, 18,* 56–60.
American Psychological Association. (1968). Ethical standards of psychologists. *American Psychologist, 23,* 357–361.
American Psychological Association. (1977, March). Ethical standards of psychologists. *APA Monitor,* pp. 22–23.
American Psychological Association. (1979). *Ethical standards of psychologists.* Washington, DC: Author.
American Psychological Association. (1981). Ethical principles of psychologists. *American Psychologist, 36,* 633–638.
American Psychological Association. (1990). Ethical principles of psychologists (Amended June 2, 1989). *American Psychologist, 45,* 390–395.

Request copies of the APA's Ethical Principles of Psychologists and Code of Conduct from the APA Order Department, 750 First Street, NE, Washington, DC 20002–4242, or phone (202) 336–5510.

---

[1] Professional materials that are most helpful in this regard are guidelines and standards that have been adopted or endorsed by professional psychological organizations. Such guidelines and standards, whether adopted by the American Psychological Association (APA) or its Divisions, are not enforceable as such by this Ethics Code, but are of educative value to psychologists, courts, and professional bodies. Such materials include, but are not limited to, the APA's *General Guidelines for Providers of Psychological Services* (1987), *Specialty Guidelines for the Delivery of Services by Clinical Psychologists, Counseling Psychologists, Industrial/Organizational Psychologists, and School Psychologists* (1981), *Guidelines for Computer Based Tests and Interpretations* (1987), *Standards for Educational and Psychological Testing* (1985), *Ethical Principles in the Conduct of Research With Human Participants* (1982), *Guidelines for Ethical Conduct in the Care and Use of Animals* (1986), *Guidelines for Providers of Psychological Services to Ethnic, Linguistic, and Culturally Diverse Populations* (1990), and *Publication Manual of the American Psychological Association* (3rd ed., 1983). Materials not adopted by APA as a whole include the APA Division 41 (Forensic Psychology)/American Psychology–Law Society's *Specialty Guidelines for Forensic Psychologists* (1991).

state psychological associations, other professional groups, psychology boards, other state or federal agencies, and payors for health services. In addition to actions for violation of the Ethics Code, the APA Bylaws provide that APA may take action against a member after his or her conviction of a felony, expulsion or suspension from an affiliated state psychological association, or suspension or loss of licensure.

Preamble

Psychologists work to develop a valid and reliable body of scientific knowledge based on research. They may apply that knowledge to human behavior in a variety of contexts. In doing so, they perform many roles, such as researcher, educator, diagnostician, therapist, supervisor, consultant, administrator, social interventionist, and expert witness. Their goal is to broaden knowledge of behavior and, where appropriate, to apply it pragmatically to improve the condition of both the individual and society. Psychologists respect the central importance of freedom of inquiry and expression in research, teaching, and publication. They also strive to help the public in developing informed judgments and choices concerning human behavior. This Ethics Code provides a common set of values upon which psychologists build their professional and scientific work.

This Code is intended to provide both the general principles and the decision rules to cover most situations encountered by psychologists. It has as its primary goal the welfare and protection of the individuals and groups with whom psychologists work. It is the individual responsibility of each psychologist to aspire to the highest possible standards of conduct. Psychologists respect and protect human and civil rights, and do not knowingly participate in or condone unfair discriminatory practices.

The development of a dynamic set of ethical standards for a psychologist's work-related conduct requires a personal commitment to a lifelong effort to act ethically; to encourage ethical behavior by students, supervisees, employees, and colleagues, as appropriate; and to consult with others, as needed, concerning ethical problems. Each

psychologist supplements, but does not violate, the Ethics Code's values and rules on the basis of guidance drawn from personal values, culture, and experience.

General Principles
Principle A: Competence

Psychologists strive to maintain high standards of competence in their work. They recognize the boundaries of their particular competencies and the limitations of their expertise. They provide only those services and use only those techniques for which they are qualified by education, training, or experience. Psychologists are cognizant of the fact that the competencies required in serving, teaching, and" or studying groups of people vary with the distinctive characteristics of those groups. In those areas in which recognized professional standards do not yet exist, psychologists exercise careful judgment and take appropriate precautions to protect the welfare of those with whom they work. They maintain knowledge of relevant scientific and professional information related to the services they render, and they recognize the need for ongoing education. Psychologists make appropriate use of scientific, professional, technical, and administrative resources.

Principle B: Integrity

Psychologists seek to promote integrity in the science, teaching, and practice of psychology. In these activities psychologists are honest, fair, and respectful of others. In describing or reporting their qualifications, services, products, fees, research, or teaching, they do not make statements that are false, misleading, or deceptive. Psychologists strive to be aware of their own belief systems, values, needs, and limitations and the effect of these on their work. To the extent feasible, they attempt to clarify for relevant parties the roles they are performing and to function appropriately in accordance with those roles. Psychologists avoid improper and potentially harmful dual relationships.

Principle C: Professional and Scientific Responsibility

Psychologists uphold professional standards of conduct, clarify their professional roles and obligations, accept appropriate responsibility for their behavior, and adapt their methods to the needs of different populations. Psychologists consult with, refer to, or cooperate with other professionals and institutions to the extent needed to serve the best interests of their patients, clients, or other recipients of their services. Psychologists' moral standards and conduct are personal matters to the same degree as is true for any other person, except as psychologists' conduct may compromise their professional responsibilities or reduce the public's trust in psychology and psychologists. Psychologists are concerned about the ethical compliance of their colleagues' scientific and professional conduct. When appropriate, they consult with colleagues in order to prevent or avoid unethical conduct.

Principle D: Respect for People's Rights and Dignity

Psychologists accord appropriate respect to the fundamental rights, dignity, and worth of all people. They respect the rights of individuals to privacy, confidentiality, self-determination, and autonomy, mindful that legal and other obligations may lead to inconsistency and conflict with the exercise of these rights. Psychologists are aware of cultural, individual, and role differences, including those due to age, gender, race, ethnicity, national origin, religion, sexual orientation, disability, language, and socioeconomic status. Psychologists try to eliminate the effect on their work of biases based on those factors, and they do not knowingly participate in or condone unfair discriminatory practices.

Principle E: Concern for Others' Welfare

Psychologists seek to contribute to the welfare of those with whom they interact professionally. In their professional actions, psychologists weigh the welfare and rights of their patients or clients, students, supervisees, human research participants, and other affected persons, and the welfare of animal subjects of research. When conflicts occur among psychologists' obligations or concerns, they attempt to resolve these conflicts and to perform their roles in a responsible fashion that avoids or minimizes harm. Psychologists are sensitive to real and ascribed differences in power between themselves and others, and they do not exploit or mislead other people during or after professional relationships.

Principle F: Social Responsibility

Psychologists are aware of their professional and scientific responsibilities to the community and the society in which they work and live. They apply and make public their knowledge of psychology in order to contribute to human welfare. Psychologists are concerned about and work to mitigate the causes of human suffering. When undertaking research, they strive to advance human welfare and the science of psychology. Psychologists try to avoid misuse of their work. Psychologists comply with the law and encourage the development of law and social policy that serve the interests of their patients and clients and the public. They are encouraged to contribute a portion of their professional time for little or no personal advantage.

Ethical Standards
1. General Standards

These General Standards are potentially applicable to the professional and scientific activities of all psychologists.

1.01 Applicability of the Ethics Code

The activity of a psychologist subject to the Ethics Code may be reviewed under these Ethical Standards only if the activity is part of his or her work-related functions or the activity is psychological in nature. Personal activities having no connection to or effect on psychological roles are not subject to the Ethics Code.

1.02 Relationship of Ethics and Law

If psychologists' ethical responsibilities conflict with law, psychologists make known their commitment to the Ethics Code and take steps to resolve the conflict in a responsible manner.

1.03 Professional and Scientific Relationship

Psychologists provide diagnostic, therapeutic, teaching, research, supervisory, consultative, or other psychological services only in the context of a defined professional or scientific relationship or role. (See also Standards 2.01, Evaluation, Diagnosis, and Interventions in Professional Context, and 7.02, Forensic Assessments.)

1.04 Boundaries of Competence

(a) Psychologists provide services, teach, and conduct research only within the boundaries of their competence, based on their education, training, supervised experience, or appropriate professional experience.

(b) Psychologists provide services, teach, or conduct research in new areas or involving new techniques only after first undertaking appropriate study, training, supervision, and/or consultation from persons who are competent in those areas or techniques.

(c) In those emerging areas in which generally recognized standards for preparatory training do not yet exist, psychologists nevertheless take reasonable steps to ensure the competence of their work and to protect patients, clients, students, research participants, and others from harm.

1.05 Maintaining Expertise

Psychologists who engage in assessment, therapy, teaching, research, organizational consulting, or other professional activities maintain a reasonable level of awareness of current scientific and professional information in their fields of ac-

tivity, and undertake ongoing efforts to maintain competence in the skills they use.

1.06 Basis for Scientific and Professional Judgments

Psychologists rely on scientifically and professionally derived knowledge when making scientific or professional judgments or when engaging in scholarly or professional endeavors.

1.07 Describing the Nature and Results of Psychological Services

(a) When psychologists provide assessment, evaluation, treatment, counseling, supervision, teaching, consultation, research, or other psychological services to an individual, a group, or an organization, they provide, using language that is reasonably understandable to the recipient of those services, appropriate information beforehand about the nature of such services and appropriate information later about results and conclusions. (See also Standard 2.09, Explaining Assessment Results.)

(b) If psychologists will be precluded by law or by organizational roles from providing such information to particular individuals or groups, they so inform those individuals or groups at the outset of the service.

1.08 Human Differences

Where differences of age, gender, race, ethnicity, national origin, religion, sexual orientation, disability, language, or socioeconomic status significantly affect psychologists' work concerning particular individuals or groups, psychologists obtain the training, experience, consultation, or supervision necessary to ensure the competence of their services, or they make appropriate referrals.

1.09 Respecting Others

In their work-related activities, psychologists respect the rights of others to hold values, attitudes, and opinions that differ from their own.

1.10 Nondiscrimination

In their work-related activities, psychologists do not engage in unfair discrimination based on age, gender, race, ethnicity, national origin, religion, sexual orientation, disability, socioeconomic status, or any basis proscribed by law.

1.11 Sexual Harassment

(a) Psychologists do not engage in sexual harassment. Sexual harassment is sexual solicitation, physical advances, or verbal or nonverbal conduct that is sexual in nature, that occurs in connection with the psychologist's activities or roles as a psychologist, and that either: (1) is unwelcome, is offensive, or creates a hostile workplace environment, and the psychologist knows or is told this; or (2) is sufficiently severe or intense to be abusive to a reasonable person in the context. Sexual harassment can consist of a single intense or severe act or of multiple persistent or pervasive acts.

(b) Psychologists accord sexual-harassment complainants and respondents dignity and respect. Psychologists do not participate in denying a person academic admittance or advancement, employment, tenure, or promotion, based solely upon their having made, or their being the subject of, sexual harassment charges. This does not preclude taking action based upon the outcome of such proceedings or consideration of other appropriate information.

1.12 Other Harassment

Psychologists do not knowingly engage in behavior that is harassing or demeaning to persons with whom they interact in their work based on factors such as those persons' age, gender, race, ethnicity, national origin, religion, sexual orientation, disability, language, or socioeconomic status.

1.13 Personal Problems and Conflicts

(a) Psychologists recognize that their personal problems and conflicts may interfere with their effectiveness. Accordingly, they refrain from undertaking an activity when they know or should know that their personal problems are likely to lead to harm to a patient, client, colleague, student, research participant, or other person to whom they may owe a professional or scientific obligation.

(b) In addition, psychologists have an obligation to be alert to signs of, and to obtain assistance for, their personal problems at an early stage, in order to prevent significantly impaired performance.

(c) When psychologists become aware of personal problems that may interfere with their performing work-related duties adequately, they take appropriate measures, such as obtaining professional consultation or assistance, and determine whether they should limit, suspend, or terminate their work-related duties.

1.14 Avoiding Harm

Psychologists take reasonable steps to avoid harming their patients or clients, research participants, students, and others with whom they work, and to minimize harm where it is foreseeable and unavoidable.

1.15 Misuse of Psychologists' Influence

Because psychologists' scientific and professional judgments and actions may affect the lives of others, they are alert to and guard against personal, financial, social, organizational, or political factors that might lead to misuse of their influence.

1.16 Misuse of Psychologists' Work

(a) Psychologists do not participate in activities in which it appears likely that their skills or data will be misused by others, unless corrective mechanisms are available. (See also Standard 7.04, Truthfulness and Candor.)

(b) If psychologists learn of misuse or misrepresentation of their work, they take reasonable steps to correct or minimize the misuse or misrepresentation.

1.17 Multiple Relationships

(a) In many communities and situations, it may not be feasible or reasonable for psychologists to avoid social or other nonprofessional contacts with persons such as patients, clients, students, supervisees, or research participants. Psychologists must always be sensitive to the potential harmful effects of other contacts on their work and on those persons with whom they deal. A psychologist refrains from entering into or promising another personal, scientific, professional, financial, or other relationship with such persons if it appears likely that such a relationship reasonably might impair the psychologist's objectivity or otherwise interfere with the psychologist's effectively performing his or her functions as a psychologist, or might harm or exploit the other party.

(b) Likewise, whenever feasible, a psychologist refrains from taking on professional or scientific obligations when preexisting relationships would create a risk of such harm.

(c) If a psychologist finds that, due to unforeseen factors, a potentially harmful multiple relationship has arisen, the psychologist attempts to resolve it with due regard for the best interests of the affected person and maximal compliance with the Ethics Code.

1.18 Barter (With Patients or Clients)

Psychologists ordinarily refrain from accepting goods, services, or other nonmonetary remuneration from patients or clients in return for psychological services because such arrangements create inherent potential for conflicts, exploitation, and distortion of the professional relationship. A psychologist may participate in bartering *only* if (1) it is not clinically contraindicated, *and* (2) the relationship is not exploitative. (See also Standards 1.17, Multiple Relationships, and 1.25, Fees and Financial Arrangements.)

1.19 Exploitative Relationships

(a) Psychologists do not exploit persons over whom they have supervisory, evaluative, or other authority such as students, supervisees, employees, research participants, and clients or patients. (See also Standards 4.05–4.07 regarding sexual involvement with clients or patients.)

(b) Psychologists do not engage in sexual relationships with students or supervisees in training over whom the psychologist has evaluative or direct authority, because such relationships are so likely to impair judgment or be exploitative.

1.20 Consultations and Referrals

(a) Psychologists arrange for appropriate consultations and referrals based principally on the best interests of their patients or clients, with appropriate consent, and subject to other relevant considerations, including applicable law and contractual obligations. (See also Standards 5.01, Discussing the Limits of Confidentiality, and 5.06, Consultations.)

(b) When indicated and professionally appropriate, psychologists cooperate with other professionals in order to serve their patients or clients effectively and appropriately.

(c) Psychologists' referral practices are consistent with law.

1.21 Third-Party Requests for Services

(a) When a psychologist agrees to provide services to a person or entity at the request of a third party, the psychologist clarifies to the extent feasible, at the outset of the service, the nature of the relationship with each party. This clarification includes the role of the psychologist (such as therapist, organizational consultant, diagnostician, or expert witness), the probable uses of the services provided or the information obtained, and the fact that there may be limits to confidentiality.

(b) If there is a foreseeable risk of the psychologist's being called upon to perform conflicting roles because of the involvement of a third party, the psychologist clarifies the nature and direction of his or her responsibilities, keeps all parties appropriately informed as matters develop, and resolves the situation in accordance with this Ethics Code.

1.22 Delegation to and Supervision of Subordinates

(a) Psychologists delegate to their employees, supervisees, and research assistants only those responsibilities that such persons can reasonably be expected to perform competently, on the basis of their education, training, or experience, either independently or with the level of supervision being provided.

(b) Psychologists provide proper training and supervision to their employees or supervisees and take reasonable steps to see that such persons perform services responsibly, competently, and ethically.

(c) If institutional policies, procedures, or practices prevent fulfillment of this obligation, psychologists attempt to modify their role or to correct the situation to the extent feasible.

1.23 Documentation of Professional and Scientific Work

(a) Psychologists appropriately document their professional and scientific work in order to facilitate provision of services later by them or by other professionals, to ensure accountability, and to meet other requirements of institutions or the law.

(b) When psychologists have reason to believe that records of their professional services will be used in legal proceedings involving recipients of or participants in their work, they have a responsibility to create and maintain documentation in the kind of detail and quality that would be consistent with reasonable scrutiny in an adjudicative forum. (See also Standard 7.01, Professionalism, under Forensic Activities.)

1.24 Records and Data

Psychologists create, maintain, disseminate, store, retain, and dispose of records and data relating to their research, practice, and other work in accordance with law and in a manner that permits compliance with the requirements of this Ethics Code. (See also Standard 5.04, Maintenance of Records.)

1.25 Fees and Financial Arrangements

(a) As early as is feasible in a professional or scientific relationship, the psychologist and the patient, client, or other appropriate recipient of psychological services reach an agreement specifying the compensation and the billing arrangements.

(b) Psychologists do not exploit recipients of services or payors with respect to fees.

(c) Psychologists' fee practices are consistent with law.

(d) Psychologists do not misrepresent their fees.

(e) If limitations to services can be anticipated because of limitations in financing, this is discussed with the patient, client, or other appropriate recipient of services as early as is feasible. (See also Standard 4.08, Interruption of Services.)

(f) If the patient, client, or other recipient of services does not pay for services as agreed, and if the psychologist wishes to use collection agencies or legal measures to collect the fees, the psychologist first informs the person that such measures will be taken and provides that person an opportunity to make prompt payment. (See also Standard 5.11, Withholding Records for Nonpayment.)

1.26 Accuracy in Reports to, Payors and Funding Sources

In their reports to payors for services or sources of research funding, psychologists accurately state the nature of the research or service provided, the fees or charges, and where applicable, the identity of the provider, the findings, and the diagnosis. (See also Standard 5.05, Disclosures.)

1.27 Referrals and Fees

When a psychologist pays, receives payment from, or divides fees with another professional other than in an employer–employee relationship, the payment to each is based on the services (clinical, consultative, administrative, or other) provided and is not based on the referral itself.

2. Evaluation, Assessment, or Intervention

2.01 Evaluation, Diagnosis, and Interventions in Professional Context

(a) Psychologists perform evaluations, diagnostic services, or interventions only within the context of a defined professional relationship. (See also Standard 1.03, Professional and Scientific Relationship.)

(b) Psychologists' assessments, recommendations, reports, and psychological diagnostic or evaluative statements are based on information and techniques (including personal interviews of the individual when appropriate) sufficient to provide appropriate substantiation for their findings. (See also Standard 7.02, Forensic Assessments.)

2.02 Competence and Appropriate Use of Assessments and Interventions

(a) Psychologists who develop, administer, score, interpret, or use psychological assessment techniques, interviews, tests, or instruments do so in a manner and for purposes that are appropriate in light of the research on or evidence of the usefulness and proper application of the techniques.

(b) Psychologists refrain from misuse of assessment techniques, interventions, results, and interpretations and take reasonable steps to prevent others from misusing the information these techniques provide. This includes refraining from releasing raw test results or raw data to persons, other than to patients or clients as appropriate, who are not qualified to use such information. (See also Standards 1.02, Relationship of Ethics and Law, and 1.04, Boundaries of Competence.)

2.03 Test Construction

Psychologists who develop and conduct research with tests and other assessment techniques use scientific procedures and current professional knowledge for test design, standardization, validation, reduction or elimination of bias, and recommendations for use.

2.04 Use of Assessment in General and With Special Populations

(a) Psychologists who perform interventions or administer, score, interpret, or use assessment techniques are familiar with the reliability, validation, and related standardization or outcome studies of, and proper applications and uses of, the techniques they use.

(b) Psychologists recognize limits to the certainty with which diagnoses, judgments, or predictions can be made about individuals.

(c) Psychologists attempt to identify situations in which particular interventions or assessment techniques or norms may not be applicable or may require adjustment in administration or interpretation because of factors such as individuals' gender, age, race, ethnicity, national origin, religion, sexual orientation, disability, language, or socioeconomic status.

2.05 Interpreting Assessment Results

When interpreting assessment results, including automated interpretations, psychologists take into account the various test factors and characteristics of the person being assessed that might affect psychologists' judgments or reduce the accuracy of their interpretations. They indicate any significant reservations they have about the accuracy or limitations of their interpretations.

2.06 Unqualified Persons

Psychologists do not promote the use of psychological assessment techniques by unqualified persons. (See also Standard 1.22, Delegation to and Supervision of Subordinates.)

2.07 Obsolete Tests and Outdated Test Results

(a) Psychologists do not base their assessment or intervention decisions or recommendations on data or test results that are outdated for the current purpose.

(b) Similarly, psychologists do not base such decisions or recommendations on tests and measures that are obsolete and not useful for the current purpose.

2.08 Test Scoring and Interpretation Services

(a) Psychologists who offer assessment or scoring procedures to other professionals accurately describe the purpose, norms, validity, reliability, and applications of the procedures and any special qualifications applicable to their use.

(b) Psychologists select scoring and interpretation services (including automated services) on the basis of evidence of the validity of the program and procedures as well as on other appropriate considerations.

(c) Psychologists retain appropriate responsibility for the appropriate application, interpretation, and use of assessment instruments, whether they score and interpret such tests themselves or use automated or other services.

2.09 Explaining Assessment Results

Unless the nature of the relationship is clearly explained to the person being assessed in advance and precludes provision of an explanation of results (such as in some organizational consulting, preemployment or security screenings, and forensic evaluations), psychologists ensure that an explanation of the results is provided using language that is reasonably understandable to the person assessed or to another legally authorized person on behalf of the client. Regardless of whether the scoring and interpretation are done by the psychologist, by assistants, or by automated or other outside services, psychologists take reasonable steps to ensure that appropriate explanations of results are given.

2.10 Maintaining Test Security

Psychologists make reasonable efforts to maintain the integrity and security of tests and other assessment techniques consistent with law, contractual obligations, and in a manner that permits compliance with the requirements of this Ethics Code. (See also Standard 1.02, Relationship of Ethics and Law.)

3. Advertising and Other Public Statements

3.01 Definition of Public Statements

Psychologists comply with this Ethics Code in public statements relating to their professional services, products, or publications or to the field of psychology. Public statements include but are not limited to paid or unpaid advertising, brochures, printed matter, directory listings, personal resumes or curricula vitae, interviews or comments for use in media, statements in legal proceedings, lectures and public oral presentations, and published materials.

3.02 Statements by Others

(a) Psychologists who engage others to create or place public statements that promote their professional practice, products, or activities retain professional responsibility for such statements.

(b) In addition, psychologists make reasonable efforts to prevent others whom they do not control (such as employers, publishers, sponsors, organizational clients, and representatives of the print or broadcast media) from making deceptive statements concerning psychologists' practice or professional or scientific activities.

(c) If psychologists learn of deceptive statements about their work made by others, psychologists make reasonable efforts to correct such statements.

(d) Psychologists do not compensate employees of press, radio, television, or other communication media in return for publicity in a news item.

(e) A paid advertisement relating to the psychologist's activities must be identified as such, unless it is already apparent from the context.

3.03 Avoidance of False or Deceptive Statements

(a) Psychologists do not make public statements that are false, deceptive, misleading, or fraudulent, either because of what they state, convey, or suggest or because of what they omit, concerning their research, practice, or other work activities or those of persons or organizations with which they are affiliated. As examples (and not in limitation) of this standard, psychologists do not make false or deceptive statements concerning (1) their training, experience, or competence; (2) their academic degrees; (3) their credentials; (4) their institutional or association affiliations; (5) their services; (6) the scientific or clinical basis for, or results or degree of success of, their services; (7) their fees; or (8) their publications or research findings. (See also Standards 6.15, Deception in Research, and 6.18, Providing Participants With Information About the Study.)

(b) Psychologists claim as credentials for their psychological work, only degrees that (1) were earned from a regionally accredited educational institution or (2) were the basis for psychology licensure by the state in which they practice.

3.04 Media Presentations

When psychologists provide advice or comment by means of public lectures, demonstrations, radio or television programs, prerecorded tapes, printed articles, mailed material, or other media, they take reasonable precautions to ensure that (1) the statements are based on appropriate psychological literature and practice, (2) the statements are otherwise consistent with this Ethics Code, and (3) the recipients of the information are not encouraged to infer that a relationship has been established with them personally.

3.05 Testimonials

Psychologists do not solicit testimonials from current psychotherapy clients or patients or other persons who because of their particular circumstances are vulnerable to undue influence.

3.06 In-Person Solicitation

Psychologists do not engage, directly or through agents, in uninvited in-person solicitation of business from actual or potential psychotherapy patients or clients or other persons who because of their particular circumstances are vulnerable to undue influence. However, this does not preclude attempting to implement appropriate

collateral contacts with significant others for the purpose of benefiting an already engaged therapy patient.

4. Therapy

4.01 Structuring the Relationship

(a) Psychologists discuss with clients or patients as early as is feasible in the therapeutic relationship appropriate issues, such as the nature and anticipated course of therapy, fees, and confidentiality. (See also Standards 1.25, Fees and Financial Arrangements, and 5.01, Discussing the Limits of Confidentiality.)

(b) When the psychologist's work with clients or patients will be supervised, the above discussion includes that fact, and the name of the supervisor, when the supervisor has legal responsibility for the case.

(c) When the therapist is a student intern, the client or patient is informed of that fact.

(d) Psychologists make reasonable efforts to answer patients' questions and to avoid apparent misunderstandings about therapy. Whenever possible, psychologists provide oral an/or written information, using language that is reasonably understandable to the patient or client.

4.02 Informed Consent to Therapy

(a) Psychologists obtain appropriate informed consent to therapy or related procedures, using language that is reasonably understandable to participants. The content of informed consent will vary depending on many circumstances; however, informed consent generally implies that the person (1) has the capacity to consent, (2) has been informed of significant information concerning the procedure, (3) has freely and without undue influence expressed consent, and (4) consent has been appropriately documented.

(b) When persons are legally incapable of giving informed consent, psychologists obtain informed permission from a legally authorized person, if such substitute consent is permitted by law.

(c) In addition, psychologists (1) inform those persons who are legally incapable of giving informed consent about the proposed interventions in a manner commensurate with the persons' psychological capacities, (2) seek their assent to those interventions, and (3) consider such persons' preferences and best interests.

4.03 Couple and Family Relationships

(a) When a psychologist agrees to provide services to several persons who have a relationship (such as husband and wife or parents and children), the psychologist attempts to clarify at the outset (1) which of the individuals are patients or clients and (2) the relationship the psychologist will have with each person. This clarification includes the role of the psychologist and the probable uses of the services provided or the information obtained. (See also Standard 5.01, Discussing the Limits of Confidentiality.)

(b) As soon as it becomes apparent that the psychologist may be called on to perform potentially conflicting roles (such as marital counselor to husband and wife, and then witness for one party in a divorce proceeding), the psychologist attempts to clarify and adjust, or withdraw from, roles appropriately. (See also Standard 7.03, Clarification of Role, under Forensic Activities.)

4.04 Providing Mental Health Services to Those Served by Others

In deciding whether to offer or provide services to those already receiving mental health services elsewhere, psychologists carefully consider the treatment issues and the potential patient's or client's welfare. The psychologist discusses these issues with the patient or client, or another legally authorized person on behalf of the client, in order to minimize the risk of confusion and conflict, consults with the other service providers when appropriate, and proceeds with caution and sensitivity to the therapeutic issues.

4.05 Sexual Intimacies With Current Patients or Clients

Psychologists do not engage in sexual intimacies with current patients or clients.

4.06 Therapy With Former Sexual Partners

Psychologists do not accept as therapy patients or clients persons with whom they have engaged in sexual intimacies.

4.07 Sexual Intimacies With Former Therapy Patients

(a) Psychologists do not engage in sexual intimacies with a former therapy patient or client for at least two years after cessation or termination of professional services.

(b) Because sexual intimacies with a former therapy patient or client are so frequently harmful to the patient or client, and because such intimacies undermine public confidence in the psychology profession and thereby deter the public's use of needed services, psychologists do not engage in sexual intimacies with former therapy patients and clients even after a two-year interval except in the most unusual circumstances. The psychologist who engages in such activity after the two years following cessation or termination of treatment bears the burden of demonstrating that there has been no exploitation, in light of all relevant factors, including (1) the amount of time that has passed since therapy terminated, (2) the nature and duration of the therapy, (3) the circumstances of termination, (4) the patient's or client's personal history, (5) the patient's or client's current mental status, (6) the likelihood of adverse impact on the patient or client and others, and (7) any statements or actions made by the therapist during the course of therapy suggesting or inviting the possibility of a posttermination sexual or romantic relationship with the patient or client. (See also Standard 1.17, Multiple Relationships.)

4.08 Interruption of Services

(a) Psychologists make reasonable efforts to plan for facilitating care in the event that psychological services are interrupted by factors such as the psychologist's illness, death, unavailability, or relocation or by the client's relocation or financial limitations. (See also Standard 5.09, Preserving Records and Data.)

(b) When entering into employment or contractual relationships, psychologists provide for orderly and appropriate resolution of responsibility for patient or client care in the event that the employment or contractual relationship ends, with paramount consideration given to the welfare of the patient or client.

4.09 Terminating the Professional Relationship

(a) Psychologists do not abandon patients or clients. (See also Standard 1.25e, under Fees and Financial Arrangements.)

(b) Psychologists terminate a professional relationship when it becomes reasonably clear that the patient or client no longer needs the service, is not benefiting, or is being harmed by continued service.

(c) Prior to termination for whatever reason, except where precluded by the patient's or client's conduct, the psychologist discusses the patient's or client's views and needs, provides appropriate pretermination counseling, suggests alternative service providers as appropriate, and takes other reasonable steps to facilitate transfer of responsibility to another provider if the patient or client needs one immediately.

5. Privacy and Confidentiality

These Standards are potentially applicable to the professional and scientific activities of all psychologists.

5.01 Discussing the Limits of Confidentiality

(a) Psychologists discuss with persons and organizations with whom they establish a scientific or professional relationship (including, to the extent feasible, minors and their legal representatives) (1) the relevant limitations on confidentiality, including limitations where applicable in group, marital, and family therapy or in organizational consulting, and (2) the foreseeable uses of the information generated through their services.

(b) Unless it is not feasible or is contraindicated, the discussion of confidentiality occurs at the outset of the relationship and thereafter as new circumstances may warrant.

(c) Permission for electronic recording of interviews is secured from clients and patients.

5.02 Maintaining Confidentiality

Psychologists have a primary obligation and take reasonable precautions to respect the confidentiality rights of those with whom they work or consult, recognizing that confidentiality may be established by law, institutional rules, or professional or scientific relationships. (See also Standard 6.26, Professional Reviewers.)

5.03 Minimizing Intrusions on Privacy

(a) In order to minimize intrusions on privacy, psychologists include in written and oral reports, consultations, and the like, only information germane to the purpose for which the communication is made.

(b) Psychologists discuss confidential information obtained in clinical or consulting relationships, or evaluative data concerning patients, individual or organizational clients, students, research participants, supervisees, and employees, only for appropriate scientific or professional purposes and only with persons clearly concerned with such matters.

5.04 Maintenance of Records

Psychologists maintain appropriate confidentiality in creating, storing, accessing, transferring, and disposing of records under their control, whether these are written, automated, or in any other medium. Psychologists maintain and dispose of records in accordance with law and in a manner that permits compliance with the requirements of this Ethics Code.

5.05 Disclosures

(a) Psychologists disclose confidential information without the consent of the individual only as mandated by law, or where permitted by law for a valid purpose, such as (1) to provide needed professional services to the patient or the individual or organizational client, (2) to obtain appropriate professional consultations, (3) to protect the patient or client or others from harm, or (4) to obtain payment for services, in which instance disclosure is limited to the minimum that is necessary to achieve the purpose.

(b) Psychologists also may disclose confidential information with the appropriate consent of the patient or the individual or organizational client (or of another legally authorized person on behalf of the patient or client), unless prohibited by law.

5.06 Consultations

When consulting with colleagues, (1) psychologists do not share confidential information that reasonably could lead to the identification of a patient, client, research participant, or other person or organization with whom they have a confidential relationship unless they have obtained the prior consent of the person or organization or the disclosure cannot be avoided, and (2) they share information only to the extent necessary to achieve the purposes of the consultation. (See also Standard 5.02, Maintaining Confidentiality.)

5.07 Confidential Information in Databases

(a) If confidential information concerning recipients of psychological services is to be entered into databases or systems of records available to persons whose access has not been consented to by the recipient, then psychologists use coding or other techniques to avoid the inclusion of personal identifiers.

(b) If a research protocol approved by an institutional review board or similar body requires the inclusion of personal identifiers, such identifiers are deleted before the information is made accessible to persons other than those of whom the subject was advised.

(c) If such deletion is not feasible, then before psychologists transfer such data to others or review such data collected by others, they take rea-

sonable steps to determine that appropriate consent of personally identifiable individuals has been obtained.

5.08 Use of Confidential Information for Didactic or Other Purposes

(a) Psychologists do not disclose in their writings, lectures, or other public media, confidential, personally identifiable information concerning their patients, individual or organizational clients, students, research participants, or other recipients of their services that they obtained during the course of their work, unless the person or organization has consented in writing or unless there is other ethical or legal authorization for doing so.

(b) Ordinarily, in such scientific and professional presentations, psychologists disguise confidential information concerning such persons or organizations so that they are not individually identifiable to others and so that discussions do not cause harm to subjects who might identify themselves.

5.09 Preserving Records and Data

A psychologist makes plans in advance so that confidentiality of records and data is protected in the event of the psychologist's death, incapacity, or withdrawal from the position or practice.

5.10 Ownership of Records and Data

Recognizing that ownership of records and data is governed by legal principles, psychologists take reasonable and lawful steps so that records and data remain available to the extent needed to serve the best interests of patients, individual or organizational clients, research participants, or appropriate others.

5.11 Withholding Records for Nonpayment

Psychologists may not withhold records under their control that are requested and imminently needed for a patient's or client's treatment solely because payment has not been received, except as otherwise provided by law.

6. Teaching, Training Supervision, Research, and Publishing

6.01 *Design of Education and Training Programs*

Psychologists who are responsible for education and training programs seek to ensure that the programs are competently designed, provide the proper experiences, and meet the requirements for licensure, certification, or other goals for which claims are made by the program.

6.02 *Descriptions of Education and Training Programs*

(a) Psychologists responsible for education and training programs seek to ensure that there is a current and accurate description of the program content, training goals and objectives, and requirements that must be met for satisfactory completion of the program. This information must be made readily available to all interested parties.

(b) Psychologists seek to ensure that statements concerning their course outlines are accurate and not misleading, particularly regarding the subject matter to be covered, bases for evaluating progress, and the nature of course experiences. (See also Standard 3.03, Avoidance of False or Deceptive Statements.)

(c) To the degree to which they exercise control, psychologists responsible for announcements, catalogs, brochures, or advertisements describing workshops, seminars, or other non-degree-granting educational programs ensure that they accurately describe the audience for which the program is intended, the educational objectives, the presenters, and the fees involved.

6.03 *Accuracy and Objectivity in Teaching*

(a) When engaged in teaching or training, psychologists present psychological information accurately and with a reasonable degree of objectivity.

(b) When engaged in teaching or training, psychologists recognize the power they hold over students or supervisees and therefore make reasonable efforts to avoid engaging in conduct that is personally demeaning to students or supervisees. (See also Standards 1.09, Respecting Others, and 1.12, Other Harassment.)

6.04 *Limitation on Teaching*

Psychologists do not teach the use of techniques or procedures that require specialized training, licensure, or expertise, including but not limited to hypnosis, biofeedback, and projective techniques, to individuals who lack the prerequisite training, legal scope of practice, or expertise.

6.05 *Assessing Student and Supervisee Performance*

(a) In academic and supervisory relationships, psychologists establish an appropriate process for providing feedback to students and supervisees.

(b) Psychologists evaluate students and supervisees on the basis of their actual performance on relevant and established program requirements.

6.06 *Planning Research*

(a) Psychologists design, conduct, and report research in accordance with recognized standards of scientific competence and ethical research.

(b) Psychologists plan their research so as to minimize the possibility that results will be misleading.

(c) In planning research, psychologists consider its ethical acceptability under the Ethics Code. If an ethical issue is unclear, psychologists seek to resolve the issue through consultation with institutional review boards, animal care and use committees, peer consultations, or other proper mechanisms.

(d) Psychologists take reasonable steps to implement appropriate protections for the rights and welfare of human participants, other persons affected by the research, and the welfare of animal subjects.

6.07 Responsibility

(a) Psychologists conduct research competently and with due concern for the dignity and welfare of the participants.

(b) Psychologists are responsible for the ethical conduct of research conducted by them or by others under their supervision or control.

(c) Researchers and assistants are permitted to perform only those tasks for which they are appropriately trained and prepared.

(d) As part of the process of development and implementation of research projects, psychologists consult those with expertise concerning any special population under investigation or most likely to be affected.

6.08 Compliance With Law and Standards

Psychologists plan and conduct research in a manner consistent with federal and state law and regulations, as well as professional standards governing the conduct of research, and particularly those standards governing research with human participants and animal subjects.

6.09 Institutional Approval

Psychologists obtain from host institutions or organizations appropriate approval prior to conducting research, and they provide accurate information about their research proposals. They conduct the research in accordance with the approved research protocol.

6.10 Research Responsibilities

Prior to conducting research (except research involving only anonymous surveys, naturalistic observations, or similar research), psychologists enter into an agreement with participants that clarifies the nature of the research and the responsibilities of each party.

6.11 Informed Consent to Research

(a) Psychologists use language that is reasonably understandable to research participants in obtaining their appropriate informed consent (except as provided in Standard 6.12, Dispensing With Informed Consent). Such informed consent is appropriately documented.

(b) Using language that is reasonably understandable to participants, psychologists inform participants of the nature of the research; they inform participants that they are free to participate or to decline to participate or to withdraw from the research; they explain the foreseeable consequences of declining or withdrawing; they inform participants of significant factors that may be expected to influence their willingness to participate (such as risks, discomfort, adverse effects, or limitations on confidentiality, except as provided in Standard 6.15, Deception in Research); and they explain other aspects about which the prospective participants inquire.

(c) When psychologists conduct research with individuals such as students or subordinates, psychologists take special care to protect the prospective participants from adverse consequences of declining or withdrawing from participation.

(d) When research participation is a course requirement or opportunity for extra credit, the prospective participant is given the choice of equitable alternative activities.

(e) For persons who are legally incapable of giving informed consent, psychologists nevertheless (1) provide an appropriate explanation, (2) obtain the participant's assent and (3) obtain appropriate permission from a legally authorized person, if such substitute consent is permitted by law.

6.12 Dispensing With Informed Consent

Before determining that planned research (such as research involving only anonymous questionnaires, naturalistic observations, or certain kinds of archival research) does not require the informed consent of research participants, psychologists consider applicable regulations and institutional review board requirements, and they consult with colleagues as appropriate.

6.13 Informed Consent in Research Filming or Recording

Psychologists obtain informed consent from research participants prior to filming or recording them in any form, unless the research involves simply naturalistic observations in public places and it is not anticipated that the recording will be used in a manner that could cause personal identification or harm.

6.14 Offering Inducements for Research Participants

(a) In offering professional services as an inducement to obtain research participants, psychologists make clear the nature of the services, as well as the risks, obligations, and limitations. (See also Standard 1.18, Barter [With Patients or Clients].)

(b) Psychologists do not offer excessive or inappropriate financial or other inducements to obtain research participants, particularly when it might tend to coerce participation.

6.15 Deception in Research

(a) Psychologists do not conduct a study involving deception unless they have determined that the use of deceptive techniques is justified by the study's prospective scientific, educational, or applied value and that equally effective alternative procedures that do not use deception are not feasible.

(b) Psychologists never deceive research participants about significant aspects that would affect their willingness to participate, such as physical risks, discomfort, or unpleasant emotional experiences.

(c) Any other deception that is an integral feature of the design and conduct of an experiment must be explained to participants as early

as is feasible, preferably at the conclusion of their participation, but no later than at the conclusion of the research. (See also Standard 6.18, Providing Participants With Information About the Study.)

6.16 Sharing and Utilizing Data

Psychologists inform research participants of their anticipated sharing or further use of personally identifiable research data and of the possibility of unanticipated future uses.

6.17 Minimizing Invasiveness

In conducting research, psychologists interfere with the participants or milieu from which data are collected only in a manner that is warranted by an appropriate research design and that is consistent with psychologists' roles as scientific investigators.

6.18 Providing Participants With Information About the Study

(a) Psychologists provide a prompt opportunity for participants to obtain appropriate information about the nature, results, and conclusions of the research, and psychologists attempt to correct any misconceptions that participants may have.

(b) If scientific or humane values justify delaying or withholding this information, psychologists take reasonable measures to reduce the risk of harm.

6.19 Honoring Commitments

Psychologists take reasonable measures to honor all commitments they have made to research participants.

6.20 Care and Use of Animals in Research

(a) Psychologists who conduct research involving animals treat them humanely.

(b) Psychologists acquire, care for, use, and dispose of animals in compliance with current federal, state, and local laws and regulations, and with professional standards.

(c) Psychologists trained in research methods and experienced in the care of laboratory animals supervise all procedures involving animals and are responsible for ensuring appropriate consideration of their comfort, health, and humane treatment.

(d) Psychologists ensure that all individuals using animals under their supervision have received instruction in research methods and in the care, maintenance, and handling of the species being used, to the extent appropriate to their role.

(e) Responsibilities and activities of individuals assisting in a research project are consistent with their respective competencies.

(f) Psychologists make reasonable efforts to minimize the discomfort, infection, illness, and pain of animal subjects.

(g) A procedure subjecting animals to pain, stress, or privation is used only when an alternative procedure is unavailable and the goal is justified by its prospective scientific, educational, or applied value.

(h) Surgical procedures are performed under appropriate anesthesia; techniques to avoid infection and minimize pain are followed during and after surgery.

(i) When it is appropriate that the animal's life be terminated, it is done rapidly, with an effort to minimize pain, and in accordance with accepted procedures.

6.21 Reporting of Results

(a) Psychologists do not fabricate data or falsify results in their publications.

(b) If psychologists discover significant errors in their published data, they take reasonable steps to correct such errors in a correction, retraction, erratum, or other appropriate publication means.

6.22 Plagiarism

Psychologists do not present substantial portions or elements of another's work or data as their own, even if the other work or data source is cited occasionally.

6.23 Publication Credit

(a) Psychologists take responsibility and credit, including authorship credit, only for work they have actually performed or to which they have contributed.

(b) Principal authorship and other publication credits accurately reflect the relative scientific or professional contributions of the individuals involved, regardless of their relative status. Mere possession of an institutional position, such as Department Chair, does not justify authorship credit. Minor contributions to the research or to the writing for publications are appropriately acknowledged, such as in footnotes or in an introductory statement.

(c) A student is usually listed as principal author on any multiple-authored article that is substantially based on the student's dissertation or thesis.

6.24 Duplicate Publication of Data

Psychologists do not publish, as original data, data that have been previously published. This does not preclude republishing data when they are accompanied by proper acknowledgment.

6.25 Sharing Data

After research results are published, psychologists do not withhold the data on which their conclusions are based from other competent professionals who seek to verify the substantive claims through reanalysis and who intend to use such data only for that purpose, provided that the confidentiality of the participants can be protected and unless legal rights concerning proprietary data preclude their release.

6.26 Professional Reviewers

Psychologists who review material submitted for publication, grant, or other research proposal review respect the confidentiality of and the proprietary rights in such information of those who submitted it.

7. Forensic Activities

7.01 Professionalism

Psychologists who perform forensic functions, such as assessments, interviews, consultations, reports, or expert testimony, must comply with all other provisions of this Ethics Code to the extent that they apply to such activities. In addition, psychologists base their forensic work on appropriate knowledge of and competence in the areas underlying such work, including specialized knowledge concerning special populations. (See also Standards 1.06, Basis for Scientific and Professional Judgments; 1.08, Human Differences; 1.15, Misuse of Psychologists' Influence; and 1.23, Documentation of Professional and Scientific Work.)

7.02 Forensic Assessments

(a) Psychologists' forensic assessments, recommendations, and reports are based on information and techniques (including personal interviews of the individual, when appropriate) sufficient to provide appropriate substantiation for their findings. (See also Standards 1.03, Professional and Scientific Relationship; 1.23, Documentation of Professional and Scientific Work; 2.01, Evaluation, Diagnosis, and Interventions in Professional Context; and 2.05, Interpreting Assessment Results.)

(b) Except as noted in (c), below, psychologists provide written or oral forensic reports or testimony of the psychological characteristics of an individual only after they have conducted an examination of the individual adequate to support their statements or conclusions.

(c) When, despite reasonable efforts, such an examination is not feasible, psychologists clarify the impact of their limited information on the reliability and validity of their reports and testimony, and they appropriately limit the nature and extent of their conclusions or recommendations.

7.03 Clarification of Role

In most circumstances, psychologists avoid performing multiple and potentially conflicting roles in forensic matters. When psychologists may be called on to serve in more than one role in a legal proceeding—for example, as consultant or expert for one party or for the court and as a fact witness—they clarify role expectations and the extent of confidentiality in advance to the extent feasible, and thereafter as changes occur, in order to avoid compromising their professional judgment and objectivity and in order to avoid misleading others regarding their role.

7.04 Truthfulness and Candor

(a) In forensic testimony and reports, psychologists testify truthfully, honestly, and candidly and, consistent with applicable legal procedures, describe fairly the bases for their testimony and conclusions.

(b) Whenever necessary to avoid misleading, psychologists acknowledge the limits of their data or conclusions.

7.05 Prior Relationships

A prior professional relationship with a party does not preclude psychologists from testifying as fact witnesses or from testifying to their services to the extent permitted by applicable law. Psychologists appropriately take into account ways in which the prior relationship might affect their professional objectivity or opinions and disclose the potential conflict to the relevant parties.

7.06 Compliance With Law and Rules

In performing forensic roles, psychologists are reasonably familiar with the rules governing their roles. Psychologists are aware of the occasionally competing demands placed upon them by these principles and the requirements of the court system, and attempt to resolve these conflicts by making known their commitment to this Ethics Code and taking steps to resolve the conflict in a responsible manner. (See also Standard 1.02, Relationship of Ethics and Law.)

8. Resolving Ethical Issues

8.01 Familiarity With Ethics Code

Psychologists have an obligation to be familiar with this Ethics Code, other applicable ethics codes, and their application to psychologists' work. Lack of awareness or misunderstanding of an ethical standard is not itself a defense to a charge of unethical conduct.

8.02 Confronting Ethical Issues

When a psychologist is uncertain whether a particular situation or course of action would violate this Ethics Code, the psychologist ordinarily consults with other psychologists knowledgeable about ethical issues, with state or national psychology ethics committees, or with other appropriate authorities in order to choose a proper response.

8.03 Conflicts Between Ethics and Organizational Demands

If the demands of an organization with which psychologists are affiliated conflict with this Ethics Code, psychologists clarify the nature of the conflict, make known their commitment to the Ethics Code, and to the extent feasible, seek to resolve the conflict in a way that permits the fullest adherence to the Ethics Code.

8.04 Informal Resolution of Ethical Violations

When psychologists believe that there may have been an ethical violation by another psychologist, they attempt to resolve the issue byng it to the attention of that individual if an informal resolution appears appropriate and the intervention does not violate any confidentiality rights that may be involved.

8.05 Reporting Ethical Violations

If an apparent ethical violation is not appropriate for informal resolution under Standard 8.04 or is not resolved properly in that fashion, psychologists take further action appropriate to the situation, unless such action conflicts with confidentiality rights in ways that cannot be resolved. Such action might include referral to state or national committees on professional ethics or to state licensing boards.

8.06 Cooperating With Ethics Committees

Psychologists cooperate in ethics investigations, proceedings, and resulting requirements of the APA or any affiliated state psychological association to which they belong. In doing so, they make reasonable efforts to resolve any issues as to confidentiality. Failure to cooperate is itself an ethics violation.

8.07 Improper Complaints

Psychologists do not file or encourage the filing of ethics complaints that are frivolous and are intended to harm the respondent rather than to protect the public.

Name Index

Weiner, I. B., 240–241
Weinrach, S. G., 101
Weisberg, L. S., 181
Westerlund, E., 175
Wheeler, B. R., 175, 176
Williams, R. F., 184
Williamson, E. G., 224

Winborn, B., 168
Winiarski, M. G., 183
Wittmer, J. M., 14, 21, 22
Wolberg, L. R., 107, 117
Wolf, T., 180
Wolpe, J., 87, 91

Yalom, I. D., 74, 203

Zeig, J. K., 3
Zytowski, D. G., 230

Subject Index

Acceptance, 125, 127
Accountability, of counselors, 264
Accreditation, 13–15
Achievement tests, 11, 247–248
Acquired Immune Deficiency Syndrome (AIDS), 181–184
Active listening, 65, 141, 152–153, 201–202, 209
Actualizing tendency, 58–59, 61, 67
Addictive behaviors, 181. *See also* Substance abuse counseling
Adult survivors of child sexual abuse, 174–178
Advanced empathy, 159–160
Advice, 126
Affective approaches to counseling, 57–77, 112, 114, 115
Affectiveness, 122–123
Aging population, 184–186, 263
American Association of Counseling and Development, 178
American Counseling Association (ACA), 12, 13, 16, 180, 184, 255–256, 263
American Mental Health Counselors Association, 16
American Personnel and Guidance Association (APGA), 2, 13, 15
American Psychological Association, 12, 13, 242, 251, 255
Anal stage, 43
Anchoring, 100
Anecdotal records, 245
Anxiety, 40–42, 50, 51, 61, 62, 67, 75, 83, 91–92, 166, 175, 195
Aptitude tests, 248
Assertion training, 93, 167
Assessment, 243–252
   communicating results in, 252
   purposes of, 244
   testing in, 246–251
   types of, 245–246
Association for Counselor Education and Supervision (ACES), 13, 15, 26
Attending behaviors, 149–150
Authenticity, 29, 62, 76, 129
Autobiography, 245

Beck Depression Inventory, 250
Behavioral counseling, 87–94, 166–167
Behavior change, 6
Behavior contracts, 92–93, 166
Beliefs, 28

Bender-Gestalt interpretations, 250
Birth order, 48
Bisexuality, 180
Body image, 175
Boundary issues, 177
Buckley-Pell Amendment, 259–260
Burnout, 183

California Psychological Inventory (CPI), 249
California Test of Mental Maturity, 247
Career Assessment Inventory, 248
Career counseling, 10, 221–236, 264
   and changing world of work, 222–223
   computer technology in, 236
   process of, 231–234
   and theories of career development, 223–230
   tools for, 234–236, 248–249
Certification, 15, 16, 185–186
Child sexual abuse (CSA), 174–178
Clarification, 163
Classical conditioning, 88
Clients
   of counselors versus psychotherapists, 4–6
   effectiveness of, 212–213
   expectations of, 9
   responsibility of, 33–34, 67–73, 75, 76, 83, 84
Client variables, 268
Clinical psychology, counseling versus, 23
Cognitive-behavioral approaches to counseling, 80–104, 113–114, 115, 116
Cognitive processes, 51
Cognitive therapy, 100–101
Commission on Rehabilitation Counselor Certification, 16
Communication
   barriers to, 125–128
   basic skills in, 150–156
   nonverbal behaviors in, 132, 144–150, 209
   privileged, 260–262
   of results of tests, 252
Compensation, 42, 47
Competence, 262
Computers, 236, 243, 250–251, 264
Concreteness, 132–133
Conditioning, 88
   counter-, 91, 166
Confidentiality, 139, 183, 257–262

Confrontation, 163–165, 201–202, 210–211
Congruence, 129, 131
Conscience, 39
Consultants, counselors as, 182, 193–197
Continuum of awareness, 71
Contracts
   behavior, 92–93, 166
   consulting, 196
Control groups, 266–267
Control issues, 177
Control theory, 95
Coping skills, 7
Council for the Accreditation and Related Educational Programs (CACREP), 13–17, 186
Counseling
   affective approaches to, 57–77, 112, 114, 115
   clinical psychology versus, 23
   cognitive-behavioral approaches to, 80–104, 113–114, 115, 116
   credentials in, 13–16
   defined, 2–3
   ethical considerations in, 139, 178–179, 183, 255–259
   goals of, 4, 6–9
   helping relationship in, 122–136, 197–218
   historical development of profession, 10–13
   legal considerations in, 259–262
   personal theory of, 107–119
   psychoanalytic approaches to, 38–55, 112, 114, 115
   psychotherapy versus, 3–6
   research and evaluation in, 265–268
   and role of counselor, 21–22
   specialty areas in, 16–21
   therapeutic techniques in, 44–45, 48–49, 51–52, 63–65, 71–73, 76, 85–86, 91–93, 95–96, 115–116, 138–171, 209–212, 217
   trends in, 262–265
   See also Training
Counseling environment, 138–139, 185
Counseling groups, 198
Counselors
   as consultants, 182, 193–197
   development process for, 34–35
   education of, 13–16, 30–32, 178, 183–186, 198, 265
   nonverbal behavior of, 148–150